foundations of education

COMMITMENT TO TEACHING, VOLUME I

foundations of education ✓

COMMITMENT TO TEACHING, VOLUME I

James C. Stone
Professor of Education and
Director of Teacher Education
University of California, Berkeley

Frederick W. Schneider
Associate Professor of Education, San Jose State College

THOMAS Y. CROWELL COMPANY
Established 1834, New York

3-1303- 00041-3592

127348

foreword

There is no course of professional preparation with so diverse a set of demands as that for prospective teachers. They must delve into the philosophical underpinnings of educational goals. They must achieve an understanding of our entire social system as it affects both behavior in the classroom and the ways our schools are governed. They must discern the structure of the nation's largest profession. They must recognize the psychological principles that underlie the learning process. They must appreciate the factors of human growth and development that form the context for pupil progress in schools. They must grasp the thrust of educational history to know where they are and why. And, in a time of revolution in education, they must welcome changes in the techniques of teaching even as they learn them.

To bring together in one book the basic materials in all of these fields is no mean feat, but the authors have accomplished it. Here are the facts, the viewpoints, the data, and—I am happy to note—a healthy dose of the day-to-day realities that every teacher must face.

There is, of course, much more to learn about each of the subjects presented here. But the basic ideas, the fundamental data, the organizing principles are laid out clearly, with a wealth of material drawn from many sources. The authors are frank about such provocative topics as the teacher's clerical and babysitting roles, the tyrannies of curricula and schedules, and the need to deal boldly with the problems of disadvantaged children.

Moreover, they realize fully, and convey dramatically, the exhilaration of this extraordinary profession. They know full well that to become a teacher is to put yourself into a professional role, the significance of which cannot be overemphasized. This has always been true; the difference is that now the large majority of Americans have become aware of the fact. In the school, where young minds are nurtured and character crystallizes, the future of a person, a community, a nation, a world, are in large part determined. To have a hand in such an enterprise should yield any young person a justified sense of his own worth.

I hope that this book will be your gateway to the exasperating, exhilarating, extraordinary profession of teaching.

ALVIN C. EURICH
*President, Aspen Institute
for Humanistic Studies*

preface

Considerable time and effort have gone into the design of this book. If it is unique—and we are convinced it is—it is because of the way in which it was developed.

Several hundred beginning students in education at San Jose State College responded in writing to the question: What would you most have liked to know about education when you were considering it as a career choice?

A group of students completing their student teaching and another group completing their year of internship teaching at the University of California, Berkeley, were interviewed with regard to the general question: Looking back over the field of education, what topics would you most have liked to know about, and in what order?

The results of the two surveys agreed both as to the concepts which should be covered and the priority which should be given to them. So we have here a book organized and structured from the viewpoint of college and university students of teacher education as learners. In this, *the student interest approach to education,* the authors believe their book is a first. For this, we are indebted to these students and beginning teachers—too numerous to list—for their invaluable assistance.

JAMES C. STONE
FREDERICK W. SCHNEIDER

contents

i

American education can be as good as the American
people want it to be, and no better.

JOHN W. GARDNER

the milieu

As the title for this first chapter, we have used the French word *milieu,*
which means surroundings or environment, because we believe it more accurately than any English word describes the cultural and social setting of a
people from which the system of education receives its chief characteristics
and its commitment. As the historian Arnold J. Toynbee has written:

A society enters on the process of civilization as soon as it can afford to maintain a minority, however small, whose time and energy is not wholly taken up
in producing food and the other primary necessities of life. The leisured
minority is the social milieu in which an unorganized and unself-conscious
apprenticeship in the older generation's way of life comes to be supplemented,
more and more, by the organized and self-conscious kind of instruction which
is what we commonly mean today in our society when we use the word "education." [1]

Education—instruction of the young by the older generation—the passing
on and improving of the cultural heritage—the preparation of youth for adult
responsibilities—this is (and has been) done in different *ways* by different
societies. Not only are the ways different, but the nature of the heritage which
is passed on and the type of preparation for adulthood also are different from
one society to another, from epoch to epoch, from time to time, from nation
to nation.

Why are the nature of the process and the nature of what is passed on so
different? What is distinctly different about American education, and why?
These are the questions to be considered in this chapter.

THE NATURE OF CULTURE

In using the word *culture,* the reader should keep in mind that social
scientists have a special meaning for it. Culture to them means the entire way

[1] Arnold J. Toynbee, "Education: The Long View," in *American Education
Today,* ed. Paul Woodring and John Scanlon (New York: McGraw-Hill, 1963),
p. 272.

of life of a society or, in a complex society, of each particular and distinguishable subgroup within the society. In analyzing a society's "way of life"—its "life-style," its entire "social heritage"—the sociologist talks about customs (folkways), traditions (mores), attitudes, skills, and ideals which are held by the members of the society.

A man who grew up apart from human association would lack culture because he had not communicated with other men and would, therefore, not share the knowledge of earlier generations. He would, however, solve problems and learn from experience, as do other animals. By the acquisition of culture, by tapping the heritage of his past, man becomes distinctively human. Man has, therefore, been called the culture-bearing animal.[2]

Man dies, but his culture lives on. The elements of a society which "live on"—folkways, mores, skills, attitudes, ideals—these have a particular relevance for education because they provide the framework of a given society's educational system. They shape education, and in turn they are shaped by the educational enterprise. Furthermore, since the school is made up of individuals —students and teachers—who form a group with common behavior and thought patterns, the school constitutes a subculture of society. "Subcultures are distinguishable from one another and from the dominant culture forms by such manifest characteristics as language, clothing, gesture, and etiquette."[3] Thus we speak of the "teen-age subculture," the "peer group subculture," and the like. In this way, the school—an instrument for the preservation of American culture—is at the same time a social entity with a distinctive subculture.

Differences in Cultures

Close your eyes and imagine that the awful event on which Nevil Shute based his novel *On the Beach* has actually occurred: the bomb has fallen and the world as we know it and everything on it have disappeared. Imagine further that you are a man from Mars who just landed on this recently blown-to-bits planet. Life in all its forms has disappeared. All evidence of buildings, streets, cities, houses—these too have disappeared. As you survey the bleak surroundings, your wandering eye is attracted to something bright in the sand. You pick it up. It is round and copper-colored and has some figures and writing on it. What does it tell you about the civilization that once inhabited this planet?

Open your eyes, take a penny out of your pocket (or purse), and examine it as a visitor from Mars would examine it. What does it tell you about the civilization that once inhabited this planet? The people wore clothes. They had mastered the art of metallurgy. They knew more than one language and had a complex number system.

Assuming that you can decode one of the languages, you will discover

[2] Leonard Broom and Philip Selznick, *Sociology*, 3d ed. (New York: Harper & Row, 1963), p. 52.

[3] *Ibid.*, p. 60.

Teen-age Tyranny

Teen-age, like birth and death, is inevitable. It is nothing to be ashamed of. Nor is it a badge of special distinction worthy of a continuous birthday party. And while teen-agers should be afforded mitigating circumstances for some of their actions and views, on the basis of natural immaturity, they should neither be placed in an aquarium tank for purposes of exhibition and analysis nor be put on a pedestal to be extolled for that admittedly enviable condition—youth.

For several decades now, the most insecure and most immature members of adult society have permitted, often in the name of self-expression and pseudo-psychology, the most insecure and most immature adolescents to establish their own independent and sovereign culture: teen-age. The task now is to make it clearly understood that adolescence is a state of human development, not an empire or even a colony. The mission of the adult world is to help teen-agers become adults by raising their standards and values to maturity rather than by lowering adulthood to insecure immaturity. The task for the adult world is to make adolescence a step toward growing up, not a privilege to be exploited.

[Teen-age tyranny] dominates most brutally the teen-agers themselves. What starts with relatively innocent conforming to the ways of the crowd soon turns into manipulation of those crowd mores by a combination of inept adult leadership and plain commercial exploitation. The longer it continues the harder it becomes, as in the case of every artificially imposed regime for dissenters to declare their independence.

The adolescent question to mother, "Don't you trust me?", asked with proper dash of teen-age drama and hurt, needs often to be answered: "I trust you on your own, but not when you think you must be part of the crowd."

In addition to having the courage to set their own standards without submitting blindly to hard pressures, parents as well as schools must be brave enough to establish rules and set limits for their own children without waiting for society or even the community to reach an agreement. If they do so they may learn to their surprise that adolescents really want such limitations and a clear understanding of how far they can go. Since teen-agers are uncertain about their actions and their maturity, they will, if left without regulations, keep probing and, in the absence of brakes, run into trouble. They will follow the group.

Grace and Fred M. Hechinger, *Teen-age Tyranny* (New York: William Morrow, 1963), pp. ix–xi *passim*, 233–43 *passim*. Copyright © 1963 by Grace Hechinger and Fred M. Hechinger.

further that they believed in one God. They had a system of exchange involving money. They had a central government made up of a number of states. They believed in liberty.

Yes, you can deduce these things and a lot more about the civilization and its *culture* simply by examining the coin. For culture consists of *artifacts*—tools, buildings, clothes, and other physical things man has made—and *mentifacts*—the ideas, ideals, values, customs and other nonphysical things man has created. Because both artifacts and mentifacts are man-made, they differ from one society to another.

The physical environment is one of the chief causes of differences between cultures, because it provides the all-important basic resources that determine everything from the materials with which artifacts are made, to the framework within which the culture develops. For example, the contrast between dry desert and luxuriant woodland explains many of the differences between the Hopi Indians of Arizona and New Mexico and the Iroquois of the East. Furthermore, if there is a struggle with the environment for essential needs, the society will not be prosperous enough to support a leisured class to think and create.

In addition to being different because of indigenous reasons, cultures vary because of invention and borrowing. The wheel, for instance, was unknown to the closed society of the American Indian, who had to settle for his own crude inventions as substitutes, like the travois developed by the Plains Indians. And since the Indian was not exposed to a culture having the wheel, he could not borrow it. In contrast, we find that most of our present-day American culture has been borrowed from past cultures or from other countries. Just how extensive and important an element borrowing of artifacts has been to our American culture is dramatically illustrated by the quotation on pages 6 and 7 from Ralph Linton's book *The Study of Man.*

More significant than artifacts, however, are the mentifacts, which express the fundamental, most cherished beliefs and values of a society and which, just like artifacts, are different from culture to culture.

Because societies place such importance on their ideals and values, they have established specific agencies to promote and safeguard them. These are called social *institutions.* One example of such is the *family,* another the *church,* another the *school.*

And now we come to the crux of this discussion of culture and education and are ready to consider three generalizations which have profound significance for teachers.

> *First* (the obvious generalization)
>> Because cultures differ from place to place, nation to nation, epoch to epoch, the values, ideals, and goals of each also differ one from another.
> *Second* (the generalization which logically follows)
>> Because values and goals differ from society to society, from culture to culture, the means or system for passing on these values and inculcating them in the minds and hearts of the next generation also varies.

Third (the concluding generalization)

If societies differ in their values, if they differ in the *modus operandi* of the educational system, it is because all forms of "schooling" derive their chief characteristics from the society which nurtures and sustains them.

Role of Goals

In every culture—ancient, primitive, and modern—the purpose of the educational enterprise, however simple or complicated it may be, is to inculcate the values of the culture, to prepare the young to live harmoniously in that society.

Did the educational system of ancient Sparta differ from the educational system of ancient Athens? Yes, and the differences were rooted in the different *goals* of these two peoples. Does the educational enterprise of Soviet Russia today differ from the educational enterprise of the United States? Yes, and the differences are rooted in the different *goals* of the two cultures. We have expressed a simple fact—yet one which is most often overlooked or ignored in discussions of American education.

How often have you heard someone say, "Why aren't our American high schools the equal of the British secondary schools?" or "Why can't our American fifth graders equal French fifth graders in achievement in arithmetic?" The answer is not to be found in a debate over which educational system is better than the other. The clue to the answer to any such question is that America, Britain, France, Russia each differs in its goals. It would be difficult to transplant one country's educational system on top of another's goals. Similarly, before you can change a nation's educational enterprise, you first have to change its goals, for these are what the schools are designed to preserve, pass on, improve, and foster.

CULTURAL CHANGE

At this point, the reader might well retort, "This discussion of the relation of cultural values to education seems to imply a fixed and somewhat static relationship—one which says, in fact, that since education passes on the values of the past, obviously it doesn't change." We know though that it does. Yes, education does change, but *only as the culture itself changes*. Remember we said the school was a social institution—like the church or the family—designed to preserve society's values. This implies that it is somewhat resistant to change and can be changed only as the total culture and its values change.

Change and the School

In a delightful parody on education, *The Saber-tooth Curriculum*, Harold Benjamin tells the story of a primitive people whose very existence was de-

The 100% American

Our solid American citizen awakens in a bed built on a pattern which originated in the Near East but which was modified in Northern Europe before it was transmitted to America. He throws back covers made from cotton, domesticated in India, or linen, domesticated in the Near East, or wool from sheep, also domesticated in the Near East, or silk, the use of which was discovered in China. All of these materials have been spun and woven by processes invented in the Near East. He slips into his moccasins, invented by the Indians of the Eastern woodlands, and goes to the bathroom, whose fixtures are a mixture of European and American inventions, both of recent date. He takes off his pajamas, a garment invented in India, and washes with soap invented by the ancient Gauls. He then shaves, a masochistic rite which seems to have been derived from either Sumer or ancient Egypt.

Returning to the bedroom, he removes his clothes from a chair of southern European type and proceeds to dress. He puts on garments whose forms originally derived from the skin clothing of the nomads of the Asiatic steppes, puts on shoes made from skins tanned by a process invented in ancient Egypt and cut to a pattern derived from the classical civilizations of the Mediterranean, and ties around his neck a strip of bright-colored cloth which is a vestigial survival of the shoulder shawls worn by the seventeenth-century Croatians. Before going out for breakfast he glances through the window, made of glass invented in Egypt, and if it is raining puts on overshoes made of rubber discovered by the Central American Indians and takes an umbrella, invented in southern Asia. Upon his head he puts a hat made of felt, a material invented in the Asiatic steppes.

On his way to breakfast he stops to buy a paper, paying for it with coins, an ancient Lydian invention. At the restaurant a whole new series of borrowed elements confronts him. His plate is made of a form of pottery invented in China. His knife is of steel, an alloy first made in southern India, his fork a medieval Italian invention, and his spoon a derivation of a Roman original.

He begins breakfast with an orange, from the eastern Mediterranean, a cantaloupe from Persia, or perhaps a piece of African watermelon. With this he has coffee, an Abyssinian plant, with cream and sugar. Both the domestication of cows and the idea of milking them originated in the Near East, while sugar was first made in India. After his fruit and first coffee he goes on to waffles, cakes made by a Scandinavian technique from wheat domesticated in Asia Minor. Over these he pours maple syrup, invented by the Indians of the Eastern woodlands. As a side dish he may have the egg of a species of bird domesticated in Indo-China, or thin strips of the flesh of an animal domesticated in Eastern Asia which have been salted and smoked by a process developed in northern Europe.

When our friend has finished eating he settles back to smoke, an American Indian habit, consuming a plant domesticated in Brazil in either a pipe, derived from the Indians of Virginia, or a cigarette, derived from Mexico. If he is hardy enough he may even attempt a cigar, transmitted to us from the Antilles by way of Spain. While smoking he reads the news of the day, imprinted in characters invented by the ancient Semites upon a material invented in China by a process invented in Germany. As he absorbs the accounts of foreign troubles he will, if he is a good conservative citizen, thank a Hebrew deity in an Indo-European language that he is 100% American.

Ralph Linton, *The Study of Man* (New York: Appleton-Century, 1936), pp. 326–27. Reprinted by permission of Alfred A. Knopf, Inc.

---

pendent upon their ability to catch fish with their bare hands, club little woolly horses, and drive away the saber-tooth tiger with fire. Consequently the skills of "fish-grabbing," "woolly-horse-clubbing," and "saber-tooth-tiger-scaring-with-fire" were the basic curriculum of the school.

In time, a change occurred in the physical environment of these paleolithic people. A great glacier descended from the north, muddying the streams, so that "No matter how good a man's fish-grabbing education had been, he could not grab fish when he could not find fish to grab." The great glacier also caused the little woolly horses to migrate to a drier climate and killed the saber-tooth tigers. Under these changed conditions, the tribe would have perished had there not been some inventions. Survival now became dependent upon the people's ability to catch fish in the muddy water with newly invented nets, to snare the elusive antelopes who had replaced the horses, and to trap bears in pits. Meanwhile, "back at school," they continued to teach the skills of fish-grabbing, horse-clubbing, and tiger-scaring.

Now there were a few thoughtful tribesmen who criticized the schools. "These new activities of net-making, snare-setting, and pit-digging are indispensable to modern existence," they said. "Why can't they be taught in school? *After all, you will have to admit that times have changed.*"

But the wise old men who controlled the schools pointed out that the school curriculum already was too crowded with teaching the intricate details of the "standard cultural subjects"—fish-grabbing, horse-clubbing, and tiger-scaring. No, they couldn't possibly consider adding such "fads and frills" as net-making, antelope-snaring, and bear-killing, because "the essence of true education is timelessness. It is something that endures through changing conditions like a solid rock standing squarely and firmly in the middle of a raging torrent. You must know that there are some eternal verities, and the saber-tooth curriculum is one of them." [4]

To an equally significant, but perhaps somewhat less obvious, degree, American culture has changed and is changing. Does this mean that our schools should change? Are we now experiencing some resistance to change by those who fear losing the "basics" in the school curriculum?

[4] Harold Benjamin, *The Saber-Tooth Curriculum* (New York: McGraw-Hill, 1939), p. 44.

The Significance of Change

The noted anthropologist Margaret Mead has stated our biggest problem today is that *"no one will live all his life in the world into which he was born, and no one will die in the world in which he worked in his maturity."* [5]

This is because we are living in a world that is changing faster than ever before. Previously, change was slow enough to be "assimilated and taught to the next generation by teachers who learned it as they went along."

Now, thanks to rapid technological and social changes, we in America have moved to a position where the system of education that relies on the teacher as a "passer on" of the cultural heritage just won't work. And this is new to the concept of teaching today. Our trouble, says Margaret Mead, is that we are crying over our failure to live in a way in which we have never been called upon to live before, to which we are completely unaccustomed.

Confronted face to face with the realities of rapid cultural change, adults no longer know enough. This puts teachers and parents (the experienced) in the same boat with the youth (the inexperienced) whom they are responsible to educate. What can the teacher do?

The experienced persons can give the general rules, set a style, give the system, *and then they and the child can go on together to meet something neither one of them has ever seen* [or known].

It's easy and safe to find certainty early and then to rest upon it. It requires intellectual bravery to learn to live constantly with a sense of change. This is much harder to do. Our times thus demand a kind of "open-ended" education—preparation to face "the blank page," preparation for life in a complex world where the ability to live with uncertainty and change and still act effectively is a fundamental requirement. To complete Margaret Mead's survey of the situation, "We need to teach students to think, when we don't know what method to use, about a problem which is not yet formulated." [6]

Cultural Trends

Is it enough simply to recognize the fact that our culture is changing and some of the implications for education? We need also to know in what ways it is changing if we are to be properly equipped to help our students develop the attitudes compatible with change.

Summarized here are some of the most important cultural trends:

1. Knowledge in every subject field has increased as more of our resources are directed toward research. "Knowledge has certainly never before

[5] Margaret Mead, "Thinking Ahead: Why Is Education Obsolete?" *The Harvard Business Review,* pp. 23–37, 164–70, November-December, 1958.

[6] *Ibid.,* "Changing Teacher in a Changing World," in *The Education of Teachers,* ed. G. K. Hodenfield and T. M. Stinnett (Englewood Cliffs, N.J.: Prentice-Hall, 1961), pp. 121–34.

in history been so central to the conduct of an entire society. What the railroads did for the second half of the last century and the automobile for the first half of this century may be done for the second half of this century by the 'knowledge' industry: that is, to serve as the focal point for national growth." [7]

2. Specialization, interdependence, and complexity are growing.

3. Our population is increasing. In our fastest growing state, California, a new child is "born every minute and a half. At this rate, a new city the size of San Diego can be populated every year. To accommodate these children, five new schools need to open their doors every Monday morning." [8]

4. Our population is becoming more mobile. For example, "one in four Californians moves each year." [9] And the distribution of our population is changing. In 1930, about 60 per cent lived in big cities or on farms; in the 1960's, about 60 per cent live in either suburbs or small towns.

5. Family patterns are changing; youth are marrying earlier than their parents and grandparents did and, thanks to TV, the home again is becoming a family center (at least in a physical sense).

6. New sources of power and automation are raising standards of living and the minimum competence necessary for initial employment.

7. The amount of time for leisure has increased and will continue to increase. "Within a quarter of a century, automation will produce such an ocean of free time that each person's working life will include a decade of disposable time." [10]

8. Advances in mass communication and increased standardization of products have brought increased pressures toward conformity at a time when increased individuality and creativity are needed.

9. Scientific and technological advances have outstripped our social institutions and value standards, that is, have grown faster than our ability to adjust to them.

10. The separation between the generations is becoming wider and communications between adults and the young is becoming more difficult, cynicism and skepticism have increased, the ebb of religion has grown greater, ideological conflicts have sharpened, and the importance of education has greatly increased.

With all these current cultural changes occurring, what is left? Are there any longer some eternal verities? If education is the tool by which we prepare young Americans to live a fruitful life in a culture dominated by change, do we teach only for change? Or are there still some over-all dominant values, some *real* eternal verities, which do and will likely continue to characterize our society. If so, what are these values—the goals of Americans?

[7] Clark Kerr, *University Bulletin* (University of California Press), No. 9, p. 53, September 30, 1963.

[8] James C. Stone, *California's Commitment to Public Education* (New York: Thomas Y. Crowell, 1961), p. 1.

[9] *Ibid.*, p. 7.

[10] Robert Lazarus, as quoted in the *San Francisco Chronicle*, May 17, 1963.

GOALS FOR AMERICANS

It has been said that America is not one culture but many. For America is the nation which said to the world:

> . . . *Give me your tired, your poor,*
> *Your huddled masses yearning to breathe free,*
> *The wretched refuse of your teeming shore.*
> *Send these, the homeless, tempest-tost to me,*
> *I lift my lamp beside the golden door.*[11]

Conflicting Goals

If we are a nation of many cultures, then it follows that we are a nation of many values, a nation of conflicting values. That we are a nation of conflicting values is attested to by the well-known novelist Erskine Caldwell, who wrote:

What of life in the United States of America at this particular time of our century?

Dynamic. Depressing. Open—all night. Closed-for-the-season. Everybody welcome. White only. Colored entrance. Bloated with wealth and despairing in poverty. Aggressive and reactionary. Devoutly religious and amorally uninhibited. Charge it. Pay later. Something for nothing. A day's work for a day's pay. Ban the bomb. Remember Pearl Harbor.[12]

Is America going all ways at once? And are the schools thus reduced to teaching different values to different children, depending on which direction the teacher assumes they are going? Or are there some basic values—some fundamental goals to which all Americans give allegiance? Which goals give direction to the educational enterprise?

In an effort to define for the 1960's the goals for Americans, President Dwight D. Eisenhower established the President's Commission on National Goals. The commission was requested by the President to "develop a broad outline of coordinated national policies and programs" and "to set up a series of goals in various areas of national activity." An excerpt from the commission's report appears on page 12.

The Fundamental Goals

The major domestic goals for Americans, as defined in the report, are *equality* and *education*. These goals, in turn, depend overwhelmingly on the individual attitudes and actions of each American.

[11] Inscription, from a poem by Emma Lazarus, on the Statue of Liberty, New York City.

[12] Erskine Caldwell, *Erskine Caldwell's USA* (San Francisco: The Chronicle Publishing Co., 1963), p. 1.

Our faith is that man lives, not by bread alone, but by self-respect, by regard for other men, by convictions of right and wrong, by strong religious faith.

Man has never been an island unto himself. The shores of his concern have expanded from his neighborhood to his nation, and from his nation to the world. Free men have always known the necessity for responsibility. A basic goal for each American is to achieve a sense of responsibility as broad as his world-wide concerns and as compelling as the dangers and opportunities he confronts.[13]

The job of the school—the teacher's primary obligation—then is to teach the knowledge and skills inherent in the preservation and enhancement of our democratic values. John Gardner states the issue succinctly in the concluding paragraph to his chapter on "National Goals for Education":

And in striving for excellence, we must never forget that American education has a clear mission to accomplish with every single child who walks into the school. Modern life has presented some urgent and sharply defined tasks on education, tasks of producing certain specially needed kinds of educated talent. For the sake of our future we had better succeed in these tasks—but they cannot and should not crowd out the great basic goals of our educational system: to foster individual fulfillment and to nurture the free, rational and reasonable men and women without whom our kind of society cannot endure. *Our schools must prepare all young people, whatever their talents, for the serious business of being free men and women.*[14]

Another way of stating the goals identified in the commission's report is that our basic ideal is the importance of people as individuals worthy of human dignity, or respect for personality. From this basic goal flow the three major ideals that have guided American thought, action, and feeling:

> human freedom and rights
>
> equality of opportunity
>
> social responsibility and self-discipline

Regardless of the words used, the important idea which needs to be reinforced is that the concepts represented by the various phrases embody the essential idealism which has come to characterize what we today call glibly "the American way of life." These ideals are the most precious element in our national heritage; they have been evolved over generations, with the basic core of beliefs remaining constant, but enlarging and expanding as each new historical epoch has unfolded and as each new generation has sought to apply them to its times.

Reinterpretation and expansion, superimposed upon a central theme—this has been a fundamental characteristic of the historical development of American ideals. In their inception, they were largely political and legal in character,

---

[13] *Goals for Americans* (Report of the President's Commission on National Goals) (Englewood Cliffs, N.J.: Prentice-Hall, 1960), p. 23.

[14] *Ibid.,* p. 100.

but their original political and legal framework has been expanded into social and economic areas for a single sovereign nation . . . the ideals for a single nation have been reinterpreted and broadened into a "one world" conception of establishing these ideals for all people everywhere. . . . The primary function of American education is the preservation and extension of these ideals.[15]

[15] James C. Stone, "A Curriculum for the Teaching of American Ideals," unpublished doctoral dissertation, Stanford University, 1949.

Goals for Americans

The paramount goal of the United States was set long ago [authors' italics]. It is to guard the rights of the individual, to ensure his development and to enlarge his opportunity. It is set forth in the Declaration of Independence drafted by Thomas Jefferson and adopted by the Continental Congress on July 4, 1776. The goals we here identify are within the framework of the original plan and are calculated to bring to fruition the dreams of the men who laid the foundation of this country.

They stated their convictions quite simply:

"We hold these truths to be self-evident, that all men are created equal, that they are endowed by their Creator with certain unalienable Rights, that among these are Life, Liberty and the pursuit of Happiness. That to secure these rights, Governments are instituted among men, deriving their just powers from the consent of the governed."

It was a mighty vision. In the echo of those fateful words can be heard the onrolling thunder of a new age. It was an even broader and bolder declaration than those who made it knew. Its soaring vision enabled our society to meet the trials of emerging nationhood. It placed the young republic securely behind the principle that every human being is of infinite worth. In time it led the nation out of the morass of human slavery. It inspires us still in the struggle against injustice.

To make this vision a reality, a framework of self-government was established nationally and in each state. It rested upon two fundamental principles—the election of representatives from among competing candidates, and the constitutional limitation of power of those elected.

The way to preserve freedom is to live it [authors' italics]. Our enduring aim is to build a nation and help build a world in which every human being shall be free to develop his capacities to the fullest. We must rededicate ourselves to this principle and thereby strengthen its appeal to a world in political, social, economic, and technological revolution.

. . . . .

To preserve and enlarge our own liberties, to meet a deadly menace, and to extend the area of freedom throughout the world: these are high and difficult goals. Yet our past performance justifies confidence that they can be achieved if every American will accept personal responsibility for them.

. . . . .

. . . Choices are hard, and costs are heavy. They demand subordination of lesser goals to the greater. But the rewards are beyond calculation, for the future of our nation depends on the result.

Goals for Americans (Report of the President's Commission on National Goals (Englewood Cliffs, N.J.: Prentice-Hall, 1961), pp. 1, 2. © 1960 by The American Assembly, Columbia University, New York, New York. Reprinted by permission of Prentice-Hall, Inc., Englewood Cliffs, New Jersey.

OUR COMMITMENT

To accomplish these goals for Americans, in the second half of the twentieth century, involves a continuing or continuous commitment by the people of the extent to which our resources will be devoted to achieving these ends.

One state—our most populous one—has expressed her commitment in these terms:

California's commitment to public education includes *all* its children and youth—regardless of skin color, intelligence, physical deformities, geographical location, socioeconomic status, or vocational aim. The commitment is not one that can be restricted or turned on or off at will. California's commitment extends to the provision of free public education from kindergarten through the university for all boys and girls in the state.

This commitment is anchored in California's constitution, is supported by a most voluminous set of laws and the largest proportionate outlay of money of any state, and is more inclusive of all aspects of public education than that found in most other states. In addition to elementary and high schools, California provides free education at sixty-five public junior colleges, fifteen state colleges, and seven branches of the state university. . . .

In the report of the Governor's Conference on Education, the following beliefs, deeply rooted in the American tradition, were reiterated:

1. We have established a system of free public education from the kindergarten through the university—open and available to each young person to the extent that he can profit from it.

2. The heart of the educational system is the teacher. Everything else about schools—the buildings, the money, the organization—is designed to enable good teaching to take place.

3. There is no substitute for the good teacher.

4. Every child, by his birthright, is entitled to the education which good teachers provide through their daily and immediate contact with a group of youngsters whom they know as individuals.

No other state but California makes a more generous effort to husband all of its resources in support of its one greatest natural resource—its children and its youth.[16]

[16] Stone, *op. cit.*, pp. 15–18.

THE COMMITMENT LAG

Although the different parts of culture are interdependent, they may change at different rates. And the delay during which one thing catches up with another is called the culture lag. In a similar manner, in this country we find a difference between what our commitment is, ideally speaking, and what the situation is, realistically speaking. In this section we will trace our commitment lag, through the reactions of the well-known English critic Denis Brogan and the very controversial Fidel Castro, Prime Minister of the Republic of Cuba, plus two Americans—Mrs. Eleanor Roosevelt and Max Lerner. The chapter will conclude with a review of relevant facts about the status of American education today—the present situation, its challenge, and its possibilities.

From the English Point of View

Following a tour of America in 1961, Denis W. Brogan—historian and professor of political science, as well as Britain's foremost authority on the United States and its people—sprinkled an account of his trip with such observations as "America is tense and worried," "I notice a steady deterioration in American self-confidence and trust in the 'American way of life,'" "I think the irritation and malaise that I encountered . . . [are] more a matter of the whole moral tone of the American way of life than immediate deficiencies that an intelligent Administration can rapidly cure."

He cites particularly the "intelligent worry" about America's public schools, especially because he believes that *all* Americans want to send "and soon hope to send" their children to a college or university. He underscores the fact that there are great variations both among states and within states in the level of educational opportunity offered and in "the theoretical equality" promised as part of the American dream. "It [says Brogan] is too often an equal right to unequal things."

Brogan concludes his perceptive analysis of America by saying:

The American people are looking in the mirror at the moment, and are not, I fear, very pleased with what they see. So I have had to pass a good deal of my time in recent months cheering up my American friends and telling them that it has been worse, a sentiment with which they are sheepishly glad to agree. It could be worse, but it could be a great deal better, and it is very difficult at the moment to see where the improvement is to come from.[17]

From an American Point of View

Are these the doddering words of a headline-seeking English critic? Let us turn to a great American woman, Mrs. Franklin D. Roosevelt. In 1962, *The*

---

[17] *San Francisco Chronicle*, September 27, 1961, pp. 1, 16.

Autobiography of Eleanor Roosevelt was published and widely reviewed. One reviewer commented as follows:

She [Mrs. Roosevelt] is a very wise woman and it would be correspondingly unwise not to take notice of her hopes—and fears. Her hope is that the vision of good will and neighborly justice that inspired the years of the New Deal can now be extended to the family of man. Her fear is that the West has neither the drive nor the discipline to take on the task in time. It is significant that what chiefly impressed and troubled her in Russia was the comparison between the disciplined dedication demanded of Russian youth and the lack of preparation for service in American education. "Great things," said Mrs. Roosevelt, "cannot be accomplished in America by slack and listless instruments." [18]

From the Communist Point of View

Let's go away and look at this matter of the "disciplined dedication demanded of Russian youth." But we need not go to Russia. A hundred miles south of Florida is far enough. Fidel Castro is speaking to Cuba's youth at the dedication of a new college, which was formerly an army base.

We had first intended to make this into a regular college campus, but we came to the conclusion it would be better to create an institute of Science and Technology—a center of learning to teach engineering, to train experts who will know about factories and who will acquire from engineering, physics, and chemistry all the technical and scientific knowledge necessary to industrialize our country.

Because of capitalistic imperialism, you children are suffering the consequences of all the neglect in which the people of our nation have lived. However, you will not suffer many things that we have suffered because we are going to educate you so that things will turn out all right in the future.

Do you believe that the revolutionary reconstruction and reform of Cuba is finished now?

Children: "No."

Then if it is not yet finished, who is going to finish it?

Children: "We are."

You are the ones who must rebuild and reform Cuba. Do you want to be good patriotic citizens?

Children: "Yes, yes."

Then what is the first thing you must do?

Children: "Study."

Yes. Study! Any child who does *not* study is not a good citizen. Anybody who refuses to study is not patriotic and cannot be one of us nor help us, because we all have a lot of important things to do and in order to do them it is necessary to learn *how* to do them.

The people of Cuba used to come by and see a fortress here where now they will see a scholastic center. Cuba is the only country in the world that has been able to do this—to conquer a military fortress and convert it into a school. What do we need fortresses for? What we need are institutions of learning.

[18] *Saturday Review,* 44:23, September 30, 1961.

This intellectual fortress will never be seized by anybody else. This is no longer the headquarters of a gang of bullies. It is the fortress of the Cuban people.

THE CHALLENGE

How strong is America's intellectual and moral fortress? Are we equal to the Russians? Or at least to the Cubans? Let's see what one critical observer of America during thirty-five years as author, syndicated newspaper columnist, and teacher has to say on the subject of our commitment lag. The observer is Max Lerner, now a Professor of American Civilization at Brandeis University. To thoroughly appreciate the flavor of his analysis, read first what he says about élan, élite, and ethos in the side-insert, page 17.

Professor Lerner believes that our society has developed a definite set of goals

that I'm not very happy about. I don't mean that they are entirely empty. I do suggest that part of the problem of education is to understand the national and personal goals by which we live and die. When I wrote my *America as a Civilization* I talked of the five-goal system that we have in America, of success and power, and money and prestige, and security, and I added that we are a happiness civilization. We use happiness as the test of so much.

There is nothing basically wrong with success if you are talking of the capacity to see your problem through, but if you mean by success that others should recognize you as having arrived, if you mean by success that you have been able to trample upon others, then I see very little in it.

. . . Instead of power for the individual, I would suggest that we shift to a sense of the functioning of the individual to the limit of his powers . . . of reaching to the very depth of his capacity.

Instead of money as a goal, I suggest the doctrine of work and, through work, achieving the things that money cannot buy . . . Instead of prestige, which we largely think of in terms of seeing ourselves in the mirror of the esteem of others, I suggest that we care about the good opinion only of our fellow craftsmen, of our friends, the people who form part of us and of whom we form a part, so that we are not continually bedeviled by the question of what the world as a whole thinks of us. Instead of security, I suggest that we shift to the capacity for risk, for a sense of selfhood, sense of identity.

Instead of happiness, I suggest joyousness, a feeling for nature, for the tent of the sky, for the carpet of the earth, for the world of sight and sound and sense all around us. In our industrialized urban society we very badly need a re-education of the senses.

If you put these together, and if along with this you take a creative America with a creative élite, and if along with that you take a sense of élan, a sense of a country still unfinished, a sense of the authentic revolutionary tradition which is our history and which we can project into the future—if you put those together then I suggest to you that perhaps we'll be able to do something with our youngsters in our educational system. Perhaps we'll be able to win the future.[19]

[19] Max Lerner, "Humanist Goals," in *Education: An Instrument of National Goals,* ed. Paul R. Hanna. Copyright, 1962. McGraw-Hill Book Company.

ÉLAN, ÉLITE, ETHOS

I want to start with one aspect of national purpose, the aspect that I call *élan*. I use a French term because I don't know of any English term. What I mean by *élan* is the feeling of commitment, the feeling of being on fire, a sense of mission, a sense that there are things worth dying for and worth living for.

We've got to recapture what seems to me the *élan* of American history, and that's the authentic idea of a revolutionary America. I think it means we've got to stop being afraid of the term "revolution." I found that the image of America (which many people in other countries have) . . . is the image of a fat, rich, prosperous, complacent country which was the last bulwark of the *status quo,* and they didn't like it.

If we think in terms of this authentic revolutionary tradition and if we keep alive, as I hope we will keep alive, the life of the mind and the spirit so as to give meaning to these dynamic energies of ours, then I think that we can answer the problem of *élan.* And with this energy we have great tasks to perform. I think that I can put them all in a single phrase, and the phrase for me is that of finishing the unfinished business of democracy.

I break down the concept of national purpose into a second portion. To this also I give a foreign name, *élite,* the idea of an educated, creative *élite.* . . . If we are to win what I regard as the crucial race, not the weapons race but the entire *intelligence race,* it can be done only by using our educational plant and resources for the development of the best potentials of our most promising youngsters.

The problems of the school system of a generation ago, two generations ago, three or four or five generations ago are no longer the problems of today. We've gone through a great educational revolution, a revolution of trying to give a substratum of necessary cohesion to the society. We are, as Walt Whitman said, not just a nation but a nation of nations. America was built up by streams of immigration from every part of the world. And it was necessary during our history to use our educational system in such a way that youngsters coming from families with different religions, with different ethnic traditions, with different cultural traditions, should have something in common, they should have some cohesion, some cement. The problem today is different. It is that of a creative America.

In every realm of activity, in every discipline in our lives, there is a small group of people who are training themselves, educating themselves, stretching themselves in order to transcend themselves. I see emerging a new creative America which will develop a democratic élite and make use of it for strengthening the culture.

I've spoken of *élan* and of a creative American *élite.* I end by suggesting a third element of the larger concept of national purpose. That is an *ethos,* a sense of values to live by and to die by if necessary.

Max Lerner, "Humanist Goals," in *Education: An Instrument of National Goals,* ed. Paul R. Hanna. Copyright, 1962. McGraw-Hill Book Company.

All Americans

To "win the future" which Max Lerner talks about, all Americans must ask themselves the question "What kind of society do we want America to be?" If we want it to become a society of weapons-producers and technicians, this will establish one set of goals for our schools. On the other hand, if Americans want to become a society willing to "live and die" by ideals such as those of Orin Knox, then this means a priority of another sort for our schools.

In the following section from Allen Drury's *Advise and Consent*, Orrin Knox, the senior senator from Illinois, is addressing the members of the United States Senate at a time of momentous crisis in the history of the United States. The time is 197?, and the Russians have just announced to the world the completion of the first successful flight to the moon. They have claimed the moon on behalf of the USSR and have sent the President of the United States a telegram ordering him to meet in Geneva with representatives of the Russian government within forty-eight hours. With America on the brink of capitulation or disaster, Senator Knox rises and addresses his colleagues:

"Mr. President," he began slowly looking thoughtfully about the room, "I see before me Senators of the United States, seated in the Senate of the United States, here in this great Capitol of the United States, with our sister house of the Congress just across the way and all around us the great symbols of our heritage and our purpose and our future. And I ask myself, and I put to you these questions:

"Are these things suddenly turned to nothing in half an hour's time?

"Are a few words from the moon sufficient to erase all we have stood for and all we are?

"Should we who have done so much, and have so much, and have yet before us such great tasks for ourselves and for all humankind, be struck dumb and paralyzed because we have been temporarily bested in our continuing contest with the Soviet Union?

"Does this suddenly cancel everything that America is?

"Mr. President," he said quietly, "I cannot believe it. I know not how others feel, but I know how I feel.

"There are certain things in this life that are still valid, and will always be.

"There are ways of dealing with other people which are just and honest and honorable and decent; and these have not been changed.

"There are standards of character and of integrity which honorable men, while they may not always achieve them, at least have before them for their goal; and these have not been changed.

"There is human good will and loving-kindness and tolerance towards one's fellow man in all his shortcomings, whatever they may be and bearing in mind one's own; and these have not been changed.

"There is a great nation and a great people and a great mission of liberty and freedom and justice for all, coming out of the past and moving on gloriously into the future, insofar as God helps us to achieve it; and neither have these been changed.

"Nothing of the essentials of the human heart or the human character or the human story as good men see it have been changed.

"Senators," he said softly, and in the utter silence there was a powerful emotion in his voice that powerfully moved them all, "I commend to you your country; a very great nation, which has a job to do.

"Let us get on with it!" [20]

All Teachers

While Americans sit by the fire and spin, debating the various alternatives, what more should the teacher be doing? As early as 1932, George S. Counts raised the question of the professional practitioner's place in the scheme of things in his book *Dare the School Build a New Social Order?* Nearly thirty-five years later, the question is still appropriate. In a large measure, the answer to the question of the direction of the future of the American school lies in the hands of its teachers. It depends on their wisdom, their insight, their character, their devotion to the task of educating the next generation. For it is the teacher who, through guiding the mind and hearts of our children and youth, determines not only their future, but through them the future of our state, our nation, and our world.

CONCLUSION

We began by examining the nature of culture and its relation to education. We learned that from society at large come the aims, content, and organization of our schools, that the school and its purposes change as the body politic from which the school draws its life blood changes. We have examined some of the challenges, conflicts, and shortcomings of the values, held by most Americans, to which the school owes allegiance. We have concluded that, given our over-all societal and educational commitment, within this the teacher has a great opportunity for determining the nature of the future American citizen.

There is no such thing as "mass education." Every use of the phrase is a denial of a vital reality; education is a wholly individual process. The life of the mind—despite all pressures to invade it—remains a private life. It occurs in each person uniquely. We do democracy no service in seeking to inhibit thought—free, wide-ranging, hazardous.

Henry M. Wriston, in *Goals for Americans* (Report of the President's Commission on National Goals) (Englewood Cliffs, N.J.: Prentice-Hall, 1961), p. 56.

---

[20] From *Advise and Consent*, pp. 714–15, by Allen Drury. Copyright © 1959 by Allen Drury. Reprinted by permission of Doubleday & Company, Inc.

Questions for Discussion

1. What is the distinct role of each of the following social institutions: the school, the family, the church.
2. What functions do each of the above social institutions share in common?
3. Are all groups equally acceptable to the idea of cultural change? Think of examples of groups which resist change. What accounts for their resistance?
4. Are there values or goals which are "eternal," that is, never change? List some examples.
5. Reread the cultural trends listed on pages 8 and 9. What educational implications are growing out of each trend?
6. What is the school's role in reducing the "commitment lag"?
7. Do you agree with Max Lerner's analysis of contemporary America in terms of élan, élite, and ethos? What can teachers do to bring our ideals into everyday living?
8. What responsibility does each teacher have for inculcating American ideals and values? Do teachers of all grades and all subjects have equal responsibility?
9. Are some classes, subject fields, or units of study uniquely suited to teaching values?
10. Do you believe in the education of the élite as proposed by Thomas Jefferson? Why or why not?

Activities and Projects

1. Interview an elementary or secondary school counselor and ask him to tell you what's "the latest" in the peer culture of his pupils.
2. Read a chapter in Stuart A. Queen's *The Family in Various Cultures* and prepare an analysis of its implications for you as a teacher.
3. Interview one representative of each of the following social groups regarding the point of view his organization takes toward teaching American ideals:
   Boy Scouts of America
   AFL-CIO
   National Association of Manufacturers
   American Legion
   American Association of University Women
   League of Women Voters
   American Civil Liberties Union
4. Make a special study of education in some other culture or nation, noting especially how its schools are "the mouthpiece of the culture."
5. Make a survey of the faculty at your college on the degree to which they accept or reject Margaret Mead's notions about culture and cultural change.
6. Think about the community in which you were raised as a child. List the

changes that have taken place since then in the economy, the population, the buildings, the ages of the residents, etc. After you have made your list, for each change indicate whether the school had a significant part in it, was neutral, or slowed it down.

7. Visit an Americanization class in the adult education program of a nearby school and report to your class what you observed.
8. Analyze the front page of the local newspaper over a period of several weeks. What values are being headlined? What implications does your conclusion have for the school?

References

"CULTURE"

BENEDICT, RUTH, *Patterns of Culture* (New York: New American Library, 1959).

BROOM, LEONARD, and PHILIP SELZNICK, *Sociology*, 3d ed. (New York: Harper & Row, 1963), Chapter 3, "Culture"; Chapter 4, "Socialization"; Chapter 5, "Primary Groups."

CLARK, BURTON R., *Educating the Expert Society* (San Francisco: Chandler, 1962), Chapter I, "Education as a Cultural Agent."

COOK, LLOYD, and ELAINE COOK, *A Sociological Approach to Education* (New York: McGraw-Hill, 1960), Parts I and II.

ELKIN, FREDERICK, *The Child and Society* (New York: Random House, 1960).

KING, EDMUND J., *World Perspectives in Education* (Indianapolis: Bobbs-Merrill, 1962), Chapters 3, 5, 6.

LEVIN, MARTIN, ed., *Five Boyhoods* (New York: Doubleday, 1962).

LINTON, RALPH, *The Study of Man* (New York: Appleton-Century, 1936).

MEAD, MARGARET, *Growing Up in New Guinea, Coming of Age in Samoa, Cultural Patterns and Technical Change* (New York: New American Library, 1959).

———, "Thinking Ahead: Why Is Education Obsolete?" *The Harvard Business Review*, pp. 23–27, 164–70, November-December, 1958.

SPINDLER, GEORGE D., *Education and Culture* (New York: Holt, Rinehart & Winston, 1963), Part II, "Education in American Culture"; Part III, "Education Viewed Cross-culturally."

———, *The Transmission of American Culture* (Cambridge, Mass.: Harvard University Press, 1960).

"SOCIAL INSTITUTIONS"

BOSSARD, JAMES S., *The Sociology of Child Development*, rev. ed. (New York: Harper & Row, 1954).

BROOM and SELZNICK, Chapter 10, "The Family"; Chapter 11, "Religion."

COOK and COOK, Part II, "Social Institutions."

KING, Chapter 12, "Social and Family Change."

MURDOCK, GEORGE P., *Social Structure* (New York: Macmillan, 1949).

QUEEN, STUART A., *et al.*, *The Family in Various Cultures* (Philadelphia: Lippincott, 1961).

"CULTURAL CHANGE—CULTURAL TRENDS"

BENJAMIN, HAROLD, *The Saber-Tooth Curriculum* (New York: McGraw-Hill, 1939).

BROOM and SELZNICK, Part III, "Master Trends."

COUNTS, GEORGE S., *Dare the Schools Build a New Social Order?* (New York: John Day, 1932).

HANDLIN, OSCAR, *The Uprooted* (New York: Grosset & Dunlap, 1951).

HODGKINSON, HAROLD L., *Education in Social and Cultural Perspectives* (Englewood Cliffs, N.J.: Prentice-Hall, 1962), Chapter 4, "Cultural Lag, Social Change, and Education."

MEAD, MARGARET, "Changing Teachers in a Changing World," in *The Education of Teachers,* G. K. Hodenfield and T. M. Stinnett (Englewood Cliffs, N.J.: Prentice-Hall, 1961).

PACKARD, VANCE, *The Status Seekers* (New York: David McKay, 1959).

PETERSEN, WILLIAM, and DAVID MATZA, *Social Controversy* (Belmont, Calif.: Wadsworth, 1963), "Does 'Mass Culture' Threaten Culture?" pp. 316–41.

SIMPSON, HOKE S., ed., *The Changing American Population* (New York: Inst. of Life Insurance, 1962).

THOMPSON, DANIEL C., The Negro Leadership Class (Englewood Cliffs, N.J.: Prentice-Hall, 1963), Chapters 2 and 3.

"THE CULTURE OF SCHOOLS"

BROOKOVER, WILBUR B., and DAVID GOTTLIEB, A *Sociology of Education* (New York: American Book, 1964, Part III, "The School Society."

CLARK, Chapter 7, "Student Cultures."

COLEMAN, JAMES S., *Social Climates in High Schools* (Washington, D.C.: U.S. Department of Health, Education and Welfare, 1961).

GRAMBS, JEAN D., and L. MORRIS MC CLURE, *Foundations of Teaching* (New York: Holt, Rinehart & Winston, 1964), Chapter 7, "The Culture of the School–Elementary"; Chapter 8, "The Culture of the School–Secondary."

HECHINGER, GRACE and FRED, *Teen-age Tyranny* (New York: Morrow, 1963).

"SOCIAL GOALS AND VALUES"

CURTI, MERLE, *The Social Ideas of American Educators* (Paterson, N.J.: Littlefield, Adams, 1959).

Goals for Americans (Report of the President's Commission on National Goals) (Englewood Cliffs, N.J.: Prentice-Hall, 1960).

HECHINGER, FRED, *The Big Red Schoolhouse* (New York: Doubleday, 1962).

HODGKINSON, *Education in Social and Cultural Perspectives,* Chapter 7.

TOYNBEE, ARNOLD J., "Education: The Long View" in *American Education Today,* ed. Paul Woodring and John Scanlon (New York: McGraw-Hill, 1963).

TRAGER, HELEN G., and MAREAN R. YARROW, *They Learn What They Live* (New York: Harper & Row, 1952).

TRUMP, J. LLOYD, and DORSEY BAYNHAM, *Focus on Change: Guide to Better Schools* (Chicago: Rand McNally, 1961).

ii

There are doubts concerning the business [of education] since all people do not agree in those things which they would have a child taught, both with respect to improvement in virtue and a happy life; nor is it clear whether the object of it should be to improve the reason or rectify the morals. From the present mode of education we cannot determine with certainty to which men incline, or what tends to virtue, or what is excellent; for all these things have their separate defenders.

ARISTOTLE

the goals

THE PUBLIC VERSUS THE EDUCATORS

Public schools belong to the people. Thus, parents and taxpayers believe the schools are *their* businesss. School administrators and teachers, specially prepared for their jobs and committed to education as a lifelong career, also believe that the schools are *their* business. Herein lies a basis for possible differences in points of view.

While this natural conflict between taxpayers and teachers has been with us for years, it has assumed much greater importance since the Russians launched Sputnik I on October 4, 1957. Ever since the cold war moved into outer space, the American people have been newly discovering education. As one state governor has put it, "In this futuristic contest, we [the American people] have discovered that our classrooms are the launching platforms." [1]

In too many instances, the newly stirred public concern for better schools has overlooked the teacher's natural interest in the same goal, and too often self-appointed experts have taken a radical, somewhat hysterical point of view. A review of headlines which have appeared over recent newspaper articles will illustrate the point:

[1] Address by Governor Edmund G. Brown before the annual conference of the California School Boards Association, December 10, 1960.

American Education—Unhealthy Monopoly of Professional School Administrators and Politicians.

Schools Being Run according to Foggy Patent Philosophies and Pedagogic
Gobbledy-Gook.

American Educators Equate Interest with Entertainment and Underesti-
mate the Brains and the Ambitions of Our Children.

University Professors Condemn San Francisco Schools.

Artificiality and Insecurity in Teachers' Relationships with Pupils.

Bright Children Allowed to Drift—Special Abilities Not Developed.

If one analyzes the conflicting statements and points of view carefully, the
divergent philosophies of education underlying the differences between
groups of taxpayers and educators become apparent. In other words, there
exists a conflict or a lack of agreement on what our schools should accomplish.

THE OBJECTIVES OF EDUCATION

Is the purpose of education to prepare for life, for jobs, for citizenship,
for college? Has intellectual training and development been neglected in favor
of life adjustment or the whole child? Is intellect any more important in a
scale of values than good citizenship, getting along with others, loyalty to our
democratic traditions, ability to get and keep a job? These are the questions
that still are before us today just as they have been over the last hundred
years—in fact, ever since the establishment of public schools.

Just as each age creates its women's fashions, so it has its own particular
ideas about education. For example, following World War I and the shock over
the number of young men physically unqualified for military service came a
period when "healthful living" was the number one aim of the schools. And
following the uproar which resulted from the Russians' launching of the first
satellite, the new fashion in education—its central purpose—came to be "training the mind." Thus, to the question "What should be the purposes of education?," each generation has offered an answer appropriate to the social
conditions and climate of opinion of the epoch. An understanding of this historical development is necessary as we work out our answer in the second half
of the twentieth century.

What Knowledge Is of Most Worth?

We begin this review and analysis of statements of the purpose of education with an essay by Herbert Spencer, a sociologist who has been variously
described as "the founder of sociology as a science," "*the* philosopher of the
nineteenth century," and "the father of modern social science." Whatever his
title, the question he has raised—"What knowledge is of most worth?"—is certainly *the* basic issue for education. Since Spencer first asked it in 1860, it has
continued to provoke, dismay, and stimulate educators.

To Spencer, the basic issue is the "relative values of knowledges." The school's task is to discover what subjects are of most worth, and to design a curriculum which gives these subjects top priority. His criterion of true education is utilitarian: "Of what use is it?"; the true aim of education: "preparation for complete living." John Dewey and his followers were to say the same thing a half century later, and this philosophy is apparent in several of the later statements included in this chapter.

If there requires further evidence of the rude, undeveloped character of our education, we have it in the fact that the comparative worths of different kinds of knowledge have been yet scarcely even discussed—much less discussed in a methodic way with definite results. Not only is it that no standard of relative values has yet been agreed upon; but the existence of any such standard has not been conceived in any clear manner. And not only is it that the existence of any such standard has not been clearly conceived; but the need for it seems to have been scarcely even felt. Men read books on this topic, and attend lectures on that; decide that their children shall be instructed in these branches of knowledge, and shall not be instructed in those; and all under the guidance of mere custom, or liking, or prejudice; without ever considering the enormous importance of determining in some rational way what things are really most worth learning. . . . Before devoting years to some subject which fashion or fancy suggests, it is surely wise to weigh with great care the worth of the results, as compared with the worth of various alternative results which the same years might bring if otherwise applied.

Spencer discusses the need to establish priorities:

In education, then, this is the question of questions, which it is high time we discussed in some methodic way. The first in importance, though the last to be considered, is the problem—how to decide among the conflicting claims of various subjects on our attention. Before there can be a rational *curriculum,* we must settle which things it most concerns us to know; or, to use a word of Bacon's, now unfortunately obsolete—we must determine the relative value of knowledges.

To this end, a measure of value is the first requisite. And happily, respecting the true measure of value, as expressed in general terms there can be no dispute. Every one in contending for the worth of any particular order of information, does so by showing its bearing upon some part of life. In reply to the question, "Of what use is it?" the mathematician, linguist, naturalist, or philosopher, explains the way in which his learning beneficially influences action —saves from evil or secures good—conduces to happiness. When the teacher of writing has pointed out how great an aid writing is to success in business—that is, to the obtainment of sustenance—that is, to satisfactory living; he is held to have proved his case. And when the collector of dead facts (say a numismatist) fails to make clear any appreciable effects which these facts can produce on human welfare, he is obliged to admit that they are comparatively valueless. All then, either directly or by implication, appeal to this as the ultimate test.

How to live?—that is the essential question for us. Not how to live in the mere material sense only, but in the widest sense. The general problem which comprehends every special problem is—the right ruling of conduct in all directions under all circumstances. In what way to treat the body; in what way to treat the mind; in what way to manage our affairs; in what way to bring up a family; in what way to behave as a citizen; in what way to ultilize all those sources of happiness which nature supplies—how to use all our faculties to the greatest advantage of ourselves and others—how to live completely? And this being the great thing needful for us to learn is, by consequence, the great thing which education has to teach. To prepare us for complete living is the function which education has to discharge; and the only rational mode of judging of any educational course is, to judge in what degree it discharges such function. . . .

When Spencer answers his own question "What knowledge is of most worth?" by citing the subject of science, he means the natural *and* social sciences:

To the question with which we set out—What knowledge is of most worth? —the uniform reply is—Science. This is the verdict on all the counts. For direct self-preservation, or the maintenance of life and health, the all-important knowledge is—Science. For that indirect self-preservation, which we call gaining a livelihood, the knowledge of greatest value is—Science. For the due discharge of parental functions, the proper guidance is to found only in—Science. For that interpretation of national life, past and present, without which the citizen cannot rightly regulate his conduct, the indispensable key is—Science. Alike for the most perfect production and highest enjoyment of art in all its forms, the needful preparation is still—Science. And for purposes of discipline—intellectual, moral, religious—the most efficient study is, once more—Science. The question which at first seemed so perplexed, has become, in the course of our inquiry, comparatively simple. We have not to estimate the degrees of importance of different orders of human activity, and different studies as severally fitting us for them; since we find that the study of Science, in its most comprehensive meaning, is the best preparation for all these orders of activity. We have not to decide between the claims of knowledge of great though conventional value, and knowledge of less though intrinsic value; seeing that the knowledge which we find to be of most value in all other respects, is intrinsically most valuable; its worth is not dependent upon opinion, but is as fixed as is the relation of man to the surrounding world. Necessary and eternal as are its truths, all Science concerns all mankind for all time. Equally at present, and in the remotest future, must it be of incalculable importance for the regulation of their conduct, that men should understand the science of life, physical, mental, and social; and that they should understand all other science as a key to the science of life. . . .[2]

The Seven Cardinal Objectives

One of the first and best-known specific definitions of the school's purposes was formulated in 1918 by the Commission on the Reorganization of Secondary Education. The commission proposed for the schools a set of Seven Cardinal Objectives:

[2] Herbert Spencer, *Education: Intellectual, Moral and Physical* (New York: Appleton, 1860), pp. 4–5, 6–7, 49–50.

1. health
2. command of fundamental processes
3. worthy home membership
4. vocational competence
5. effective citizenship
6. worthy use of leisure time
7. ethical character

To evaluate this statement properly one must recall its setting. World War I was ending and Americans were disturbed over the large number of young men rejected for service in the armed forces because of physical unfitness and inability to read and write. If such disabilities and inabilities were to be reduced, the schools obviously had a major job to perform, and the commission sought to give emphasis to this job by the place it gave to health and command of the fundamental processes in a hierarchy of purposes.

The Aims of Education

About the same time, Alfred North Whitehead, then a University of London professor of mathematics, came to Harvard as professor of philosophy and, in 1922, published *The Aims of Education*. While the statement had a greater initial impact on higher rather than elementary or secondary school education, it is included here because of its contrast in point of view to the Seven Cardinal Objectives, as well as because of the importance it has attained with today's greater emphasis on the intellectual side of education and on teaching subject matter per se in a deductive rather than by the traditional inductive process.

One main idea runs throughout Whitehead's chapters: students are alive and the purpose of education is to stimulate and guide their self-development. It follows from this that teachers also should be alive with living thoughts. The whole book is a protest against dead knowledge, against inert ideas. "There is only one subject-matter for education, and that is Life in all its manifestations."

Culture is activity of thought, and receptiveness to beauty and humane feeling. Scraps of information have nothing to do with it. A merely well-informed man is the most useless bore on God's earth. What we should aim at producing is men who possess both culture and expert knowledge in some special direction. Their expert knowledge will give them the ground to start from, and their culture will lead them as deep as philosophy and as high as art. We have to remember that the valuable intellectual development is self-development, and that it mostly takes place between the ages of sixteen and thirty. As to training, the most important part is given by mothers before the age of twelve. A saying due to Archbishop Temple illustrates my meaning. Surprise was expressed at the success in after-life of a man, who as a boy at Rugby had been somewhat undistinguished. He answered, "It is not what they are at eighteen, it is what they become afterwards that matters."

In training a child to activity of thought, above all things we must beware of what I will call "inert ideas"—that is to say, ideas that are merely received into the mind without being utilised, or tested, or thrown into fresh combinations.

In the history of education, the most striking phenomenon is that schools of learning, which at one epoch are alive with a ferment of genius, in a succeeding generation exhibit merely pedantry and routine. The reason is, that they are overladen with inert ideas. Education with inert ideas is not only useless; it is, above all things, harmful—*Corruptio optimi, pessima.* Except at rare intervals of intellectual ferment, education in the past has been radically infected with inert ideas. That is the reason why uneducated clever women, who have seen much of the world, are in middle life so much the most cultured part of the community. They have been saved from this horrible burden of inert ideas. Every intellectual revolution which has ever stirred humanity into greatness has been a passionate protest against inert ideas. Then, alas, with pathetic ignorance of human psychology, it has proceeded by some educational scheme to bind humanity afresh with inert ideas of its own fashioning.

Let us now ask how in our system of education we are to guard against this mental dryrot. We enunciate two educational commandments, "Do not teach too many subjects," and again, "What you teach, teach thoroughly."

Note that at the turn of the century, Whitehead was discussing the "discovery" that modern curriculum reformers emphasize:

The result of teaching small parts of a large number of subjects is the passive reception of disconnected ideas, not illumined with any spark of vitality. Let the main ideas which are introduced into a child's education be few and important, and let them be thrown into every combination possible. The child should make them his own, and should understand their application here and now in the circumstances of his actual life. From the very beginning of his education, the child should experience the joy of discovery. The discovery which he has to make, is that general ideas give an understanding of that stream of events which pours through his life, which is his life. By understanding I mean more than a mere logical analysis, though that is included. I mean "understanding" in the sense in which it is used in the French proverb, "To understand all, is to forgive all." Pedants sneer at an education which is useful. But if education is not useful, what is it? Is it a talent, to be hidden away in a napkin? Of course, education should be useful, whatever your aim in life. It was useful to Saint Augustine and it was useful to Napoleon. It is useful, because understanding is useful.

I pass lightly over that understanding which should be given by the literary side of education. Nor do I wish to be supposed to pronounce on the relative merits of a classical or a modern curriculum. I would only remark that the understanding which we want is an understanding of an insistent present. The only use of a knowledge of the past is to equip us for the present. No more deadly harm can be done to young minds than by depreciation of the present. The present contains all that there is. It is holy ground; for it is the past, and it is the future. At the same time it must be observed that an age is no less past if it existed two hundred years ago than if it existed two thousand years ago. Do not be deceived by the pedantry of dates. The ages of Shakespeare and of Molière are no less past than are the ages of Sophocles and of Virgil. The communion of saints is a great and inspiring assemblage, but it has only one possible hall of meeting, and that is, the present; and the mere lapse of time through which any particular group of saints must travel to reach that meeting-place, makes very little difference.

Passing now to the scientific and logical side of education, we remember that here also ideas which are not utilised are positively harmful. By utilising an idea, I mean relating it to that stream, compounded of sense perceptions, feelings, hopes, desires, and of mental activities adjusting thought to thought, which forms our life. I can imagine a set of beings which might fortify their souls by passively reviewing disconnected ideas. Humanity is not built that way—except perhaps some editors of newspapers.

In scientific training, the first thing to do with an idea is to prove it. But allow me for one moment to extend the meaning of "prove"; I mean—to prove its worth. . . .

Whitehead expresses a pragmatic philosophy of education which seems to have been ignored in his time by the followers of John Dewey:

. . . Education is the acquisition of the art of the utilisation of knowledge. This is an art very difficult to impart. Whenever a text-book is written of real educational worth, you may be quite certain that some reviewer will say that it will be difficult to teach from it. Of course it will be difficult to teach from it. If it were easy, the book ought to be burned; for it cannot be educational. In education, as elsewhere, the broad primrose path leads to a nasty place. . . .

. . . There is no royal road to learning through an airy path of brilliant generalisations. There is a proverb about the difficulty of seeing the wood because of the trees. That difficulty is exactly the point which I am enforcing. The problem of education is to make the pupil see the wood by means of the trees.

The solution which I am urging, is to eradicate the fatal disconnection of subjects which kills the vitality of our modern curriculum. There is only one subject-matter for education, and that is Life in all its manifestations. Instead of this single unity, we offer children—Algebra, from which nothing follows; Geometry, from which nothing follows; Science, from which nothing follows; History, from which nothing follows; a Couple of Languages, never mastered; and lastly, most dreary of all, Literature, represented by plays of Shakespeare, with philological notes and short analyses of plot and character to be in substance committed to memory. Can such a list be said to represent Life, as it is known in the midst of the living of it? The best that can be said of it is, that it is a rapid table of contents which a deity might run over in his mind while he was thinking of creating a world, and had not yet determined how to put it together. . . .

Emphasizing the value of trained intelligence (and sounding much like a writer of the 1960's), Whitehead says:

. . . When one considers in its length and in its breadth the importance of this question of the education of a nation's young, the broken lives, the defeated hopes, the national failures, which result from the frivolous inertia with which it is treated, it is difficult to restrain within oneself a savage rage. In the conditions of modern life the rule is absolute, the race which does not value trained intelligence is doomed. Not all your heroism, not all your social charm, not all your wit, not all your victories on land or at sea, can move back the finger of fate. To-day we maintain ourselves. To-morrow science will have moved forward yet one more step, and there will be no appeal from the judgment which will then be pronounced on the uneducated. . . .[3]

The Purposes of Education in American Democracy

Following the Great Depression of the early 1930's, there developed among Americans a renewed concern for the individual—a special concern for the dignity and worth of each man and his rights, not only for the traditional freedoms but also for rights in the economic sphere. These new concerns called for re-evaluation of the purposes of the school, and in response to the times, the Educational Policies Commission of the National Education Association developed a statement of aims known as *The Purposes of Education in American Democracy*.

This highly influential statement opens with a quotation from John Dewey:

If philosophy is for anything—if it is not a kind of mumbling in the dark, a form of busy work—it must shed some light upon the path. Life without it must be a different sort of thing from life with it. And the difference which it makes must be in us. Philosophy, then, is reflection upon social ideals, and education is the effort to actualize them in human behavior.

The use of the quotation was not incidental: the philosophy of Dewey is reflected in the four major goals for the school, and the goals are stated in behavioral terms—that is, as outcomes which will be apparent in the way students act. The complete list of objectives in the statement follows:

I. The Objectives of Self-Realization

The Inquiring Mind. The educated person has an appetite for learning.

Speech. The educated person can speak the mother tongue clearly.

Reading. The educated person reads the mother tongue efficiently.

Writing. The educated person writes the mother tongue effectively.

Number. The educated person solves his problems of counting and calculating.

Sight and Hearing. The educated person is skilled in listening and observing.

Health Knowledge. The educated person understands the basic facts concerning health and disease.

Health Habits. The educated person protects his own health and that of his dependents.

Public Health. The educated person works to improve the health of the community.

Recreation. The educated person is participant and spectator in many sports and other pastimes.

[3] Alfred N. Whitehead, *The Aims of Education* (New York: Macmillan, 1929), pp. 13–16, 18, 19, 26. Reprinted by permission of The Macmillan Company.

Intellectual Interests. The educated person has mental resources for the use of leisure.

Esthetic Interests. The educated person appreciates beauty.

Character. The educated person gives responsible direction to his own life.

II. The Objectives of Human Relationship

Respect for Humanity. The educated person puts human relationships first.

Friendships. The educated person enjoys a rich, sincere, and varied social life.

Cooperation. The educated person can work and play with others.

Courtesy. The educated person observes the amenities of social behavior.

Appreciation of the Home. The educated person appreciates the family as a social institution.

Conservation of the Home. The educated person conserves family ideals.

Homemaking. The educated person is skilled in homemaking.

Democracy in the Home. The educated person maintains democratic family relationships.

III. The Objectives of Economic Efficiency

Work. The educated producer knows the satisfaction of good workmanship.

Occupational Information. The educated producer understands the requirements and opportunities for various jobs.

Occupational Choice. The educated producer has *selected* his occupation.

Occupational Efficiency. The educated producer succeeds in his chosen vocation.

Occupational Adjustment. The educated producer maintains and improves his efficiency.

Occupational Appreciation. The educated producer appreciates the social value of his work.

Personal Economics. The educated consumer plans the economics of his own life.

Consumer Judgment. The educated consumer develops standards for guiding his expenditures.

Efficiency in Buying. The educated consumer is an informed and skillful buyer.

Consumer Protection. The educated consumer takes appropriate measures to safeguard his interests.

IV. The Objectives of Civic Responsibility

Social Justice. The educated citizen is sensitive to the disparities of human circumstance.

Social Activity. The educated citizen acts to correct unsatisfactory conditions.

Social Understanding. The educated citizen seeks to understand social structures and social processes.

Critical Judgment. The educated citizen has defenses against propaganda.

Tolerance. The educated citizen respects honest differences of opinion.

Conservation. The educated citizen has a regard for the nation's resources.

Social Applications of Science. The educated citizen measures scientific advance by its contribution to the general welfare.

World Citizenship. The educated citizen is a cooperating member of the world community.

Law Observance. The educated citizen respects the law.

Economic Literacy. The educated citizen is economically literate.

Political Citizenship. The educated citizen accepts his civic duties.

Devotion to Democracy. The educated citizen acts upon an unswerving loyalty to democratic ideals.[4]

The Ten Imperative Needs of Youth

In 1944, the National Association of Secondary School Principals published *Planning for American Youth.* Written during World War II, the book reflects progressive education's "life adjustment"[5] concept as well as war-time conditions. In the Foreword, the authors state: "The war has reminded us of many virtues and ideals that we had forgotten. One of them is the duty we owe to our youth in the provision of their education, not education merely in terms of books, credits, diplomas, and degrees, but education in terms of preparation for living and earning."

Planning for American Youth points out how birth and environment have made boys and girls different and how they all must have equal opportunities to live and learn, but emphasizes that *all* youth have certain educational needs in common.

"Youth have specific needs they recognize; society makes certain requirements of all youth; together these form a pattern of common educational needs." It is *the* job of the school to see that these needs are met and satisfied. The Ten Imperative Needs of Youth are:

1. All youth need to develop salable skills.
2. All youth need to develop and maintain good health and physical fitness.
3. All youth need to understand the rights and duties of the citizen of a democratic society.
4. All youth need to understand the significance of the family for the individual and society.
5. All youth need to know how to purchase and use goods and services intelligently.

[4] Educational Policies Commission, *The Purposes of Education in American Democracy* (Washington, D.C.: Educational Policies Commission of the National Education Association and the American Association of School Administrators, 1938), pp. 50, 72, 90, 108.

[5] "Progressive education" is the name of the movement resulting from the attempts to implement John Dewey's philosophy of education (see Chapter 11). His concept was to educate the "whole" child—intellect, emotions, etc.—and to do so by capitalizing on the child's own interests. Life adjustment, as the name implies, means educating the student for life as he is living it now—today—rather than education as preparation for adulthood—tomorrow.

6. All youth need to understand the influence of science on human life.
7. All youth need an appreciation of literature, art, music, and nature.
8. All youth need to be able to use their leisure time well and to budget it wisely.
9. All youth need to develop respect for other persons.
10. All youth need to grow in their ability to think rationally.[6]

It is important for the reader to understand that ever since the publication of *The Purposes of Education in American Democracy* and the *Ten Imperative Needs of Youth*, the question has been appropriately raised of the extent to which these statements by professional groups of educators—the National Education Association and the National Association of Secondary School Principals—represent the purposes of the schools as seen by the public itself.

The White House Conference on Education

In a monumental attempt to utilize the insights of the American public at large on the problems of public education, President Eisenhower called the 1955 White House Conference on Education. Two-thirds of the three thousand persons called to Washington for this three-day conference were laymen, a group of distinguished Americans who had had experience either as members of local boards of education or as members of college boards of regents. In a significant document entitled *The Committee for the White House Conference on Education, A Report to the President*, the group sought to identify the purposes of education.

WHAT SHOULD OUR SCHOOLS ACCOMPLISH?

1. A general education as good as or better than that offered in the past, with increased emphasis on the physical and social sciences.
2. Programs designed to develop patriotism and good citizenship.
3. Programs designed to foster moral, ethical, and spiritual values.
4. Vocational education tailored to the abilities of each pupil and to the needs of the community and Nation.
5. Courses designed to teach domestic skills.
6. Training in leisure-time activities such as music, dancing, avocational reading, and hobbies.
7. A variety of health services for all children, including both physical and dental inspections, and instruction aimed at bettering health knowledge and habits.
8. Special treatment for children with speech or reading difficulties and other handicaps.
9. Physical education, ranging from systematic exercises, physical therapy, and intramural sports, to interscholastic athletic competition.
10. Instruction to meet the needs of the abler students.

[6] *Planning for American Youth* (An Educational Program for Youth of Secondary School Age) (Washington, D.C.: National Association of Secondary School Principals, 1949).

11. Programs designed to acquaint students with countries other than their own in an effort to help them understand the problems America faces in international relations.
12. Programs designed to foster mental health.
13. Programs designed to foster wholesome family life.
14. Organized recreational and social activities.
15. Courses designed to promote safety. These include instruction in driving automobiles, swimming, civil defense, etc.

During the past two generations, this list of school goals has grown with increased speed. This is a phenomenon which has excited both admiration and dismay. After several decades of experimentation, should this broadening of the goals be recognized as legitimate?

This Committee answers *Yes.* Nothing was more evident at the White House Conference on Education than the fact that these goals, representing as they do an enormously wide range of purposes, are the answer to genuine public demand. These goals have, after all, been hammered out at countless school board meetings during the past quarter-century throughout the land. The basic responsibility of the schools is the development of the skills of the mind, but the overall mission has been enlarged. Schools are now asked to help each child to become as good and as capable in every way as native endowment permits. The schools are asked to help children to acquire any skill or characteristic which a majority of the community deems worthwhile. The order given by the American people to the schools is grand in its simplicity: in addition to intellectual achievement, foster morality, happiness, and any useful ability. The talent of each child is to be sought out and developed to the fullest. Each weakness is to be studied and, so far as possible, corrected. This is truly a majestic ideal, and an astonishingly new one. Schools of that kind have never been provided for more than a small fraction of mankind.

Although it is new, this ideal of schools which do everything possible for all children is a natural development in the United States. The moving spirit of this Nation has been from the beginning a sense of fairness. Nowadays equality of opportunity for adults means little without equality of educational opportunity for children. Ignorance is a greater obstacle than ever to success of most kinds. The schools have become a major tool for creating a Nation without rigid class barriers. *It is primarily the schools which allow no man's failure to prevent the success of his son.*

In still another way, this new ideal for the schools is a natural development of this country: it recognizes the paramount importance of the individual in a free society. Our schools are asked to teach skills currently needed by the Nation, but never at the expense of the individual. This policy of encouraging each child to develop his individual talents will be of the greatest use to the Nation, for in the long run, if no talent is wasted in our land, no skill will be lacking.[7]

The purposes of education identified by the White House Conference group are all-encompassing in their coverage. For the first time in the world's history, the schools are to educate all youth to an extent never before con-

[7] *The Committee for the White House Conference on Education, A Report to the President* (Washington, D.C.: U.S. Government Printing Office, 1956), pp. 8–10.

ceived. No other nation has ever tried it. If American schools have failed for some, have neglected some of the most able, it should not be surprising. In fact, it would be most remarkable if American schools did well by all. In this connection, the English author Denis Brogan was prompted to remark that the American school "is undertaking to do more than it can (which is very American) and doing much more than it seems to do (which is also very American)." [8]

The Council for Basic Education

One of the groups which agrees thoroughly with Brogan that the schools are "doing too much" as well as failing to give priority to "the proper goals" is the Council for Basic Education. Its president and chief spokesman is James D. Koerner, who feels that

almost all children are capable of sustained academic study and that it is the proper business of a public school system to give this study to them through the medium of what Matthew Arnold called "the best that has been thought and said in the world." In this system all students run on the same track but at their own best speeds; and all concentrate their education in a relatively few areas that encompass the most significant of man's knowledge.

Koerner then addresses himself to the question of these "areas that encompass the most significant of man's knowledge" and the criteria by which one identifies them.

In the process of his own intellectual development—as he uncovered great knowledge, mostly through trial and error over eons of time—man finally was able to refine particular techniques for investigating phenomena, techniques that over long periods were found to produce results that were more fruitful than those produced in other ways. Through man's passion for classifying and codifying his knowledge, in order to continue improving it, some few fields have attained pre-eminence because they are generative, because they form the nucleus of other, secondary fields, because they represent pinnacles of human achievement, and because they now constitute bodies of knowledge of proven power and research techniques of proven effectiveness.

These basic fields include the major languages of mankind, the instrument without which all of us would still live like pre-Neolithic sub-men; they also include that other indispensable language, the language of mathematics, without which all of us would likewise still be primitives; they include history, which in its largest sense encompasses all the records of all the ages, without which the race would be as intellectually impotent as a man without a memory; and they include the natural sciences, which by becoming highly qualified and capable of extremely reliable predictions about the major phenomena of nature, have radically transformed the modern world. These fields, I suggest, are clearly the chief ones in which man has recorded his experience on earth and his understanding of life. One might justly argue that other fields are nearly as basic, or that what is basic in one age is not so in another, and that the

[8] Denis Brogan, *Unity and Liberty* (New York: Knopf, 1944), p. 135.

pattern of educational programs must change accordingly. My only point is that the foregoing fields have been the chief means by which man has become what he now is and that they remain paramount at this particular point in his history. As such they have earned a pre-eminent place in the education of each new generation. In the common schools of our society, the question of priorities is compelling, for there is time only for those subjects which best serve the need of all men, as citizens and human beings.[9]

Clearly, the council would assign to the schools those goals which it alone could achieve. Thus, by implication, it would leave other goals for other social institutions to achieve. And it also would place the academic (or "solid") subjects in a position of paramount importance, thus—again by implication— relegating all other subject fields either to the scrap heap or at least to a lesser position of importance.

The Reconstruction of Education

Another well-known critic of the educational status quo during the late 1950's and early 1960's was Arthur Bestor, a professor of history at the University of Illinois. Bestor reacted vigorously to what he called the "soft" effects of the progressive education movement of the 1920's and 1930's. Like Koerner, Bestor proposes and argues for a return to the "solid" subjects—to the teaching of the intellectual disciplines as the distinctive function of the school. By implication, vocational, social, and other objectives would be eliminated. Through his many publications—*Educational Wastelands, Backwoods Utopias*, and *The Restoration of Learning*—he gained the reputation as the most serious and influential critic of education to appear during the fifties and sixties. His point of view is in sharp contrast to the Educational Policies Commission statement and the Ten Imperative Needs of Youth, with their "life adjustment" philosophy of the objectives of education.

"In its education," Admiral Rickover has said, paraphrasing Lord Haldane, "the soul of a people mirrors itself." A mirror, one must remember, is undiscriminating. It reflects the good and the bad, the beautiful and the ugly, with crystalline impartiality. Education is such a mirror. Defects in our educational system are reflections of weakness and shortcomings in our national life. This is a hard truth to accept, but a truth nonetheless. The danger lies in confusing explanation with justification. Because racial discrimination can be explained historically is no reason for viewing it in any other light than as an abomination. So with defects and weaknesses in American education. To explain them is not to condone them.

.   .   .   .   .

The school, the college, and the university were created to perform a specific and recognized function. Their facilities and techniques—classrooms, libraries, laboratories, recitations, lectures, seminars, and examinations—were designed and developed for the particular purpose of intellectual training. To

[9] James D. Koerner, "Theory and Experience in the Education of Teachers," *Sixteenth Yearbook* (Washington, D.C.: American Association of Colleges for Teacher Education, 1963), pp. 15, 16–17.

enable the school to carry out any other function, it must be altered and adapted, and its performance in the new role is usually haphazard, fumbling, and defective. Moreover, if intellectual training is pushed aside or neglected by schools and colleges, society is thereby impoverished of intellectual training, because it possesses no other resources, no other agencies, no other techniques for making up the loss. That the primary function of the educational system is to furnish intellectual training is as completely self-evident as any statement that can possibly be made about the function of a social institution, whether one approaches the matter from the point of view of logic or history or sociology.

The distribution of functions that I have described is never more than approximate, of course. Most institutions perform, in an incidental and indirect way, functions that belong primarily to institutions of another sort. Thus business and industry, not only in the "breaking in" of employees but also in advertising, attempt a good deal of social indoctrination, particularly in what are held to be the "economic virtues." The home carries on a good deal of vocational instruction and also a good deal of intellectual training. The school, even in its strictly academic work, maintains, and therefore helps to inculcate, the ethical standards of the surrounding culture, whenever issues involving these standards—for example, the matter of honesty in examinations—arise in the classroom. In providing the intellectual foundations for professional work, moreover, the school at times cannot avoid crossing the line that theoretically separates intellectual training from apprenticeship. A blurring of lines, in the degree which these examples represent, is both natural and inescapable, and it raises no question worth discussing.

That American public schools have enormously expanded their functions is so obvious a fact that I do not suppose the point calls for elaboration or demonstration. Those who most vigorously oppose the point of view I take on educational policy do not deny this expansion of scope; indeed they acknowledge it and take pride in it. One of the most influential statements of the function of the public school, *Planning for American Youth*, a program published by the National Association of Secondary School Principals, says: "Youth have specific needs they recognize; society makes certain requirements of all youth; together these form a pattern of common educational needs. . . . It is the Job of the School to Meet the Common and the Specific Individual Needs of Youth."

The "needs" that are particularized (in the ten points that make up the body of the statement) include those forms of training that I have described as job training and social conditioning. The responsibility of the school, in other words, is supposed to extend to all the areas in which society has customarily furnished some form of deliberate training.

. . . . .

Is it really necessary or desirable for the school to expand its responsibility to this extent? In fact, is the school capable of discharging such extended responsibility? Can it perform the tasks involved without fatally neglecting its primary social obligation—that of providing intellectual training?

Bestor discusses "life adjustment," but in terms of a "mature and disciplined intellect":

The adjustment to life that we must strive for through the school is the kind of adjustment that results from applying the varied resources and the developed powers of a mature and disciplined intellect to each successive problem as it arises. Adjustment in this highest sense is an outcome of education. It is not an outcome that can be reached by short cuts, by a miscellany of experiences, by playroom imitations of the mere externals of adult activity. "There is no *royal road* to geometry," said Euclid to his sovereign, Ptolemy I. "There is no royal road to intelligent citizenship" is the message that educators should deliver to the sovereign people of today. Serious, sustained, systematic labor, in libraries, laboratories, and classrooms, is the only way of producing educated men and women in the twentieth century, as in every preceding century.[10]

Report of the Rockefeller Brothers Fund

The Pursuit of Excellence, a laymen's report issued by the Rockefeller Brothers Fund in 1958, considers what our schools should accomplish and the extent to which present goals can realistically be achieved in view of (1) the increase in number of students to be taught, (2) the new and expanded facilities to be provided, and (3) the competition for the tax dollar from so many different social agencies. After reviewing these three major problems which face the American people, the report comes to this conclusion:

Not only must our educators handle a huge increase in number of students; they must offer higher quality in education. From time to time, one still hears arguments over *quantity* versus *quality* education. Behind such arguments is the assumption that a society can choose to educate a few people exceedingly well or to educate a great number of people somewhat less well, but that it cannot do both. But a modern society such as ours cannot choose to do one *or* the other. It has no choice but to do both. Our kind of society calls for the maximum development of individual potentialities *at all levels*.

Fortunately the demand to educate everyone up to the level of his ability and the demand for excellence in education are not incompatible. We must honor both goals. We must seek excellence in a context of concern for all.[11]

The Central Purpose of American Education

Seek "excellence," says the Rockefeller Brothers Fund. Excellence in what? Have "concern for all." Concern for all that they achieve what? In 1961 in a long-awaited statement, the Educational Policies Commission of the NEA issued a twenty-one-page pamphlet which attempts to put aside vagueness and triviality and come to grips with the issue of priorities. *The* goal: how to think. "The purpose which runs through and strengthens all other educational pur-

---

[10] Arthur Bestor and J. L. Childs, "Education and the American Scene," in *Education in the Age of Science*, ed. Brand Blanshard (New York: Basic Books, 1959), pp. 55, 56, 60–63, 71.

[11] Rockefeller Brothers Fund, *The Pursuit of Excellence* (New York: Doubleday, 1958), p. 22.

poses—the common thread of education—is the development of the ability to think."

Does this then mean the schools have been off the track in following the commission's 1918 and 1938 pronouncements on this same subject? Hardly.

In any democracy, education is closely bound to the wishes of the people, but the strength of this bond in America has been unique. The American people have traditionally regarded education as a means for improving themselves and their society. Whenever an objective has been judged desirable for the individual or the society, it has tended to be accepted as a valid concern of the school. The American commitment to the free society—to individual dignity, to personal liberty, to equality of opportunity—has set the frame in which the American school grew. The basic American value, respect for the individual, has led to one of the major charges which the American people have placed on their schools: to foster that development of individual capacities which will enable each human being to become the best person he is capable of becoming.

The schools have been designed also to serve society's needs. The political order depends on responsible participation of individual citizens; hence the schools have been concerned with good citizenship. The economic order depends on ability and willingness to work; hence the schools have taught vocational skills. The general morality depends on choices made by individuals; hence the schools have cultivated moral habits and upright character.

.   .   .   .   .

The rapid increase in man's ability to understand and change the world and himself has resulted from increased application of his powers of thought. These powers have proved to be his most potent resource, and, as such, the likely key to his future.

The rational powers of the human mind have always been basic in establishing and preserving freedom. In furthering personal and social effectiveness they are becoming more important than ever. They are central to individual dignity, human progress, and national survival.

The individual with developed rational powers can share deeply in the freedoms his society offers and can contribute most to the preservation of those freedoms. At the same time he will have the best chance of understanding and contributing to the great events of his time. And the society which best develops the rational potentials of its people, along with their intuitive and aesthetic capabilities, will have the best chance of flourishing in the future. To help every person develop these powers is therefore a profoundly important objective and one which increases in importance with the passage of time. By pursuing this objective, the school can enhance spiritual and aesthetic values and the other cardinal purposes which it has traditionally served and must continue to serve.

The purpose which runs through and strengthens all other educational purposes—the common thread of education—is the development of the ability to think. This is the central purpose to which the school must be oriented if it is to accomplish either its traditional tasks or those newly accentuated by recent changes in the world. To say that it is central is not to say that it is the sole purpose or in all circumstances the most important purpose, but that it must be a persuasive concern in the work of the school. Many agencies contribute to achieving educational objectives, but this particular objective will not be generally attained unless the school focuses on it. In this context, therefore, the development of every student's rational powers must be recognized as centrally important.[12]

IV. ESTABLISHING PRIORITIES FOR THE SCHOOL

- What are the distinctive responsibilities of the school in contrast to those that properly belong to the family, the church, industry, and various youth-serving agencies?
- What responsibilities should the school share with other institutions and agencies?
- What, then, should be included in the school program? What should be excluded from it?

Recommendation 10. Priorities for the school are the teaching of skills in reading, composition, listening, speaking (both native and foreign languages), and computation . . . ways of creative and disciplined thinking, including methods of inquiry and application of knowledge . . . competence in self-instruction and independent learning . . . fundamental understanding of the humanities and the arts, the social sciences and natural sciences, and mathematics . . . appreciation of and discriminating taste in literature, music, and the visual arts . . . instruction in health education and physical education.

Responsibilities best met by joint efforts of the school and other social agencies include: development of values and ideals . . . social and civic competence . . . vocational preparation.

The decision to include or exclude particular school subjects or outside-of-class activities should be based on: (a) the priorities assigned to the school and to other agencies; (b) data about learners and society, and developments in the academic disciplines; (c) the human and material resources available in the school and community.

To determine specifically just what the school's distinctive responsibilities are, each school must find answers to the following questions:

What knowledge, values, and skills do children and youth in our culture need to learn?

Which of these goals can best be achieved by the school?

What knowledge, skills, and values can best be taught by the home, the church, and other social institutions?

Which learnings require the joint efforts of the school and other agencies?

Ole Sand, A Summary of the Report of the NEA Project on Instruction, *Schools for the Sixties, NEA Journal,* 53:27, January, 1964.

---

[12] Educational Policies Commission, *The Central Purpose of American Education* (Washington, D.C.: Educational Policies Commission of the National Education Association, 1961), pp. 1, 11–12.

To achieve this "central purpose" within a reaffirmation of all its other previously stated purposes, the report says:

1. It is "crucial that the teacher possess a thorough knowledge of the material to be taught, a mature mastery of a variety of teaching procedures, an understanding of his pupils, and the quality of judgment that will enable him to blend all in making decisions."

2. The school must foster both the desire and the respect for knowledge as well as the inquiring spirit. "It must encourage the pupil to ask: 'How do I know?' as well as 'What do I know?'"

3. Schools should teach the "strategies of inquiry—by which man has sought to extend his knowledge and understanding of the world."

4. The overriding need is for "that kind of education which frees the mind and enables it to contribute to a full and worthy life. To achieve this goal is the high hope of the nation and the central challenge to its schools." [13]

At the Local Level

While these statements of purpose have been made at national and state levels, local boards of education, local citizen groups, and local teacher groups also have been wrestling with the problem of identifying and establishing a priority for their efforts. The most significant of such statements have been those which have resulted from a team effort by citizens and teachers working together. A recent example, and one which should be considered typical of a local school system's statement of its goals, is the one for the Santa Monica schools, which appears on this page.

A FRAMEWORK FOR THE EDUCATIONAL PROGRAM OF THE
SANTA MONICA SCHOOLS

We Believe

. . . that a system of free and universal public education provides the most effective means of strengthening and advancing the basic ideals of democracy. It is therefore the responsibility of the public schools to provide learning experiences which promote and emphasize the fundamental objectives of our democratic society.

We Believe

. . . that education should lead to the knowledge, skills, and understandings needed by each individual to live effectively as a person and as a responsible citizen. It is the obligation of the public schools to strive to help each student (1) to become competent in using the esential skills of mathematics, reading, writing, speaking, and listening; (2) to acquire knowledge of and appreciation for the history and significance of our culture and its basic institutions; (3) to develop understanding of other nations of the world and of our country's re-

[13] *Ibid.*, pp. 17, 19, 21.

lationship to them; and (4) to acquire knowledge of the sciences as a resource for man's understanding and control of his environment.

We Believe
. . . that moral and spiritual values are essential elements of the school curriculum. The development of ethical ideals and appreciation for high standards of conduct should be emphasized throughout the instructional program. The public schools, while leaving religious instruction in the home and the church, should at all times in all ways maintain a respectful attitude toward the religious beliefs taught by the home.

We Believe
. . . that the development of the highest potential of each individual is the major purpose of education. Evaluation of special abilities, talents and needs should serve as the basis for assisting students with the selection of appropriate individual goals, early and realistic vocational choices, and learning experiences which assure maximum educational achievement.

We Believe
. . . that the understanding and support necessary for the realization of these principles is possible only from a community which is fully informed about the needs and purposes of the public schools.

We Believe
. . . that the school environment and the instructional program should contribute to the healthful living necessary for desirable personal development.

We Believe
. . . that all people have some measure of creative ability. The educational program should offer opportunities in the arts which encourage the development of creative expression and appreciation in all students.

We Believe
. . . that education is more than the assimilation of subject matter and the acquisition of skills. Since education fulfills its purpose only as it also develops ability to evaluate ideas and concepts and to use the methods of critical thinking to form independent judgments, these abilities should be an important outcome of the instructional program.

We Believe
. . . that education should help prepare students for the wise selection of worthwhile leisure-time activities.

We Believe
. . . that in an era of rapid technological and social development and in a world increasingly characterized by change, the school curriculum should prepare individuals for adaptation to change.

We Believe
. . . that the educational program is continuously developing. As society meets the challenges of new social, political, economic and scien-

tific frontiers, and as the education process continues to become better understood, the schools should be prepared to adapt to changing needs and conditions in order to fulfill their assigned task.

We Believe
. . . that education is a cooperative enterprise. Although the public schools assume responsibility for the education of individuals in our society, other phases are shared by the home and the community. The full and wholesome development of our young people requires a cooperative relationship among all these agencies.

We Believe
. . . that good education provides for the development of responsible self-direction. Guidance of student learning should lead to continuous growth in ability to select appropriate tasks, to choose wise courses of action, and to accept responsibility for choices made.

Reprinted by permission of the Santa Monica Unified School District.

THE TEACHER'S ROLE

This great debate on the aims of education has not ended. As mentioned previously, the ends of education will change and grow as society itself changes and evolves, and with these changes will come conflict among laymen, among educators, and between laymen and educators.

No matter what the current trend, certain constants remain for the teacher: (1) Teachers need to formulate their own statement of purposes as a guide to daily instruction of pupils in their classes, (2) teachers' purposes will change in emphasis as the pupils they teach reflect differing socioeconomic levels of the community, and (3) teachers will be asked to do more than there will be the means readily and successfully to achieve.

As a guide to enable teachers to cut their way through the discussions and arrive at decisions concerning their own beliefs about the ends of education, the following quotation from Norman Cousins, editor of the *Saturday Review*, is offered: "Education fails unless the three R's at one end of the schools' spectrum lead ultimately to the four P's at the other—PREPARATION FOR EARNING, PREPARATION FOR LIVING, PREPARATION FOR UNDERSTANDING, PREPARATION FOR PARTICIPATION in the problems involved in the making of a better world." [14]

CONCLUSION

The schools are supported by the people for the education of their children. Thus they want to say what the basic job of the school is. Teachers, as professional practitioners of their craft, also have well-established ideas on the subject of the purposes of education. And each of these groups, plus the many

[14] *The Clearing House,* 31:158 (Nov., 1956).

groups between the layman and the professionals, has expressed its views in relation to the temper of the times.

So in this chapter, we have reviewed statements reflecting the concerns of Deweyists to basic educationists, from the disciples of the 1900's to the prophets of the sixties. Each new age will bring new demands on the schools and renewed efforts to define its distinctive and unique role.

The job of the teacher is to recognize the historical and sociological tenets of school purposes and to resolve for himself the question of what his teaching is designed to accomplish. Only in this way will he be able to direct the education of others; only in this way will he be able to choose the means of arriving at his goals; only in this way will he be in a position to determine the extent to which the ends of education have been achieved for his class or any individual in it.

The primary concern of American education today is not the development of the appreciation of the "good life" in young gentlemen born to the purple.

Our purpose is to cultivate in the largest possible number of our future citizens an appreciation of both the responsibilities and the benefits which come to them because they are Americans and are free.

JAMES BRYANT CONANT

Questions for Discussion

1. Is the true purpose of education to prepare for life, for jobs, for citizenship, for college? Is your answer the same for all students, or might the purpose be different for some?
2. Do you agree with Spencer's criterion that the most useful knowledge is of most worth?
3. Take the Seven Cardinal Objectives and for each one list the school subjects that contribute the most to it. How do you rationalize or explain your classification?
4. Despite Whitehead's protest against "inert ideas," is there still considerable dead knowledge in the school curriculum? Where? Why? So what?
5. What relationship do the 1938 and 1961 Educational Policies Commission statements of purpose bear to each other? Do you agree that the second is a "slick cover-up job" to minimize the real difference between it and the progressive education influence reflected in the 1938 statement?
6. Assume agreement with the White House Conference statement, "It is primarily the schools which allow no man's failure to prevent the success of his son." What implications does this have for education?
7. Some have said that James Koerner's concept of purpose is appropriate for bright, college-bound students, but not for others. Do you agree or disagree? Why?

8. Can Americans enjoy the luxury of both quantity and quality in education?
9. Analyze the Santa Monica statement "A Framework for the Educational Program." Does it reflect the influence of Bestor, of the Ten Imperative Needs of Youth, of both, or of neither?
10. Do teachers' purposes change as the pupils they teach reflect differing socioeconomic levels of the community? Should they?
11. Is there a direct relation between the liberal education given by elementary and secondary schools and that available in liberal arts colleges? Why?

Activities and Projects

1. Write the State Department of Education of your state for a statement of objectives and purposes. How does it compare with the two EPC statements reproduced in this chapter?
2. Organize your class into a little White House Conference to discuss the question "What should our schools accomplish?" Conclude with an analysis of similarities and differences in the points of view expressed.
3. Secure a statement of purpose from your local school. How does it compare with the Santa Monica statement?
4. Make up an opinionnaire using statements from the Council for Basic Education. Use it with (a) a group of retired people (senior citizens), (b) college seniors. Compare the results.
5. Do driver-training, civil defense, and ROTC belong in the school curriculum? Justify your answer on philosophical grounds.
6. Within the same school, interview a teacher of each of the following subjects regarding their purposes: (a) foreign language, (b) physical education, (c) remedial reading. In what ways do their purposes agree and disagree?
7. Go to a series of school board meetings, and write a report of the purposes which seem inherent in the system *from what the members say in discussions.*

References

"PUBLIC VERSUS PROFESSION"

BESTOR, ARTHUR, *Education in the Age of Science* (New York: Basic Books, 1959), pp. 55–75.

BROUDY, HARRY S., *Paradox and Promise* (Englewood Cliffs, N.J.: Prentice-Hall, 1961), Part II, "Paradoxes in School and Society."

The Committee for the White House Conference on Education, A Report to the President (Washington, D.C.: U.S. Government Printing Office, 1956).

KOERNER, JAMES, *The Miseducation of Teachers* (Boston: Houghton Mifflin, 1963).

RIESMAN, DAVID, *Constraint and Variety in American Education* (Lincoln: University of Nebraska Press, 1956).

ROCKEFELLER BROTHERS FUND, *The Pursuit of Excellence* (New York: Doubleday, 1958).

STONE, JAMES C., *California's Commitment to Public Education* (New York: Thomas Y. Crowell, 1961), Chapter 6, "Education Role of Parents and Taxpayers."

THELEN, HERBERT A., *Education and the Human Quest* (New York: Harper & Row, 1960).

"CLASSICAL POINTS OF VIEW"

ADLER, MORTIMER, and MILTON MAYER, *The Revolution in Education* (Chicago: University of Chicago Press, 1958).

RUSSELL, BERTRAND, *Education and the Modern World* (London: George Allen & Unwin, 1932).

SIMON, LOUIS, *Shaw on Education* (New York: Columbia University Press, 1958).

SMILEY, MARJORIE B., and JOHN S. DIEKHOFF, *Prologue to Teaching* (New York: Oxford, 1959), Part 3.

SPENCER, HERBERT, *Education: Intellectual, Moral and Physical* (New York: Appleton, 1860).

TOYNBEE, ARNOLD J., *Education in the Perspective of History* (New York: Harper & Row, 1960).

WHITEHEAD, ALFRED N., *The Aims of Education and Other Essays* (New York: New American Library, 1949).

"GOALS: THE 20's TO THE 70's"

AIKIN, WILFORD M., *The Story of the Eight-year Study* (New York: Harper, 1942).

The Central Purpose of American Education (Washington, D.C.: Educational Policies Commission, NEA, 1961).

CLARK, BURTON R., *The Open Door College* (New York: McGraw-Hill, 1960).

CONANT, JAMES B., *The American High School Today* (New York: McGraw-Hill, 1959), Section I, "The Characteristics of American Education"; Section II, "A Unique Feature—The Comprehensive High School."

EURICH, ALVIN C., "Higher Education in the Twenty-first Century," *Atlantic*, 211:53–57 (June, 1963).

GWYNN, J. MEINOR, *Curriculum Principles and Social Trends*, 3d ed. (New York: Macmillan, 1960), Chapters 8 and 12.

KEARNEY, NOLAN C., *Elementary School Objectives* (Report Prepared for the Mid-century Committee on Outcomes in Elementary Education) (New York: Russell Sage Foundation, 1953), 42–113.

KING, EDMUND J., *World Perspectives in Education* (Indianapolis: Bobbs-Merrill, 1962), Chapter 8, "Further and Higher Education."

LEE, J. MURRAY, "Elementary Education: 1985," *Educational Leadership*, 17:475–79, May, 1960.

MCCONNELL, THOMAS, "Diversification in Higher Education" in *Talks on American Education*, ed. Henry Chauncey (New York: Bureau of Publications, Teachers College, Columbia University, 1962).

MEDSKER, LELAND, "The Community College" in *Talks on American Education*, ed. Henry Chauncey (New York: Bureau of Publications, Teachers College, Columbia University, 1962).

Planning for American Youth (Washington, D.C.: National Association of Secondary School Principals, 1949).

The Purposes of Education in American Democracy (Washington, D.C.: Educational Policies Commission and American Association of School Administrators, NEA, 1938).

STRANG, RUTH, "Getting Off Self-center," *National Parent-Teacher*, 55:24–26, November, 1960.

WILES, KIMBALL, "Education of Adolescents: 1985," *Educational Leadership*, 17:480–83, May, 1960.

ZERAN, FRANKLIN R., ed., *Life-adjustment in Action* (New York: Chartwell House, 1953).

"ROLE OF THE TEACHER"

BRUNER, JEROME S., *The Process of Education* (Cambridge, Mass.: Harvard University Press, 1960).

FREDERICK, ROBERT W., *The Third Curriculum* (New York: Appleton-Century-Crofts, 1959).

HAVIGHURST, ROBERT J., *Development Tasks and Education* (New York: Longmans, Green, 1960).

KELLEY, EARL C., *In Defense of Youth* (Englewood Cliffs, N.J.: Prentice-Hall, 1962).

ROSS, LEONARD Q., *The Education of Hyman Kaplan* (New York: Harcourt, Brace & World, 1937).

SAND, OLE, and RICHARD I. MILLER, "New Goals in Instruction," *CTA Journal*, 59:25–28, May, 1963.

STENDLER, CELIA B., *Teaching in the Elementary School* (New York: Harcourt, Brace & World, 1958).

iii

The art of teaching is the art of assisting discovery.

MARK VAN DOREN

teaching

One of the best ways to learn about teaching, or about any profession, is to talk with someone in the field. Accordingly, so that the prospective teachers reading this book might have the benefit of knowledgeable opinions, the authors asked a number of teachers, some with one year of experience and others with a number of years in the classroom, to present unsigned statements of how they feel about teaching and of what it means in their lives. Most of the respondents indicated that the work was hard and seemingly endless, with small monetary returns, but that it was rewarding in many ways that deny verbal description. It seems that for the most part those who remain in the field for several years become attached to their work and plan to devote the remainder of their active professional years to it.

Teaching is dynamic work with ever-new challenges daily as teachers work with children and youth in the nation's classrooms. Attesting to this idea is the following statement from a primary teacher with more than twenty years of experience:

Teaching has a constantly changing face. As a teacher, I seem to be something different to each pupil in the classroom, and often my role changes from hour to hour as each child's needs change. One great reward of teaching is trying to fulfill the needs of the pupils. Each child is a real challenge; my small part in each child's life represents some of the rewards of teaching. The association with the child in the classroom is a concrete value upon which a teacher can count. Maybe this teacher is learning more than she is teaching.

The satisfaction—the reward—of seeing children progress in their learning because of something the teacher has done or has caused to be done in the classroom is certainly one of the abstract compensations enjoyed by every teacher. One teacher in the early high school grades, who entered the profession after spending a number of years in business and personnel work, expresses this feeling as follows:

I considered other professions, such as petroleum engineer and commercial aviation, since I have been actively flying since 1951, but I chose teaching because I like working with boys and girls. I felt there would be more satisfaction in teaching than any of these other professions since I would be contributing to the development of young people. . . . It is very satisfying to see a young person grow and develop partially under my guidance. Teaching is very interesting work, because one is constantly meeting new challenges. After having taught for six years, I am happy that I chose this profession and still can not think of any other profession I would rather be in.

Teaching provides individuals with the opportunity of being of service to mankind, and this, to some, is a strong motivation when the time comes for choosing their life's work. A thirty-eight-year-old man with fourteen years of teaching experience in the upper grades feels that teaching is the field in which he can serve his fellow men most effectively. He writes:

Teaching is the most complex profession in the world. To be a teacher, one is presented with the most challenging, frustrating, and yet highly rewarding occupation. To deal with human minds is the greatest responsibility on earth. To help young people succeed and taste the joy of achievement is most gratifying. To experience with them the thrill of victory and the agony of defeat is really living for others. I feel that it is in teaching that I can make my greatest contribution to the good of mankind.

Paradoxically, the most constant aspect of teaching is that it is continually changing. Nothing, or very little, is done in exactly the same way twice. A teacher who works with 25 or more unique—and alive!—youngsters must expect anything to happen at any moment and be able to make the appropriate adjustment to the situation. One bright young woman, just completing her first year in the middle grades, has this to say:

I like teaching very much, but my opinion of teaching changes from day to day just as the children I teach change from day to day. . . . Teaching isn't all a joy. At 3:30 or 4:00, when others are leaving their jobs, a teacher has papers to correct, children to keep after school to catch up with their lessons or other reasons, meetings to attend, lesson plans to be altered for the next day's work, parents to contact, work to be typed and duplicated and research to be done. These are things that must be done more than several times a week—many of them nightly. This list hasn't even begun to include the extra chores by which a teacher is confronted, such as report cards, cumulative record folders, etc.

It is very disappointing when a teacher encourages children to ask questions and come in for extra help in projects or for class work only to have to turn them away to attend a teachers' meeting, parent conference, etc.

A teacher can be compared to a frustrated mother of 30 (plus) children, trained to see their needs, to know how to meet them, and unable to meet all of them. A teacher will never be able to go home at night and feel that he or she has completed his or her work. There is always more work to be done.

Since teachers work with active ingredients and many times unknowns, reactions are often unexpected. Children don't always seem to appreciate what is being done for them. In fact, some days pass when one isn't quite sure if they have learned anything the day before or not. Unlike some chemical reactions, teachers are not catalysts; they are very much affected by the children they teach. Thankfully, every day is different, and every child is an individual.

Teaching is one of the most creative occupations in the world. Many times rewards don't come when they are needed most, and the work load seems overpowering. But I am a teacher, and I wouldn't trade occupations with anyone else.

Although one particular aspect of teaching may be the predominant motivating force, professional educators choose teaching for a number of reasons—not just one. Such is the situation of a kindergarten teacher who has taught more than twenty years:

I teach because I love children. I feel pride in teaching because it is a profession and is given respect and importance in the community. I enjoy contact with children and their parents. I have much freedom within my job—I can choose when and what I will do today and no one is checking to see if I am earning my salary every minute; I get to drive myself. There are many hours of homework, but I don't mind; I earn more money than I could in an office, without the homework.

From these statements, it is clear that teaching means different things to different teachers. This is to be expected, since each teacher is unique, is an individual with a personality peculiar to his own self, just as each child is unique. To some teachers, the work is one exciting challenge after another; to others, the experiences in the classroom are nothing short of drudgery. Underlying all the statements, however, are certain threads of consistency: the work is hard and demanding of time and energy, there are new challenges each day, and there are compensations which are not reflected in the monthly paycheck.

WHY DO YOU WANT TO TEACH?

At this point in your development, you have tentatively, at least, chosen teaching to be your life's work. Why have you chosen this profession? Some of you are members of a teaching family; perhaps your father or mother, or both, are educators, and perhaps their parents, too, and it is natural for you to fall in line. Some of you have decided to become a teacher because back in elementary or high school you idolized one or more of your teachers and then and there vowed to become like them. Some of you have chosen teaching because you feel that the working conditions will be to your liking; some of you sincerely wish to be of service to your fellow human beings; some of you have been forced into teaching by well-meaning parents or other adults who feel that this will always be a good job if you need one or that it will be an excellent stepping-stone until you can get into something else. Just as teachers now in service have chosen the profession for a number of reasons, so have you.

Perhaps it would be interesting and valuable to know the varied reasons for entering the profession given by others at approximately the same point in

WHY TEACH?

Let's face it. Teaching *is* frustrating, nerve-wracking, demanding, tiring work. Do what he may, the teacher remains the butt of poor jokes, the object of endless criticism, and the scapegoat for many of society's most widely shared shortcomings.

But it is the teacher to whom parents and politicians, businessmen and clergymen turn, time after time, to set straight whatever is wrong with youth or the world. Are children unmindful of their elders' unrealized ambitions? Are the national goals neglected? Is free enterprise endangered? Do we lack the moral strength we ought to have? See the teacher!

Any teacher can find dozens of reasons, many of them plausible, to feel sorry for himself. But there are more convincing reasons for teachers to feel quite differently about their work and about themselves. For when due allowance has been made for the irresponsible criticism, the foolish expectations, the fuzzy thinking, and the exaggerated claims, the truth comes through, clear and unassailable: The teacher is a most important person.

This new appreciation of the teacher reflects one of the more curious—and welcome—paradoxes of our time. It has taken the enormous increase in the quantity of physical energy within man's reach to remind us that the central element in all our power, in all our plans for using power, is the educated man. We have had to be reminded, for many had forgotten, that technical proficiency, although it is essential, is insufficient, either to build this world nearer to our dreams or to carry us to other regions of the universe.

Fortunately for all of us, the value of education and the urgent need for good teaching are being recognized not only by those who write statements of national policy on education but by growing numbers of able and discerning young people. Wanting most of all to spend their lives in worthy causes, thousands of our best young men and women are choosing to teach. Improved salaries and working conditions are helping to attract new teachers and to retain experienced people, and continued progress along these tangible lines is highly necessary. But these are at best secondary matters; the more significant change is not in the salaries but in the attention teachers are receiving.

The change is not, however, without its unpleasant side, for while the glare of the spotlight may lend the teacher something of a halo, it also reveals his flaws with a minimum of mercy. No longer can teaching be a sinecure for those who want a job with long vacations or a monthly check to tide them over until something better comes along. Nor is there room in modern schools for teachers who lack the capacity for self-criticism or the willingness to work at a task that is endless and ever-changing.

Why teach? Whether the question is asked by a college student on the threshold of a career or by a forty-year veteran with chalk dust in his blood, the answer can be given many ways. Twenty years ago Lyman Bryson put it gracefully and well when he called the teacher "the friend who makes men free."

Running through all the answers, if they are honest and wise, will be a thread of commitment—a note of faith. To find success or satisfaction in his work, a teacher must begin and end with faith—in the worth of all men and especially in his students; in all learning and particularly in what he teaches. But most of all, the teacher must believe in himself and in the value of what he is attempting to accomplish.

In the days in which we live and teach, it should not be difficult to sustain that faith. Wherever men have believed that the human mind and spirit should be illuminated, the good teacher has been held in esteem and respect. It is so here and now, as it always will be where freedom, opportunity, and excellence are valued. In twenty centuries, no one has been able to answer Cicero's question: "What greater or better gift can we offer the republic than to teach and instruct our youth?"

John H. Fischer, *NEA Journal*, 51:31, April, 1962.

---

their preparation as you. For that reason, from students in the initial stages of their professional training, the authors have solicited statements which reveal some of the reasons for their choice. It is interesting to note a rather close relationship between what teachers indicate the profession means to them as presented in the preceding section and what educational trainees believe teaching will mean to them.

One student in a beginning professional class said,

I want to teach because I love working with children. . . . I want to see children grow and learn and know that in some way I helped them. The security, the pleasant surroundings, and the convenient hours which can be worked around a family all helped me decide to go into teaching. However, my main reason was that children are the most interesting and complex things in the world and to teach them is one of the most enjoyable jobs in the world.

Another student in an introductory education course expressed this mature point of view:

What profession offers a person the opportunity to shape and guide the thoughts, values, and knowledge of thousands of future citizens . . . the chance to know intimately thousands of fresh young minds . . . a position in which year after year he is looked up to as an "oracle of all wisdom"? Teaching offers the closest thing to a real fountain of youth. A teacher cannot help but share some of the young ideas and outlooks offered by the students. Just as courtesy and good manners are "catching," so is the youthful enthusiasm of children. To be truly effective in the classroom, a teacher must keep up with world affairs, new discoveries, the latest song and dance hits, the current World Series. This aspect of teaching makes it appeal to an active person whose desire to grow "with the times" is as keen as his willingness to learn from youngsters the interests and fears and joys of a new generation.

It has been said that a person in the teaching profession can stay young; he *must* stay young! The student just quoted has this point of view in mind, and, in addition, alludes to the idea that, in teaching, a person may continually quench his thirst for more and new knowledge.

WHY DO I TEACH?

As an elementary teacher for 20 years I have been asked many times —"Why do you teach?" This is my answer:

For me the teaching profession is the essence of creative living. In this materialistic age, it remains, intrinsically, the artist, molding, with painstaking care, the lives of boys and girls. At its fingertips is the wisdom valiantly won by our scholars.

Teaching combines two of my great interests, books and people. What, then, could be a more satisfying occupation? What could be more free from monotony than work which involves such resources as ideas and children? The elementary teacher must have many techniques and a deep understanding of children, for she deals with students in their most formative years. Besides basic skills and fundamentals, she must inculcate good work and behavior patterns. Unless she is a specialist, she deals with all the children of all the people in a community.

I like a task that keeps me on my toes both literally and figuratively. A teacher in the grades uses all her abilities, for she must be many people in one: a mother in domestic gear; a scientist in an artist's smock; a diplomat at the council table, a psychiatrist without a certificate. She must bring cohesion to any knowledge of any profession that can help her children.

I like teaching because it is a quiet and solid force in a world of confusion. I like to think my classroom an oasis in the din of blaring noises and worthless guarantees. Here, for a little while, I have a chance to expose my children to classical values and high principles. I like to think that my kind of discipline is a cogent force against juvenile delinquency, for I teach my boys and girls to be courteous, to be honest, and to be resourceful.

The respectability of my work pleases me. In contrast to some occupations, teaching demands the best of one, not only in efficiency, but in character. The public is deeply interested in the life of its children's teacher. Immorality in a Peter Pan collar may be a slick chick in some fields, but she's a dead duck in mine.

Neither does one's ultimate success depend on superficialities. Glamour can be an asset, but it is not an indispensable commodity; and time, so disastrous to veneer and youth, can add to the worth of a teacher. High fashion, while neither objectionable nor commendable, is often economically impossible. On the other hand, dullness in any dress is not disguised, and the true beauty of style can be outward expression of the instructor's personal attractiveness.

Because communism is riding the winds of today's history, I want to be part of a force that combats this evil. If, according to UNESCO authority, over half of the world is illiterate, and if, according to Lenin, the ignorant are outside the field of politics, then a teacher is America's strongest internal security against the 'isms that sweep the world. It is in a teacher's power to create a patriot's love of democracy through comparisons and dramatizations, through the arts, and in student participation in activities that develop good citizens.

Above all, though it is not in the domain of the public school teacher to teach religion as such, ethics by any name remains the same, and by example and subtle guidance, she leads students to moral decisions.

To like her work is not enough for a teacher; she must be dedicated to it. Surely, with Eternity's evaluation of service, close to the parents and strengthening them, will be the teacher. God grant her wisdom and charity and keep her free!

Ethel Hofflund, *CTA Journal,* April, 1959.

From a student in her first professional course—a young mother who has decided to fulfill the education requirements for teaching—come these reasons:

The desire to teach was firmly established approximately eight years ago when I first became aware of the teaching process, as my oldest child learned to read and write. The opportunity to help open up this new world to children appealed to me then, and has remained a fervent desire. Teaching brings a thrill, as children respond to the newness of any situation. . . . To teach, to serve mankind, is a worthy goal. It does require proper preparation, though, and if one intends to operate within the framework of the public schools, a certain amount of formal education is necessary. After definitely settling in my own mind what my goal was, it was necessary to find out the legal requirements, and fit these requirements into my established life as a wife and mother. This has required a great deal of careful planning and adjusting, both on my part and the part of my family.

As this student points out, it is important for one with home responsibilities to do some careful planning as he contemplates pursuing a teacher education program. It is no less important for a person who does not have such responsibilities to plan carefully for his future work. He needs to look in a mirror and study himself to ascertain whether he is really suited for working with children; he must consider all aspects of the teaching-learning situation to see whether he has the stamina and patience which such a situation requires; he must try to determine just what he wants to give to the job as well as what he expects to get from it. You should remember that when you have elected to go into teaching, or into any other position or profession, you have made one of the most important decisions in your life, and you should make every effort to be sure that your decision is the right one for you.

What Will You Learn about Yourself?

Once your decision is made and you proceed with your teacher education program and as you finally take your place in front of one of the nation's classrooms, there are many things that will need to be learned. Among them are a number of things about yourself. Indeed, you will no doubt learn to know yourself better than you have before. You will learn that as a teacher you will face many problems, and you will have to learn how to solve them. You will learn that as a teacher your time is not exactly yours to do with as you please;

it must be sacrificed to help students and parents. You will learn how to co-operate with administrators and fellow teachers in trying to evolve the finest educational program for boys and girls and youth in your community. You will learn that teaching is a profession in which there is no room for selfish people. You will learn whether you are realistic or foolhardy in the choice of your life's work and that you must be honest in your evaluation of yourself and your goals if the results are to satisfy your needs and interests. You will realize the importance of an honest assessment of your strengths and weaknesses. You will certainly learn whether you are able to get along with many different kinds of people. You will, of course, learn whether you have the ability to motivate youngsters and to arrange an environment in which maximum learning will take place in each individual in your classroom. You will have in true focus your real values and ideals in life. As you progress toward becoming an effective member of the profession, you certainly will learn self-control and unselfishness, and you will develop a better sense of humor than you probably now possess. As you become more and more involved in pursuing later courses in education and then begin teaching in the classroom, you will find you will be involved in a testing period far more important and more difficult than any final examination you have faced up to this point.

What Will You Learn about Others?

A teacher who makes an attempt to learn the mystery of human behavior can go a long way toward solving the intricacies of man's relationship to society and to the culture. In becoming individually acquainted with students of varied backgrounds and environments, a teacher can gain a much greater understanding of the complex social problems within the communities of the states and nation.

As a teacher, you will find out what people in the school and community expect from you, and if you are dedicated to your work, you will find out how you can respond to their expectations. You will learn that it is necessary to try to understand other people of all ages, to accept them for what they are with all of their idiosyncrasies. As you work with children, colleagues, and lay persons in your community, you are bound to gain increasing insight into other people's attitudes, beliefs, interests, goals, and efforts, and this insight will help you understand why they behave as they do. Through working with others, you may be able to modify and clarify your own ideals and beliefs.

What Will You Learn about Knowledge?

In the ever-changing world and universe in which we live today, you, as a guide of children's growth and learning, have an obligation to your students and to the people in your community to keep abreast of innovations and advancements in all areas of living. A basic foundation of knowledge in such areas as literature, composition, mathematics, science, social sciences, and fine arts is, of course, essential as you begin to teach. You will need to know the *what, how,* and *why* not only for the "three R's," but also for our form of government, for our democracy based on the rights of the individual.

There will no doubt be times when you will be frustrated by how little knowledge you actually possess, even though you possess at least one college degree. These times will provide you with the opportunity to learn to appreciate the amount of knowledge that has accumulated throughout history and to recognize the struggle that pioneers in all fields of knowledge have had and are having in discovering, organizing, and presenting this knowledge for all the world to use. No doubt you will come to have a deep appreciation for having an opportunity to probe, no matter how slightly, into a vast reservoir of information.

You will learn that knowledge, if it is to have full value, must be realized and comprehended by each individual learner; only in this way will the knowledge be a working part of him. It will be your responsibility to help the pupil prepare himself for acquiring knowledge, to teach him to think for himself to help him increase his capacity to understand, and to aid him in recognizing truth for himself.

In the classroom you and your pupils will discover knowledge principally through the various disciplines to be studied. It is most important that you and your class learn, as Foshay says, to approach the disciplines directly, to "grasp the intellectual means through which knowledge is discovered, in the hope that they may thus become active, not passive, learners." [1] It is possible for children to become producers of knowledge, not mere passive consumers of it.

IMPORTANCE OF TEACHERS IN OUR SOCIETY

The importance of teachers and teaching in the schools of our country is undeniably great. One has only to read a popular magazine or a daily newspaper to sense the general public's interest in, and demand for, quality programs in schools. Indeed, the future of our democratic way of life is dependent upon the kinds of learning experiences our future leaders and citizens have as they progress through the elementary and secondary school classrooms in the United States. Authorities in all fields of knowledge are collaborating in an effort to provide the ultimate in programs for the education of students of all ages in America and abroad, and teachers are in a pivotal position from the standpoint of organizing and implementing these programs for classroom use.

It is of great concern, then, that only the best possible people be assigned to the classrooms of the nation to guide the growth and learning of children and youth. Teachers are assuming no small responsibility when they set out to help pupils learn the subject matter of the various disciplines, as well as acquire the numerous skills and attitudes that accompany this knowledge, because these

---

[1] Arthur W. Foshay, "A Modest Proposal for the Improvement of Education," *What Are the Sources of the Curriculum? A Symposium* (Washington, D.C.: Association for Supervision and Curriculum Development, NEA, 1962), p. 3.

are essential for productive, happy, and creative lives in a democratic culture where dynamic changes occur almost daily.

Number and Types of Teachers

In most communities in the United States, the schools constitute the largest business, and the corps of teachers and other school personnel is the largest working force in the area. According to 1961 statistics, there were 1,400,000 teachers in public elementary and secondary schools; 220,000 teachers in private elementary and secondary schools; 130,000 administrators, supervisors, consultants, research experts, and other specialists in elementary and secondary schools; 350,000 professional personnel in higher education institutions; and 25,000 professional staff members in professional organizations, in government offices of education, and in private agencies with educational programs. These figures total 2,125,000 persons who are connected in one way or another with teaching.[2] And the number is growing rapidly! One source in 1964 indicated that there were 1,800,000 teachers in schools of America in that year—and that 2,200,000 would be needed by 1975.[3]

As indicated above, education as a field offers persons who enter it many kinds of opportunities to serve in interesting, dynamic positions. Possibly the most interesting and challenging of all jobs is that of the classroom teacher, and in this category the schools employ individuals at the preschool (nursery and kindergarten), elementary, secondary, and college or university levels. Within these levels are found teachers of separate or combined grades; teachers of special subjects such as art, music, English, foreign languages, social studies; teachers of physically and mentally handicapped children and youth; and critic teachers in laboratory or experimental schools.

Aiding the important work that teachers perform in the classroom are other personnel in positions where classroom teaching experience often is a prerequisite. Many teachers aspire to such positions as superintendent of schools, principal or vice-principal of a school, general or special supervisor, librarian, speech correctionist, school psychologist, guidance counselor, nurse, curriculum consultant, athletic coach, research director, registrar, business manager, head of department, dean of boys or dean of girls, or director of audio-visual materials. Most large school systems employ all these types of personnel in addition to many others, whereas smaller systems do not offer so many different kinds of positions. In general, the smaller the district, the fewer the personnel available in certain of the special services.

There are also employment opportunities for educators in certain of the national, regional, and local professional organizations such as the National

---

[2] Margaret Lindsey, ed., *New Horizons for the Teaching Profession* (Washington, D.C.: National Commission on Teacher Education and Professional Standards, NEA, 1961), p. 5.

[3] *Phi Delta Kappan,* 46:37, September, 1964.

Education Association, in state departments of education, in civic or private or religious organizations, in federal agencies, and in foreign service.

The Influencing of Behavior by Teachers

Teachers are in constant contact with impressionable children and youth in the classrooms of this country; the effectiveness of any school depends upon the knowledge, skills, convictions, character, and ability in human relations of the teachers on the staff.

Good teachers exude a contagious enthusiasm, faith, and confidence in life and learning which are needed by young people as they strive to solve their problems and to reach their goals. Often only in the school classroom do children and youth find the intelligent, sympathetic guidance needed to chart a course through the bafflement and bewilderment in world and national politics, changes in ways of living and in social institutions, and emotional disturbances in homes and communities.

The job of the teacher—in fact, the job of all persons employed in a school system—is to facilitate and motivate learning by the learners. In a real sense, learning is change of behavior, because, as a result of learning, a person's behavior is changed. Thus, the job of teachers and other school personnel is to influence desirable changes in pupil behavior. To do this job effectively, teachers not only must be knowledgeable in subject areas and adept in how to teach them, but also must be aware of backgrounds—the physical condition of the pupils, the skills and knowledges they possess, and their socioeconomic status. Only after these things are known about his pupils can the teacher really proceed, with the cooperation of the children, to the business of initiating and directing experiences which result in optimum learning.

Good teachers use methods which are effective in helping all students grow toward understanding their social environment and ways to improve it, and which provide opportunities for students to participate in the democratic planning and carrying out of learning activities. Children should learn to use the scientific method of problem-solving so that when they leave school they will be able to meet all problems head-on and follow through to satisfactory solutions. It is important, too, for teachers to encourage creativity in pupils' approaches to problems and learning situations.

Teachers of Tomorrow

The foreseeable future promises to be a period of changing values and extended horizons in all areas of living and learning, a critical era in history, carrying with it a burning need for individuals who can make intelligent decisions. As we have noted previously, the years immediately ahead will demand that teachers be able not only to "hand down the culture" but, more importantly, to provide each child with an opportunity to develop his abilities to the fullest so that he can completely help the nation and himself solve problems which do not even exist in today's complex world society.

As the world's population continues to explode, throwing people into extremely close proximity, teachers of tomorrow must be increasingly concerned with human values, motives, and aspirations that must have scientific, historical, traditional, and artistic roots to condition and help shape human behavior into socially acceptable channels. More than this, though, teachers of the future must be able to inspire their pupils to be creative in their approach to problems they will be facing at that time. Students must be taught *how* to learn; this is much more important than having the ability to parrot facts and figures which ten or fifteen years hence, or less, will be outmoded or obsolete.

Since the will of the student to learn is in some measure prompted by the emulation of his most effective teachers, it is imperative that tomorrow's teachers be well grounded in a liberal education, which really means a preparation for enlightened citizenship and character development. The behavior and character of the nation's future teachers, tempered by their knowledge of the humanities and social and physical sciences, will have a deep and abiding influence upon the quality of our future citizens.

Armed with a background of substantial academic preparation, and sound professional education in psychological, curricular, and applied aspects of teacher preparation, and carefully screened for their work, the nation's future teachers will be the most competent corps of professional persons the schools have ever known. The advances in knowledge and the demands of the profession and the public will insist upon such competency. The survival of mankind may demand such competency!

THE JOB OF TEACHING

In her address before the 1963 national convention of the National Education Association, NEA President Hazel A. Blanchard, principal of an elementary school, succinctly described the work of the teacher in the following words:

Prepared to cope with a changing society, today's teachers fit no mold. . . . Every day they become what they must be—instructor, disciplinarian, psychologist, supervisor, coach, counselor, banker, nurse, and, on occasion, even a baby sitter. Able, attractive young men and women possessing an ever-increasing amount of professional training, skill, experience, and competence replace the old concept of the proverbial pedagogue. . . . In addition to rendering a service to society, a profession must establish minimum standards for preparation and competence; develop and enforce a code of ethics; set requirements for membership therein.

The teacher who brings the most to his classroom is the one who has an understanding of the political, social, physical, and intellectual world; who helps children develop skills, knowledges, understandings, good work and study habits, aesthetic appreciations, and their own innate and creative abilities; who is sensitive to individual differences within the class group as a whole; who understands child growth and development and learning principles, especially as they apply to the age-group he is teaching; who frees the child to recognize, express, actualize, and experience his own uniqueness. And in addition to these relationships with children, the effective teacher also has normal relationships with other adults in political, social, intellectual, and spiritual areas of life.

Public and private school teachers generally strive to accomplish these many objectives at one of three levels: (1) the elementary school, (2) the junior high school, (3) the secondary school, including the senior high school and the first two years of college. To set forth the many actual duties and responsibilities of teachers at any one of these levels would be a task of impossible magnitude; a cursory overview of the three levels should be sufficient at this point.

Teachers at Work: the Elementary School

When a teacher's education prepares him for elementary school teaching, he will probably be assigned to one of the grades between kindergarten and grade six, or grade eight if this is the terminal grade in the district's elementary school organization. The usual range of chronological ages of pupils in the elementary school is five years to eleven years in the K–6 school, or five to thirteen in the K–8 school. The learning activities of boys and girls in the elementary school stress physical, social, and emotional growth and also emphasize the development of social relations, ethical behavior and character, as well as the more traditional areas of social studies, science, language arts, mathematics, and fine arts. As children progress through the elementary grades, their teachers attempt to help bring about desirable changes in behavior commensurate with the particular age and grade level. It should be emphasized at this point that a teacher will find quite a wide range of ability and achievement among children in his classroom, regardless of what grade or subjects he may be teaching; in fact, it should be added, if the teacher does an effective job of teaching, the range should widen perceivably.

Children begin their formal education in the first four years of the elementary school, usually referred to as the primary grades, and consisting of kindergarten and grades one, two, and three. Grades four, five, and six, usually considered the intermediate grades, continue the learning begun in the primary grades and proceed to learning activities of ascending difficulty. Typically, especially in the primary grades, the classrooms are self-contained; that is, one teacher teaches the same children each day in all subject areas. For the past several years, however, a number of elementary schools in America have been experimenting with different types of organizational structure. The three types most in evidence currently are known as (1) the ungraded, nongraded, multigraded, or continuous progress plan; (2) the dual progress, platoon, or core plan; and (3) team teaching.

Under the ungraded plan, children generally are grouped according to achievement levels instead of in grades, and each child advances step by step through the various levels at his own particular rate. Teachers do not teach at grade levels; they teach usually in the primary or the intermediate department. They advance each child to the next achievement level as rapidly as he is qualified for it, regardless of whether school has just gotten underway in the fall, or whether it is ready to be dismissed for the summer vacation; there are no promotion crises in the ungraded school. A typical elementary school under this plan may comprise as many as seventeen to twenty different "levels" of achievement, based primarily upon the child's reading abilities, though other aspects of his development are considered also. The ungraded plan of organization thus (1) provides for the continuous growth and learning of each child through flexible groupings; (2) eliminates, or minimizes, grade level lines; and (3) provides a plan of promotions whereby a child's development in all aspects of his being may be considered, not just the intellectual aspect.

A program of instruction containing some aspects of both the graded and ungraded plans and both the self-contained and departmentalized plans is the dual progress plan. Here the grades are retained in language arts, social studies, and physical education, but grade lines are ignored in other subjects such as arithmetic, science, music, arts and crafts, recreation, and health. Proponents of this plan hold that every person in our culture should have a definitely set knowledge of the basic tools of everyday living—language arts and the social studies; they hold, also, that no such universal obligation exists in subjects like arithmetic, music, art, and science, and children progress only as their abilities permit. A homeroom teacher is responsible for registration, counseling, and teaching reading and social studies for half a day; children then, for the other half of the day, are assigned to special teachers for all their other subjects.

The team teaching plan operates in this general manner. Instead of each teacher having charge of a class of 25, 30, or 35 pupils, two or more teachers who are subject matter specialists pool their pupils for part of each week in a large classroom, and one of the team presents a series of lessons in his special field. Meanwhile, other teachers on the team prepare lessons and curriculum materials for the next sequence. At times, small groups of 12 to 20 pupils meet for discussion; at other times, pupils do individual study in libraries or laboratories. Some teams include teacher assistants and clerks who take care of the more or less routine duties for the team. The team teaching plan makes use of large classes, perhaps of 75 to 100 pupils, small groups, and individual study. Television teaching is usually accomplished via the team plan, and many teacher teams employ such innovations as teaching machines and programmed lessons.

The newer plans of organization are not restricted to elementary schools in this country; in fact, a number of secondary and junior high schools are experimenting with all these innovations in various sections of the nation.

Teachers at Work: the Junior High School

The transition school in a large number of communities in the United States is known as the junior high school; here youngsters between the ages of twelve and fourteen or fifteen attend grades seven, eight, and nine. During these years young adolescents are making rapid changes in their growth patterns, so that teachers must provide dynamic learning experiences which will fit a wide variety of interests and needs and varying psychological readiness levels. Broad fields of humanities, social studies, the arts, and the sciences are provided for youngsters in the junior high school, and students have opportunities for experiences in many fields which they may study in more detail in the secondary or senior high school.

The typical organizational plan in the junior high school is departmental; however, the core program, similar to the dual progress plan described above, has met with its greatest success at the junior high school level. Teachers who are subject matter specialists, but who, at the same time, are well grounded in methodology, curriculum, and early adolescent psychology, are usually found in the junior high school classrooms of the country.

Educational and social guidance plays an important role in the junior high school; teachers must help students assume a healthy, natural acceptance of adolescent growth patterns so that learning will be fostered with a minimum of emotional stress and embarrassment. Junior high school teachers strive to help boys and girls grow naturally through the early adolescent years rather than risk permanent emotional damage by forcing students through premature adult patterns.

In the democratic junior high school classroom, a prime responsibility of the teacher is to see that his pupils learn how to work effectively together, to recognize and to respect their responsibilities toward one another, and to control self-desires while working for the benefit of the entire group. In short, the important responsibility of the junior high school teacher is to provide learning experiences through which students not only may acquire knowledge, but also may make some long strides toward becoming ready for effective citizenship in our democratic culture.

Teachers at Work: the Senior High School

Students of ages fifteen through seventeen or eighteen, in grades ten, eleven, and twelve, are taught usually by teachers who have had college subject matter majors, with strength in professional education foundation and methods courses. In these upper grades the teachers help the students continue to perfect their knowledges, skills, and attitudes which will eventually help them succeed as effective members of our democratic society. Besides gaining increased power in written and oral communication and expression, increased understanding of science principles and social sciences areas, increased maturity in physical and mental health habits and social responsibility, senior high school students begin to prepare themselves in vocational areas for which they seem best suited. Teachers at this level help students plan their educational programs and their life careers to mesh with their capabilities.

The secondary school teacher's work usually involves teaching several subjects, but often, especially in middle-sized to large school districts, the subjects lie within one broad field. For example, a teacher of English may have classes in American literature, English literature, composition, grammar, or linguistics; a teacher of business subjects may teach typewriting, shorthand, secretarial practice, accounting, or office procedures. If a young person preparing for a teaching position tends to prefer subjects in one broad field rather than subjects in several different fields, and tends to prefer working with adolescent-age youth rather than with youngsters of elementary school age, he should seriously consider the senior high school field.

The typical senior high school is organized according to the departmentalization plan; that is, teachers are members of the social sciences department, the physical sciences department, the music department, the business department, the industrial arts department, etc. Most teachers at this level are subject matter specialists in one field or another. This does not, however, preclude the importance of teachers' learning to know their students as individuals so that they may help them satisfy their needs and interests. A knowledge of how to care for individual differences is especially important with teen-age youngsters because in these upper grades of the public schools the widest range in achievement levels is apparent.

QUALIFICATIONS OF THE PROFESSIONAL EDUCATOR

The profession of teaching invites persons with the brightest minds, the most outstanding personalities, and the soundest moral commitments. Since teaching is not only the oldest of the professions, but is also the nurturer of all the others, it is imperative that only the best choose this field of endeavor. Educators, now recognized as professional leaders in their communities, engage in complex and demanding work and thus must possess and develop a large number of varied competencies.

Elsewhere in this book, in chapters dealing with the pressures and problems of teachers, the authors point up the importance of good physical and mental health of teachers. In this section we discuss the necessity for prospective teachers to develop other kinds of competencies.

An Awareness of the Importance of Education

To be a really professional person, a teacher must have great faith in education—greater even than that of Americans generally whose belief in free, public education is so strong that they entrust their dearest possessions to it. It is imperative for the professional educator to recognize that teaching is essential in the development of man's intellectual, social, economic, and ethical life if he is to progress and survive. An informed individual possesses tremendous power for good in an enlightened society.

When a society supports schools so that children, youth, and adults can become educated, it expresses the belief that such schools will enable members of the culture to perpetuate its traditions and values and will, also, improve the society itself. Teachers, above all in the social organization, must be aware of and have faith in the significance and potential of education, and guide their actions and evolve their values with the importance of the profession in mind.

A Keen Sensitivity to the Needs, Interests, and Welfare of Children

A good portion of this book is devoted to the importance of meeting the needs and interests of children and of providing for their general welfare, and of the teacher's role in this endeavor. What happens during the twelve or more years that children are in the public school classrooms will have a lifetime effect upon their lives. Each year a child spends in school adds to, or detracts from, his total stature.

The chief responsibility of the teacher is that of helping young people to help themselves, of helping them define their most pressing needs, interests, and problems and helping them understand their environment and how to cope with it. The teacher must help children learn how to learn, to relate the facts they discover in their learning experiences to their everyday lives.

A Desire to Be in a "Service" Field

Inherent in almost everyone's makeup is the urge to be of service to mankind. What nobler goal could one have than that of living and working so that fellow human beings might be helped in their struggle to meet life's problems and vicissitudes? For the person with such a philosophy, there are probably few, if any, types of work that offer the opportunities for fulfilling life's goals the way teaching does.

There is never a day, and seldom an hour, in the life of a teacher but that there are countless opportunities to help some boy or girl or adult to meet some problem. And as any experienced teacher will attest, these opportunities are not just in the area of the intellect; they occur in the areas of physical, social, emotional and spiritual development as well.

A Willingness to Carry on Continued Study in the Field

Education is a dynamic profession! Nothing is so constant as change in the teaching field where each new year brings added knowledge in such abundance as to challenge the brightest of minds. Teaching is one field in which continued study is not only suggested; it is demanded. New knowledge with respect to how children grow and develop and learn is evolving at a very rapid rate; new techniques of teaching are being tested in increasingly larger numbers of schools each year; information in all fields of knowledge is forthcoming with such rapidity that much in last year's textbooks is obsolete. Those persons charged with guiding the learning activities of children must be familiar with as much new knowledge as possible; the only way one may gain this awareness is through continued formal or informal study.

A Broad Liberal Arts Background with Depth in Subject Matter

Of all persons in our society, a teacher must be the best educated. This demands of one a broad background in all subject or academic areas and depth of subject matter in the area or areas he teaches. The active minds of children are forever conjuring up ideas and questions that bear on academic areas outside the particular class or subject with which they are presently involved, so the teacher must be prepared to follow their thinking to any field of knowledge. Then, too, for his own personal self-realization, a teacher must have a solid background in subject areas fundamental to his well-being in our society.

Between 75 and 90 percent of the prospective teacher's academic work toward the baccalaureate degree in college is spent in the liberal arts, including course work in general education—the humanities, communication, social studies, natural science, and personal health and development—and in the student's major subject area.

An Adequate Background in Professional Preparation

It is easy enough—and obvious enough—to say that an adequate preparation is necessary in any field in which one will practice. The problem comes in defining what an adequate preparation is, as shown by the considerable controversy of recent years over professional education courses. There is a wide variety of opinion as to the actual amount of necessary professional work in a prospective teacher's college preparatory program. Most authorities, however, claim that out of a four or five year preparatory program, the largest part of one year should be adequate for professional work. This would provide adequate preparation in foundation courses, directed teaching, and methods and materials. It is interesting to note that, whereas the requirements in liberal arts courses over the past 100 years have been increasing in numbers of units of work, the requirements in professional education in a prospective teacher's program have remained approximately the same since the days of Horace Mann.

On Teacher Preparation

Are teacher preparation program geared to the needs of teachers? The air is full of conflicting opinions on this question. The controversy revolves around how much emphasis should be placed on teaching methods versus how much emphasis should be placed on academic subject matter.

On the basis of experience, classroom teachers are uniquely suited to provide informed opinion on this issue. Therefore the NEA Research Division recently gave a scientifically selected cross section of the nation's 1.5 million public school teachers an opportunity to have their say about how their college preparation fitted them for teaching. Ninety-seven percent of the sample replied to this question:

In terms of your actual teaching needs, to what extent did your *undergraduate* teacher preparation program prepare you in the following areas?

	PREPARATION WAS:		
	Too little	*About right*	*Too much*
Depth of knowledge in subject fields in which you specialized	27.0%	71.2%	1.8%
General education—some knowledge in many fields	19.9	75.9	4.2
Psychology of learning and teaching	25.8	66.4	7.8
Human growth and development	23.2	72.1	4.7
Teaching methods	40.6	49.1	10.3
History and philosophy of education	15.1	64.2	20.7
Use of audiovisual equipment and materials	60.1	38.1	1.8

It is interesting to note that while only 27 percent of the teachers felt that they had received too little preparation in their subject field, nearly 41 percent felt that they had received too little preparation in teaching methods.

A still greater percentage of teachers felt that they should have had more preparation in the use of audiovisual equipment and materials. In this area, the highest proportion, 60 percent, registered a need for more preparation than they had received.

If undergraduate teacher preparation programs are overloaded with methods courses at the expense of academic subjects, as some people allege, then the imbalance would presumably be more pronounced at the secondary teaching level than at the elementary level. Yet the data in the chart show that 78 percent of secondary teachers as compared with 70 percent of elementary teachers found the emphasis on specialized subject matter about right or too much.

The area in which the highest percentage of teachers believed they had received too much preparation was in history and philosophy of education. Perhaps some of the criticism of teaching methods is really intended for this area.

NEA Research Division, Teacher Opinion Poll, *NEA Journal*, LII:34, December, 1963.

During the the late 1950's and early 1960's, popular magazines and newspapers have carried articles denouncing the education of public school teachers, their writers claiming that prospective teachers take too many professional courses and not enough classes in the liberal arts. The June 1963 *Changing Times* magazine presented some interesting facts and ideas on this subject:

. . . the charge that teacher preparation programs are weighted down with professional courses does not hold up for the majority of education schools. The typical teacher training institution requires between 35 and 40 semester hours in professional education for elementary teachers. That's about one-third of the total hours of study. For those planning to be secondary teachers, the average requirement in education is between 20 and 25 hours, which is about one-fifth of their total program, and 30 to 40 hours in their subject field.

In general, the time an education major spends on required subjects isn't greater than the time required of other majors. At the University of Maryland, for example, a student in elementary education must devote about 33% of his time to professional courses. In engineering, requirements take 33% to 40% of the total time; in physical therapy, 30%; in business administration, 40%; in premedicine, 40%; in history, 50%. A student in secondary education puts 20% of his time into professional courses and 25% to 30% into the subject he will teach.

.   .   .   .   .

Courses on methods and techniques are important, too. The most common cause of failure among teachers . . . is lack of knowledge of *how* to teach. The argument that anyone who knows a subject can teach it may hold for college or even for a class of high-IQ high school students with similar backgrounds and strong motivation. But a scholar who knows nothing about teaching methods would have a hard time handling the average high school class or a room full of elementary school kids.[4]

The magazine states that "all colleges and universities and all departments within them must become more interested in, and involved with, the preparation of teachers," and that this means "greater stress on liberal arts education for teachers wherever they take their training; but it also means that liberal arts colleges must strengthen their professional education courses, too."[5]

THE PRACTICAL ASPECTS OF CHOOSING TEACHING: A SUMMARY

The preceding section of this chapter dealt with the qualifications of the professional educator, with the competencies required of an effective teacher. At this point the authors present what might be termed some "practical" aspects of the job of teaching, some reactions to certain questions that naturally will come to the minds of young people contemplating entering into the profession of education.

[4] "How Good *Are* Our Teachers?" *Changing Times*, 17:26–27, June, 1963. Reprinted by permission. Copyright 1963 by The Kiplinger Washington Editors, Inc., 1729 H St., N.W., Washington, D.C. 20006.
[5] *Ibid.*, p. 31.

Will I Be in a Field Where I'm Needed?

Since before World War II there has been a shortage of qualified teachers for the public schools in the United States, and there are indications that there will continue to be a shortage for some time to come. As pointed out earlier in this chapter, about 2,125,000 persons are in some type of professional position at the present time; this figure represents an all-time high. The fact that more teachers are employed each year in itself indicates that there is an increasing need for persons in public school classrooms.

It is possible, of course, that a first-year teacher will not be able to find a position in the exact location he desires, or at the exact grade level or in the subject matter field for which he feels he is best suited. Many school systems find little difficulty in filling their staff vacanies; others experience considerable difficulty and must occasionally resort to employing teachers with emergency licenses who are not completely qualified. Also, certain academic areas, such as social studies and physical education, seem to have an adequate supply, while certain other areas, such as languages, English, and elementary grades—especially primary grades—are, at this time, in short supply.

A prospective teacher should consult the annual publication of the National Education Association Research Division, entitled "Teacher Supply and Demand in Public Schools," for an up-to-date analysis of supply and demand in the profession. The picture is constantly changing, and the current situation may change within the next very few years. Such factors as birth rates, economic conditions, trends in the profession, and the status of certain instructional fields cause supply and demand to vary. Personnel in the education department of the college you are attending have information regarding the supply and demand of teachers nationally and in the specific locality in which you prefer to teach; it would be well for you to confer with them regarding the current status and the trends that appear to be emerging.

Will I Have Enjoyable Work?

Most teachers enjoy their work. Like any type of work, teaching has its share of headaches, disappointments, and problems, but these are outweighed by the challenges it presents and by the satisfactions it affords.

There are unfortunately a few persons in the profession who for one reason or another do not enjoy teaching. Perhaps they do not enjoy working with children and youth; perhaps they do not understand why young people do the things they do; perhaps they do not like the dynamic atmosphere of the public school classroom. Whatever their reason, they should not remain in the profession; there are few things worse than being discontented with one's life's work. For this reason prospective teachers should take advantage of every opportunity to work in children's or youth groups and should take courses in introduction to education early in their college career as "self-screening" measures.

Will I Make a Reasonable Salary?

Teachers' salaries generally have been improving in recent years, and there are indications that they will continue to improve in the future. Historically, the wages of teachers have been pitifully low, but the organized efforts

---

MONEY

Good teachers—like good engineers, good hygienists, good doctors, good help in any profession or business—cost money. Starting salaries, it's true, have been rising and are becoming competitive with other occupations open to college graduates. But the long-range economic outlook in teaching still isn't very enticing—especially to a young man who will have a family to support.

What's the answer? More money for all teachers, unlimited ceilings? Too expensive, say opponents, and it rewards mediocrity. Merit pay for the best? Who'll judge? Merit schemes, say opponents, tend to reward apple-polishers rather than teachers interested in students.

The solution may be the kind of middleground plan being put into effect in Arlington, a county in northern Virginia long known for its excellent schools. The program has three scales. The first or Basic Scale will have a pay range of $5,000–$7,900 for holders of the bachelor's degree and $5,500–$8,300 for a master's, with a three-year probation period and regular increments contingent on satisfactory evaluation. (Average teacher pay for the country is $5,735.)

The next scale is the crucial one. It's called the Career Scale and offers those with a bachelor's a range of $6,400–$10,500 and a master's a range of $6,900–$12,000. To get on this scale, a teacher must have five years' experience, three of them consecutively in Arlington immediately prior to entering the scale; must have taken six semester hours of approved additional work in his field and agree to continue with extra study; and must request transfer to the Career Scale. A "Career Service Committee" composed of teachers and administrators evaluates the applicant's qualifications. Teachers who don't want to commit themselves to a long-range career or continuing college study can remain on the Basic Scale.

Ultimately, a third scale called the Resource Scale will be set up with a range of $8,400–$14,400 for teachers of outstanding ability who are called on to help new teachers and act as leaders to maintain high teaching quality.

Arlington has been raising starting salaries regularly, but the chief result has been to reward transients without reducing turnover. The new system aims to attract good teachers to make a permanent career in Arlington.

"How Good *Are* Our Teachers?" *Changing Times,* 17:30, June, 1963. Reprinted by permission. Copyright 1963 by The Kiplinger Washington Editors, Inc., 1729 H St., N.W., Washington, D.C. 20006.

of educators and others, especially since World War II, have caused the general public to become increasingly concerned over teachers' low remuneration, and the result has been improved salaries and other economic benefits.

The range in salaries of teachers over the nation is great. With a little over $5,700 being the current national average for classroom teachers, salaries range from about $3,500 to more than $10,000. Generally, teachers' starting salaries compare favorably with other professions and occupations, but it is only fair to say that over a period of years they do not as a rule keep pace with the incomes of persons in such professions as medicine and law.

Larger school systems pay higher salaries than smaller ones; cities in northern and western states, as a rule, have higher teacher salary schedules than cities in the South. There is a trend, within the various states, toward a minimum salary for beginning teachers, and, also, toward the establishment of single salary schedules within districts so that teachers with the same background of experience and education receive the same salary. It is advisable for teacher applicants to consider, in addition to the annual salary, the cost of living; a salary of $5,000 in one community may mean almost as much purchasing power as a salary of $6,000 in another location.

Will I Have Reasonable Leisure Time?

In teaching, as in most other lines of work, practitioners need time for activities which will give them release from their regular occupational duties and responsibilities. While there are many occasions which keep teachers at school after hours, and while many hours are spent in planning and preparing after the dismissal bell rings, teachers do—and should—have their evenings and weekends relatively free of professionally associated duties. For two or three months in the summer, also, teachers have the opportunity to participate in activities other than those directly associated with school, though many improve themselves professionally by attending summer sessions on college campuses, by reading, by travel, or by participating in children's and youths' camps and other activities. It is important for teachers to plan their lives so that they have a proper balance of work and rest and relaxation or participation in activities that are *different* from their usual routine.

Are There Real Opportunities for Service?

As indicated in a previous section of this chapter, opportunities for service to children and adults abound in the field of teaching. There are also opportunities to serve organizations of various kinds in the profession, the community, the state, and the nation. Teachers make up the membership of committees and official staffs of national, state, regional, and local professional organizations. They serve as Sunday School teachers or other church-affiliated officials; workers with Boy or Girl Scouts; members of service clubs and other organizations in the community; organizers of social, recreational, and religious activities. Some enter into political affairs and a few run for public office. Opportunities for teachers to serve are legion; oftentimes the problem is to limit themselves to the most worthwhile activities so that they do not spread themselves too thinly and thereby accomplish little, if anything, of importance.

Am I Properly Equipped to Do the Job?

To the sincere prospective teacher, the idea of being responsible for guiding the learning activities of 25 or more youngsters in the classroom is a challenge of considerable magnitude, and it is natural for him to question whether he is prepared to undertake such a responsibility. Dedicated teachers have always pondered this question from the first day they teach until the day they retire.

Good teaching requires physical and mental stamina, so the successful teacher will maintain satisfactory personal health. Good teaching demands a broad background in the liberal and practical arts, so the effective teacher will include in his prebaccalaureate and postbaccalaureate college program a series of courses and other experiences which will make him a well educated individual. Good teaching calls for an adequate background in the profession and a know-how in the art of guiding learning activities for young people, so in his college curriculum the professional teacher will have an adequate balance of education courses which will include psychological, historical, social, and philosophical foundations of education, a study of the curriculum, and methodology.

The effective teacher keeps in mind that the pupils must learn things today that will be beneficial to them in tomorrow's world. Thus, he must keep abreast of happenings and trends in all areas and places of living. Most important of all, he must gain and maintain the ability to teach children how to learn so that the experiences they have in today's classrooms will transfer to the world outside the classroom when they become adults. Children of today will need to know how to survive in a world of tomorrow that will be completely different.

Effective teachers will keep up with happenings and trends in all areas of living, especially in fields closely allied to their profession. New knowledge is continually being disseminated in fields of psychology, growth and development, learning, methodology, audio-visual materials. It is imperative that teachers keep abreast of this knowledge through such activities as reading in professional books and journals and attending professional meetings, as well as attending evening classes and summer sessions at colleges and universities.

Can I Have Pride in the Profession?

Teachers in America's public schools have had no small part in making this the great nation that it is today. Their pupils have graduated from their classes to become world leaders in science, medicine, government, politics, art, music, and communications. Their pupils have contributed to making this country the one with the highest standard of living in all the world. Public school teachers *have* done, and are doing, a highly commendable job in the classrooms of the nation.

The profession itself has risen in public esteem in recent years. The myriad of written and spoken words attests to the fact that respect for the profession on the part of the public has risen to peak proportions. This has resulted in increased moral and financial support of teachers and their work. Respect for educators by persons in business, industry, and the home has never been higher than at the present time.

Prospective teachers have every right to be proud of the accomplishments of their predecessors and of those currently employed in carrying on work of greatest importance. It is of utmost urgency, for our culture and for the profession, that tomorrow's teachers continue to hold high the standards of a profession that has made great strides since the early days of our country's history.

Questions for Discussion

1. Why have you chosen teaching as the profession you wish to follow? Before you can adequately answer this question, you must do two things: write down on paper your philosophy of life and, also, write down your philosophy of education.
2. To what position in the schools do you ultimately aspire? Why?
3. Specifically, how can a teacher teach his pupils *how* to learn? In what specific ways does a good liberal education make a better classroom teacher? What is the rationale currently in vogue for the belief that an elementary school teacher educated in depth in one particular area will be a better teacher in the classroom, no matter how the instructional program is organized?
4. Explain why the range of achievement in academic areas should widen within a grade or subject area if the teacher is performing effectively.
5. Of the three types of experimentation in organizational structure at the elementary school level described in this chapter (ungraded, dual progress, and team teaching), which do you believe holds the most promise? Explain your answer. Do you feel that any of these plans might be adaptable to the junior high or senior high school levels? Which ones and why?
6. In the light of the facts from *Changing Times* magazine regarding professional education—as presented in this chapter and in the companion book of readings—how do you explain the criticisms of professional programs in colleges and universities?
7. Mrs. Hofflund's essay on "Why Do I Teach?" mentions the importance of a teacher's ability to "inculcate good work and behavior patterns." What are these, and how could a teacher "inculcate" them? Also, in what ways

is a teacher "America's strongest internal security against the 'isms that sweep the world?"

8. In what ways does the work of the elementary teacher differ from that of the secondary teacher? From the junior high teacher?

9. What are some of the ways teachers can keep up with the immense amount of new knowledge that is forthcoming almost daily?

10. How many teachers are employed in your community? How does this compare with the number of doctors, dentists, and filling station operators?

Activities and Projects

1. In some of the authors' foundation courses, certain students have found it interesting and informative to return to the public school which they attended or from which they were graduated, and to interview some of their former teachers about the profession. If such a project interests you, be certain you are equipped with a set of questions for which you wish answers; remember, teachers are busy people, and with them time is a precious commodity. If your former school is not convenient, try this project at one that is. Either way, be certain to arrange an appointment in advance of your visit. An oral report of your interview will be of interest to others in your college class.

2. Refer to some self-rating scale for determining fitness for teaching, such as the one in Robert W. Richey's *Planning for Teaching*, or E. E. Samuelson, *et al.*, *You'd Like Teaching*, to see how you stand as a prospect for the profession. After reading Dr. Combs' article in the companion text of readings, how do you feel your personality fits you for the profession?

3. If you aspire to an administrative position, such as a principalship, interview a person in that position regarding its advantages and disadvantages, and report your findings to the class.

4. Make a list of qualities you think teachers should possess. Talk to your friends about the qualities they think teachers should possess. Which ones predominate? Are there any evidences of differences in those proposed by women and those by men? How does your list compare with an authority's list?

5. Check over your transcript of college work thus far. Is 75 to 90 per cent of it in the liberal arts? How do you feel your major subject area will help you in teaching classes at the elementary or secondary level? What professional courses you've taken so far do you feel will benefit you most on the job? Least?

6. Check with the teacher placement office in your college and determine which teaching areas seem to be most in demand currently. In which does the supply seem to be adequate? How does your particular teaching interest stand in the supply and demand figures?

7. Secure the salary schedule from the district in which you are interested

in securing a position. How does the beginning salary compare with the national average? Approximately how does the starting wage compare with the first-year income for doctors, lawyers, and ministers in your area?

8. Look through several college bulletins in your library and compare their teacher education programs. How does your program compare with those described? What are the respective percentages of work in the liberal arts and in professional education in each instance?

9. Choose the field of your greatest interest from these: science, medicine, government, politics, art, music, communications. By consulting encyclopedias and other references, choose the world's leaders in the area of your choice. Which are products of America's public schools?

References

"PLANNING FOR TEACHING"

ALEXANDER, WILLIAM M., *Are You a Good Teacher?* (New York: Holt, Rinehart & Winston, 1959).

CHANDLER, B. J., *Education and the Teacher* (New York: Dodd, Mead, 1961), Chapters 7, 15.

Classroom Teachers Speak on Teaching as a Profession (Washington, D.C.: Department of Classroom Teachers, NEA, 1960).

CRESSMAN, GEORGE R., and HAROLD W. BENDS, *Public Education in America*, 2d ed. (New York: Appleton-Century-Crofts, 1961), Chapters 1, 7.

HASKEW, LAURENCE D., and JONATHON C. MC LENDON, *This Is Teaching*, rev. ed. (Chicago: Scott, Foresman, 1962), Chapters 1, 5, 11.

RAGAN, WILLIAM B., *Teaching America's Children* (New York: Holt, Rinehart & Winston, 1961), Chapter 1.

RICHEY, ROBERT W., *Planning for Teaching*, 3d ed. (New York: McGraw-Hill, 1963), Chapters 1, 2, 4.

STINNETT, T. M., and ALBERT J. HUGGETT, *Professional Problems of Teachers*, 2d ed. (New York: Macmillan, 1963), Chapters 3, 5, 6.

THOMAS, LAWRENCE G., LUCIEN B. KINNEY, ARTHUR P. COLADARCI, and HELEN A. FIELSTRA, *Perspective on Teaching* (Englewood Cliffs, N.J.: Prentice-Hall, 1961), Chapters 13–15.

Who's a Good Teacher? (Washington, D.C.: American Association of School Administrators, NEA, 1961).

"THE WORK OF THE TEACHER"

ANDERSON, ROBERT H., "Team Teaching," *NEA Journal*, 50:52–54, March, 1961.

BROWN, B. FRANK, "The Non-Graded High School," *Phi Delta Kappan*, 44:206–9, February, 1963.

CHANDLER, Chapters 9–13.

CONANT, JAMES B., *The American High School Today* (New York: McGraw-Hill, 1959).

——, *Education in the Junior High School Years* (Princeton, N.J.: Educational Testing Service, 1960).

CRESSMAN, Chapters 5, 7, 10.

DRUMMOND, HAROLD D., "Team Teaching: An Assessment," *Educational Leadership,* 19:160–65, December, 1961.

FOSHAY, ARTHUR W., "A Modest Proposal for the Improvement of Education," *What Are the Sources of the Curriculum? A Symposium* (Washington, D.C.: Association for Supervision and Curriculum Development, NEA, 1962), pp. 1–13.

GRAMBS, JEAN D., CLARENCE G. NOYCE, FRANKLIN PATTERSON, and JOHN ROBERTSON, *The Junior High School We Need* (Washington, D.C.: Association for Supervision and Curriculum Development, NEA, 1961).

Group Processes in Elementary and Secondary Schools, What Research Says Series No. 19 (Washington, D.C.: Department of Classroom Teachers, NEA, 1959).

HANSEN, KENNETH H., *High School Teaching* (Englewood Cliffs, N.J.: Prentice-Hall, 1957), Chapter 14.

HASKEW, Chapters 2, 6–8.

HEFFERNAN, HELEN, and VIVIAN EDMISTON TODD, *The Kindergarten Teacher* (Boston: Heath, 1960).

HUTCHINSON, JOSEPH C., *Modern Foreign Languages: The Language Laboratory* (Washington, D.C.: U.S. Office of Education, Bulletin No. 23, 1961).

JOHNSON, MAURITZ, JR., "School in the Middle Junior High: Education's Problem Child," *Saturday Review,* 40–43, July 21, 1962.

KLAUSMEIR, HERBERT J., and KATHARINE DRESDEN, *Teaching in the Elementary School,* 2d ed. (New York: Harper & Row, 1962).

KNELLER, GEORGE F., *Foundations of Education* (New York: Wiley, 1963), Chapter 16.

MORSE, ARTHUR, *Schools of Tomorrow—Today* (New York: Doubleday, 1960), Chapters 1, 4, 5, 8.

RAGAN, Chapters 3, 6–10, 12–15.

RICHEY, Chapters 6, 7.

ROSE, GALE W., "Performance Evaluation and Growth in Teaching," *Phi Delta Kappan,* 45:48–53, October, 1963.

SHERMAN, MENDEL, "MPATI's Promise: A Summing Up," *Phi Delta Kappan,* 43:326–30, May, 1962.

STINNETT, Chapter 16.

"A Teachers' Guide to Classroom Management," *NEA Journal,* 51:21–32, October, 1962.

"Teaching Machines and Programmed Learning," *NEA Journal,* 50:15–30, November, 1961.

THOMAS, Chapters 7–9, 10, 12.

TRUMP, J. LLOYD, *Images of the Future: A New Approach to the Secondary School* (Washington, D.C.: Commission on Experimental Study of the Utilization of the Secondary School, National Association of Secondary School Principals, 1959).

――――, and DORSEY BAYNHAM, *Focus on Change: Guide to Better Schools* (Chicago: Rand McNally, 1961).

WILES, KIMBALL, *Teaching for Better Schools*, 2d ed. (Englewood Cliffs, N.J.: Prentice-Hall, 1959).

――――, and FRANKLIN PATTERSON, *The High School We Need* (Washington, D.C.: Association for Supervision and Curriculum Development, NEA, 1959).

Year-round Schools (Washington, D.C.: American Association of School Administrators, NEA, 1960).

"ECONOMICS OF TEACHING"

BUDER, LEONARD, "Report from New York City: The Teachers' Revolt," *Phi Delta Kappan*, 43:370–76, June, 1962.

CHANDLER, Chapter 14.

Credit Unions for Teachers, NEA Discussion Pamphlet No. 6 (Washington, D.C.: Research Division and Department of Classroom Teachers, NEA, 1960).

EASTMOND, JEFFERSON N., *The Teacher and School Administration* (Boston: Houghton Mifflin, 1959), Chapters 17, 18.

Economic Status of Teachers (Washington, D.C.: Research Division, NEA, latest issue).

GAGE, N. L., ed., *Handbook of Research on Teaching* (Chicago: Rand McNally, 1963).

GROSS, E., "Sociological Aspects of Professional Salaries in Education," *Educational Record*, 41:130–37, April, 1960.

HASKEW, Chapter 10.

LILLYWHITE, RAY L., "Trends in Teacher Retirement," *NEA Journal*, 50:45–46, February, 1961.

MCNAMARA, PAT, "Why Federal Money for Teachers' Salaries?" *NEA Journal*, 50:12–14, February, 1961.

MASON, WARD S., *The Beginning Teacher: Status and Career Orientations* (Washington, D.C.: U.S. Office of Education, Circular 644, 1961).

"Merit Pay for Teachers," *Saturday Review*, December 16, 1961.

MICHAL-SMITH, HAROLD, "It Takes Self-understanding," *NEA Journal*, 49:37–40, April, 1960.

"Proper Use of Sick Leave," *NEA Journal*, 51:11, May, 1962.

RICHEY, Chapters 9, 10.

STINNETT, Chapters 7–12.

STOVER, WILLIAM R., "The What and Why of Tenure," *NEA Journal*, 50:47–48, March, 1961.

"Teacher Supply and Demand in Public Schools," *Research Report* (Washington, D.C.: Research Division, NEA, issued annually).

WOLLNER, ROBERT C., and M. AURILLA WOOD, *Requirements for Certification of Teachers, Counselors, Librarians, Administrators for Elementary Schools, Secondary Schools, Junior Colleges* (Chicago: University of Chicago Press, revised annually).

WOODRING, PAUL, "The New York Teachers' Strike," *Saturday Review,* 45:51–52, May 19, 1962.

"EDUCATION OF TEACHERS"

CHANDLER, Chapter 8.

CONANT, JAMES B., *The Education of American Teachers* (New York: McGraw-Hill, 1963).

CRESSMAN, Chapter 6.

DENEMARK, GEORGE W., ed., *Criteria for Curriculum Decisions in Teacher Education* (Washington, D.C.: Association for Supervision and Curriculum Development, NEA, 1963).

HASKEW, pp. 6–13.

HODENFIELD, G. K., and T. M. STINNETT, *The Education of Teachers* (Englewood Cliffs, N.J.: Prentice-Hall, 1961).

"How Good *Are* Our Teachers?" *Changing Times,* 17:25–31, June, 1963.

LINDSEY, MARGARET, ed., *New Horizons for the Teaching Profession* (Washington, D.C.: National Commission on Teacher Education and Professional Standards, NEA, 1961).

MC GRATH, EARL J., "The Ideal Education for the Professional Man," in *Education for the Professions,* ed. NELSON B. HENRY, Sixty-first Yearbook of the National Society for the Study of Education, Part II (Chicago: University of Chicago Press, 1962), pp. 281–301.

MISNER, PAUL J., FREDERICK W. SCHNEIDER, and LOWELL G. KEITH, *Elementary School Administration* (Columbus, Ohio: Charles E. Merrill, 1963), Chapter 3.

RAGAN, Chapter 2.

RICHEY, Chapter 4.

SCHOOLING, H. W., "Partnership in Teacher Preparation," *NEA Journal,* 51:61–62, May, 1962.

STILES, LINDLEY J., *et al., Teacher Education in the United States* (New York: Ronald, 1960).

STINNETT, Chapters 4, 18.

———, and LAURENCE D. HASKEW, *Teaching in American Schools* (New York: Harcourt, Brace & World, 1962).

THOMAS, Chapter 15.

"We Must Prepare the Best," *California Teachers Association Journal,* 58:16–17ff., October, 1962.

"What Is a Well Educated Man?" *NEA Journal,* 51:22–25, April, 1962.

iv

All the high hopes which I entertain for a more
glorious future for the human race are built upon
the elevation of the teacher's profession and the en-
largement of the teacher's usefulness.

HORACE MANN

pressures and problems of teaching

DAY-BY-DAY TEACHING: THE TRUE PICTURE

The Typical Work Day

Mrs. M., third-grade teacher at Willow School, arrived at the school building at 8:00 A.M., went immediately to the teachers' lounge where she picked
up the principal's "Bulletin for the Day," hurriedly read it, and then took out
of her folder five Ditto masters she had prepared at home the night before. She
ran off on the duplicator forty copies of each master for distribution to her
children; they would use the sheets for seat work later in the day. Mrs. M. then
went to her room to get supplies ready for the children and to ready the room
for the opening of the class sessions.

When the 8:30 bell rang, Mrs. M. greeted the children who had lined up
at the classroom door, according to their usual procedure. She allowed the
children to enter the room and for 5 minutes the boys and girls sat quietly,
resting their heads on their desks. Until 9:00, the time in the classroom was
spent by the entire class repeating the Pledge of Allegiance to the flag, con-
ducting a health inspection, and collecting cafeteria money. Between 9:00 and
9:45, the teacher and children planned together for the day's work in social
studies, and the teacher distributed and explained the duplicated sheets in
language usage, spelling, and writing. On days when time allowed, part of this
time was used in conversational Spanish or English activities.

At 9:45, Mrs. M. took the children to the playground where she super-
vised their playing a game she had introduced earlier in the year, and at 10:00

the children returned to the classroom for reading instruction. During the ensuing hour, Mrs. M. first worked with reading group III while group I worked on the language work-study sheets and group II worked on work-study sheets for social studies; she then worked with reading group II while group I worked on social studies work-study sheets and group III worked on language work-study activities; and finally, she worked with reading group I while group II worked on language work-study sheets and group III completed the social studies sheets. On alternate days, the children worked on science instead of social studies activities.

The 20-minute period beginning at 11:00, which Mrs. M. designated as the directed writing and spelling period for the entire group, usually proved to be insufficient, because the class was in the process of making the transition from manuscript to cursive writing. Between 11:20 and 11:30, the teacher always, and wisely so, allowed time for an evaluation of the work that had taken place during the morning; a list of "Things We Learned This Morning," drawn out from members of the class, was written on the chalkboard for all to see.

During the lunch hour, Mrs. M. had half of the period for rest and relaxation, but she spent the other half hour in supervising in the cafeteria, a "duty" which fell her way for three weeks each semester. On three other weeks during the semester, Mrs. M. had "yard duty" on the playground for half of her lunchhour time.

At 12:25 the bell sounded and the children once more lined up at the classroom door; Mrs. M. admitted them to the room and they once more rested for a 5-minute period. At 12:35, Mrs. M. began the arithmetic lesson, which she taught by entire group and small group activities. During the 45-minute period between 1:05 and 1:50, Mrs. M. again called each of the three reading groups to the reading circle for 15-minute sessions for each, but this time the emphasis was upon recreational reading instead of developmental reading, as it had been in the morning. While the teacher was discussing with each group their recreational reading activities, the other groups were doing additional recreational reading at their seats. Between 1:50 and 2:20, Mrs. M. led the class in an art lesson with tempera paints; on other days at this period she provided experiences for the class in music, literature, dramatization, story-telling, or choral speaking. During the final 10 minutes before dismissal at 2:30, all completed papers were turned in by the children and another evaluation period ensued in which the children provided statements under a chalkboard heading of "Things We Learned Today."

During the day, two mothers came to visit the classroom—one in the morning and the other in the afternoon. Of course, some time had to be spent with each mother discussing the achievement of her child. Twice during the day children from the rooms nearby came to the room to borrow certain pieces of equipment and each time interrupted Mrs. M. in whatever she happened to be doing, and once the principal popped into the room to ask Mrs. M. if she would serve on the refreshments committee for the next meeting of the Parent-

Teacher Association. On this afternoon, as on each Wednesday afternoon, Mrs. M. joined her colleagues in a regular faculty meeting which ran from 3:00 to 4:15. Faculty meetings at Willow School were not the drudgery they are in some schools, however, as time was spent in worthwhile in-service education activities which involved participation by all teachers on the building staff.

By the time Mrs. M. returned to her room and picked up papers to be graded at home that evening, it was a little after 4:15, and she had completed an 8-hour and 15-minute day. It seemed that despite her best organization it was never possible to complete the day at the building in less time than that, what with parent conferences, organizational meetings, and other kinds of activities. Furthermore, Mrs. M. often returned to the school building in the evening to attend programs by pupils in the school, PTA meetings, and gatherings of other organizations and groups in the school community.

Mr. S. is a business education teacher in Pioneer Senior High School. He leaves his home at 7:35 each morning to reach his one-mile-distant school by 7:50; when he arrives at the building he reads the principal's bulletin to teachers and makes last-minute preparations for the first class session which begins at 8:05. During the first class session, office practice, Mr. S. has students work on clerical office practice sets, and when the various jobs are complete they turn them in to the teacher to be checked.

Mr. S.'s preparation period comes between 9 and 9:45. After listening to the daily bulletin read from the principal's office, he studies shorthand for a class period later in the day; checks some student papers handed in the previous period; goes to see the Dean of Girls about curriculum offerings in the business education department next year, including class size, total enrollments, and number of sections; and talks with his student teacher who reports to the school each day.

Between 9:50 and 10:45, Mr. S. supervises the student teacher as the latter teaches a clerical office practice class, helps students who need individual attention in the course, and then confers with the student teacher's college supervisor who has come to observe the student's work in the classroom. Mr. S.'s lunch hour this year is between 10:50 and 11:35; on this day during lunch he confers with another business education teacher regarding subject offerings for the next year, about certain techniques of teaching shorthand, and about the possibility of building a class in secretarial practice.

From 11:40 to 12:20 Mr. S. teaches the class in typing III and IV, in which students learn how to do tabulation reports of an accounting and executive nature, and from 12:25 to 1:15 he teaches the second section of the same class. The beginning shorthand class meets between 1:20 and 2:15; for the first 5 minutes of the period, students practice brief forms with their flash cards; then Mr. S. dictates home work and new matter to the class. Juniors in the class remain a few minutes after class is dismissed for a check-up with Mr. S. to find out whether they were recommended for next year's secretarial practice class.

The period between 2:20 and 3:15 is free on all days except Wednesdays, when Mr. S. sponsors the American Field Service club in the high school. At this day's meeting, a foreign student in a neighboring high school speaks to the club about her homeland of Barbados.

After the 3:15 dismissal bell, Mr. S grades the shorthand papers, counsels a student about transferring to an earlier morning class in shorthand, talks with four students about the next speaker for the American Field Service Club's meeting, writes two letters asking for free teaching materials, closes the windows in the classroom and checks it for orderliness. On the way to the parking lot, Mr. S. talks with another business education teacher regarding textbook orders, curriculum reports, and the school's proposed semester examinations. By this time, the clock reads 4:00, and Mr. S. has completed a better than 7½-hour day at school, and in the evening at home he spends another 2 hours in grading papers and planning for the next day's classes.

The two examples given above are true stories in the lives of two teachers, one at the elementary school level and one at the secondary level. They are mythical typical days, because in teaching there are no "typical" days, since teachers, pupils, and schools vary so greatly from day to day that it is impossible to call anything typical. But the preceding accounts of two days of two actual teachers should give the reader some conception of what teachers do during the day. At least it can be seen that for a certainty the teacher's day is not what is commonly thought, a 9:00 to 2:30 job in which the teacher spends his time "hearing lessons" and disciplining children, and which ends for the day when the children go home. It can be seen that the usual day in teaching is about 8 hours in length, plus whatever time is spent on school work after regular school hours.

The Typical Work Week

The typical length of the work week for teachers is about 50 hours. Here again, no week is typical, but one professional association has broken down the average teacher's work week as follows: [1]

	HOURS WEEKLY	
Duty	*Ele. Tchr.*	*Sec. Tchr.*
Teaching and other duties during school hours	36.7	37.7
Lesson planning, correcting papers, clerical work and other duties outside school	9.6	10.1
Extra occasional duties—such as trips, pupil activities, and PTA meetings	. . .	1.0
Professional activities not sponsored by the schools, such as study	1.5	1.5
Total	47.8	50.3

[1] *New York State Education*, 47:48–49, October, 1959.

Both elementary and secondary teachers, on the average, spend more than 3 hours per week outside school in lesson planning and more than 1 hour per week in clerical work. Elementary teachers average about 3.5 hours per week and secondary teachers about 5 hours per week in correcting papers.[2]

The Typical Summer

Teaching is the one profession which affords its members a long summer vacation period. Because most school systems in the United States dismiss pupils for the summer vacation in mid-June or late June, teachers are relatively free from their classrooms until early or mid-September. Although the trend is toward extending the school year, it will probably be some time before teachers can no longer look forward to a 2- to 3-month summer vacation which they can pretty well use as they see fit. Like the typical school day, there is no typical pattern of teacher activities during this free period.

More school districts each year are offering their teachers opportunities to supplement their annual income by jobs in the district's summer sessions for the enrichment of many pupils' programs and for special make-up or remedial classes. Many teachers, too, gain salary increments through completing district in-service education classes and courses on college campuses; the large college enrollments during summer sessions are made up predominantly of teachers who are taking advantage of this time to improve their professional status and to grow. An increasing number of teachers are combining travel and further education in colleges and universities in different parts of this country and abroad. Many teachers supplement their income by working in jobs outside the teaching profession during the summer months; others take part in such creative activities as writing, painting, composing, and playing or singing in musical organizations.

The mythical typical days in the lives of two teachers which began this chapter clearly point up the fact that persons in the profession have a multitude of responsibilities, both inside and outside the classroom. Their duties are many and varied; most of them are challenging and interesting; some of them are routine and dull.

Typical Daily Planning

An analysis of the two teachers' days at the opening of this chapter points up something of the amount of behind-the-scenes effort expended by teachers so that their pupils might participate in many kinds of learning experiences. Most teachers spend literally hours of time in study and in planning and organizing teaching-learning procedures.

Teachers must plan for certain instructional units to be taught to their

[2] Arvid J. Burke, "Do Teachers Have 'Short' Hours?," in *Teaching in America,* ed. Anthony C. Riccio and Frederick R. Cyphert (Columbus, Ohio: Charles E. Merrill, 1962), pp. 125–26.

pupils; often this presents a need for either writing a resource unit or choosing one which will be adaptable to the present group of children in the class. From the units, the teachers plan individual lessons with the needs and interests of members of the class in mind. Teachers must determine which types of instructional materials and audio-visual aids will most effectively carry out the activities of the individual lessons, and see that they are on hand when needed.

In good schools today, teachers employ many types of instruction methods at both elementary and secondary school levels, and do not depend on one single approach to accomplish their objectives. Much use is made of teacher-pupil planning and problem-solving techniques, and from them spring such procedures as dramatizations, film presentations, demonstrations, presentations by resource persons, field trips, laboratory experiences, and individual and group evaluations. If the teachers give more than lip-service to the idea that learning is an *individual* matter, then pupil-centered and cooperative group projects to which all children can contribute will be the bases of methodology. Since there is no one best way to teach, teachers must be encouraged to experiment in the classroom and to use their ingenuity in instructional approaches.

Classroom management is an important aspect of a teacher's daily work. This many-faceted area includes a number of things discussed previously—planning for units and lessons, arranging for instructional materials, and deciding upon appropriate methodology. Attendance-checking, assignment-making, and paper-collecting are also obvious parts of this important teacher responsibility. Another aspect of classroom management, one that looms large in the viewpoint of many teachers, particularly first-year teachers, is that of discipline. Some teachers seemingly have more than their share of behavior problems; others apparently have very few or none at all. The difference, generally, is that those who have few or no behavior problems have learned to avoid them subtly by creating classroom environments where industry and interest abound, or they have learned to sense impending misbehavior and have taken steps to prevent its happening. Despite the most subtle planning to avoid behavior incidents, they still occasionally arise. When they do, teachers, realizing that all behavior is caused, should attempt to find the cause of the problem and insofar as possible take steps to alleviate or eliminate the cause. The causes that make children behave in ways which are not socially acceptable are legion, but teachers who do not attempt to find specific reasons for misbehavior and remedy them are not worthy of their titles. Unless causes of misbehavior are found and acted on, children can hardly be expected to grow into socially acceptable ways of behavior.

During the course of each learning experience, teachers and pupils must evaluate their progress toward whatever are the agreed objectives of the class. Procedures and techniques must constantly be appraised so that the teacher and the class will know whether they can be continued or whether other processes should be employed. Tests of various kinds, written reports, anecdotal records, check lists, and questionnaires are among the tools used in evaluation,

My First School

The question was settled; the die was cast. The matter which had been under consideration by myself and friends for some length of time was finally decided. *I was to teach.*

With a vigorous and confident hand, I grasped the reins of government in the little domain of my classroom. All went well for a time. But then, to my dismay, my pupils began to exhibit signs of restlessness and insubordination. I tightened the reins of discipline, assumed more sternness of demeanor, but in vain. The hitches and jerks in the machinery would come.

Weeks and months passed, and, in spite of all my effort, the school would often be noisy; the children, unruly. I was utterly heartsick and discouraged until, gradually, permanent thought and experience took the place of anxiety and discouragement. I discovered I had been reaching after the unattainable, that I had been wasting my strength in vain endeavor to keep quiet, and to drill into perfection that which God never meant should be quiet.

A healthy growth can best be secured by that very restlessness which is the bane of the teacher's experience. Indeed I may say, the teacher's proper task is not to destroy restlessness, but to seek to turn it into the right channel, and thus promote the development of both physical and mental faculties. He or she who learns to do this has found the "philosopher's stone" in teaching.

My short experience has brought to my mind the fact that a very great evil in country schools is keeping the children in school too long, and especially too long at a time. But I enforce the policy of keeping them busy, let it be whatever you choose—printing, drawing, writing on a slate, or whatever is assigned.

And then when they have done the best they can and all that has been asked of them for the time, I let them go out to play to work off the superabundant vitality that is in them. Fresh air and exercise is what they need to keep their bodies sound and their minds bright and active for work in the school room.

This, my humble experience in my first effort to "teach the young ideas how to shoot," I give for what it is worth. If it will be any help or any encouragement to my fellow teachers, who like myself have just begun to tread the thorny pathway of the profession and whose hearts groan, as did mine, for light, sympathy, and help in their calling, my object will be attained.

Written sometime between 1880 and 1883 by Amanda Crabtree, *NEA Journal*, Vol. 55, No. 4, p. 18.

and it is the responsibility of the teacher to administer and interpret the results of these evaluative media.

Reporting to parents is an extremely important part of the teacher's work. This demands of a teacher the ability to measure pupils' achievements and accomplishments accurately and to report to parents objectively regarding children's growth in skills, knowledges, understandings, attitudes, and behavior. Such reporting can hardly be done effectively through many of the traditional systems of grading. Individual teacher-parent conferences provide possibly the most mutually beneficial method of reporting, since the parent and the teacher may learn from each other what procedures may be taken by each for the ultimate benefit of the child. The traditional letter marks or percentage scores are frequently confusing and misleading, and the written paragraphs, while superior to the marks, have their grave limitations also. It is unfortunate that here, in the third quarter of the twentieth century, the trend in reporting seems to be back in the direction of the five-level letter marks: A–B–C–D–F.

Other aspects of a teacher's daily work are also obvious from an analysis of the activities described at the beginning of this chapter. Many times each day, teachers who have proper rapport with pupils are called upon to counsel boys and girls and youth as they attempt to solve problems involving educational, social, or vocational plans. Also, in most schools in the country, teachers have the opportunity to direct at least one activity which is termed, variously, as co-curricular or extracurricular; these activities are concerned with many areas, such as music, speech, journalism, athletics, hobbies, or social life. The daily work of the teacher also includes professional study and cooperative professional contacts and projects with other teachers on the school's staff.

THE TEACHER'S ROLES

The teacher "wears many hats." Some fit very well; others do not. But the teacher must wear them all, for associating and working with pupils and parents and other lay persons and professional colleagues forces him to fill many different roles, a number of which have been indicated previously. Besides being a director of learning, a motivator, a confidant, a disciplinarian, and a resource person, the teacher at different times also finds himself in the roles of a clerk, a "baby-sitter," an executive, a recreational leader, and a joiner.

The Clerk

There is a great deal of paper work involved in the teacher's job; in fact, the record-keeping required of teachers seems to increase almost annually. Much of the work is of a clerical nature, but a great amount of it, such as making entries in cumulative records, is highly professional and is necessary for an effective teaching-learning situation. Daily attendance records are usually kept by teachers; these are important since the state money allotments are based on average daily attendance records. Pupils' cumulative records must be kept up-to-date in areas where teachers are involved. Lunch records, excuses for pupil absences or tardiness, teacher registers, pupil permits to take field trips—all of these, as well as others, bid for their time in the daily life of the teacher.

What Is A Teacher?

The teacher is a prophet. He lays the foundations of tomorrow. *The teacher is an artist.* He works with the precious clay of unfolding personality. *The teacher is a friend.* His heart responds to the faith and devotion of his students. *The teacher is a citizen.* He is selected and licensed for the improvement of society. *The teacher is an interpreter.* Out of his maturer and wider life he seeks to guide the young. *The teacher is a builder.* He works with the higher and finer values of civilization. *The teacher is a culture-bearer.* He leads the way toward worthier tastes, saner attitudes, more gracious manners, higher intelligence. *The teacher is a planner.* He sees the young lives before him as a part of a great system which shall grow stronger in the light of truth. *The teacher is a pioneer.* He is always attempting the impossible and winning out. *The teacher is a reformer.* He seeks to remove the handicaps that weaken and destroy life. *The teacher is a believer.* He has abiding faith in the improvability of the race.

Joy Elmer Morgan, *NEA Journal*, March, 1958, back cover.

The "baby-sitter"

Some parents apparently feel that one of the responsibilities of the teacher is to "sit" with their children. One of the authors vividly recalls an incident wherein a mother brought her child back to school after the child had had a "not-too-sick" experience with chicken pox, and the relief the parent verbalized now that the school would have the child on its hands and out from under the mother's feet. What teacher has not had a parent suggest, "Anything the school can do for the child will be appreciated, as I can't do a thing with him"? On the other hand, the teacher has a legal role of *loco parentis*, "in place of the parent," in which the laws and traditions of this country have given parental status to the teacher for supervision of pupils on playgrounds and on trips of various kinds.

The Executive

As an employee of a local school district, teachers are expected to abide by and to enforce the state laws and rules and regulations of the local board of education as they apply to the school and to the classroom. At the same time, however, it is important for teachers to remember that, even though they are employees of a local district and as such are agents of the state, they are legally liable for any injuries caused by negligent acts, just as are any other persons in this nation. The teacher, too, is the real executive officer in the classroom; even though the activities are cooperatively planned and executed, the teacher, in the final analysis, is the person responsible for what goes on in the classroom.

The Recreation Leader

Because of a teacher's background of training and his ability to work with youngsters and adults, he is often called upon to take an active leadership role in recreational activities in the community. Whether he is sought out in this capacity, he most certainly will be, at times, the recreational leader of the boys and girls in his classroom, especially in the elementary school. With the desired goals of social and physical well-being, recreational activities in the classroom or school consist of games, sports, and certain recreational clubs which are usually promoted through contests or tournaments. A relatively new and increasingly important recreational activity in the schools—one in which increasing numbers of teachers are being involved—is that of camping and outdoor education. Many colleges are increasing their programs in which pupils work, play, live, and learn together under the direction of public school and student teachers.

The Joiner

Teachers, of course, are key persons in the important community area of education, but they are also participants in other activities of the community such as the church, civic organizations, and other clubs and political groups. They also join professional organizations at national, state, and local levels.

Most school districts expect teachers to become associated with churches in the community, and studies have shown that, whereas less than half of the general population of the nation are members of religious organizations, over 90 per cent of the country's teachers participate in church activities. Teachers are sought for membership in local service clubs in most communities, and they are often asked to give leadership to such agencies as the Community Chest, the Red Cross, and Boy and Girl Scout troops. Members of teaching staffs generally take their political responsibilities seriously, and many of them run for and are elected to political offices. Most teachers belong to two or three professional organizations, such as the National Education Association, state teachers' associations, and national, state, and local groups affiliated with the NEA; some school districts apply considerable pressure to get teachers to join professional groups.

PROFESSIONAL AND PUBLIC RELATIONSHIPS

Parents and Community Groups

Schools, like other institutions, cannot long continue to operate at a high level of efficiency if they do not have the goodwill and support of the patrons they serve. While the schools do not "sell" in the same sense that commercial institutions do, they nonetheless must develop a grass-roots understanding and appreciation of their programs through interaction with parents and other lay persons. Since almost every person in America has attended public schools at one time or another, and since millions of people have children now attending their classes, the schools are close to the people and are likely to remain so for a long time to come. The schools must maintain an effective program of keeping the people informed of their needs, purposes, and achievements, and at the same time develop a sensitivity to the needs and desires of the community.

It is inevitable that teachers, whether they are new to the system or are veterans of some tenure, will have many contacts with parents of children and with various groups of lay persons in the community. Parents have a special concern for the school, and, in most cases, feel a kindred interest with the teachers in the education of their children. In a sense, teachers pick up the educational task from the children's first teachers—the parents—and carry on from that point in collaboration, it is hoped, with the mothers and fathers. The further teachers can go in developing good relationships with parents, the greater will be the possibility of an effective team approach to the education of the children.

Whether or not the school is considered a "good" school depends to a large extent on the stories children bring home to mothers and fathers. If the learning experiences at school have been satisfying, meaningful, interesting, and pleasant for children, the principal effort for satisfactory parent-teacher relationships will be won, and the way will be open to effective team effort toward the education of boys and girls and youth.

With proper rapport between teachers and parents usually will come the necessary effective cooperation for the children's optimum learning; parents will often contact the teachers and will contribute, as well as receive, much information which will be of mutual benefit in the education of the children. The goal of both parents and teachers should be the optimum development of the children, and both have much to share toward this end.

Teachers invariably feel a sense of frustration when the time comes to communicate with parents at "reporting" time, especially if the reporting system involves letter grades or percentage marks. The reporting time could and should be a time when some of the most effective interaction takes place between teachers and parents for the benefit of the children. But it can be so only if parents and teachers are able to sit down together in mutual trust and confidence and exchange information about the children which will materially affect their growth and development. Thus the reporting time becomes a two-way affair in which those concerned with an evaluation of the children's achievement may discuss ways of improvement, rather than a one-way report in which teachers tell parents in ways often not understood, or else misunderstood, about the progress of the children.

Parents may be brought into closer cooperation with the school in ways other than individual conferences. Often they serve on committees with teachers and administrators, such as curriculum, report card, and social committees. Many interested teachers and parents affiliate with the local chapter of the National Congress of Parents and Teachers, an organization founded in 1897, consisting of more than 12 million members, and dedicated to the education and welfare of children and youth. Meetings of local PTA's can be used constructively for informing parents and teachers of school affairs and activities and their purposes. It cannot be denied that parent-teacher organizations of this type over the years have made some outstanding contributions to public school education.

An organization which exists in many communities, named the community coordinating council or simply community council, is made up of lay leaders from most of the civic and social organizations in the area. Such a council is often active in studying the educational programs of schools in the community, and it is not unusual for such a group to make recommendations to the local board of education or to the local school district's corps of administrative officials. Teachers are usually represented in one way or another on Community Councils; at any rate, it is well for teachers to know of such groups and their purposes and activities.

It is not unusual for the school district's board of education to appoint committees for special purposes. It is popular at this time, for example, for boards to appoint committees to study the programs of the schools in the local district and to make recommendations for changes or improvements. Members of such committees sometimes visit teachers' classrooms to evaluate the activities they find there. Sometimes these committees are composed of teachers and lay persons, but at other times teachers are not included.

Space does not permit a complete listing of the numerous clubs and societies in the community with which the schools must work from time to time. Certain of these are "youth-serving" groups, such as church-sponsored organizations, Boy and Girl Scouts, Hi-Y, Rainbow Girls, DeMolay, and 4-H, in all of which teachers are often solicited to serve. Adult groups active in most communities which, in one way or another, have education as one of their purposes include Kiwanis, Rotary, and Lions in the service club area; Masons and Knights of Columbus among the religious-social-philanthropic groups; American Legion, Veterans of Foreign Wars, and Daughters of the American Revolution in the patriotic club category; and the League of Women Voters and the Fortnightly Club in the study and social groups. All these organizations have varying degrees of influence and, upon occasion, have been quite effective in exercising this influence on the school curriculum and curriculum materials, personnel, finance, and methodology.

Labor organizations in the various American cities historically have been strong supporters of public education and have been very effective at times in organizing public opinion about certain educational issues. Commercial and industrial groups, such as the powerful U.S. Chamber of Commerce and the National Association of Manufacturers, have, particularly in recent years, joined the group of public education's best friends. A review of the legislative records of both major political parties—Republican and Democrat—reveals that, in general, they have favored strong educational systems in the 50 states.

Boards of Education

A district is a division to which the state legislature delegates most of the actual administration of the schools within its boundaries; its size may vary from less than a square mile to several thousand square miles embracing an entire township or an entire county. And the legally constituted community group which is charged with complete responsibility and authority for the operation of the schools in a single district is the board of education. Composed usually of five to seven members elected in most states by popular vote in the community, the board usually serves without pay and spends much time in exercising duties in connection with the schools. Legally, the board can exercise direct supervision of the school program, and in some communities, particularly in small ones, individual members actually take this right seriously. However, when the board of education is not in session, its members have no more authority in school matters than have other citizens, unless the board has delegated them such authority.

In actual practice, the board does not as a rule become involved in the actual running of the school, but rather serves as a policy-making, legislative, and evaluative organization, delegating the executive powers to the school's superintendent and his staff; the superintendent is the board's chief executive officer. The board generally approves or rejects the superintendent's nominations for teaching positions in the district, though it is not uncommon practice in small districts for the teacher applicants to be interviewed by members of the board individually or as a group.

The board approves or disapproves the superintendent's budget and other matters that come to its attention from school employees through the district's chief school officer. State legislatures and state departments of education, which are charged by law with education within the state, generally delegate most of this responsibility to the local board of education.

Administrators; Other Teachers

When a teacher accepts a position in a school district, he will come in contact with other persons employed in the district in many different capacities. Here he will find fellow teachers, administrators, supervisors, custodians, the nurse, cafeteria employees, and, in some instances, doctors, dentists, psychologists, and others.

From the day the teacher is interviewed throughout his entire tenure he is constantly associating on the job with school administrators. In small districts, he may come in daily contact with the superintendent of schools; in large districts, he may see the superintendent only once or twice a year, if that often, and then only in large district-wide staff meetings. The teacher may see the assistant superintendent in charge of instruction a bit oftener, but here again, very little individual contact with him will be possible.

The administrator with whom the teacher has the most direct contact is the building principal. The national trend is toward the principalship as a supervisory as well as administrative position; in fact, national and state principals' organizations have subscribed to the idea that at least 50 per cent of the principal's time should be spent in supervision, teacher evaluation, and the general improvement of instruction. If all principals would adhere to this recommendation, it is clear that a great deal of their work would be devoted to helping teachers.

It is natural for a beginning teacher to want to know what will be the relationship between himself and the principal, what each can expect from the other. As a starting point, it is reasonable to expect that, since administrators are former teachers, they are acquainted with most of the trials and tribulations of instructors; as principals, they are now charged with the coordination of all teachers' efforts in and contributions to the instructional program. With the administrator's background being thus, it would be reasonable that the beginning teacher could expect him to be an educational leader, one whose professional leadership the teacher could expect to follow. The teacher can also expect the administrator to be competent in his position, to be fair in his dealings with all teachers, and to display an understanding attitude toward the instructors' problems, since he himself has experienced similar problems. By his actions, the administrator should also allow the teacher to share in much of the administrative problem-solving and action with respect to school affairs.

TEACHER EVALUATION

TEACHER: *Socrates*   A. PERSONAL QUALIFICATIONS

	Rating (high to low)	*Comments*
	1 2 3 4 5	
1. Personal appearance	☐ ☐ ☐ ☐ ☑	Dresses in an old sheet draped about his body
2. Self-confidence	☐ ☐ ☐ ☐ ☑	Not sure of himself—always asking questions
3. Use of English	☐ ☐ ☐ ☑ ☐	Speaks with a heavy Greek accent
4. Adaptability	☐ ☐ ☐ ☐ ☑	Prone to suicide by poison when under duress

B. CLASS MANAGEMENT

	1 2 3 4 5	
1. Organization	☐ ☐ ☐ ☐ ☑	Does not keep a seating chart
2. Room appearance	☐ ☐ ☐ ☑ ☐	Does not have eye-catching bulletin boards
3. Utilization of supplies	☑ ☐ ☐ ☐ ☐	Does not use supplies

C. TEACHER-PUPIL RELATIONSHIPS

1. Tact and consideration ☐ ☐ ☐ ☐ ☑ Places student in embarrassing situation by asking questions

2. Attitude of class ☐ ☑ ☐ ☐ ☐ Class is friendly

D. TECHNIQUES OF TEACHING

1. Daily preparation ☐ ☐ ☐ ☐ ☑ Does not keep daily lesson plans

2. Attention to course of study ☐ ☐ ☑ ☐ ☐ Quite flexible—allows students to wander to different topics

3. Knowledge of subject matter ☐ ☐ ☐ ☐ ☑ Does not know material—has to question pupils to gain knowledge

E. PROFESSIONAL ATTITUDE

1. Professional ethics ☐ ☐ ☐ ☐ ☑ Does not belong to professional association or PTA

2. In-service training ☐ ☐ ☐ ☐ ☑ Complete failure here — has not even bothered to attend college

3. Parent relationships ☐ ☐ ☐ ☐ ☑ Needs to improve in this area —parents are trying to get rid of him

RECOMMENDATION: *Does not have a place in Education. Should not be rehired.*
John Gauss, *Phi Delta Kappan,* 43:4, January, 1962, back cover.

In return, the administrator can expect the teacher to be competent in the ability to teach the subjects and to guide the learning activities of children at whatever grade level the teacher is assigned. He should expect the teacher to assume a professional attitude and an ethical countenance in his dealings with others, and to participate in projects of various types that will immediately or eventually be of benefit to the school system.

Teachers work with other teachers. Oftentimes, too, since teachers have similar backgrounds and experiences, the relationships are extended into their social activities. Teachers share ideas individually and in group meetings, they travel together to professional meetings, they participate together in teacher institutes and workshops, and they pool their ideas in college summer session classes or other professional activities held during times school is in recess. In some schools, arrangements are made for intervisitation of teachers in each other's classrooms or in schools in distant parts of the city or in other communities; such activities have proved interesting and helpful in the area of improvement of the teachers' own instruction.

Demonstration teaching is often a part of a building's in-service education program. Here, teachers or supervisors demonstrate some particular technique or techniques—often with pupils present—for the benefit of their colleagues.

Professional Organizations

The various organizations to which a teacher might belong are described in Chapter 12, "The Profession," page 281. Teachers should study the many organizations available to them and decide for themselves the ones with which they want to become affiliated.

Of course, a teacher cannot afford the dues or the time to belong to very many of the professional organizations, so he must weigh them in relation to his own needs, interests, and financial ability. To gain the most from membership in professional groups, just as in other organizations, a teacher must participate actively; this can be a drain on a teacher's time, energy, and finances.

CONCLUSION

There are many problems and pressures that a teacher faces when he enters into the largest profession in the nation. In the first place, he faces long work days which often extend late into the night; he faces weeks which extend well beyond the 40 hours usually accepted as a typical work week. Then, too, the teacher assumes a number of different roles as he works with children, parents, and others in the community in direct educational activities and in closely related projects. He has certain obligations and responsibilities with respect to lay persons and his professional colleagues with whom he associates each day.

Questions for Discussion

1. How can we reconcile the fact that teachers work nearly a 50-hour week, while the normal work week in other occupations is 40 hours—with prospects of 32 hours?
2. The one aspect of teaching about which prospective teachers are most apprehensive is that of discipline, or, more accurately, misbehavior. How do you account for the fact that some teachers just never have any behavior problems, while others have many?
3. Which of the several media for reporting pupil progress do you prefer? Explain why you feel that your preference does the best job of letting parents know how their children are progressing.
4. Can you think of ways that might alleviate some of the responsibilities now assumed by teachers in roles which have little direct relation to the teaching-learning situation?
5. What are the organizations in your community which are education oriented? With which of these should teachers have some acquaintance? Which seem to be most sincerely devoted to the well-being of children and to their education? Which organizations do you think would be good ones

for elementary school teachers to join? Why? Which ones would probably be more interested in secondary-age children? Why do you think so?

6. How can a beginning teacher determine what his relationship with his professional colleagues should be? If a beginning teacher wishes to act in a professional manner, how should he consider and deal with the news he hears in a typical teachers' lounge?

7. Compare the work of the elementary teacher and the secondary teacher described at the beginning of this chapter. In what ways should their teacher preparation programs be different? How should they be similar? Which deals more in subjects and which deals more with children? Should this be true? Why?

8. How do modern teachers' methods compare with those indicated in the selection "My First School," written in the early 1880's? How do they differ and how are they similar? What should be a teacher's goal in this respect?

9. In what ways do you think parents and teachers can work together as a team in the education of children?

10. Do you think it is fair and ethical for communities to insist that teachers in their schools join and attend churches in the local communities, spend their wages in the local places of business, wear business clothing while they are in the classroom, and refrain from patronizing certain businesses or amusement places which the public generally may patronize? Why or why not?

Activities and Projects

1. Divide a sheet of paper into two columns by drawing a line vertically through the center of the paper. Label the lefthand column "The teacher is . . . ," and then in the column, list each predicate nominative included in the selection "What Is a Teacher?" In the righthand column, entitled "As such, he . . . ," insert as many instances as you can of how teachers personify each of the nominatives. Example:

The Teacher Is . . .	*As Such, He . . .*
1. A prophet	1. Helps pupils become prepared to meet future questions by teaching them how to solve problems scientifically.
	2. Projects into the future, basing projections on experiences of the past and present.
	3. Helps pupils see the possible results of courses of action they take daily.
	4.
2. An artist	1.

2. Visit a meeting of a civic, social, or religious organization which stresses education as one of its major objectives. Make a list of the educational projects of the group, and indicate what, specifically, is being taught. What techniques are being used by those doing the teaching? Can you detect similarities and differences in the methodology used by trained professionals and those doing the teaching in the organization?

3. Interview two or three teachers at the level of your interest (elementary or secondary) on their typical summertime activities. Note similarities and differences.

4. Visit, or write to, two or three schools in different districts and obtain copies of their report cards and contrast these in such areas as the subjects reported on, the type of marks given, the means of parental contributions, the terminology used in explaining the marks, etc.

5. In collaboration with other members of your class, dramatize a spontaneous teachers' room meeting of several members of a school's staff. With a different "teacher" assuming each of the various roles of the teacher—the clerk, the "baby-sitter," the executive, the recreation leader, and the joiner —discuss recent activities in each of these areas, including the demands made upon each one's time and energies. See if your group can arrive at any courses of action which might relieve the pressures in each area.

6. Attend a meeting of a school's PTA or Parents' Club. Note the activities of the group which you feel contribute to the children's education, and those which do not. What suggestions would you make regarding those which are not learning-oriented? In what specific ways do the activities which purportedly contribute to the children's education actually do so?

7. Attend a meeting of a local board of education. Make notes of the types of topics considered by the board. Is any time spent in considering topics extraneous to the operation of the school system?

8. Talk to a school principal, after making an appointment with him, regarding what he believes should be the appropriate relationships between the teachers on his staff and himself with respect to (a) the schools, and (b) activities of a social nature.

References

"TEACHERS' RELATIONSHIPS WITH OTHERS"

BERNARD, HAROLD W., *Mental Hygiene for Classroom Teachers,* 2d ed. (New York: McGraw-Hill, 1961), Chapter 20.

BRUCE, WILLIAM F., and A. JOHN HOLDEN, JR., *The Teacher's Personal Development* (New York: Holt, Rinehart & Winston, 1957).

BUCK, R. C., "Extent of Social Participation among School Teachers," *Journal of Educational Sociology,* 33:311–19, April, 1960.

CHAMBERLAIN, LEO M., and LESLIE W. KINDRED, *The Teacher and School Organization* (Englewood Cliffs, N.J.: Prentice-Hall, 1958), Chapter 21.

CHANDLER, B. J., *Education and the Teacher* (New York: Dodd, Mead, 1961), Chapter 11.

CRESSMAN, GEORGE B., and HAROLD W. BENDA, *Public Education in America* (New York: Appleton-Century-Crofts, 1961), Chapters 5, 14–16.

EASTMOND, JEFFERSON N., *The Teacher and School Administration* (Boston: Houghton Mifflin, 1959), Chapter 12.

HASKEW, LAURENCE D., and JONATHON C. MC LENDON, *This Is Teaching*, rev. ed. (Chicago: Scott, Foresman, 1962), Chapter 6.

HILLS, R. J., *New Concept of Staff Relations* (Chicago: University of Chicago Press, Midwest Administration Center, 1960).

LEESE, JOSEPH, KENNETH FRASURE, and MAURITZ JOHNSON, JR., *The Teacher in Curriculum Making* (New York: Harper, 1961), Chapters 3, 4, 14, 15.

MISNER, PAUL J., FREDERICK W. SCHNEIDER, and L. G. KEITH, *Elementary School Administration* (Columbus, Ohio: Charles E. Merrill, 1963), Chapters 14–16.

Perceiving, Behaving, Becoming: A New Focus for Education, 1962 Yearbook (Washington, D.C.: Association for Supervision and Curriculum Development, NEA, 1962).

RAGAN, WILLIAM B., *Teaching America's Children* (New York: Holt, Rinehart & Winston, 1961), Chapter 14.

RICHEY, ROBERT W., *Planning for Teaching*, 3d ed. (New York: McGraw-Hill, 1963), Chapter 6.

STINNETT, T. M. and ALBERT J. HUGGETT, *Professional Problems of Teachers*, 2d ed. (New York: Macmillan, 1963), Chapter 2, 4.

"Teacher, Superintendent, Board Members: What Traits Do They Value in Each Other?" *NEA Journal*, April, 1961.

THOMAS, LAWRENCE G., LUCIEN B. KINNEY, ARTHUR P. COLADARCI, and HELEN A. FIELSTRA, *Perspective on Teaching* (Englewood Cliffs, N.J.: Prentice-Hall, 1961), Chapter 5.

WILES, KIMBALL, *Teaching for Better Schools* (Englewood Cliffs, N.J.: Prentice-Hall, 1959), Chapters 13, 14.

"PROFESSIONAL ORGANIZATIONS"

BUFORD, JOHN LESTER, "Why Belong to an NEA Department?," *NEA Journal*, 52:47, February, 1963.

CHANDLER, Chapter 10.

Handbook for Local, State and National Associations (Washington, D.C.: National Education Association, latest issue).

Professional Organizations in American Education (Washington, D.C.: Educational Policies Commission, NEA, 1957).

RICHEY, Chapter 8.

STINNETT, Chapter 5.

———, *The Teacher and Professional Organizations* (Washington, D.C.: National Education Association, 1956).

THOMAS, pp. 284–99.

"REPORTING TO PARENTS"

AHMAN, J. STANLEY, *et al.*, *Evaluating Elementary School Pupils* (Boston: Allyn & Bacon, 1960).

CHANDLER, Chapter 12.

GWYNN, J. MINOR, *Theory and Practice of Supervision* (New York: Dodd, Mead, 1961), pp. 276–80.

HANNA, LAVONE A., GLADYS L. POTTER, and NEVA HAGAMAN, *Unit Teaching in the Elementary School*, rev. ed. (New York: Holt, Rinehart & Winston, 1963), Chapter 15.

LEE, J. MURRAY, and DORRIS M. LEE, *The Child and His Curriculum*, 3d ed. (New York: Appleton-Century-Crofts, 1960), Chapter 15.

MISNER, pp. 276–80.

RAGAN, Chapter 15.

RICHEY, Chapter 5.

ROTHNEY, JOHN W. M., *Evaluating and Reporting Pupil Progress*, What Research Says Series No. 7 (Washington, D.C.: Department of Classroom Teachers, American Educational Research Association, 1960).

STONE, JAMES C., *California's Commitment to Public Education* (New York: Thomas Y. Crowell, 1961), Chapter 10.

STRANG, RUTH, *How to Report Pupil Progress* (Chicago: Science Research Associates, 1955).

THOMAS, pp. 284–88.

WITZLER, WILSON F., "Reporting Pupil Progress," *The Grade Teacher*, 76:20–21, April, 1959.

v

We face a crisis in education. The exploding school
population is bursting open inadequate classrooms.

JOHN F. KENNEDY

pressures and problems of the school

The preceding chapter pointed up certain pressures and problems which the teacher encounters as he attempts to meet the responsibilities connected with his multi-faceted position. It is only fair to advise the prospective teacher that there are yet additional pressures and problems which he must face; as long as there are schools and instructors, there will be pressures of time and facilities, and there will also be problems of husbanding resources so that the pressures can be satisfactorily met and relieved.

PRESSURES OF TIME AND FACILITIES

In their attempt to arrange learning activities so that their pupils can learn the very most that is possible, teachers invariably find that there simply are not enough hours of the day or that there are insufficient facilities available to them. Successful teaching requires a great amount of organizational ability, so that more can be accomplished in a short amount of time, and it also requires considerable ability in improvising in situations where needed physical facilities are not available.

Tyranny of the Curriculum

Generally speaking, when a new teacher joins the staff of a school district, he will find a curriculum that is pretty well established, and will be expected to carry on his teaching within the framework of that program. Perhaps a part of the curriculum has been legislated by lawmakers in the state capitol; perhaps a part of it has been established by professionals who made up the teaching staff of the school in years past; perhaps a part of it has been imposed previously by boards of education which, for one reason or another, deemed it necessary that certain things be included in the school's program.

State legislatures with a concern for education and general welfare within their boundaries have enacted laws proposing curriculum additions or changes that have a real effect not only upon what teachers teach in their classrooms, but also, in some instances, upon how it is to be taught. Generally these laws have been reasonable, especially when one considers that law-makers, most of whom are not teachers, do not have an opportunity for a comprehensive and continuing study of the school curriculum.

The laws in the state of California, probably the most detailed of any of the states, for example, provide for the entire course of study at the elementary level, and for a part of the secondary school curriculum. The following paragraphs, appearing in the 1961 *Education Code* for the West Coast state, present an indication of the extent to which legislation determines the curriculum in the public schools:

The courses of study in the elementary schools shall include instruction in the following prescribed branches in the several grades in which each is required pursuant to this article:

(a) Beginning in grade 1, and continuing through grade 6 or 8, as the case may be, instruction shall be given in all of the following: (1) reading; (2) writing; (3) spelling; (4) arithmetic, with emphasis on basic principles and techniques.

(b) Beginning not later than grade 4 and continuing through grade 6 or 8, as the case may be, instruction shall be given in all of the following: (1) English as a separate subject with emphasis on thoroughness, and as a discipline separate from the social studies; (2) geography; (3) history, including the early history of California and the history of the United States.

(c) Beginning not later than grade 6, and continuing through grade 6 or 8, as the case may be, instruction shall be given in all of the following: (1) civics; (2) a foreign language or languages; (3) health.

(d) The course of study in the elementary schools shall include instruction, in the grade or grades, prescribed by the county board of education of the city, county, or city and county, in all of the following: (1) art; (2) music.

(e) Such other studies, not to exceed three, as may be prescribed by the board of education of the city, county, or city and county.[1]

The Code includes a statement relating to the minimum time requirements to be devoted to various subject areas at the elementary school level, as follows:

A minimum of 50 percent of each school week shall be devoted to reading, writing, language study, spelling, arithmetic, and civics in grades one to six, inclusive, and a minimum of 600 minutes of each school week shall be devoted to such subjects in grades seven and eight.[2]

[1] *Education Code* (Sacramento: State of California, Documents Section Printing Division, 1961), vol. I, pp. 372–73.

[2] *Ibid.*, p. 373.

With respect to the curriculum at the secondary school level, the 1961 *Code* prescribes the following:

. . . the course of study shall require of all pupils in grades 7 to 12, inclusive:

(a) Five years of instruction in the use of English, designed to teach the student to read rapidly and perceptively, to write clearly and correctly, and to present ideas orally. Such instruction shall include the principles of grammar and punctuation as instruments of reading and writing. Also a core of reading designed to familiarize the student with the variety of literary forms and to improve his reading ability shall be taught.

(b) Five years of history commencing with grade 7, to include all of the following: (1) twenty semester periods of American history emphasizing American institutions and ideals, and California history; (2) twenty semester periods of history, the history of Western civilization, and world geography; (3) ten semester periods of American government emphasizing principles of the Constitution and the Declaration of Independence, and the principles of state and local government under the Constitution of this State.[3]

The Code further states that the legislature declares the policy of the state is to "encourage foreign language programs in the elementary and secondary schools" so that the children of California might speak and write in the languages with the same facility that children in other countries speak and read foreign languages.[4] In addition, the Code provides that each teacher shall endeavor to impress on pupils' minds the principles of "morality, truth, justice, and patriotism, to teach them to avoid idleness, profanity, and falsehood," and that,

Instruction shall be given in all grades of school and in all classes during the entire school course, in manners and morals. Instruction upon the nature of alcohol and narcotics and their effects upon the human system as determined by science shall be included in the curriculum of all elementary and secondary schools.[5]

The Code prescribes that regular courses in the Constitution of the United States, American history, the Constitution of the state of California, and California history shall be given in all public and private schools located in the state, such courses to begin in grade eight and continue in the high school and in colleges and universities and in educational departments of state, municipal, and private institutions.[6]

In most states the curriculum has not been so thoroughly prescribed by state legislation as in California. Rather, the curriculum in those states has come about by professionals and lay persons working individually and in groups and recommending additions and changes to the local boards of education. But the "do-it-yourself" curriculum-building of the past has served its usefulness. Trends now indicate that in the future the curriculum may be developed on a

[3] *Ibid.*, pp. 374–75.
[4] *Ibid.*, p. 373.
[5] *Ibid.*, pp. 378–79.
[6] *Ibid.*, pp. 379–80.

national basis by teams of recognized scholars, as evidenced by the work and published materials of such organizations as the School Mathematics Study Group and the National Science Foundation.

Whereas in the past only the community was concerned with the education and welfare of its people, now the nation is concerned. The National Defense Education Acts of 1961 and 1964, for example, show the deep concern of the federal government for education. Millions of dollars have been made available by these legislative acts to provide materials and equipment for experimental programs in the schools in the curriculum areas of mathematics, science, foreign languages, English, reading, history, geography, and civics; in higher education, financial assistance for institutions provides for added preparation of teachers of these subjects and for teachers of disadvantaged youth, school librarians, and educational media specialists. The provisions of the 1964 National Defense Education Act extend through 1967, and, as with the earlier NDEA, not only are the controls over funds very few in number, but also they are very general in scope. Funds are administered by the United States Office of Education through the various state departments of education. School districts willing to match federal funds draw up a proposed program and submit it to the state authorities. If the state approves the program, it submits the program to the U.S. Office of Education, and if that office approves the program, the funds are made available to the districts through the state authorities. The Eighty-eighth Congress also passed, in August, 1964, the Economic Opportunity Act of 1964, commonly referred to as the antipoverty bill. This act is, in effect, a youth-training act which, in addition to its other provisions, provides nearly one billion dollars to fight poverty through work-training and work-study programs for youth.

The real criterion as to whether curriculum *improvement* takes place when there is curriculum change is whether the pupils learn; thus, the curriculum is not effective, regardless of its origin, except at the teaching-learning situation. Here lie the real opportunity and responsibility of the teacher in the area of curriculum improvement in the public schools.

Tyranny of the Daily Schedule

Since the curriculum of today's public schools provides for so many teaching-learning activities, and since it becomes more crowded each year with new areas that seem to deserve a place in an already crowded program, it is imperative that teachers and children evolve some kind of daily schedule. Effective planning of daily programs is not easy, though it is of utmost importance. Time must be provided for the teacher to work with the class as a whole, with small groups, and with individuals; daily schedules must make provisions for each child in the class. Flexibility with balance and variety are the ingredients of an effective daily schedule which provides for satisfying and adequate learning experiences.

One teacher attended an entire summer session of a state university for the expressed purpose of writing daily plans for her elementary school class for the next school year, but after the first two weeks of school the following fall, she found that she had to relegate the entire summer's work to the "circular file." Her plans were not flexible to the point that they provided for *this* particular group of children *this* particular semester. Moreover, they did not allow for learning possibilities that presented themselves unexpectedly. Daily schedules, if they are to allow for opportunities for optimum learning, must be flexible enough to provide for such activities as field trips, attendance at concerts or plays, use of television or special radio programs, and special school programs of various types as they arise. They must also be of such a nature that if the activity demands a longer period of time than anticipated, an extension can be made with no serious damage to the program generally.

Balance in the daily program is one of the most important and challenging aspects of the teacher's schedule. Just as the "What knowledge is of most worth?" question constantly plagues the curriculum-maker, the question of "How much time shall be given to each learning activity?" continually rears its challenge to the classroom program arranger. Both, obviously, are problems of balance. Hanna, in Figure 1, presents a configuration on which balance in the program is indicated at the various levels from the primary grades through senior high school. Adequate attention in the schedule must be given to all areas of learning—but the big question is, and has always been, what is "adequate"? It may be that this question can never really be answered for all situations— just as the one posed by the curriculum-maker has never really been answered —except with the words, "It depends." Inherent in the problem of scheduling

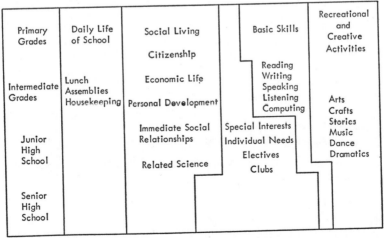

Figure 1. Balance in the Total Life of the School. Source: Lavone A. Hanna, *Unit Teaching in the Elementary School, rev. ed.* (New York: Holt, Rinehart and Winston, Inc., 1963), p. 105. Adapted from Henry Harap, *Social Living in the Curriculum* (Nashville, Tenn.: George Peabody College for Teachers, 1952), p. 65. Used by permission of the author.

the school day are such limiting factors as the length of the school day, which varies from about 3 hours in the kindergarten to 6 to 8 hours in the high school; the legally prescribed features of the program, mentioned in the preceding section; the number of grades in the classroom; and the varying needs and interests of the learners.

In many schools, teachers will find a program already scheduled and worked out by administrators or teachers. Pupils and teachers in such situations know what happens in which order. This is especially true in high schools and many elementary schools whose "periods" are regulated by a master clock and bell system. Experience has shown that primary children, especially, become accustomed to a routine and a deviation from the set procedure can be frustrating to them. It is questionable, of course, whether teachers' programs should become so routinized that children come to depend on certain things happening in a certain order or at certain hours. Besides, there are bound to be interruptions to upset rigid routines. There is, in fact, a trend away from closely designed daily schedules, especially in elementary schools; certain classes or activities often require more or less time at certain places in their development than they do at others, and learning experiences should not be chopped off before they are completed.

Hanna suggests the following daily program for elementary teachers who use the unit approach in the social and related sciences:[7]

Time	Subject	Approximate Minutes per Day
9:00-10:00	Unit work	60
10:00-10:10	Recess	10
10:10-11:10	Reading (two groups)	50
11:10-11:30	Physical Education	20
11:30-12:00	Arithmetic	30
12:00- 1:00	Noon [Lunch]	
1:00- 1:40	Language Arts	40
1:40- 2:00	Music	20
2:00- 2:10	Recess	10
2:10- 2:30	Appreciations (Art, literature, music)	20

The same author suggests the following program for another day when almost all activities might be related to the social studies unit:[8]

9:00- 9:20	Planning
9:20-10:20	Reading—three groups, twenty minutes each (children not in reading group working on letters to be mailed at the "post office")
10:20-10:35	Recess
10:35-10:50	Seeing film on distributing the mail

[7] Lavone A. Hanna, *Unit Teaching in the Elementary School*, rev. ed. (New York: Holt, Rinehart & Winston, 1963), p. 106.

[8] *Ibid.*, pp. 106–7.

10:50-11:10	Discussing what they had learned from the motion picture and planning the construction period
11:10-11:40	Working in committees in building the "post office"
11:40-12:00	Cleaning up and evaluating
12:00- 1:00	Lunch
1:00- 1:40	Reading and correcting letters and making spelling list of words used in the letters
1:40- 2:00	Music
2:00- 2:15	Recess
2:15- 2:35	Making up an original rhythm expressing "sorting the mail"
2:35- 3:10	Buying stamps and making change. Computing time it would take letters to reach their destination

For school districts employing a split-day in which smaller groups are in reading classes during the first and last hours of the school day, Hanna suggests the following schedule for grades one and two: [9]

9:00-10:00	Reading (half of class)
10:00-10:10	Recess
10:10	Arrival of other half of class
10:10-10:40	Language arts: spelling and oral and written expression
10:40-11:00	Music
11:00-11:10	Recess
11:10-11:30	Physical Education
11:30-12:00	Arithmetic, science, health, safety
12:00- 1:00	Lunch
1:00- 2:00	Social studies
2:00	Children who came at 9:00 are dismissed
2:00- 2:10	Recess
2:10- 3:10	Reading (half of class—children who came at 10:00)

At the secondary level, flexibility and balance in planning lessons are still important considerations, but at the same time, teachers must realize that the rigid time limits of the daily period are aspects with which they must reckon. Since there are individual differences among teachers just as among children, the detail of the plan for each day's activities depends upon the individual teacher; generally, a considerable degree of detail provides some assurance for many instructors, especially those in their first year of teaching.

McKean emphasizes that the quickest way for the first-year teacher to start to build an instructional time sense is for him to make daily estimates of the amount of time needed for various parts of the lesson. He suggests that a secondary teacher's time estimate for a 1-hour period might be as follows: [10]

| 8:30- 8:35 | Take roll |
| 8:35- 8:40 | Read announcements; collect parent questionnaires due today |

[9] *Ibid.*, p. 107.
[10] Robert C. McKean, *Principles and Methods in Secondary Education* (Columbus, Ohio: Charles E. Merrill, 1962), p. 140.

8:40- 8:55   Pass out assignment sheets for in-class theme. Discuss the assignment. Answer questions. Review the use of *to*, *two* and *too* which they are to pay special attention to in this written work

8:55- 9:25   Students work on themes at their seats. Teacher moves about the room to supervise the writing. (Check to see that Rex is using quotation marks correctly.)

9:25- 9:30   Collect the papers. (Ask Sandra to stop by the room after school to talk about the class newspaper.) Remind the class that the unit examination will be given Friday.

Adequacy of Facilities

Many are the teachers who have learned good practices and procedures in the courses in professional education in college, only to go out to teach in school situations where it is impossible to put the practices and procedures into effect because of inadequate facilities. If the principal responsibility of teachers is motivating children and arranging the environment so that they may learn, which is the authors' thesis as explained in Chapter 6, then adequate physical facilities should be available to help instructors.

The school building. The building itself is a facility which is important to the teaching-learning situation. Despite the trend, begun before World War II, to build school plants that are more functional, comfortable, healthful, and long lasting, there remain thousands of buildings throughout the nation that do not meet these criteria and, thus, are not adapted to modern educational programs. Many pupils are housed in unsafe, unsanitary, poorly constructed school buildings, the remnants of a period when the philosophy was to build the school and then fit the program into it. Not all of the antiquated, drab, dismal, and dark school buildings are located in isolated rural areas of this country. One has only to observe the older buildings in many towns, cities, and large metropolitan areas to see conditions deplorable for teaching and learning. It will take a great deal of planning and many dollars before such situations will be improved.

Modern school buildings present a marked contrast in appearance to those constructed before 1925. But even more important than improved appearance is the better structural and functional features of the newer plants. Increased use of windows and glass-brick in appropriate portions of the buildings has, for example, allowed for more natural light, and increased attention to artificial lighting has also resulted in improvements. School building planners have provided for better orientation to the site where the plant is located, and have promoted one-story structures for greater safety and, in many instances, for outside entrances to each room. Roomier corridors, recessed water fountains and lockers, acoustically treated ceilings and walls, automatic temperature controls, hygienic furniture, pastel colors throughout—all of these, and many more features, combine to make today's modern school plant a proper environment for children's learning.

The classroom. The most important work in the school building takes place, of course, in the individual classrooms. For the sake of health, working efficiency, and comfort, school classrooms should provide optimum conditions for pupils who spend from 5 to 6 hours within their confines each day. The use of proper lighting, adequate heating and ventilation equipment, combined with newer shades of color in the painted walls, chalkboards, and other items of furniture and equipment, will help protect teachers' and pupils' physical and mental health. Attention should be given to the shape and size of the chairs and tables in the classroom, also. The trend in today's public schools is away from "fixed" seating.

Classroom size is an important aspect of schoolhouse planning. Most authorities today recommend that classrooms for both elementary and secondary schools contain a minimum of 30 square feet of floor space per pupil; a room containing at least 900 square feet would thus be the minimum suggested for a class of 30 pupils. The authorities' suggestion for primary and activity rooms, in which there is a great amount of pupil movement, is that they contain from 1000 to 1200 square feet. There should, of course, be considerable flexibility in room sizes. With today's emphasis upon such organizational structures as team teaching, for example, the classrooms should be of a size to accommodate large groups—up to 75 or 100 in elementary school, and up to 250 in secondary school—and small groups, and should have some facilities to accommodate pupils working on individual research projects.

Ideally, an elementary school self-contained classroom of approximately 1200 square feet will have space for necessary work areas; exhibit, display, and storage areas; boys' and girls' lavatories; a stage for dramatization; and movable shelving and storage cabinets for books and other materials. Laboratory and water facilities will also be provided within the room. Darkening shades and projection screens will be provided for the use of audio-visual materials and, if possible, radios and television receivers will be part of the room's equipment.

Regardless of the type of room in which a teacher finds himself, he can do much to make it educationally livable. Attractively arranged bulletin boards and special areas of the room can be planned by the teacher and children. Furniture and other equipment can be well-placed about the room to improve its appearance and functional aspects. Light-colored panels made from materials such as oak tag board can lighten up drab or dark places within the room. And the teacher can watch himself to see that he does not stand between the pupils and the windows so that pupils have to look into the light as they watch and listen to him.

Effective learning today calls for pupils' doing, as well as reading and listening. This presupposes a flexible situation in which classroom furniture and other equipment can be moved about. Instead of the old types of combined seat-desks (usually screwed to the floor!) tables and chairs, or tablet armchairs, are used in today's modern classrooms so that effective individual and group work and construction projects can be carried out. Bookcases and some storage cabinets on casters provide for moving books and other materials to various parts of the room with maximum efficiency and speed and, at the same time, may serve as dividers for partitioning off special areas. Tackboard on the backs of cabinets provides additional bulletin or pinning board space.

Books and materials. For more than 100 years, a dominant factor in instruction in the schools of the United States has been the textbook. Educational conditions in the early period of American history may explain, in part, the traditional importance attached to textbooks: in most schools teachers were poorly trained, reference material was for the most part nonexistent, and formal or memoriter conceptions of education prevailed. Even though several national committees, including the Committee of Ten in 1892, condemned the use of a single textbook in each subject, to this day the textbook largely dominates classroom instruction in American schools.

In many schools, particularly in elementary grades, resourceful teachers now are employing the multiple textbook approach and are divorcing themselves from the traditional practice of using one textbook for each course. These teachers are accepting the balanced development of intellectual skills and independence of thought of the pupil as the fundamental objective of education and are seeing the fallacy of class adherence to a single textbook with the assignment-recitation cycle in daily repetition. They hold that in their challenge of attempting to meet the needs of pupils, teachers must have at their disposal textbooks which are at the level of the slower-learning or the retarded readers, the average, and the bright, and, in addition, they must have many and varied instructional materials of other types.

Broader, more flexible teaching plans are possible with the multiple textbook approach. Teachers employ groups of pupils equipped with textbooks and other materials appropriate to topics of a common nature and to the range of the pupils' abilities in classroom activities pursued in the development of subject units. Textbooks used in this approach are most often employed in small sets for individual or small committee reference and are not followed page by page from cover to cover; rather, teachers and pupils select portions from them to best serve their needs. Mastery of the tools of learning is the goal, and in this endeavor much use is made of many textbooks, collateral readings, audio-visual aids, excursions, construction activities, and the like, which are intended to be compatible with plans of teachers and pupils, plans that are not restricted to the activities suggested in any of the teaching materials. Under this approach, pupils are taught to reserve judgment, seek evidence, and exchange ideas before forming opinions. Value goals sought with boys and girls and youth include desirable attitudes, appreciations, abilities, habits, and skills, and attention is given to such attributes as cooperation, leadership, integrity, responsibility, and critical thinking.

In a study made at a midwestern elementary school in 1957 by one of the authors, it was found through objective tests that pupils using multiple textbooks in the classroom had no significant advantage over pupils using a single textbook as far as acquisition of social studies subject matter is concerned and that the multiple textbook group had no significant advantage over the single textbook group with improvement in such characteristics as cooperation, friendliness, integrity, responsibility, leadership, and critical thinking. However, it was found that in the concomitant area of related sciences, the multiple textbook group had a slight advantage over the single textbook group; also, probably of more importance, it was found that children of superior mental ability who used the multiple textbook technique surpassed the children in the control group with superior mental abilities by a 10 per cent level of significance. In addition, in areas of work-study skills and understandings, as measured subjectively by the teachers in the experiment, the multiple textbook approach appeared to hold more merit and potential.[11]

All of this points up the importance of many books and other teaching materials in the truly effective teaching-learning situation. If teachers accept the broader purposes of education—if they want boys and girls to learn to think critically and to understand what they learn—a multiplicity of references and textbooks and varied other materials are a necessity. The books and equipment such as maps, charts, globes, various types of projectors, and tape recorders should be stored in or near the classroom, readily accessible to teachers at the time they are needed.

The fact is, however, that a large number of school systems do not have a large supply of books and other materials. Good teachers can teach, and are teaching, acceptably every day under adverse classroom conditions and with inadequate supplies of books and other materials; however, it is reasonable to assume that they would do a better job if they were provided with the tools and facilities they need.

The traveling teacher. Another problem faced by certain teachers when they join a district's staff is that of finding a place to "hang their hats," a place which they can call home. Many school districts employ special teachers who travel from building to building to assist in the instructional program in the manner in which they are best suited. Included in this group of teachers are those whose training and experience have been in specialized areas such as exceptional children, including the mentally retarded, physically handicapped, emotionally disturbed, culturally disadvantaged, and academically talented; art, music; physical education; science; foreign language; television teaching; speech correction; occupational therapy; and remedial reading. It is not unusual for teachers with specialties to spend perhaps one or two periods in a building and then move to other buildings for about the same period of time. Very often these "traveling" teachers teach very seldom, but rather spend their time assisting classroom teachers with problems in their special-

[11] Frederick W. Schneider, "An Experimental Study Comparing the Effects of the Multiple Textbook Approach and the Single Textbook Approach to Elementary School Social Studies," unpublished doctoral dissertation, University of Colorado, 1957.

ized areas. If the prospective teacher plans to specialize in areas such as those named above, it is quite possible that he will find himself employed in a district with no particular home base.

Generally, traveling teachers work directly out of the central offices of the district, which in a sense are their headquarters. Their work, however, is done out in the various schools, so very little time is spent in their offices. They sometimes find it necessary to haul much of their equipment and materials in their automobiles; they can ill afford to dash to the central offices between each school visit to leave materials and pick up additional equipment. Some districts try to provide materials used by special teachers at each building on a more or less permanent basis, but this obviously runs into considerable expense. Various kinds of rooms are provided for the traveling teachers; these may range from a nicely furnished, regular size classroom to a clothes-closet type room, if regular classrooms are deemed impossible to spare. In some schools, the philosophy of the principal with respect to the special areas taught by traveling teachers determines the facilities provided.

Still another type of traveling teacher may be found in areas, especially in fast-growing sections of the United States, where classrooms must be scheduled rather tightly because of space shortages. Thus, it is entirely possible for teachers to find themselves without a home base right in their own building and to have to move about to different rooms for their classes so that the available classrooms can be used to the optimum. The extent of such situations in California was indicated in a study made at the University of California. In the 1959–60 class of 60 graduate intern teachers, 37 remained in one location for the entire day, but 11 had two locations, 7 had three, 3 had four, and 2 teachers worked in five different locations during the day.

HUSBANDING YOUR RESOURCES

The Fatigue Problem

It goes without saying that individuals who are able to withstand the rigors of teaching should be in good physical and mental condition. Many states, in fact, require that applicants pass a physical examination prior to the issuance of teaching licenses. And an annual physical examination should be on each teacher's calendar.

Few jobs exceed teaching when it comes to hard work. The strain and stress of guiding the learning activities of 25 or more pupils, each unique and each with differing needs and problems, places exceptional pressures on the physical and emotional reserves of teachers. Then there is the length of the work week, up to 50 hours in many instances. Furthermore, many teachers' schedules are overloaded, the pupil-teacher ratio is extremely high in many instances, and innumerable buildings and classrooms are inadequate from the standpoint of structural and physical facilities; all of these cause fatigue on the part of the instructors. Insecurity of position and finance are often causes

TEACHER FATIGUE

Fatigue as related to our energy and performance can be both harmful and beneficial. Constructively, it can induce us to refreshing sleep or sound the warning signal that exhaustion is not far off. Destructively, it can destroy initiative or transform us from exuberant, active human beings into tired, lifeless creatures oblivious of our responsibilities.

Teaching is one of the most fatiguing of all the professions: Students sap the teacher's energy; papers to be graded or extracurricular activities drain vitality; evening meetings or other after-school responsibilities interrupt rest.

Teacher fatigue can be alleviated by action proceeding from an analysis of the factors causing it and an understanding of how they can be minimized.

Environmental factors may contribute to fatigue. A teacher's bank account of energy may be depleted in schools that are located next door to noisy factories or that have poor systems of ventilation, dim lighting, overheated classrooms.

Type of work can also affect degree of fatigue. Too much work, or work that is unsatisfying or monotonous can result in mental fatigue. Too much physical labor can cause muscular weariness.

The attitude of a teacher toward his work may be a source of trouble. Whether he regards the position as challenging or boring makes a big difference. The poor physical condition of the instructor or a lack of cultural, recreational, or community interests may be the culprit. Emotions such as hate, frustration, and anxiety are notable trouble-makers. The teacher's daily habits with regard to diet, exercise, relaxation, rest, and play can also contribute to or help alleviate fatigue.

Cutting down on fatigue requires the help of the teacher and the school. Here are some things that you as a teacher can do to deal with the problem:

1. Be inwardly motivated and propelled toward accomplishing your school tasks. If you do not recognize the importance of teaching and do not derive satisfaction from your job, you are probably fatigued as a result of sheer boredom.

2. Try to cut down on emotional turmoil by planning, by facing problems realistically, and by setting attainable standards. Work to develop self-control and try not to become involved in feelings of anger, fear, hate, and frustration.

3. Eliminate monotony by varying your tasks. Throw out the class plan you have been using for 20 years. Vary your daily schedule. Get a new look.

4. Live a balanced life which involves participating in some vigorous activity, following a nutritious diet, getting ample rest and relaxation, and spending a few moments each day in self-evaluation. All work and no play also makes dull teachers.

5. Jot down the things you do each day to see if it is possible to cut down on routine chores. Ask yourself: Is it always necessary to water the

plants at 8:01, have the fingernail-and-handkerchief check in midmorning, and make sure the window shades are in proper alignment before going home?

6. Practice some technique for relaxation. Gardening is better than TV, and making a set of bookends is often more refreshing than stretching out on the sofa.

7. Remember fatigue is cumulative; rest *before* it builds up.

Now for some suggestions as to how administrators and school boards can help:

1. Relieve the teacher of some clerical and nonprofessional duties by providing sufficient secretarial help.

2. Contribute to the teacher's feelings of belonging and security by giving respect and prestige to the position; paying good salaries; and providing sick leaves, insurance, retirement plans, sabbaticals, and leaves of absence.

3. Eliminate unnecessary noises or other disturbances. Provide a healthful, attractive school environment: Dingy walls and gloomy classrooms should be ruled out.

4. Provide rooms where teachers can rest and relax.

5. Develop a climate of friendliness in the school.

6. Assign reasonable work loads. Creative teaching is difficult when the teacher's entire day is filled with a breathless round of classes and meetings.

Charles A. Bucher, *NEA Journal*, 48:29, December, 1959.

---

of further mental stress, though the trend toward adoption of tenure regulations and single salary schedules in more and more districts is helping to alleviate these conditions. Further strain in the life of a teacher is caused by the various roles he must play, as described in the preceding chapter.

Despite the stresses and activities of teachers, the profession is not considered particularly hazardous physically. In fact, teachers in most districts are provided special rates for insurance policies.

A teacher should develop, if he does not already possess, an ability to meet an emotionally charged situation in a calm manner, an appropriate sense of humor, a balanced emotional countenance, a respect and acceptance of himself for what he is, and a sincere interest in and compassion for other people. A study by Ryans reveals that superior teachers tend to manifest superior emotional adjustment.[12] The teacher should pursue activities and interests outside the realm of teaching and in company with adults other than teachers; this will provide a healthy avenue for release of pent-up physical and emotional stresses.

[12] David G. Ryans, *Characteristics of Teachers* (Washington, D.C.: American Council on Education, 1960), pp. 386, 398.

The Enthusiasm Problem

There are times when teachers have difficulty in keeping their morale on a high plane, in keeping their enthusiasm operating at high gear. This is true of all jobs, but teaching is particularly susceptible to an elusive characteristic that periodically causes morale to hit new lows and at such times exerts an especially debilitating effect. Some capable persons even leave the profession because of it.

One aspect of teaching which often produces a debilitating effect on dedicated persons is the intangibility of the educational product. In contrast to the work of persons in other professions or vocations, the results of education cannot be guaranteed. The success of the teacher's work depends largely upon the cooperation and effort of his students. Part of the compensation of teaching is seeing progress in pupils' achievement, but since progress is often not forthcoming for some time—months or even years—and since credit for this progress may never find its way to the right person, teachers often become distressed and feel that their efforts are producing no results.

YOUR MENTAL HEALTH

Even without the extra stresses caused by the cultural growing pains of today's society, the emotional environment in which teachers work holds considerable strain and tension. The psychological interaction involved in teaching a roomful of lively youngsters is not easy to handle hour after hour and day after day. In addition, teachers have to adjust to administrative direction from above and to the pressures of parental and public opinion from without. And more than in most occupations, the teacher's job is likely to carry over into his personal life.

Yet how important it is that teachers, as people, be mentally healthy and reasonably happy, since their attitudes and moods have such influence on children in the intimate classroom environment.

Realizing the impact of their own personalities on their pupils, almost all teachers make a real effort to keep their emotions on an even keel and their reactions healthy and constructive. This is difficult and at times impossible to do. But there are ways for teachers to make it easier for themselves to maintain reasonably good mental health even under present conditions. Here are some suggestions that might help.

Don't push your worries behind you where they can heckle you out of your sight. Bring them out in front of you, line them up, and look them over. Decide which ones you can do something about and which ones you'll just have to learn to live with. Don't waste your energies on things you can't change, but go into action on those you can.

Don't accept personally public criticism of the schools. Try to view it objectively and realize that it results largely from public anxiety in this period of painful social change. Do what you can to reassure those who approach you with their worries about the schools, but don't take on your own shoulders problems that involve the whole educational system.

Try not to let your work crowd other interests out of your life. Teaching can be a 24-hour-a-day job if you let it, but you can't keep mentally healthy on a diet of nothing but work. In some of your out-of-school hours, forget you're a teacher; relax and be just a human being. Have fun: Go bowling, take hikes, or practice some hobby you enjoy. Make friends in the community; enter into the activities of church, social, or civic groups engaged in projects of interest to you.

Give some preventive attention to annoyances and tensions in the classroom. Think over what happens during the day. What problems seem to come up regularly? Are there recurring patterns of misbehavior? Are there certain times during the day when restless pupils tend to get out of hand? Are certain pupils always mixed up in whatever happens? In planning your day's program, consider these different angles and figure out what you can do to prevent or diminish the impact of behavioral problems.

Don't let school become a monotonous grind. Have some high point to build the day around and some particularly interesting point to bring out in each lesson. Take time to smile, to get a little humor into the learning situation. Try to make the day pleasant and interesting for yourself as well as for the children.

If a problem seems too big for you to handle, break it down into smaller components. Tackle these one at a time, and when you are through, you have solved the big problem.

Don't keep resentments and other burdensome feelings pent up inside yourself. Develop safe relationships with a few other people and talk your troubles out to them. And, of course, give them an understanding ear when they have problems. This kind of reciprocal relationship not only gives opportunity for safely venting one's feelings but helps fill the need that every person has for feeling cared about.

If, in spite of all you can do, you find yourself constantly tense and exhausted with worry, go to someone trained to give you professional help, just as you would consult your doctor about physical ailments that fail to respond to everyday remedies.

R. H. Felix, *NEA Journal*, 48:9, January, 1959.

Sometimes, too, teachers find that conditions in the schools stymie, or limit, them in the very things that caused them to choose the teaching profession in the first place; they find themselves so busy with other things that they have little time left to guide the learning activities of their pupils. In some schools, the amount of bookkeeping work required of teachers demands too much time and energy that could otherwise be spent in a teaching-learning situation. Occasionally, teachers find themselves on faculties headed by authoritarian administrators who block all efforts toward creative teaching. Particularly in some communities in recent years, teachers have found themselves responsible for too many pupils or too many classes and have discovered that they attempt to spread themselves too thinly with the result that very little of importance is really accomplished. Very often, too, teachers find themselves being rated by principals or supervisors not upon their ability in the classroom learning situation, but upon their ability to patrol the halls, playgrounds, or lunchrooms, their promptness in getting in reports, their willingness to take an active part in extra-class activities or in community responsibilities. Too often teachers find themselves on a staff with other instructors not as professional and ethical as they should be, and their gripe sessions tend to have a wearing effect upon one who is dedicated to his profession.

Despite these adversities, however, the professional teacher must carry on. Again, he must assume a calm, collected countenance as he pursues his work, making whatever progress he can in the face of adverse conditions, and occasionally making inroads into situations that are difficult, but possible, to alter. Activities such as listening to good music, pursuing creative hobbies, seeing good art and drama, reading good books, raising a garden, actively participating in cultural pursuits often serve as effective morale boosters for teachers afflicted with the problem of keeping enthusiasm at a high level.

The Lack-of-Student-Response Problem

The final problem to be considered here is one experienced by every teacher in the classroom: the lack-of-student-response situation. Whether the fault lies with the pupils or with the teacher, this phenomenon occurs on occasion in even the best teaching-learning situation. Here, as with all school problems, there is no one, simple answer. The teacher must keep constant vigil for signs of the cause of lack of response so that a remedy may be sought in the procedures of the classroom. If the problem is a serious one, the solution may come only after considerable investigation of an evaluative nature. It may be a situation which calls for use of a problem-solving approach.

If the lack of response is caused by low pupil intelligence, the teacher will be obliged to plan curriculums, materials, and methods which will provide for these children of low mental ability as well as for average and fast learners. Similar planning on the teacher's part will be necessary if he finds the problem caused by retardation in children's maturing; effective teachers plan for a variety of approaches if they find the children in their classroom at different levels of maturity.

Some lack-of-response problems may be caused by an absence of motivation for learning on the part of pupils. Since pupil motives are important determiners of what is learned and how it is learned, good teachers will constantly seek motivational activities that will ensure continual learning.

In some instances of lack of pupil response, the trouble may be that the pupil cannot apply something he has learned in one situation to another situation. Pupils learn things in the classroom so that they may be able to use or apply them in other situations, but the teacher must realize that the student must learn to transfer knowledge, that he does not automatically know how to do this. Thus, the teacher who would provide for the greatest amount of positive learning transfer will see that his pupils have many opportunities to use their skills and knowledge in a variety of situations and to seek relationships among many in-school and out-of-school activities.

CONCLUSION

A universal problem of teachers is lack of sufficient time and often absence of adequate facilities. Many problems arise from a too tightly prescribed curriculum and a too crowded daily schedule. There remain too many antiquated and unsatisfactory buildings and classrooms, too few books and other learning materials to do a completely adequate job of guiding optimum learning activities. Successful teaching calls for the maximum husbanding of physical, emotional, and mental resources and ingenuity.

Questions for Discussion

1. How can a teacher, other than by means of a compartmentalized day or period, meet the provisions of the law in states where the legislatures have prescribed all or most of the curriculum?
2. In what ways do modern school plants facilitate the work of the classroom teacher?
3. Explain why children in the control group in the experimental study referred to on page 108 appeared to gain as much subject matter as did those in a group using the multiple textbook approach to the social studies.
4. If you found that you were a traveling teacher in your building, what suggestions would you have for facilitating your situation?
5. Compare the pressures and problems of elementary and secondary teachers. Do you feel that some pressures would be unique to either elementary or secondary teachers? What are they? Which pressures would probably be common to all teachers, regardless of the level on which they teach?
6. How might a teacher's association with adults outside the profession help relieve some of one's pressures? What are some of the habits or behavioral tendencies which teachers acquire in the school situation that will need to be guarded against when they associate with persons who are not teachers?
7. What do you think are the teacher's responsibilities with respect to improvement of the curriculum?
8. What are some of the traditional teacher urges that would have to be suppressed if a teacher should work in a school where the emphasis is upon the democratic approach in all aspects?
9. What kinds of help do you think teachers need to help them overcome problems of fatigue, lack of enthusiasm, and lack of student response?
10. Do you feel, as is sometimes claimed, that the curriculums in America's elementary and secondary schools have been watered down to make adjustments to needs and interests of children or to get into the program all that is supposed to be included? Explain.

Activities and Projects

1. Think back on the school you know best. Write down some proposals you would suggest for curriculum improvement in that school if you were a member of its teaching staff.
2. Make appointments to interview two teachers at the level of your choice (elementary or secondary). Ask them to tell you the difference between a textbook and a course of study, and note these differences. Ask to see their courses of study. Write down the major points included in these documents and note briefly the types of things included under each major point.
3. Prepare a one day schedule for a class of third-grade youngsters in a typical third-grade situation, or a one week program of five English classes in a secondary school. Note why you arranged the program in the manner you did.
4. Search the literature to find ideal building layouts or plans for either an elementary or a secondary school. Write an essay or draw a plan embodying the best features of the plans, and explain why you think the features are ideal. Do the same thing for an ideal classroom—one you feel meets the needs of children of the twentieth century.
5. Make a resource unit in any subject area at the grade level of your choice.
6. Search in your college library, or write to the state departments of education, to find the legal curriculum requirements of three or four states, and compare them with the California requirements included in this chapter.
7. Plan an experiment in which you would attempt to find out whether a group of students using multiple textbooks and all available audio-visual aids would gain more from a unit than a group using only a single textbook. How would you conduct the experiment? How would you allow for differences in student ability and teacher bias? How would you follow up such a study?

References

"TEACHERS' WORK LOAD"

BURKE, ARVID J., "Do Teachers Have 'Short' Hours?" in *Teaching in America,* ed. Anthony C. Riccio and Frederick R. Cyphert (Columbus, Ohio: Charles E. Merrill, 1962), pp. 125–26.

CHAMBERLAIN, LEO M., and LESLIE W. KINDRED, *The Teacher and School Organization,* 3d ed. (Englewood Cliffs, N.J.: Prentice-Hall, 1958), pp. 158–64.

"Class Size and Teacher Load" (Symposium), *NEA Journal,* 46:435–47, October, 1957.

ESBENSEN, THORWALD, "How Much Time for Teaching?" *School Executive* 79:50–51, November, 1959.

GARY, THEODORE J., "Relieving Teachers of the Clerical Burden of Reporting," *NEA Journal*, 48:24–25, December, 1959.

HANNA, LAVONE A., GLADYS L. POTTER, and NEVA HAGAMAN, *Unit Teaching in the Elementary School*, rev. ed. (New York: Holt, Rinehart & Winston, 1963.)

"How Long Is a School Day?" *Research Bulletin*, 36:8–10, February, 1961.

LAMBERT, SAM M., and DAVID IWAMOTO, "Teaching Load," in *Encyclopedia of Educational Research*, 3d ed., ed. Chester Harris (New York: Macmillan, 1960), pp. 496–502.

MCKEAN, ROBERTS C., *Principles and Methods of Secondary Education* (Columbus, Ohio: Charles E. Merrill, 1962).

MOFFITT, FREDERICK A., "The Teacher's Day," *NEA Journal*, 51:59, October, 1962.

PATRICK, THOMAS L., "Time to Teach," *Journal of Teacher Education*, 7:217–22, September, 1956.

PRIVER, JAMES, "Busy as a Classroom Teacher," *NEA Journal*, 48:29–32, March, 1959.

"Tired Teachers," *NEA Journal*, 51:8–10, November, 1962.

"CURRICULUM AND FACILITIES"

Conditions of Work for Quality Teaching (Washington, D.C.: Department of Classroom Teachers, NEA, 1959).

EASTMOND, JEFFERSON N., *The Teacher and School Administration* (Boston: Houghton Mifflin, 1959), Chapter 11.

HASKEW, LAURENCE D., and JONATHON C. MCLENDON, *This Is Teaching*, rev. ed. (Chicago: Scott, Foresman, 1962), pp. 174–75, 109–19, 136–38.

LEESE, JOSEPH, KENNETH FRASURE, and MAURITZ JOHNSON, JR., *The Teacher in Curriculum Making* (New York: Harper, 1961), Chapter 2.

PARKER, J. CECIL, T. BENTLEY EDWARDS, and WILLIAM H. STEGEMAN, *Curriculum in America* (New York: Thomas Y. Crowell, 1962), Chapter 5.

"Pressures and Concerns," *Educational Leadership*, volume 20, May, 1963, entire issue.

RICHEY, ROBERT W., *Planning for Teaching*, 3d ed. (New York: McGraw-Hill, 1963), pp. 174–77.

SCHUSTER, ALBERT H., and MILTON E. PLOGHOFT, *The Emerging Elementary Curriculum* (Columbus, Ohio: Charles E. Merrill, 1963), Chapter 1.

STINNETT, T. M., and ALBERT J. HUGGETT, *Professional Problems of Teachers*, 2d ed. (New York: Macmillan, 1963), pp. 253–69.

STONE, JAMES C., *California's Commitment to Public Education* (New York: Thomas Y. Crowell, 1961), Chapters 8, 9.

TABA, HILDA, *Curriculum Development Theory and Practice* (New York: Harcourt, Brace & World, 1962), Chapter 1.

THOMAS, LAWRENCE G., LUCIEN B. KINNEY, ARTHUR P. COLADARCI, and HELEN A. FIELSTRA, *Perspective on Teaching* (Englewood Cliffs, N.J.: Prentice-Hall, 1961), Chapter 3.

Using Current Curriculum Developments (Washington, D.C.: Association for Supervision and Curriculum Development, NEA, 1963).

What Are the Sources of the Curriculum? A Symposium (Washington, D.C.: Association for Supervision and Curriculum Development, NEA, 1962).

WRIGHT, JOHN, and JAMES T. THORNTON, eds., *Secondary School Curriculum* (Columbus, Ohio: Charles E. Merrill, 1963), Chapter 1.

"WHAT SHOULD BE TAUGHT"

ABRAHAM, WILLARD, *A Time for Teaching* (New York: Harper & Row, 1964), Chapter 1.

What Are the Sources of the Curriculum? A Symposium (Washington, D.C.: Association for Supervision and Curriculum Development, NEA, 1962).

BRUNER, JEROME, *The Process of Education* (Cambridge, Mass.: Harvard University Press, 1961).

FRAZER, DOROTHY MCCLURE, and THOMAS G. PULLEN, JR., "What to Teach?" *NEA Journal*, 44:34–36, October, 1962.

GARDNER, JOHN W., *Excellence* (New York: Harper & Row, 1961).

GOODLAD, JOHN I., "Changing Curriculum of America's Schools," *Saturday Review*, 65–67, 87–88, November 16, 1963.

GRAMBS, JEAN D., and L. MORRIS MC CLURE, *Foundations of Teaching* (New York: Holt, Rinehart & Winston, 1964), Chapter 10.

KRUGMAN, MORRIS, "Programs to Reduce School Dropouts," in *Reference Papers on Children and Youth* (Washington, D.C.: White House Conference on Children and Youth, 1960), pp. 129–36.

NEA Journal, Special Section on School Dropouts, May, 1962, p. 51ff.

PARKER, J. CECIL, T. BENTLEY EDWARDS, and WILLIAM H. STEGEMAN, *Curriculum in America* (New York: Thomas Y. Crowell, 1962).

PASSOW, HARRY A., ed., *Curriculum Crossroads* (New York: Bureau of Publications, Teachers College, Columbia University, 1962).

PETERSEN, DOROTHY G., *The Elementary School Teacher* (New York: Meredith, 1964), Chapter 8.

ROCKEFELLER BROTHERS FUND, *The Pursuit of Excellence* (New York: Doubleday, 1958).

"RESOURCES FOR TEACHERS"

ALEXANDER, WILLIAM R., *Are You a Good Teacher?* (New York: Holt, Rinehart & Winston, 1959).

BERNARD, HAROLD W., *Mental Hygiene for Classroom Teachers*, 2d ed. (New York: McGraw-Hill, 1961), Chapter 5.

BUEHRING, LEO E., "Nonteaching Duties Reduce Effectiveness of Instruction in Secondary Schools," *Nation's Schools*, 60:76–77, November, 1957.

HASKEW, Chapter 9.

HUGHES, MARIE, "What is Teaching? One Viewpoint," *Educational Leadership*, 19:251–59, January, 1962.

LEESE, Chapter 4.

MICHAL-SMITH, HAROLD, "It Takes Self-Understanding," *NEA Journal*, 49:37–40, April, 1960.

MISNER, Chapter 16.

RAGAN, WILLIAM B., *Teaching America's Children* (New York: Holt, Rinehart & Winston, 1961), Chapter 2.

RICHEY, pp. 80–81.

RYANS, DAVID G., *Characteristics of Teachers* (Washington, D.C.: American Council on Education, 1961).

STINNETT, pp. 242–53.

"What Is a Teacher?" *Look Magazine*, February 21, 1956, pp. 29–39.

Who's a Good Teacher? (Washington, D.C.: American Association of School Administrators, NEA, 1961).

WILES, KIMBALL, *Teaching for Better Schools* (Englewood Cliffs, N.J.: Prentice-Hall, 1959), Chapter 4.

. . . a child's behavior is determined by his needs; teachers are organizing the field of education so as to best meet these needs.

RUBY H. WARNER

the pupils as learners

Mark is sixteen years of age and is in the eleventh grade. He is a handsome young man, but his physical size has somewhat outgrown his coordination. Mark has an excellent home environment. As with all teen-agers, the important people in his life are the youngsters with whom he associates. All of them are interested in athletics, dancing, parties, and, yes, subjects in school; Mark is interested in everything, including the great social and religious issues of the day. While on the surface he indicates that parents and teachers couldn't interest him less, he secretly is glad they're around, especially when he has profound problems to talk over with them. Of slightly higher than average mentality, Mark is quite good in his academic work and keeps it up to date, despite his interest in school affairs and community activities for young people. He lives in a fairly large city on the West Coast and attends a senior high school with about 1600 other students. He has never been a behavior problem; all in all, he is an extremely well-rounded young man.

Johnny is an eight-year-old third-grader. He is a handsome child, with ruddy checks, wavy, golden hair, and more than his share of energy. His home environment is excellent: he has a pony to ride about on his parents' acreage at the edge of the midwestern community in which he lives, his well-to-do parents are interested in his accomplishments in and out of school and are very cooperative with teachers and other school authorities, his home contains the finest in children's books and other facilities to aid in his learning. Yet Johnny is the most consistent "customer" in the principal's office. But there is one thing for sure about him: everything he does is open and aboveboard. If he feels like doing something, he does it—and, of course, if it isn't accepted behavior, he usually gets caught at it. He has normal ability for his age, and apparently achieves up to his ability. Johnny has two older brothers.

Betty is an attractive second-grader, but is also eight years old. Although she has an I.Q. in the normal range as measured by standardized tests, she is a slow achiever. She is shy and withdrawn to the point that she very seldom speaks to anyone, even her peers, unless she is spoken to. Her parents both work, often until late at night, and she has never known any genuine affection from them. She is often left alone at night with her only brother, who is just one year her elder. There is a great amount of bickering between her parents when they are at home with her. Betty lives in a small house in a rural community of about 10,000 in the Midwest, and the house contains only the necessities for substandard living.

Bob is a ten-year-old fifth-grade youngster who, despite his high I.Q., has not achieved as well as expected in school for a variety of reasons. Because of a bad home environment, he has developed an emotional block to learning. He is reading at a second-grade level. In addition, his general physical health is below normal, and socially he is a misfit, an isolate. He has no status at home, and at times has been neglected in the classroom—but he tries to gain status with his peers through sheer physical prowess; he is forever starting fights and throwing stones at other children on the playground. He visits the principal's office a great deal because of misbehavior. Bob attends an elementary school with about 650 pupils in a middle-sized community in the eastern states. He is currently being studied by the school psychologist.

Wendy is a seventeen-year-old sophomore in high school. Her parents are in the lower socioeconomic group in an eastern community of about 20,000 population. Her father is chronically ill, and her mother does not work. She became associated with the "wrong crowd" when she was in junior high school and is currently under the supervision of juvenile authorities. Although Wendy has normal intelligence, she does not achieve to her capacity in her courses; in fact, she is quite lackadaisical about them. Her parents make her attend school, or she would not be there, because her interests are more "worldly" than those explored in the classroom. Wendy's teachers have often expressed disgust with her attitude—but have also been concerned for what will become of her in the future. In the past year, she has been in two automobile accidents while riding with questionable friends; one of the accidents was quite serious, resulting in the hospitalization for a long period of time of a three-year-old child. There are two other girls and one boy in the family.

Jerry is a popular senior in secondary school and a high achiever in his classes. He is a star athlete in three sports, having won a monogram for three years in each. Jerry is taking advanced placement work in mathematics and science and plans to become an experimental physicist after he completes the course of study in his 1200-student high school in the Midwest. Jerry goes steady with one of the popular pep squad girls, but he has no marital plans at present and intends not to have any until he is through college and has completed his military service. His is a fine home environment, and his parents have been most cooperative with school authorities ever since he began kindergarten. He is an Explorer Scout and has been active in Sunday School and church activities. In school he sticks to business and has never caused behavior problems for his teachers. He is an only child.

Mary, a twelve-year-old in the fifth grade, is mentally retarded (I.Q. about 65) and, of course, makes little or no progress in academic subjects. Most of her school work entails such activities as learning how to keep herself clean and neat and home arts activities. Her parents, too, are below average in intelligence and have been a constant thorn in the side of teachers and administrators ever since Mary started at school. Mary has five brothers, one of whom is also mentally retarded. She lives with her family in a hovel in an unattractive slum area of a city of 25,000 people in a southern state. The family receives financial assistance from the county, and charitable organizations provide some food and clothing. Mary's school attendance is quite irregular; she is often ill, especially during inclement weather. Her sex urges are beginning to develop quite strongly, and she constantly chases the boys in her school.

These seven youngsters are actual persons, though the names are fictitious. They differ one from the other, and they bring these differences to school. Even within a single building in a single school system, each pupil is different from all the others, with different problems and different interests and different native abilities. Most of the children in a single building come from different home backgrounds; all of them have different needs. But to teachers and other school authorities, all these unique individuals are the same in that they must be encouraged to learn and grow and develop as much as possible during the time they are in school.

If all pupils were alike, their growth patterns identical, their backgrounds and previous education similar and equal, teaching would be a relatively simple occupation. But a glance at the seven preceding descriptions plus the realization that these are but a few of the hundreds of thousands of children over the nation should convince teachers and prospective teachers that this is certainly not the case. The thing that makes teaching hard work—yet forever exciting and challenging—is the fact that our educational "products" are all different, and when we do a good job of teaching, we help each pupil in our charge grow and learn according to *his* own individual pattern. Educational products, our boys and girls, are not supposed to look alike when they complete their programs in school; only products that come off an assembly line en masse are intended to take on such aspects of similarity. When a pupil completes a grade or course in school he is different from what he was when he entered the grade or course, and he should be, if the teacher has done an acceptable job in guiding the learning activities of the pupils in his classroom.

The problem, then, which faces conscientious teachers is that of providing experiences which will enhance the growth and development and learning of each individual in the classroom to the extent that he may make maximum progress in accord with his ability. If teachers have a real specialty, it is, or should be, in the area of knowing how children learn and of providing for optimum learning by each pupil in the classroom. Accordingly, then, teachers and prospective teachers should pursue a study of their specialty continuously. They may accomplish this, partially at least, by keeping abreast of developments relating to the learning process and of their relationships to classroom methodology.

LEARNING AND PSYCHOLOGICAL PROPOSITIONS

Modern psychologists are by no means in agreement on a single theory of how learning takes place. This is small consolation to classroom teachers in America's schools who look to psychologists for scientific evidence which will help them in their work of arranging an environment in which boys and girls might learn. Experimental psychologists, such as Watson and Thorndike, have proposed the stimulus-response relationship as a unit of behavior from which learning processes may be inferred; each question a teacher asks is a situation acting on the learner, and his answer is a response to the situation. Thorndike's principles of rewards and punishments—simply that rewards strengthen and punishments weaken stimulus-response associations—have many times been refuted, but recent evidence tends to point up their basic accuracy. Cognitive theorists such as Tolman and Lewin, on the other hand, do not accept the stimulus-response associations as applicable to human behavior. Instead, they emphasize organization and reorganization of experience occurring in the central nervous systems of the individual; the change that occurs within the learner is the formation of a new realization or expectation. The specific stimulus-response association is, to these theorists, too small a segment to be considered a unit of behavior; their unit is a much larger whole.

Despite disagreements among schools of psychology and claims that psychology, as a research discipline, deals with its own problems rather than with those of education, some psychologists have tried to bring forth some meaning for educators from a wealth of empirical data resulting from experimentation, and they do agree on certain propositions important to the field of teaching.

Laws of Learning

The most-practiced fundamental psychological proposition appropriate to education is to the effect that rewarded, or reinforced, tendencies are those which will probably recur. Children, or animals for that matter, will react to a situation in much the same manner that they reacted to a previous situation if that reaction proved satisfactory or successful.

Part of the teacher's responsibility is to promote fruitful learning experiences involving reinforcement wherever possible. Among the techniques which teachers use to this end are self-correction devices like answer books or handwriting standards, and mechanical devices such as certain types of teaching machines, tape recorders by which students can hear themselves as they play back their recitations, and self-correcting tests of various kinds.

Some of the claims made for many of the modern teaching machines imply that reinforcement is strengthened by their use because the reward is im-

Reinforcement

In an auto-instructional program, reinforcements of various kinds are available to the student. When the student makes a response that he "knows" is right, just the fact that he can go on and complete the response is reinforcing; that is to say, the reinforcement is simply the realization that he knows, or the fact that he is able to proceed to make a response. Contrast this reinforcing event with the case of the student who comes to a test question to which he does not know the answer or who reads a passage in a book that he does not understand; not only is there no response available, but emotional reactions (e.g., frustration) can develop, involving the occurrence of behavior that actively interferes with subsequent learning. Even if the student tries to make responses to material that is not completely clear to him, wrong responses don't fit, and no self-reinforcement is available in the form of "I'm right" or "I understand." The situation is completely different when a program not only makes the correct responses available, but, in addition, indicates to the student that each response is indeed correct, thus providing additional reinforcement. The student then proceeds on to new material and this continuous progress is a kind of moving on to new, novel stimulation, an activity which has also been shown experimentally to be reinforcing.

The programmed learning situation includes more than one kind of reinforcement, and includes at least two kinds of student behavior that are being consistently reinforced: each correct response is reinforced, thereby producing the desired relationships between the content of the frames and the responses made to the content; and, in addition, the behavior called paying attention, or attending to stimuli, or reading carefully, is reinforced each time a correct response is made, with the result that the student tends to continue to pay attention and work carefully on each frame. He learns the content of the program, but he is also reinforced for using the program, which results in continued interest and motivation for using the program and responding actively to it.

William A. Deterline, *An Introduction to Programmed Instruction* (Englewood Cliffs, N.J.: Prentice-Hall, 1962), pp. 28–29.

mediate. This seems to be psychologically sound, as experimentation has indicated reinforcement immediately following the behavior sequence is more satisfactory than that which is delayed for a time. For instance, simply the word "Right" immediately following the behavior sequence is more effective than a larger reward which follows much later. Generally, reinforcements should be applied as soon as possible; pupils should know as quickly as possible whether what they are doing is correct.

In contrast to reward, which should be used generously, particularly in early stages of learning, punishment should be avoided. In certain children punished responses may encourage tendencies adverse to increased learning.

Also, punishment generally serves to disturb teacher and pupil relationships rather than to increase the likelihood of correct responses.

Intrinsic rewards, generally, are considered better than extrinsic ones and thus are the ones teachers should aim for for their pupils. When a child has a feeling of success, his chances of attaining real learning are much greater than when he receives a star or a candy bar for some achievement or other. Whereas the effects of the extrinsic reward usually depend on the giver of such rewards, the learner always has only himself to contend with when the reward system is intrinsic.

The law of readiness, also an important psychological proposition, is a concept upon which most authorities agree. Readiness relates to physiological maturity, but, just as important, it relates also to psychological maturity involving the learner's sense of the importance of, and his past preparation for, the new material to be learned. A large number of claims of superiority are made for foreign schools that begin instruction much earlier in a child's life than in public schools of the United States. In evaluating these claims, one should remember that this early teaching is based on a somewhat different approach to readiness than ours and that it is believed no great harm is done a learner if he spends two years, beginning at age six, at learning something which would take him only six months to learn at age ten.

Insight, Reflective Thinking, and Purpose

Insight is important in learning. Indeed, it is the most important part of all learning to cognitive psychologists, who contend that the problem is really solved when a pupil has the proper insight. According to Watson, "The experience of learning by sudden insight into a previously confused or puzzling situation arises when (a) there has been a sufficient background and preparation, (b) attention is given to the relationships operative in the whole situation, (c) the perceptual structure 'frees' the key elements to be shifted into new patterns, (d) the task is meaningful and within the range of ability of the subject." [1] When a student of the language arts who is assigned a composition to write is taught that an outline is an invaluable aid in organizing the composition, he has gained insight which may otherwise have escaped his attention.

Reflective thinking is also important in children's learning. This process is applicable to either reading or listening. Learning is facilitated when children are asked to read an assignment and then tell, orally or in writing, what they have read. There is some research to support the idea that children learn considerably more when they reflect upon what they have read than when they simply reread material they have already read. If, shortly after learning material, children are asked to recall what they have learned, they will likely forget less than they would if they were not asked to recall it until somewhat later. The rate of forgetting is most rapid when knowledge is first learned.

[1] Goodwin Watson, "What Do We Know about Learning?" *NEA Journal*, 52:22, March, 1963.

Student-Teacher Planning

Considerable emphasis in modern elementary and secondary schools is placed on student-teacher planning, on the psychological bases that motivation, adaptability, and learning speed may be increased when all involved in the learning situation participate in its planning. In all areas of living, children and adults are constantly planning to make intelligent decisions. In the classroom, more subject matter competence is required of the teacher when student-teacher planning is used than when it is not. Students and the teacher, in the planning procedure, attempt to answer such questions as the following:

1. What do we already know about this topic?
2. What do we need to know, or would be well to know, about the topic?
3. Why do we need to know these things about the topic?
4. How do we go about learning what we need to know?
5. Where do we find out what we need to know?
6. When do we do the things we need to do to find out about the topic?
7. Who will do what parts of the job of finding out what we need to know?

While all the questions included here are important, probably the most significant one is the "Why." It is especially important that children understand the reason for pursuing the material and that they set, within bounds, their own goals, because children need to see that success in some new undertaking is possible, though not necessarily certain, if optimum learning is to take place. Teachers who provide too much direction often create attitudes of apathetic conformity, defiance, or defeat in their pupils. An appropriate amount of permissiveness must be provided by teachers, so that increased curiosity, self-confidence, enterprise, and creativity may be generated among the students. Teachers, also, must provide an appropriate amount of encouragement to students; "Success breeds success" is especially applicable to achievement in school.

PRINCIPLES OF LEARNING

After all is considered, perhaps it is not fair to expect a full explanation of learning to come from one discipline, since the complexity of the phenomenon is quite generally accepted. Perhaps a teacher should search for an understanding of the learning process from several disciplines, starting with psychology, but also including other behavioral sciences such as sociology and anthropology. The phrase "should search" is used advisedly, because the simple truth is that at the present time there does not exist a clear-cut, concise, generally agreed-upon definition of learning that is universally applicable to all situations and all individuals. Perhaps, as experimentation and research in all the behavioral sciences proceed, a satisfactory theory of learning will one day evolve. Until that day, however, the best a teacher can do is to operate on the rather comprehensive "lore" of teaching, at the same time keeping watch on the results of experimentation reported in the literature and conducted in the classrooms across the nation.

While there is wide disagreement as to how learning *takes place*, there seems to be quite general agreement as to what learning *does*. A widely accepted axiom is that learning, evoked by stimuli from within an individual or by external stimuli acting against him, causes changes in that individual's behavior. The problem arises when the nature of the stimuli is proposed and when an explanation is attempted of how these stimuli actually affect learning. Whatever it is that happens, the results are obvious every day in classrooms across the nation as teachers observe changes in the behavior of their students, not to mention the fact that much learning goes unnoticed because it does not result in observable change of behavior.

Regardless of which psychological theory of learning a teacher accepts, if indeed he accepts any at all, there are certain aspects of learning which will help the teacher to understand how he may best direct his efforts so that optimum learning may be facilitated.

Learning Is an Individual Matter

In the first place, learning is an individual and personal matter with each learner. What a challenge it is to each teacher to know that the 30 or 40 or 250 or whatever the number of pupils in his class are unique individuals, each with a pattern of growth and development—intellectual, physical, social, emotional, spiritual—all his own! Never before has the teacher had a pupil with the same growth pattern as any pupil currently in his classroom; none of those he will have in his classroom in the future will have the same learning image as any in his room today! Furthermore, what each pupil learns is dependent entirely upon him; he will learn only what he feels is important for him to learn or what he is interested in learning. The claims of some critics of progressive education notwithstanding, an individual *cannot* open up the head of another and pour in the knowledge.

Arranging the Environment and Motivating Pupils

A person may, however, facilitate the learning process, and this is where the teacher comes in. One responsibility of the classroom teacher is to arrange the environment and motivate pupils so that they may learn. What a challenge it is, in the light of the idea expressed above, that *each* child's environment must be arranged *for him*, and *each* child must be motivated to learn whatever has been determined that he should learn.

Learning to Learn

The real job of the teacher is that of facilitating learning, not that of a hard taskmaster; the job of the learner is learning to learn, not memorizing facts and figures which tomorrow will probably become obsolete or outmoded. If children, through opportunities provided by their teachers, can learn to learn, they will continue to learn to cope with new situations and problems throughout their lives. With new knowledge evolving at such a rapid rate here in the mid-twentieth century, the world that lies in the future will be much different from the one today, and it is in that world that today's children will need to learn to live. No one alive at the present moment can foretell what knowledge people will need, but then as now, people will need to know how to solve their problems. It is here that the teacher's real specialty becomes evident: the teacher is, or should be, an expert in instructing others how to learn, an expert in helping pupils learn how to solve their problems.

THE PROBLEM-SOLVING PROCESS

Success at solving their problems and making discoveries for themselves is a thrilling, satisfying, habit-forming experience for children and youth, from the kindergarten through the most advanced levels of college graduate work. Though the problem-solving process results in a great deal of learning in the traditional sense that knowledge is transmitted, even more important is the fact that in the process real use is made of this knowledge. This context also involves attitudes, understandings, feelings, and physical activity.

The Steps

It is convenient to present a list of the steps used in the classroom in the problem-solving process. Depending upon the authority, the number of steps varies from three or four to eight or nine, and the order of these varies also. They vary greatly in wording but very little in content.

1. *Recognizing that a problem exists.* In the usual classroom situation, problems often are not easily seen. Normally there must be a change in an otherwise easy, on-going situation before a problem is recognized. Opportunities for upsetting or provocative situations in which problems are recognized often present themselves during demonstration lessons in the room, on field trips, and in the use of motion pictures.

2. *Clarifying or defining the problem.* This is often one of the most difficult steps in the problem-solving process because once a problem is recognized by the pupils in a group, each one attempts to clarify or define it from his own frame of reference. Since each member of the group has had different past experiences and since each pupil's social environment is different from that of the other members of the class, each tends to view the problem on the basis of his own perception. At this point in the process, pupils usually set up a tentative goal and their problem becomes how to achieve this goal; also, there is likely to be considerable hypothesizing, or the formulation of several possible problem solutions, at this point in the process. This should be encouraged by the teacher.

METHODS OF INQUIRY

An interesting research project, now in progress, is being conducted at the University of Illinois by [J. Richard] Suchman. His major interest is in teaching youngsters what he calls *methods of inquiry* (1961). In the process of his investigations he has found that, for example, in a typical elementary classroom, a teacher will ask from 8 to 10 times as many questions as the children. This would seem to be a very strange state of affairs when one considers the excited curiosity and interest typical of the young child. Suchman suggests that the pupils have been trained out of inquiry and wait passively to receive the knowledge presented to them. He uses films as a stimulus. In these films the children are given an experience which, from their standpoint, is unexplainable.

. . . . .

. . . For instance, a demonstration involving use of a heated brass ball and a brass ring has resulted in the following dialogue:

Pupil: Were the ball and ring at room temperature to begin with?
Teacher: Yes.
Pupil: And the ball would go through the ring at first?
Teacher: Yes.
Pupil: After the ball was held over the fire it did *not* go through the ring. Right?
Teacher: Yes.
Pupil: If the ring had been heated instead of the ball, would the results have been the same?
Teacher: No.
Pupil: If both had been heated, would the ball have gone through then?
Teacher: That all depends.
Pupil: If they had both been heated to the same temperature, would the ball have gone through?
Teacher: Yes.
Pupil: Would the ball be the same size after it was heated as it was before?
Teacher: No.
Pupil: Could the same experiment have been done if the ball and ring were made out of some other metal?
Teacher: Yes.

. . . . .

The children are taught to use a three-stage plan in developing logical, systematic approaches. First, they are asked to identify, verify, and measure the parameters of a given problem. In this process, they identify objects, observe the properties of these objects, note the conditions or states of the objects, and discover changes in the conditions. Second, they determine the relevance of particular conditions in producing the events of a scientific episode, for all conditions are not relevant. Third, they formulate and test theoretical constructs that show relationships among the variables of the observed physical event. This action calls for flexibility and imagination in asking questions.

Training sessions of an hour or less are held at intervals of several days. A silent motion picture of a physics demonstration is shown. This picture raises questions about cause and effect, and the children begin immediately to ask probing questions which are to be answered "yes" or "no." "Yes" and "no" questions test hypotheses; therefore the teacher who answers them is helping them to establish the tenability or untenability of their hypotheses. During the first stage, the children ask questions of verification. During stages two and three, they ask questions of an experimental nature, stating a set of conditions and postulating a result. Here, the teacher's answer tells whether the postulated result will or will not occur. If the teacher cannot give an unequivocal answer, he says, "That all depends," or "Tell me more," indicating that the child's "experiment" has not been sufficiently controlled. When children try to tap the teacher's understanding, the teacher's response may be, "What could you do to find out for yourself?"

After the period of inquiry through questioning, a critical review of the process is conducted by teacher, pupils, and any observers who may be present. From this review, the children are expected to learn improved strategies of inquiry. The children apparently have little interest in improving their inquiry skills *per se*, but they are willing to improve them in the context of understanding cause-and-effect relationships. The children used in the experiments have often been at sixth grade level.

This selection is drawn from material in the following sources: Harry A. Passow, ed., *Nurturing Individual Potential,* Papers and Reports from the ASCD Seventh Curriculum Research Institute (Washington, D.C.: Association for Supervision and Curriculum Development, NEA, 1964), p. 46; *Individualizing Instruction,* 1964 Yearbook (Washington, D.C.: Association for Supervision and Curriculum Development, NEA, 1964), pp. 166–67; and J. R. Suchman, "Inquiry Training in the Elementary School," *The Science Teacher,* 27:42–47, 1960. See also J. Richard Suchman, "The Child and the Inquiry Process," in *Intellectual Development: Another Look,* Papers and Reports from the ASCD Eighth Curriculum Research Institute (Washington, D.C.: Association for Supervision and Curriculum Development, NEA, 1964), pp. 59–77.

3. *Collecting data.* Information from many possible sources is collected at this point, if the information seems to have some relationship to the problem or will help in its solution. The subject matter to be pursued depends upon the particular area in which the problem falls and the goals or purposes the class has in view. Books are, of course, an excellent source from which data may be obtained, as are newspapers, journals published by learned organizations and the government, magazines, lectures, films, and community resources which may be visited by the class or brought into the classroom.

4. *Formulating, modifying, or testing hypotheses.* This step in the problem-solving process involves educated guesses, ideas, or insights and usually includes the organization and analysis of the data collected. Hypotheses may explain the data, or they may point up the necessity for further study or fact-

finding. At this point, the most logical solutions to the problem are tested; the data that have been collected and the plans that have been made are put to trial. Action is carried on until a plausible solution to the problem is found.

5. *Evaluating results.* When the final solution to the problem is found, the results of the problem-solving process need to be evaluated to determine whether the original purposes were met and whether any unexpected information was uncovered. Not only should the results of the process be evaluated, but the process itself should be appraised to see whether the procedure itself could be improved on.

6. *Generalizing.* Progressing through the various steps in the problem-solving process would be an uneconomical use of time and energy if the learning results were to end with the solution of one problem. The purpose for most learning is that the knowledge thus gained may be used in other situations. Following the arrival at a solution, then, the teacher should lead the class in making applications of the results to other circumstances so that pupils may understand that the findings do not apply only to the one particular problem under consideration. The test of children's learning about any subject or topic is what they are able to do with the knowledge they have gained.

Not until a pupil is able to apply what he has learned is he deemed to have learned at all.

Polya's Problem-Solving Formula

Polya, in four steps, presents a simple, logical approach to problem-solving which can be expanded to deal with any problem at any grade level. His approach follows:

FIRST

UNDERSTANDING THE PROBLEM

You have to *under-stand* the problem. *What is the unknown? What are the data? What is the condition?* Is is possible to satisfy the condition? Is the condition sufficient to determine the unknown? Or is it insufficient? Or redundant? Or contradictory?

Draw a figure. Introduce suitable notation.

Separate the various parts of the condition. Can you write them down?

SECOND

DEVISING A PLAN

Find the connection between the data and the unknown. You may be obliged to consider auxiliary problems if an immediate connection cannot be

Have you seen it before? Or have you seen the same problem in a slightly different form?

Do you know a related problem? Do you know a theorem that could be useful?

Look at the unknown! And try to think of a familiar problem having the same or a similar unknown.

Here is a problem related to yours and solved before. Could you use it? Could you use its results? Could you use its method? Should you introduce some found. You should obtain eventually a *plan* of the solution.

auxiliary element in order to make its use possible? Could you restate the problem? Could you restate it still differently? Go back to definitions.

If you cannot solve the proposed problem, try to solve first some related problem.

Could you imagine a more accessible related problem? A more general problem? A more special problem? An analogous problem? Could you solve a part of the problem? Keep only a part of the condition, drop the other part; how far is the unknown then determined, how can it vary? Could you derive something useful from the data? Could you think of other data appropriate to determine the unknown? Could you change the unknown or the data, or both if necessary, so that the new unknown and the new data are nearer to each other?

Did you use all the data? Did you use the whole condition? Have you taken into account all essential notions involved in the problem?

THIRD

Carry out your plan.

CARRYING OUT THE PLAN

Carrying out your plan of the solution, check each step. Can you see clearly that the step is correct? Can you prove that it is correct?

FOURTH

Examine the solution obtained.

LOOKING BACK

Can you *check the result?* Can you check the argument? Can you derive the result differently? Can you see it at a glance?

Can you use the result, or the method, for some other problem? [2]

The concept of education as problem-solving is, of course, in sharp contrast to the traditional concept that the educative process is strictly intellectual and is concerned only with ideas forced on the pupil by a textbook author, a teacher, or some other authority. In the traditional sense, the primary object is to gain knowledge; the application of this knowledge is not considered important until after the subject matter is gained. Unfortunately, the traditional approach necessitates the retraining of the learner in the application of knowledge sometime after he assumedly gains the knowledge. In the problem-solving conception, application of the knowledge is made at the time it is learned; thus, it is more meaningful and the chances of its retention are much greater than in the rote approach.

If pupils are guided by teachers in problem-solving experiences, they will gain knowledge and be able to apply it; they also will be given opportunities for forming scientific attitudes and correct work-study skills, as well as for appropriate activities in critical and reflective thinking. As pupils participate

[2] Reprinted from *How to Solve It* by G. Polya, Doubleday, 1957, by permission of the publisher.

increasingly in problem-solving, they will gain skill in the process and will become adept at meeting head on and working through to successful conclusions the myriad problems they will encounter as they go through life.

MOTIVATING AND THE ENVIRONMENT

Reference was made earlier in this chapter to the importance in learning of motivation and environmental arrangement, both of which are significant aspects of the teaching act. Actually, the two are not mutually exclusive. One of the first accomplishments of the teacher in motivating pupils is the creation of a learning environment, an environment in which youngsters will be stimulated toward interesting, appropriate, and attainable goals. This is no mean accomplishment, to say the least. It means that the teacher must learn the needs, interests, and capacities of each pupil in his class. He must establish close rapport with each individual in his group, and at the same time must supervise the peer interaction within the class. It means that the teacher must generate and communicate a vast amount of interest, enthusiasm, and creativity.

Four psychological aspects of motivation might be mentioned at this point. First is intention to learn. It seems obvious that the least teachers can do in motivating children is to let pupils know what they are expected to learn; deliberate intention to learn is an effective aid to learning. Second, ego involvement aids learning; every pupil needs to experience some degree of success and social approval. Third, frequent testing is sometimes used as a motivational technique. Although this is a somewhat questionable technique, especially at the elementary level, many teachers believe that frequent testing motivates pupils to study harder and acquire more knowledge. Fourth, knowledge of results, or of one's performance rating, may build up favorable attitudes toward improvement.

Within each individual are certain basic needs and drives which, when properly channeled, motivate him toward acceptable goals. Included in these are needs for physical security and freedom from fear; self-sufficiency and independence, personal improvement and competition with self and others; group status; personal satisfaction from accomplishment; pride and self-esteem; and emotional release. The teacher is a key person in the teaching-learning situation and, as such, must understand the needs of children and help them to satisfy these needs.

The learning environment, of course, centers in the classroom. Obviously, it should be attractive and orderly, with proper lighting, ventilation, seating, and appurtenances used in, or conducive to, the teaching-learning act. In evidence should be attractive bulletin boards; points of interest such as science tables and reading corners; listening centers where pupils can use phonographs, radios, and television equipment; individual study areas; and ample books, supplies, and other materials. These physical attributes of the classroom are, however, important only to the extent that they facilitate amenable interpersonal relationships and keep lines of communication open to members of the group, that they help the group develop a sense of responsibility and stimulate achievement motivation.

DISCOVERY AND LEARNING

Much is being made in today's classrooms of the principles involved in the "discovery" method as a technique of learning. These principles, so evident at this time in the areas of science and mathematics, are based on the fact that things to be learned have an internal connectedness and to be really learned they must be fitted together in a meaningful manner. Actual "discovery" is, of course, a rare phenomenon; in the classroom it usually involves gaining new insights as a result of the pupil's going beyond his current knowledge by re-arranging the facts involved. It seems evident that if children are to be given opportunities for discovery, they must be trained in the problem-solving process, discussed earlier in this chapter.

The discovery concept is one in which children may become "active" learners as opposed to "passive" ones. According to this idea, children may participate in making knowledge rather than simply consuming knowledge already made. Bruner relates an incident which illustrates this process:

Children in the fifth grade of a suburban school were about to study the geography of the Central States as part of a social studies unit. Previous units on the Southeastern states, taught by rote, had proved a bore. Could geography be taught as a rational discipline? Determined to find out, the teachers devised a unit in which students would have to figure out not only where things are located, but why they are there. This involves a sense of the structure of geography.

The children were given a map of the Central states in which only rivers, large bodies of water, agricultural products, and natural resources were shown. They were not allowed to consult their books. Their task was to find Chicago, "the largest city in the North Central states."

The argument got under way immediately. One child came up with the idea that Chicago must be on the junction of the three large lakes. No matter that at this point he did not know the names of the lakes—Huron, Superior, and Michigan—his theory was well-reasoned. A big city produced a lot of products, and the easiest and most logical way to ship these products is by water.

But a second child rose immediately to the opposition. A big city needed lots of food, and he placed Chicago where there are corn and hogs—right in the middle of Iowa.

A third child saw the issue more broadly—recognizing virtues in both previous arguments. He pointed out that large quantities of food can be grown in river valleys. Whether he had learned this from a previous social studies unit or from raising carrot seeds, we shall never know. If you had a river, he reasoned, you had not only food but transportation. He pointed to a spot on the map not far from St. Louis. "There is where Chicago *ought* to be." Would that graduate students would always do so well!

Not all the answers were so closely reasoned, though even the wild ones had about them a sense of the necessity involved in a city's location.

One argued, for example, that all American cities have skyscrapers, which require steel, so he placed Chicago in the middle of the Mesabi Range. At least he was thinking on his own, with a sense of the constraints imposed on the location of cities.

After forty-five minutes, the children were told they could pull down the "real" wall map (the one with names) and see where Chicago really is. After the map was down, each of the contending parties pointed out how close they had come to being right. Chicago had not been located. But the location of cities was no longer a matter of unthinking chance for this group of children.[3]

Bruner concludes, "What did the children learn?" A way of thinking about geography, a way of dealing with its raw data. They learned that there is some relationship between the requirements of living and man's habitat. If that is all they got out of their geography lesson, that is plenty. Did they remember which is Lake Huron? Lake Superior? Lake Michigan? Do you?

Foshay relates how the discovery or knowledge-making technique might be used in an American history class. He suggests that when the class has proceeded to the immediate post-Civil War period, the teacher might pursue the "ideal of intellectual excellence that is represented by an attempt to study the disciplines directly" by carrying the children to a confrontation of the historian's problem and raising with them various questions. "What kinds of events after Lincoln would be most worth knowing?" "How can we discover what these events were?" (We can read, ask, search, tell one another.) "What do historians say these events were?" (Not one historian—several, for not all historians choose to deal with the same events, and the sooner we understand this, the more liberated we are from a naïve view of our past and of the historian's place in understanding it.) "What are the principal ways the period has been interpreted by the historians?" "Do you, as a student, think of other ways?" "What information do you think the historians might include that they appear to have omitted?" "Why do you suppose they omitted this information? Because they couldn't find it? Because it didn't fit with their interpretation?" [4]

What a radical departure is this method from the old subject-centered method of teaching history! Through techniques such as those indicated in the two examples cited, teachers might confront the disciplines directly and bring pupils into knowledge-making activities instead of strictly knowledge-consuming lessons.

CONCLUSION

There are a number of theories of how learning takes place, none of which a teacher needs to adopt per se. It is important, however, for a teacher to study the psychological propositions which receive general agreement, and, together with a study of research and experimentation on his own part, arrive at some

[3] Jerome S. Bruner, "Structures in Learning," *NEA Journal*, 52:26, March, 1963.
[4] Arthur W. Foshay, "A Modest Proposal for the Improvement of Education," *What Are the Sources of the Curriculum? A Symposium* (Washington, D.C.: Association for Supervision and Curriculum Development, NEA, 1962), pp. 7–8.

sound conclusions with respect to methodology in the classroom. Problem-solving and discovery methods, when approached with the concept of teaching learners how to learn, offer some promising procedures which may help students face the important problems of the days when they will be living as adults in a precarious world.

Questions for Discussion

1. Do you agree with the idea that if a teacher has done an effective job, the range of differences in achievement between the pupils in his classroom will be wider at the end of the year than it was at the beginning? What is the rationale behind this idea?
2. In what ways do modern teaching machines implement the well-known laws of learning?
3. Why is it necessary for the teacher to have more knowledge of subject matter when teacher-pupil planning is employed than when it is not? When would be the appropriate times for a teacher to use teacher-pupil planning?
4. What is the relationship between the problem-solving approach and the reflective-thinking approach to learning? How would you justify the claim of some authorities in education that the only way people learn is by the scientific problem-solving method?
5. It is generally accepted that, broadly, learning means change in behavior. In what ways does learning new words in reading, new axioms in mathematics, or new concepts in physics change one's behavior?
6. What is the teacher's real responsibility with respect to children's learning?
7. Support or refute the idea that nothing is so constant as change.
8. What is meant by the statement that until a satisfactory theory of learning evolves, teachers will have to depend upon the "lore" of teaching?
9. B. F. Skinner has said that "the present educational process is one in which methods of imparting knowledge have changed scarcely if at all." Support or refute this statement.
10. What advice could you give to parents who want to "help" their children with school work in the evenings and during the summer recess?

Activities and Projects

1. Visit a fifth-grade elementary school classroom after first making arrangements with the principal and a teacher to do so. Notice the difference in physical appearance of the children, making notes of these differences. No names need be involved. If convenient and permissible, have the teacher tell you about the differences in mental abilities and achievement of the children in the class, again omitting all references to personalities. Note the wide range and discuss it in your class, trying to arrive at some ideas as to how individual differences found in the elementary classroom in only one area—that of the social studies, for example—might be provided for.

2. Arrange with the professor of your class to allow you to pursue the teacher-student planning procedure with your classmates, with you serving as the teacher. Plan with them as though you were in a high school history class, and use as a unit topic, "The Post-Civil War Era." Using the steps listed in this chapter under the topic "Student-Teacher Planning," go through the actual planning procedure.

3. Assume you are the science teacher in a junior high school, and you are studying the subject of air. The problem of why the length of the trombone's slide determines the varying tones of the instrument has arisen. With you serving as teacher, and your classmates as students, proceed through the steps of the problem-solving process as outlined in this chapter.

4. Practice the reflective-thinking process by asking your classmates to read silently with you any paragraph in this chapter. Then ask each one to comment on any concept or concepts he obtained from the paragraph, or any sentence in the paragraph. Encourage everyone to contribute, in his own words, what he learned from his reading; encourage, too, those students who did not learn the same concepts to express their ideas. Motivate the discussion to continue until some definite concepts are agreed upon by the class.

5. Attend a class session in an elementary or secondary school in which television or teaching machines are being used in the teaching-learning situation. Note the role of the teacher, and try to determine what new skills are needed on his part. How does this situation differ in class organization from a typical one?

6. Compare some textbooks used in today's schools with some used in the nineteenth century (these are usually available in the education library of your college). What are some of the outstanding differences? How do you account for these differences? What inferences can you make with respect to differences in authors' conceptions of pupil motivation and arrangement of environment?

7. In psychological journals or in abstracts of doctoral dissertations in your college library, look up several studies which attempt to determine the amount of subject matter retained by elementary or high school pupils after they have completed certain courses. How do you account for the "forgetting" rate?

8. Arrange to visit for a half-day in an elementary or secondary school classroom. Can you pretty well tell what the teacher's philosophy of education is? Upon what do you base your answer?

References

"LEARNING AND PROGRAMMED LEARNING"

BRUNER, JEROME S., *The Process of Education* (Cambridge, Mass.: Harvard University Press, 1961), Chapter 6.

"Building a Classroom Climate for Learning," *NEA Journal,* 39:34–38, December, 1961.

BURTON, WILLIAM H., *The Guidance of Learning Activities* (New York: Appleton-Century-Crofts, 1962), Chapter 14.

COLE, LUELLA, and IRMA NELSON HALL, *Psychology of Adolescence,* 6th ed. (New York: Holt, Rinehart & Winston, 1964).

CRESSMAN, GEORGE R., and HAROLD W. BRENDA, *Public Education in America* (New York: Appleton-Century-Crofts, 1961), Chapter 12.

FRAZIER, ALEXANDER, ed., *New Insights and the Curriculum,* 1963 Yearbook (Washington, D.C.: Association for Supervision and Curriculum Development, NEA, 1963).

GRAMBS, JEAN D., and L. MORRIS MCCLURE, *Foundations of Teaching* (New York: Holt, Rinehart & Winston, 1964), pp. 45–46 and Chapter 5.

HANNA, LAVONE A., GLADYS L. POTTER, and NEVA HAGAMAN, *Unit Teaching in the Elementary School,* rev. ed. (New York: Holt, Rinehart & Winston, 1963), Chapter 2.

HASKEW, LAURENCE D., and JONATHON C. MCLENDON, *This Is Teaching,* rev. ed. (Chicago: Scott, Foresman, 1962), Chapters 2, 3, 6.

HAWK, T. L., "School Practices and Certain Principles of Learning," *Elementary School Journal,* 64:36–41, October, 1963.

KLAUSMEIER, HERBERT J., and KATHERINE DRESDEN, *Teaching in the Elementary School,* 2d ed. (New York: Harper, 1962), Chapters 2, 3.

KNELLER, GEORGE F., *Foundations of Education* (New York: Wiley, 1963), Chapter 12.

Learning and the Teacher (Washington, D.C.: Association for Supervision and Curriculum Development, NEA, 1959).

LEESE, JOSEPH, KENNETH FRASURE, and MAURITZ JOHNSON, JR., *The Teacher in Curriculum Making* (New York: Harper, 1961), Chapter 7.

MISNER, PAUL J., FREDERICK W. SCHNEIDER, and LOWELL G. KEITH, *Elementary School Administration* (Columbus, Ohio: Charles E. Merrill, 1963), Chapter 5.

PEEL, E. A., "Some Psychological Principles Underlying Programmed Learning," *Educational Research,* 5:183–86, June, 1963.

RESNICK, L. B., "Programmed Instruction and the Teaching of Complex Intellectual Skills: Problems and Prospects," *Harvard Educational Review,* 33:439–71, Fall, 1963.

RICHEY, ROBERT W., *Planning for Teaching,* 3d ed. (New York: McGraw-Hill, 1963), Chapter 7.

SHUSTER, ALBERT H., and MILTON E. PLOGHOFT, *The Emerging Elementary Curriculum* (Columbus, Ohio: Charles E. Merrill, 1963), Chapters 2, 3.

SKINNER, B. F., "Reflections on a Decade of Teaching Machines," *Teachers College Record,* 65:168–77, November, 1963.

SMITH, LOUIS M., and BRUCE B. HUDGENS, *Educational Psychology* (New York: Random House and Knopf, 1964), Unit IV.

THOMAS, LAWRENCE G., LUCIEN B. KINNEY, ARTHUR P. COLADARCI, and HELEN FIELSTRA, *Perspective on Teaching* (Englewood Cliffs, N.J.: Prentice-Hall, 1961), Chapters 7–9.

TRAVERS, ROBERT M. W., *Essentials of Learning* (New York: Macmillan, 1963).

WAETJEN, WALTER B., ed., *New Dimensions in Learning* (Washington, D.C.: Association for Supervision and Curriculum Development, NEA, 1962).

WATSON, GOODWIN, "What Do We Know about Learning?" *NEA Journal*, 52:22, March, 1963.

"PROBLEM-SOLVING AND DISCOVERY"

BRUNER, JEROME S., "Structures in Learning," *NEA Journal*, 52:26, March, 1963.

———, "The Act of Discovery," *Harvard Educational Review*, 31:21–32, Winter, 1961.

DEWEY, JOHN, *How Do We Think?* (Boston: Heath, 1910).

FOSHAY, ARTHUR W., "A Modest Proposal for the Improvement of Education," in *What Are the Sources of the Curriculum? A Symposium* (Washington, D.C.: Association for Supervision and Curriculum Development, NEA, 1962), pp. 1–14.

FURTH, H. G., "Conceptual Discovery and Control on a Pictorial Part-Whole Task as a Function of Age, Intelligence, and Language," *Journal of Educational Psychology*, 54:191–96, August, 1963.

GUILFORD, J. P., "Creative Thinking and Problem Solving," *California Teachers Association Journal*, 60:9–10, January, 1964.

HANNA, Chapter 8.

HULLFISH, H. GORDON, and PHILIP G. SMITH, *Reflective Thinking: The Method of Education* (New York: Dodd, Mead, 1961), Chapter 3.

HUTCHINSON, ELIOT D., *How to Think Creatively* (Nashville, Tenn.: Abingdon Press, 1959).

PARKER, J. CECIL, T. BENTLEY EDWARDS, and WILLIAM H. STEGEMAN, *Curriculum in America* (New York: Thomas Y. Crowell, 1962), Chapter 3.

POLYA, G., *How to Solve It* (New York: Doubleday, 1957).

RAGAN, WILLIAM B., *Teaching America's Children* (New York: Holt, Rinehart & Winston, 1959), pp. 154–55.

RESNICK

RICHEY, pp. 213–14.

RUSSELL, BERTRAND, *The Will to Doubt* (New York: Philosophical Library, 1960).

THOMAS, pp. 172–83.

TRAVERS, Chapter 10.

TURNER, RICHARD L., and NICHOLAS A. FATTU, "Skill in Teaching, Assessed on the Criterion of Problem Solving," *Bulletin of the School of Education* (University of Indiana), vol. 37, May, 1961.

VINACHE, W. E., *The Psychology of Thinking* (New York: McGraw-Hill, 1952).

WALTER, WILLIAM GREY, *The Living Brain* (New York: Norton, 1953).

vii

> Intelligent teaching requires an understanding of individual children, their potentialities, their interests and aspirations, their problems and difficulties, and their sources of strength.
>
> RALPH W. TYLER

the pupils as boys and girls

A review of the descriptions of the seven children found at the beginning of Chapter 6 reveals that each is unique, each is different from each of the others. Even when children, like Mary and Bob, are at the same grade level—a situation in which we should expect to find some uniformity—we discover vast differences between them. There never have been two children alike, and there never will be. When this fact is considered along with the fact that there are hundreds of thousands of children attending public and private schools in this country, with hundreds of thousands more to come, it is easy to see that teachers and administrators indeed have their problems when they plan educational programs that will be applicable to each child. Variations among and between children exist in physique, chronological age, sex, achievement, intelligence and ability, nationality, interests, personality, and socioeconomic backgrounds, to name only a few.

Entire volumes have been written on individual differences among children. In this chapter, only a few of the more important considerations will be pointed out.

PUPIL DIFFERENCES

Physical Differences

One of the most obvious differences among children is that of physique: height, weight, and proportion. If one were to line up along a wall all the children of any one grade level, he could not help but be amazed at the

141

variations which exist. These wide variations in height, weight, and proportion exist for children of both sexes and of all age groups.

Boys and girls remain about the same height until age eleven, when girls are usually taller than boys; however, by age fifteen, this trend reverses and boys show averages higher than girls. Heights overlap from age to age: the tallest six-year-old youngsters are equal in height to the shortest eleven-year-olds, and the tallest eleven-year-old children are taller than the shortest eighteen-year-old youths. We find marked irregularities in rate of growth; that is, most youngsters apparently experience growth spurts and plateaus in development toward adulthood. The most rapid growth occurs during a child's pre-school years: at age three a child has attained half his adult height. As he grows older his growth rate decreases except for the adolescent growth spurt at thirteen to fifteen years of age.

Wide ranges in weight for children at all ages are also in evidence. Occasionally, a six-year-old first-grader is heavier than a sixteen-year-old eleventh-grade pupil. Usually, children attain half their adult weight at age twelve or thirteen. Whereas children reach their adult weight in the late teens or early twenties, it is obvious that weight may continue to increase until late adulthood.

A wide range of body build also exists among children at any age. Among both boys and girls, we find variations as to amount of fat and sturdiness of bones and muscles. The change in proportion as children grow older is almost endless. So long as weight stays within reasonable limits for a child's particular build, there is no cause for undue concern or anxiety.

Chronological Age Differences

In a typical school district, a wide range in chronological ages naturally exists. Typically, kindergarteners begin to attend school at age five, though some districts operate nursery schools where the lowest age may be three or four. In the same district may be found high school seniors of ages seventeen to nineteen, or students finishing junior college at ages eighteen and higher. Often there is considerable variation in chronological age at any given grade level, though the chronological age seems to be the most consistent criterion for grade placement in the public schools.

Sex Differences

Where there are no significant differences, generally, in mental ability between boys and girls in school, there are some noticeable differences between them in other areas. For school age children, the period of most rapid growth —between fourteen and fifteen years of age for boys and between twelve and thirteen years for girls—closely coincides with the beginning of sexual maturity. But the age range at the onset of sexual maturity also varies widely among individuals; there will probably be some girls in each grade between four and eleven who have reached sexual maturity, and there will also be some girls in those grades who have not. An equally wide range probably exists for boys.

If a boy and a girl have the same intelligence, the girl will usually do the better work. Girls like literature and lean toward love and "cute" stories, whereas boys generally prefer mathematics and mechanical studies and are more interested in adventure and danger stories.

Generally, schools have not been aware of sex differences in their educational programs; however, as teachers, supervisors, and administrators pursue their educational planning, they should consider some important differences. Waetjen has pointed to research which indicates the following differences between boys and girls: boys burn up more oxygen than girls; they show higher I.Q. variations; up to eight years of age, they do not use visual clues as well as girls; they can transfer their learnings better than girls; they perceive their environment more thoroughly, while girls are often misled by extraneous clues; nearly twice as many boys receive unsatisfactory marks, and the sex of the teacher makes no difference in the grades given; boys are more analytical and do better work in mathematics and science; girls are more dependent upon verbal methods of learning and do better work in the language arts.

Waetjen said that evidence does not warrant the conclusion that as children grow older some of the sex differences in school performance decrease. While indicating a willingness to try separation of the sexes, Waetjen pointed out that such a plan might present other types of problems. "What is more pertinent," he said, "is that whatever we do in education should show an awareness of and provision for sex-linked learning behavior." [1]

Achievement Differences

There are striking individual differences among school children in measures of academic achievement. Children are found in the fourth grade, for example, who, on achievement tests, may rate third grade in reading, fifth grade in arithmetic, second grade in spelling. Or the differences may be much greater, in both individuals and in groups. A child in the fourth grade may rate grade seven in vocabulary, grade five in fundamental knowledge, grade six in fundamental operations, and grade four in problem-solving. When a well-known reading achievement test was administered recently to a group of freshmen entering an eastern university, it was found that the range of achievement spread from the fourth grade to college graduate, with the median being tenth grade. Some college students are unable to read as well as pupils leaving junior high school.

In actual situations, it has been found that the spread in the range of achievement increases as children progress through school. In classrooms the

[1] Address by Walter B. Waetjen, director of the Bureau of Educational Research and Field Services at the University of Maryland, before the national meeting of the Association for Supervision and Curriculum Development, March, 1963, in St. Louis, Missouri.

range should widen if the teacher is doing an acceptable job of guiding the learning of children.

Intelligence and Ability Differences

Mental age differences among children in a single grade may total five or six years. Typically, mental ages ranging from twelve to sixteen years will usually be found in a ninth-grade group, and from seven to eleven years in a fourth-grade class. Students with intelligence quotients ranging from 80 to 130 may be found in a typical high school freshman class; in primary grades in elementary schools, I.Q.'s may be as low as the 50's and 60's. Since the I.Q. is not a constant factor but tends to become more stable as children grow older, it behooves teachers not to accept any quotient—particularly one obtained in the lower grades—as a measure of brightness throughout a child's elementary school years. Since extrinsic or accidental factors may play a part in obtaining measures of intelligence, too much precision should not be attributed to the I.Q.; it is only one approximate index to a pupil's level of intelligence.

Nationality Differences

The differences between boys and girls of different racial origins with respect to learning capacity and to character development are not significant; they are, however, significant with respect to such environmental aspects as interests, attitudes, and language troubles. In achievement, children of Jewish descent and from English and Scottish backgrounds, on the average, rate higher on tests than do children from other groups. On the same types of tests, the lower-ranking groups include children from Spanish, French-Canadian, Mexican, Polish, and Greek ancestry. Immigrants into the United States have come from all kinds of nationality backgrounds, and their children sit together in the classrooms all over this nation.

Interest Differences

It has been said that all there is to teaching is meeting the needs and interests of children or, rather, helping them meet their needs and interests. Perhaps teaching is more than that, but the statement nevertheless points up the importance of interests in the teaching-learning situation. They are of paramount importance in planning for teaching.

Teachers constantly are changing their approaches because children's interests are so variable, and as children mature their interests widen and change. What may appear a real interest today will tomorrow turn out to be only a passing whimsy. Alert teachers are, however, able to detect a thread of consistency in children's interests as they observe their work over a period of time. School personnel have at their disposal interest inventories, which are helpful in determining pupils' real interests.

ALL MUST BE EDUCATED

The descriptions of the pupils at the beginning of the previous chapter and the discussion of individual differences above serve to point up the tremendous responsibilities of teachers and other school personnel as they set about to help each child progress through school. As indicated earlier, these children are in the schools *now*, and dedicated professional workers all over the nation strive every day to help them meet their needs and prepare to become responsible citizens in our democratic society. In keeping with the spirit of the Educational Policies Commission's theme, we must seek to see that "all the children of all the people" become educated.

Teaching the Average Pupil

The superintendent and staff of a large Illinois elementary school district, after hearing so many parents relate that theirs were "superior" children, decided to find out how many "average" pupils were in the district. The entire student body of the district, numbering over 10,000, were tested against carefully drawn-up criteria to measure their "averageness." When the data were all in and tabulated, a total of only *one* pupil met the criteria for being of average ability. This true incident illustrates the fact that there really are no "average" pupils in a school, despite the fact that teachers have been accused of teaching "to the average" of their classes.

What is probably meant by the assertion that teachers teach to pupils of "average" ability is that teachers tend to teach a general diffusion of knowledge so that the largest possible number of pupils—the approximately 68 per cent of children who fall within the statistical limitations of one standard deviation on either side of the mean—may benefit from the instruction. Granted, this is not ideal because it results in neglect of pupils beyond the limitations suggested here, but it is natural for this trend to occur, and teachers need to be on constant guard against relating instruction principally toward this group. What is needed in American schools is quality education for all children regardless of where they fall along the ability continuum.

In the light of the wide ranges of ability and achievement pointed up previously, it is impossible to standardize instruction for students of "average" ability because they simply do not exist. The idea of uniform, mass instruction of homogeneous groups of children using single textbooks in the various subject areas violates recognition of the existence of individual differences in each classroom.

Grade levels actually do not indicate definite steps in academic achievement; course work requirements at any grade level cannot be prescribed for all children. To retain children at a grade level for more than one year simply on the basis of their nonacademic achievement *alone* is a direct violation of the laws of learning and of child growth and development. The idea that, if teachers do a good job of taking care of individual differences, all children in the class will be brought up to a certain predetermined standard is ridiculous; in fact, as stated earlier, good teaching results in widening the range of achievement within a group, in increasing the heterogeneity of groups. The problem of meeting "average" pupil needs is the same as that of meeting superior pupil needs: how can we best meet the needs of all children and youth in classes of widely varying capabilities?

Knowing how children can best meet their needs implies that teachers must know what these needs are. Certainly a teacher can more readily discover the needs of children if the number in the class is kept within reason. The optimum pupil-teacher ratio recommended by the Association for Supervision and Curriculum Development at its national convention in 1963 (20 to 1 for both elementary and secondary schools) would facilitate teachers' efforts in gaining knowledge about their pupils and in helping them meet their needs. A testing program which would indicate status and growth of pupils in the academic areas necessary for living in our culture would also be beneficial for teachers in these respects. Such a testing program would enable the teacher to know better the books that pupils are able to read and the kinds of problems they are able to solve. The practice of elementary teachers remaining with the same group of youngsters for as many as three years is one that provides further opportunity for teacher acquaintance with the needs of pupils.

Teaching the Slow Learner, the Handicapped

There are many children attending America's public schools who deviate from the normal in ability, intelligence, physique, or socioeconomic background to such an extent that special education programs must be provided for them if we are to educate all the children of all the people to the optimum of their capacities. While all children have the same basic needs, it is more difficult for maladjusted and handicapped children to meet their needs than for the more normal boys and girls to do so. All children, regardless of the condition of their minds and bodies, should be considered as individuals who can make contributions to democratic group living; all must learn to live in the culture in which they find themselves. Thus, in their curriculums many schools in the nation include programs for mentally retarded, physically handicapped, emotionally disturbed, and disadvantaged children who live in their districts.

Causes of retardation are legion. Children who do not make progress in school subjects may be mentally retarded, physically incapacitated, emotionally or socially disturbed, or disadvantaged because of a low socioeconomic environment. Teachers may find children whose intelligence measures well below the 90 to 100 I.Q. range considered by most authorities to be "normal." Rarely, however, will a teacher find a pupil in public school classrooms whose intelligence quotient is below 50. There are also children in the public schools who have orthopedic, heart, hearing, sight, speech, and certain other types of physical defects. Occasionally teachers encounter children in their classes who are psychotic, nervous, retiring, socially negative or who have problems of truancy, incorrigibility, or delinquency. Chiefly in the less desirable sections of the nation's largest cities, teachers may find pupils under their tutelage who have the barest of living necessities in a totally inadequate home and neighborhood environment.

Tantamount to an educational program for the maladjusted and handicapped is a proper philosophy, or attitude, with respect to these children on the part of teachers, administrators, parents, and children; sympathetic understanding of the special problems of maladjusted and handicapped children must be developed. These boys and girls must be afforded opportunities for the development of good work habits, dependability, adequate body and eating habits, and attributes of good citizenship, as well as opportunities to develop their intellectual capacities. If possible, maladjusted and handicapped children need to be integrated into activity classes in art, physical education, and music, at least for certain periods of time, so that they may learn to get along with others—a skill they will use all their lives.

In many communities in the nation, slow-learning and handicapped children have opportunities to attend special education programs in which the school tries to adjust its offerings in such a way that their abilities can be developed to the maximum. Such programs attempt to provide handicapped boys and girls with a broad basic education and with opportunities to develop certain skills, habits, and attitudes so that they can adjust to society to the best of their abilities.

Some school districts provide special education programs in segregated classes or special schools where children may be free from academic competition and may pursue individual problems at their own rate. In such an environment, too, children may be free from the stigma that sometimes exists in a regular school or classroom situation. Opponents of a plan of segregation, on the other hand, maintain that children often revolt against the isolation and distinction of special classes, that teachers sometimes feel less responsibility for handicapped children and thus stress academic subject matter rather than social development, and that such a plan tends to accentuate problems of behavior in an environment where exemplary behavior is the predominant need.

Special requirements for teachers in special education classes have been set by more than half the states; some require an advanced graduate degree and most require some teaching experience. Needless to say, effective teachers in such classes need a large amount of enthusiasm, a maximum degree of patience and understanding, and an exceptional ability to motivate children. They should approach special education classes more from the aspect of practicability than from academic emphasis.

Teaching the Superior Student

Although school and lay individuals have long recognized a need to educate mentally superior children in ways different from those used for "normal" children, only in the past twenty years has much been actually accomplished in this respect. Because mentally superior children have ben able to make progress pretty well on their own, teachers have been prone to neglect them to the point that they often have been satisfied with a level of achievement considerably below their capabilities.

While many schools accept for mentally superior classes any child who is gifted in some particular ability, most educational institutions accept favorable teacher observations and an I.Q. score of 110 or above as the most objective criteria for a pupil's participation. Whatever the method of selection, an important part of a school's program is the screening procedure it uses. Studies have revealed that mentally superior children are generally superior in most other aspects also; they are well adjusted socially and are above average in physical health. Many times they show unusual insight and possess remarkable ability to apply their learning to other situations.

While the literature and observations do not indicate that any typical program for the education of mentally superior children exists—undoubtedly because of widely varying philosophies among teachers, administrators, and lay persons—there are generally three types of plans which schools provide for these children and youth: enrichment, acceleration, and special classes. None of these is considered the final answer, however.

In programs of enrichment, the regular classroom program is embellished to a point where the mentally superior children in the class are challenged at their level of achievement. Children in the higher levels of mental acuity often provide much of their own enrichment, but this should not be left to chance; teachers need to plan for the stimulation and nurturing of the cognitive abilities of these boys and girls. The school should provide opportunities for the mentally superior to utilize individual research skills or to otherwise expand and develop more deeply their special interests.

A much-publicized and highly successful program of enrichment is provided for the superior students in the Major Work Classes of Cleveland, Ohio, in which twenty different elementary schools, three junior high schools, and three senior high schools participate. The purpose of the special classes for gifted children with I.Q.'s of 125 or over is to cover more material than is covered in the regular classroom, and to cover it more thoroughly and meaningfully. Regular courses of study set up by curriculum committees for the "average" child are the bases of study for children in the Major Work Classes. Enrichment of this program is left to the discretion of the specially trained teachers in charge of the classes, with due consideration of desires, needs, and interests of the pupils.

Possibly the oldest, mechanically the simplest, and currently the most discouraged method of handling mentally superior youngsters is acceleration. Under this plan, children are usually provided for in one of three ways: advanced to higher grade levels than their chronological ages would normally allow, assigned more advanced subject matter for study, or allowed to enter school earlier than children of "normal" mental ability. In good schools, the social, emotional, and physical development of children is always considered

---

PUPILS PARTICIPATE IN CLEVELAND MAJOR WORK PROGRAM

Visitors to elementary-school major work classes often remark on these facts:

1. The children do not hold up their hands before speaking.
2. The pupils solve disciplinary problems.
3. The pupils decide when to continue to another unit of work.
4. The group leader is responsible for seeing that everyone participates.
5. Pupils present well-prepared talks.
6. Talks and groups reports are evaluated by the pupils.
7. The study of French begins in the primary grades.
8. Each pupil is eager to learn.

Walter B. Barbe and Dorothy Norris, November 21, 1954.

---

before acceleration actually takes place. The acceleration plan calls for no differentiation of the school's curriculum. An exception, however, is the advanced placement plan whereby a superior secondary school student can gain college credit and advanced placement by taking courses at the college level or passing a college-level course examination. This plan, of course, necessitates major changes in instructional procedures and curriculum content in the high school, as the program provides for special attention to superior students and encourages independent study on the part of such students, thus giving them an advanced start on their college work.

Special class groupings, or segregation, is the third technique commonly used by school districts in taking care of mentally superior students. If the district is sufficiently large, this controversial plan may include entire schools, or it may involve only certain classes meeting for an hour or so a week in enrichment-type assignments. Many school districts employ specially trained teachers to plan for these special classes. In New York City, four specialized schools are maintained for gifted high school youngsters: Brooklyn Technical High School, the High School of Music and Art, the Bronx High School of Science, and Stuyvesant High School, each having its own philosophy, organizational structure, curriculum, and equipment centering around a specific purpose and each having a program designed to meet the superior student's special needs, interests, and abilities. Students are admitted on the basis of highly competitive examinations and interest in the area in which the school specializes.

Relationship between Intelligence and Creativity

With the technological advances of recent years has come a new interest in the identification and development of creativity. Recent studies have in-

INTELLIGENCE AND CREATIVITY

1. We need to distinguish further between intelligent thinking as measured by the IQ (and other such procedures) and creative thinking. To be sure, creative persons are intelligent. But as Guilford's and Mac-Kinnon's work with adults and our own work with children shows, this is not their most salient characteristic . . . a certain amount of intelligence is required for creativity, but . . . intelligence and creativity are by no means synonymous.

2. We need to distinguish between independence and unruliness, between individuality and rebelliousness. We have seen that our creative students were quite superior in scholastic achievement. Despite this the teachers showed no special preference for them as students, whereas they did show a special preference for the high IQ students of similar scholastic achievement. The creative students may indeed be more difficult to get along with. But it must be realized that their behavior may have had its source in independence of thought rather than in malice. Since their values differ from the values of other adolescents, they are likely to view objects and events differently than other students. Their wit may be seen as threatening and perceived as hostility. But it may be an expression only of their own deep struggle to reconcile their image of the world with the more conventional image. And, may not the feeling of threat and the perception of hostility be as much our fault as their intent? . . . If we wish to foster intellectual inventiveness, we may have to risk granting the creative student greater autonomy, and perhaps even to reward behavior that fails to comply with what we were prepared to reward.

3. We need to distinguish between healthy solitude and morbid withdrawal, between preferred separateness and compulsive isolation. The emphasis in the classroom today is too often on what has been called "togetherness," "other directedness," "group dynamics," the "enforced interactions of one with all." The most common term of opprobrium is that the child is an "isolate." . . . But . . . intellectual inventiveness and creative performance do not inevitably involve groupiness. On the contrary, it is certain that some kinds of creative performance require permitting the person to set his own problem, to proceed at his own pace, to cogitate on the issues in his own way, to play with his own ideas in his own fashion. . . .

4. We need to distinguish between tolerance for ambiguity and irresolution, between ability to delay a choice and indecisiveness. . . .

5. We need to distinguish between remembering and discovering, between information and knowledge, between the fact-filled Quiz Kid and the educated student. Possessing isolated facts is not the same as being broadly educated (either over a whole range of subjects or in one subject). To be well-informed, we need only a good memory; to be knowledgeable we must also be able to discover. The merely informed person holds on irrevocably to a once conceived fact. The educated person deals flexibly with presently conceived facts in the full realization that today's fact was yesterday's fancy, and today's fancy may very well turn out to be to-

morrow's fact. . . . The revelant educational issue might well be: are there certain areas of instruction in which opportunities are provided for "discovering" as well as for "remembering"? Is there provision in the curriculum for playing with facts and ideas as well as for repeating them? Can we teach students to be more sensitive to the nature of problems? Can we teach them that a problem may have several different interpretations and solutions? Even if there is only one right answer, as in a mathematics problem, can the student solve the problem in a number of different ways? . . .

6. We need to distinguish between sense perception and intuitive perception. . . .

7. We need to distinguish between evaluation and censorship, between judging and forejudging. . . . It is the duty of teachers to teach, but it is also their duty to encourage their students to be open to all ideas, even those that may threaten the teachers' as well as the students' own preconceptions.

8. We need to distinguish between an unattainable goal and a difficult goal, between a problem leading to dejection and resignation and a problem leading to aspiration and exertion. In attempting to avoid the assignment of frustrating tasks, teachers often shrink from setting difficult tasks. But in a sense, creative performance is called out only when the problem requires the mind to stretch for a solution, when the solution is not forthcoming through repetition and memory alone. . . .

9. We need to distinguish between organizing the curriculum with information or knowledge as the educational objective; between using repetition or discovery as the instructional method; between measuring the number of facts or evaluating the quality of wisdom as the criterion of achievement. . . .

If we are to encourage divergent thinking as well as convergent thinking, reward discovery as well as memory, we need achievement tests that are appropriate to these outcomes. And if the best we can do is essay tests, then essay tests that can be scored consistently it must be. . . .

10. The teacher is at the very center of the child's education, and there are of course differences among teachers—differences too numerous to categorize even for illustrative purposes. . . .[2]

[2] Jacob W. Getzels and Philip W. Jackson, *Creativity and Intelligence* (New York: Wiley, 1962), pp. 124–31.

---

dicated that while highly creative persons are generally above average in intelligence, the relationship between intelligence and creativity is not clear-cut. Among some persons in creative groups, the correlation between intelligence and creativity has proved to be essentially zero.

GROUPING THE PUPILS

Grouping in elementary and secondary schools in the United States has always been a matter of considerable concern, which today's demand for improved instruction and greater individualization has made even more pronounced. The problem of grouping has for many years been one of the most persistent of those challenging the ingenuity of the teacher and his professional cohorts.

Children in the public schools' classrooms are grouped, generally, according to chronological age, ability, maturity, or special characteristics. When children are grouped by chronological age, they are simply placed in a room with other pupils of their own age; this, currently, is the typical method of grouping. When grouped by ability, boys and girls are placed in a room with others of their approximate ability; when grouped by maturity, they are placed with children of the same estimated maturational level. Special characteristic grouping, mentioned previously in this chapter, refers to separate groupings of children with special interests or needs.

A number of elementary and secondary schools separate students according to ability into graded sections or groups within grades, and these groups are often designated as *H, X, Y,* or *Z.* The *H* (honors) group contains pupils who are extremely bright or who have the ability to achieve in a superior manner; the *X, Y,* and *Z* groups consist of pupils whose achievement indicates that they are fast, average, or slow, respectively. Usually, the curriculum of the school is modified to meet the needs of the pupils in each of the groups. Pupils in *H* groups pursue courses which not only meet the minimum requirements but also offer students opportunities to do extremely advanced academic work; those in *X* groups take courses which meet minimum requirements and also include a great amount of work of an enriching nature; pupils in *Y* groups take courses which meet minimum requirements and provide for a moderate amount of enrichment; and those in *Z* sections take courses which provide the minimum essentials. Students may be transferred from one group to another at the beginning of a semester or at the initiation of a new unit of instruction if their progress is sufficient to merit such a transfer.

Further refinement in grouping children for instruction is accomplished in each classroom within the school. Teachers in graded schools organize many kinds of groups, as ability groups, interest groups, and self-selection groups evolving, generally, from teacher-pupil planning of a unit about to be launched by the class. Primary level teachers usually group children according to their abilities in reading or arithmetic or in both; three or four groups in a primary room usually mean three or four levels of ability are evident in the class. In intermediate and upper grades, some ability grouping is still accomplished, though at these levels, teachers often find that other types of grouping result in more effective learning.

Ability grouping should be arranged subject by subject, so that groupings may be as different as they need to be. When considering a group for one field or subject, the teacher should use as much objective data as possible: he should consider the pupils' previous achievement in the field as well as what aptitude and intelligence tests and teacher judgment show are the children's potentialities. Flexibility in ability grouping will provide children with opportunities for moving from one group to another so that they may at times be leaders and at other times followers and at all times they may be contributors. There may be considerable advantage to some children if they are assigned to longer lasting groups; such children may need to have the feeling of security which comes from belonging to a more permanent group, or they may need to become involved in the processes of group dynamics applied to a single grouping.

Interest grouping has considerable merit in certain undertakings in the classroom. Children who are strongly motivated, who want to do a job well just because they want to, often amaze their teachers and their peers with what they accomplish. Teachers need to encourage this type of activity by appealing to pupils' real interests; these are often difficult to ascertain, but they can generally be spotted by watching children as they pursue their informal art and literature activities.

Unit teaching lends itself especially well to self-selection groupings in which children, in the pupil-teacher planning session, virtually assign themselves to carry out certain aspects of the unit. The social studies and sciences are particularly fine springboards for units in which all subject areas may be correlated. The work is often accomplished by committees of pupils—some of whom are interested in "bookish" pursuits, some of whom have particular interest in national heroes or inventors, some of whom have special interest in art or music or mechanics, some of whom are good leaders and others good followers. All may experience success by making contributions to the unit's culmination after pursuing the work of the group in which they chose membership. Often self-selection comes about because the pupils themselves recognize they have certain interests or needs.

Flexibility should be the key in whatever type of grouping is employed. While most grouping plans are undoubtedly used with the best interest of children in mind, too many of them overlook the uniqueness of each pupil. Flexible grouping within the classroom is necessary if children are to be moved freely from one group to another so as to be placed within a group working on projects which best fit their individual needs, interests, and level of maturity. Teachers who use flexible grouping procedures, who see wide ranges of differences among children at any grade level as normal and acceptable, and who know that learning is an individual matter with each unique individual within the classroom and fit their instruction to him, are well on the way to success in the important work of guiding the learning activities of children.

Some of the newer types of school organization discussed in Chapter 3 present interesting possibilities in the area of grouping. In the ungraded school, when a child is ready for the next level of achievement, he is moved into a suitable group, regardless of the time of year. Both the dual progress plan and team teaching situations also provide opportunities for pupils to be members of large groups and small groups, and present occasions for individual study or research.

PERSONALITY DIFFERENCES IN CHILDREN

It is a relatively easy matter to ascertain that there are vast differences in personality of children and youth. When faced by identical problems or by the same type of frustrations, one child will react in one way while another is reacting in an entirely different manner. Pupils who tend to be introverts, for example, attempt to adjust to their situations by rearranging their own ideas or by thinking the situations through, whereas those who have extrovert tendencies attempt to adjust by rearranging their environment.

Differences in personality seem to result from differences in perceptual fields of individuals; that is, the manner in which a person behaves will be a direct outgrowth of the way things seem to him at the moment of his behaving. If teachers are to help children improve their personalities, then, it would seem that they must first understand the nature of their pupils' perceptual fields, and, second, they must provide for the kinds of experiences which will foster in children the attainment of what Combs calls the four characteristics of the perceptual fields: a positive view of self, identification with others, acceptance of and openness to experience, and an abundance of information and understanding, which can be called on when needed and put into effective use.[3] Since effective learning experiences, among which are the mastery of symbol systems, problem-solving, reasoning, acquiring and organizing information, contribute to the fulfillment of these four characteristics, teachers must constantly be alert to and attempt to foster the close relationship that exists between learning and personality development.

While studies indicate that *individual* personalities do not vary a great deal, that they are fairly constant over the years, there are certain psychological authorities who maintain that the primary function of the schools is helping children and youth to develop healthy personalities.[4] In this respect, the responsibility for seeing that boys and girls participate in classroom activities without excessive external compulsion and that each has some degree of success falls to the teacher.

SOCIAL CLASS DIFFERENCES OF PUPILS

A glance into the classrooms of the public schools of America provides one with a cross-sectional view of the children of the nation, of boys and girls who vary as widely in their social backgrounds as in the aspects discussed previously in this chapter. Children from different social groups bring to school varying attitudes and learning patterns; at their graduation from school they will take away learning that they will use in widely varying ways.

[3] Arthur W. Combs, "A Perceptual View of the Adequate Personality," in *Perceiving, Behaving, Becoming,* 1962 Yearbook (Washington, D.C.: Association for Supervision and Curriculum Development, NEA, 1962), Chapter 5.

[4] See David Abrahamson, *Who Are Guilty?* (New York: Holt, Rinehart & Winston, 1952), p. 277, and Lawrence E. Cole, *Human Behavior* (Yonkers, N.Y.: World Book Company, 1953), Chapter 24.

Differences in social class are reflected in children's play interests and reading interests; children from higher groups play more varied games, many of them adult-type intellectual games, and their reading materials include better books and periodicals. Upper-class children generally have richer vocabularies and wider ranges of experiences to verbalize. Middle-class children generally hold a high regard for success in language arts experiences and have been taught that education holds the key for economic and social advancement. Children from lower socioeconomic backgrounds generally have lower standards for academic achievement and good conduct than do their peers from higher social strata.

Other aspects of social class differences will be considered in Chapter 8.

THE DEMAND FOR CONFORMITY

The traditional educational system has motivated boys and girls to conform and to resist change, has centered on rote memorization of facts and figures that have been discovered or agreed upon, has emphasized the "right answer" type of problem-solving activity. Such a system has had small concern for the development of creativity on the part of pupils; indeed, it has discouraged initiative and originality in students. There are teachers, even in traditional school situations, who are well meaning, who plan to give pupils opportunities for reflective thinking and original expression. But thinking and creativity are weak competitors against time and "the system" which insist that certain skills must be learned and certain basic information must be acquired *first*. In the traditional system, ready answers to any questions will be found in "the course."

Traditional school personnel, most often well meaning, have censored books, restricted discussion of critical and controversial topics, limited sharing of ideas, imposed methodology that fosters strict discipline and rote learning. Some sophisticates have advocated that schools should concern themselves only with the universal and lasting truths, and that all else is trivia. Often teachers have been made to feel that they must teach children to ape the opinions of their elders.

Forces that often operate aginst the school have sometimes driven teachers and administrators into neutral corners. Academicians, not classroom teachers, have often selected and organized knowledge for initiating pupils into the various fields of knowledge; teachers have had to come to depend on textbooks written by scholars in the various fields. Pupils have been forced to accept the written and spoken words of authorities and have been given little or no opportunity to reflect upon or question those words. Too many classrooms have been intimidated by the tyranny of the "one right answer." Sometimes the compulsion to keep the school running smoothly has forced teachers to a regimen in the areas of organization and methodology. In too many instances, thinking, if it has been stimulated at all, has been of the convergent type.

It is not intended here to imply that all that is done in traditional situations is bad; it seems only too unfortunate that the utilization of newer ideas and techniques is so infrequently in evidence. If our democratic way of life is to be perpetuated, it will be because the citizens of America know how to think critically and reflectively. They must learn how to do this during their years in the classrooms of the nation. Little fear is held for the future of the democratic way of life if children learn in school to question the things they hear and read about, check the authority of the speaker or the author, arrive at answers only after a number of different sources have been consulted, refuse to pass judgment until all the data have been collected and analyzed.

HOPES AND ASPIRATIONS VERSUS REALISTIC EXPECTATIONS

The reader of this book who is looking forward to taking his place as a teacher in a classroom in the near future is probably viewing the future with extremely optimistic anticipation. It has been the authors' observation, as they have taught college young people in their introductory or foundations courses in education, that at this point in their professional preparation, students are a bit starry eyed over the picture of guiding the learning activities of public school youngsters themselves in the near future. It would be farthest from the writers' intention to dampen such inspired aspirations; indeed, if the authors did not think that teaching was among the finest of professions, they would not have remained associated with it for these many years. They agree that "a teacher affects eternity; he can never tell where his influence stops."

As teachers-to-be read this book and others, they undoubtedly will get the feeling that they understand and are ready to tackle what is involved in caring for individual differences in children, in motivating children, in helping children to meet their needs, in involving children in pupil-teacher planning and in problem-solving processes, and in helping children develop healthy personalities and adequate countenances with which to confront the exigencies of modern society. If a student beginning the professional education sequence of course-work should not feel this way, he should probably reevaluate his objectives.

At the same time, it is important that prospective teachers understand that it is much easier to read about the responsibilities and activities of teachers than it is to actually meet and carry them out. After all, when a teacher faces a group of 25 to 35 or more unique individuals each day in the actual classroom situation, the problem of motivating and arranging an environment for each child becomes a gargantuan task. Sometimes it seems an almost impossible assignment; sometimes it proves impossible to even get to know certain children during an entire year, much less to get them on their way toward meeting their needs. Sometimes it is like "pulling teeth" to motivate children to become involved in pupil-teacher planning and in the problem-solving processes; sometimes a teacher feels that he is "making progress backwards" when today a child's responses indicate that he has unlearned everything that yesterday he had been "taught" so well. Many times it is necessary for teachers to spend so much time and energy on the "5 per cent"—the children with misbehavior problems—that they feel the day has been wasted as far as doing any real teaching is concerned. Most of the time teachers end the school day with spent energy, and often with spent temperaments. And many times it is necessary for teachers to return to the school for pupil or parent activities in the evening.

But this is teaching! It would be unfair to prospective teachers if they were left with the opinion that teaching is a "bowl of cherries," that the job is soft and free from frustrations, that it is always carried out in a pleasant and tension-free environment between the hours of 9 A.M. and 2:30 P.M., with all noonhours and vacations free of any concern for the classroom and its population. Good teachers fairly live their work, day and night and during free times. They are always concerned when Stevie isn't grasping reading as he should, or that Mary has missed so many sessions of geometry class; they lie awake nights wondering what is happening in Bobby's home tonight that will make him withdrawn and sleepy in the classroom tomorrow; they awaken early in the morning wondering how they can make American history live for 35 boys and girls in class that day.

With persistence and consistent endeavor, however, teachers can expect to do an acceptable—in many cases, outstanding—job of guiding the learning of boys and girls in their classrooms. If the teacher maintains an alert and open mind, he will learn things from each class session that will prove helpful to him in all future classes. Soon he will find himself inspired when he sees children make progress, when he sees them learn because of something he has done or has caused to happen. In a short period of time, he will begin to see each class as the best he has ever had. He will then be well on his way toward becoming a successful practitioner.

CONCLUSION

In our changing society with its changing needs, it is becoming more evident by the day that nothing short of quality education is essential to the very survival of our free way of life. With greater emphasis on quality than on quantity in our education, attention in our schools is focused on individual differences, on challenging each child to achieve his fullest potential, on developing the creative abilities of youngsters, and on meeting the needs of our dynamic society. We are now concerned about teaching the child how to think rather than what to think, how to solve problems he will meet rather than to solve ready-made problems provided by a textbook author or a teacher.

Relentless and continuous experimentation has been and is being carried on with respect to how to organize the school and its methodology for the best learning results for the nation's youngsters. When we employ improper grouping and grading practices, we ignore the very laws of child growth and development. It is impossible to maintain a standardized educational product by any name known to man; the teacher must teach children with widely varying abilities, with an emphasis upon methodology that develops creativity and competent thinking on the part of America's boys and girls.

Questions for Discussion

1. What generalizations or conclusions can you draw regarding individual differences among and between children?
2. Why is homogenous grouping of children generally impractical and, in fact, impossible? Admittedly, grouping techniques in reading and mathematics, for example, are attempts toward achieving a higher degree of homogeneity; what happens, however, when children are taught in other subject areas where no attempt at ability grouping is made?
3. Which plan of providing for mentally superior children do you favor—enrichment, acceleration, or special classes? Justify your answer.
4. Can you think of any specific activities that might be used by a teacher in a classroom to develop children's potentialities?
5. What steps can a teacher take to avoid indoctrinating children with his social status standing—usually upper-middle class?
6. Do you agree that if our free democratic culture is to survive and prosper, it is necessary for teachers to teach children to think critically and reflectively? Why? How can a teacher teach these objectives?
7. How can a teacher be flexible in his grouping procedures within the classroom? How would grouping techniques used by a teacher at the high school level differ from those used by a teacher in a typical elementary school situation?
8. How and why do teaching-learning situations in America's classrooms vary with the social makeup of the school-communities?
9. Why do so many pupils lose interest in school and drop out after they pass the legal age limit? Where are schools failing in their responsibilities to pupils? What are some other agencies or forces besides the school that may be contributing to this situation?

Activities and Projects

1. Visit an elementary school fourth-grade or a seventh-grade in a junior high school and notice the differences in height, weight, and proportion between the children. Take notes, contrasting five children whose differences appear greatest, and report on these differences to your college class.
2. If permitted by school authorities, visit three high school teachers and, avoiding names of students, obtain the range of achievement in the three different subject areas taught by those teachers. Recommended subject teachers might be those in English, history, and typewriting. Note the differences—the range—in each class and report your findings to your class at college. Discuss with your classmates some possible approaches toward

meeting the needs of students in each of the three classes—particularly of those at the high and low ends of the achievement continuum.

3. Visit either an elementary or high school in your area, after making an appointment with the principal. Talk with the principal or a special education teacher about how that school provides for mentally talented and mentally and physically handicapped children. With other members of your college class who have pursued this same project, combine your findings, duplicate what seem to be the most promising techniques, and distribute them to the entire class.

4. Arrange for a debate between class members adept in the art of argumentation on the topic, "Resolved, that creativity can be taught in a junior high school classroom."

5. Prepare a unit lesson plan for any grade level in the area of the social sciences with which you plan to correlate the other subject areas in the curriculum. Which of the subjects do you find most difficult to correlate? Why do you suppose this is so?

6. Visit a school in which team teaching is carried on. Note the activities being undertaken, and write a paper comparing this method with typical procedures. In the "Conclusions" section of your paper, state the advantages and disadvantages which you see in teaching by the team approach.

7. Attend some school activity with a child or youth of your acquaintance, and watch his reactions to occurrences. Note how he relates to what he sees and, after the event, note the things he talks about most. Do you feel he might have reacted differently had he attended the activity with another youngster instead of an adult? Why?

8. If possible, visit in the home of a culturally disadvantaged child. Note how his home environment differs from the one in which you grew up, in such aspects as type of house and furniture, availability of reading materials, presence or absence of such media as radio and television, attitudes of parents toward cultural pursuits and the school, general physical and mental health of family members. Report on what you find to your college class.

References

"INDIVIDUAL DIFFERENCES"

CHANDLER, B. J., *Education and the Teacher* (New York: Dodd, Mead, 1961), pp. 211–20.

COMBS, ARTHUR W., "A Perceptual View of the Adequate Personality," in *Perceiving, Behaving, Becoming,* 1962 Yearbook (Washington, D.C.: Association for Supervision and Curriculum Development, NEA, 1962), Chapter 5.

CRESSMAN, GEORGE R., and HAROLD W. BENDA, *Public Education in America* (New York: Appleton-Century-Crofts, 1961), Chapter 12.

"Ethnic Groups in American Life," *Daedalus,* 90:220–349, Spring, 1961.

GRAMBS, JEAN D., and L. MORRIS MC CLURE, *Foundations of Teaching* (New York: Holt, Rinehart & Winston, 1964), Chapter 5.

HASKEW, LAURENCE D., and JONATHON C. MC LENDON, *This Is Teaching,* rev. ed. (Chicago: Scott, Foresman, 1962), Chapter 3.

HAVIGHURST, ROBERT J., PAUL H. BOWMAN, GORDON P. LIDDLE, CHARLES V. MATTHEWS, and JAMES V. PIERCE, *Growing Up in River City* (New York: Wiley, 1962).

HODGES, HAROLD M., "The Acquisition of Personality," in *Education and Society,* ed. WARREN W. KALLENBACH and HAROLD M. HODGES, JR. (Columbus, Ohio: Charles E. Merrill, 1963), pp. 123–42.

KELLEY, EARL C., *In Defense of Youth* (Englewood Cliffs, N.J.: Prentice-Hall, 1962).

LANE, HOWARD, and MARY BEAUCHAMP, *Understanding Human Development* (Englewood Cliffs, N.J.: Prentice-Hall, 1959).

LEE, J. MURRAY, and DORRIS M. LEE, *The Child and His Curriculum* (New York: Appleton-Century-Crofts, 1960).

MALLERY, DAVID, *High School Students Speak Out* (New York: Harper & Row, 1962).

RAGAN, WILLIAM B., *Modern Elementary Curriculum,* rev. ed. (New York: Holt, Rinehart & Winston, 1960), Chapter 2.

———, *Teaching America's Children* (New York: Holt, Rinehart & Winston, 1961), pp. 155–58.

RICHEY, ROBERT W., *Planning for Teaching,* 3d ed. (New York: McGraw-Hill, 1963), pp. 198–99, 205–6.

SHUSTER, ALBERT H., and MILTON E. PLOGHOFT, *The Emerging Elementary Curriculum* (Columbus, Ohio: Charles E. Merrill, 1963), Chapter 2.

STEPHENS, J. M., *Educational Psychology,* rev. ed. (New York: Holt, 1956), Chapters 4–7.

SWENSON, G. A., "Acceleration vs. Enrichment," National Association of Secondary School Principals *Bulletin,* 47:9–10, October, 1963.

TABA, HILDA, *Curriculum Development Theory and Practice* (New York: Harcourt, Brace & World, 1962), pp. 477–93.

''SPECIAL EDUCATION AND DISAFFECTED CHILDREN AND YOUTH''

CUTTS, NORMA E., *et al., Providing for Individual Differences in the Elementary School* (Englewood Cliffs, N.J.: Prentice-Hall, 1960).

DE HAAN, R. F., and R. J. HAVIGHURST, *Educating Gifted Children,* rev. ed. (Chicago: University of Chicago Press, 1962).

Educational Leadership, volume 20, February, 1963, entire issue.

FLIEGLER, LOUIS A., *Curriculum Planning for the Gifted* (Englewood Cliffs, N.J.: Prentice-Hall, 1961).

FRENCH, JOSEPH L., *Educating the Gifted* (New York: Holt, 1959).

GETZELS, JACOB W., and PHILIP W. JACKSON, *Creativity and Intelligence* (New York: Wiley, 1962).

HAVIGHURST, ROBERT J., and BERNICE L. NEUGARTEN, *Society and Education*, 2d ed. (Boston: Allyn & Bacon, 1962).

HYMES, JAMES L., JR., *Behavior and Misbehavior* (Englewood Cliffs, N.J.: Prentice-Hall, 1955).

INGRAM, CHRISTINE P., *Education of the Slow-learning Child*, 3d ed. (New York: Ronald, 1960).

KOUGH, JACK, *Practical Programs for the Gifted* (Chicago: Science Research Associates, 1960).

MAGARY, JAMES F., *The Exceptional Child* (New York: Holt, Rinehart & Winston, 1960).

MISNER, PAUL J., FREDERICK W. SCHNEIDER, and LOWELL G. KEITH, *Elementary School Administration* (Columbus, Ohio: Charles E. Merrill, 1963), Chapters 9, 10.

PASCHAL, ELIZABETH, *Encouraging the Excellent* (New York: Fund for the Advancement of Education, 1960).

Perceiving, Behaving, Becoming, 1962 Yearbook (Washington, D.C.: Association for Supervision and Curiculum Development, NEA, 1962).

RIESSMAN, FRANK, *The Culturally Deprived Child* (New York: Harper & Row, 1962).

ROTHSTEIN, J. H., *Mental Retardation: Readings and Resources* (New York: Holt, Rinehart & Winston, 1962).

SHANE, HAROLD G., and E. T. MCSWAIN, *Evaluation and the Elementary Curriculum* (New York: Holt, 1958), pp. 349–53.

STAHLECKER, LOTAR V., "School Work Programs for Slow Learners," *The Clearing House*, 38:296–98, January, 1964.

STRANG, RUTH, *Helping Your Gifted Child* (New York: Dutton, 1960).

SUMPTION, MERLE R., and EVELYN M. LUECKING, *Education of the Gifted* (New York: Ronald, 1960).

THURSTON, JOHN R., "Too Close to Normalcy," *The Clearing House*, 38:296–98, January, 1964.

The Gifted Student, Cooperative Monograph Number 2 (Washington, D.C.: U.S. Department of Health, Education and Welfare, 1960).

"CREATIVITY"

California Teachers Association Journal, volume 60, January, 1964, entire issue.

DERELL, G. R., "Creativity in Education," *The Clearing House*, 38:67–91, October, 1963.

DREWS, ELIZABETH MONROE, "Profile of Creativity," *NEA Journal*, 52:26–28, January, 1963.

FLEMING, ELYSE S., and S. WEINTRAUB, "Attitudinal Rigidity as a Measure of Creativity in Gifted Children," *Journal of Educational Psychology*, 53:81–85, July, 1962.

FRAZIER, ALEXANDER, ed., *New Insights and the Curriculum,* 1963 Yearbook (Washington, D.C.: Association for Supervision and Curriculum Development, NEA, 1963), Chapters 13, 14.

GETZELS, JACOB W., and PHILIP W. JACKSON, *Creativity and Intelligence* (New York: Wiley, 1962).

GUILFORD, J. P., and P. R. MERRIFIELD, *The Structure and Intellectual Model: Its Uses and Implications* (Los Angeles: University of Southern California, 1960).

HANNA, LAVONE A., *et al., Unit Teaching in the Elementary School,* rev. ed. (New York: Holt, Rinehart & Winston, 1963), Chapter 13.

RAGAN, *Teaching America's Children,* Chapter 10.

RUBIN, L. J., "Creativeness in the Classroom," *Education Digest,* 29:49–51, September, 1963.

RUGG, HAROLD, *Imagination: An Inquiry into the Sources and Conditions That Stimulate Creativity* (New York: Harper & Row, 1963).

TAYLOR, C. W., "The Creative Individual: A New Portrait of Giftedness," *Educational Leadership,* 18:7–12, October, 1960.

TORRANCE, E. PAUL, *Education and the Creative Potential* (Minneapolis: University of Minnesota Press, 1963).

———, *Guiding Creative Talent* (Englewood Cliffs, N.J.: Prentice-Hall, 1962).

WALLACE, H. R., "Creative Thinking: A Factor in Sales Productivity," *Vocational Guidance Quarterly,* Summer, 1961, pp. 223–26.

WEIR, EDWARD C., "Choice and Creativity in Teaching and Learning," *Phi Delta Kappan,* 43:408–10, June, 1962.

WEISBURG, P. S., and KAYLA J. SPRINGER, "Environmental Factors in Creative Function," *Archives in General Psychiatry,* 5:554–64, 1961.

WILLIAMS, FRANK E., "Fostering Creativity in the Classroom," *California Teachers Association Journal,* 58:19–20, February, 1962.

ZIRBES, LAURA, *Spurs to Creative Teaching* (New York: Putnam, 1959).

"GROUPING FOR INSTRUCTION"

BILLS, ROBERT E., "Learners or Learning," *School Life,* 45:10–12, June, 1963.

BROWN, EDWIN JOHN, and ARTHUR THOMAS PHELPS, *Managing the Classroom,* 2d ed. (New York: Ronald, 1961).

DRUMMOND, HAROLD, "Grouping: A Preliminary Statement," *School Life,* 45:9–10, June, 1963.

Educational Leadership, volume 21, December, 1963, entire issue.

FRANSETH, JANE, "Research in Grouping: A Review," *School Life,* 45:5–6, June, 1963.

FRAZIER, ALEXANDER, "Learning in Groups: Some Considerations," *School Life,* 45:7–9, June, 1963.

GRAMBS, pp. 111–13.

GRIEDER, CALVIN, TRUMAN M. PIERCE, and WILLIAM EVERETT ROSENSTENGEL, *Public School Administration,* 2d ed. (New York: Ronald, 1961).

HANNA, Part II.

KNELLER, GEORGE F., ed., *Foundations of Education* (New York: Wiley, 1963), pp. 497–99.

RICHEY, pp. 471–73.

THORNDIKE, ROBERT L., *The Concepts of Over- and Underachievement* (New York: Bureau of Publications, Teachers College, Columbia University, 1963).

European schools divide the children of one class from another; American schools unite the children of one class with the others.

the pupils —
class and caste

To what extent are Americans divisible into socioeconomic classes and of what importance is this to education? Similarly, does there also exist in America, to complicate the issue of social stratification, the matter of caste, i.e., the color of one's skin as a prejudicial factor of social status? And what does this mean for education? These two basic questions form the center about which the following discussion moves.

SOCIAL STRATIFICATION

If, as stated above, American schools unite the children of one class with the others, then how many classes are there and what distinguishes one from the other? The most influential studies of social stratification were made by a group of social anthropologists at Yale University who produced the first and the classic study, *Yankee City.* By interviewing people in a New England city of 17,000 population, and asking them to rank other people they knew as above them, equal to them, or below them, a team of investigators concluded that the phenomenon of social class did, in fact, exist in America and that the people of "Yankee City" could be fitted into six social classes, as shown in Figure 2.[1]

[1] "In studies of intimate social participation it has been found that distinctions of social-class position are always made upon a basis of possible social acceptance, as illustrated by the following quotations: 'They don't fit in with our bunch.' 'We don't know her family.' 'I never saw her socially in my life.' 'They are ordinary people like us.' 'You feel at home with them.' 'They are the big shots, the society folks.' 'I wouldn't let my children play with that woman's; they are ignorant, dirty people.'" From Allison Davis, *Social Class Influences upon Learning* (Cambridge, Mass.: Harvard University Press, 1948), p. 7.

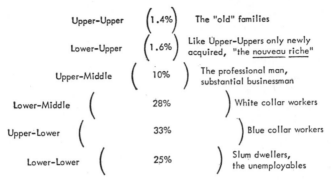

Figure 2. Social Classes in Yankee City. Based on data from Lloyd Warner and Paul Lunt, *The Social Life of a Modern Community* (New Haven: Yale University Press, 1941).

Through "Yankee City" and similar studies of other communities ("Elmtown," "Prairie City," "Jonesville," and "Old City"), the investigators have described the six classes in terms of their common and distinguishing characteristics, as follows:

The Upper-Upper Class. This is the élite group, the one to which all others aspire. It is characterized by aristocracy of birth, inherited wealth, gentility, good breeding. These are the families who are listed in the social register, whose children "go away to school," whose parents are the backbone of community social service projects. They live in fine old homes in geographically restricted areas of "Yankee City," "Elmtown," "Executive Heights," and "Yourtown."

The Lower-Upper Class. This group is made up of men of money who are on the move—captains of industry, successful entrepreneurs who are enjoying the benefits of wealth for the first time. Not until they have kept their money for three generations will they acquire the gentility which will make them acceptable to the upper-uppers. Again, generally the children "go away to school." However, many school board memberships and other civic leadership endeavors are a must for lower-uppers.

The Upper-Middle Class. This class is composed of moderately successful corporation executives, substantial businessmen, doctors, lawyers, and other professional men. The upper-middle class extols the virtues of sobriety, good work habits, economic advancement, and law enforcement. Upper-middle class men (and women) are active in civic affairs but rarely make the society page. They are hardworking, sober, upwardly mobile—the backbone of society, the bulwark of public education, the group from which most school board members and some teachers come.

The Lower-Middle Class. This is the group made up largely of the small businessman, the white-collar worker, and a few of the skilled tradesmen, but only those with the highest skills. It is a group characterized by conservatism, respectability, and similar virtues identified with the upper-middle class. It is the social class from which most of our teachers come. This is important because on how teachers view youngsters—on how willing or unwilling they are to accept those who come from the lower social classes—on this hinges the kind of education available to the youngsters who form the bulk of the young people we have to teach.

The Upper-Lower Class. Those in this group made up one-third of the population of "Yankee City." The upper-lower class is characterized by the honest workman, the clean poor people of the community. They are the semi-skilled workers, service workers, and small tradesmen.

The Lower-Lower Class. These are people who are referred to as the "poor white trash" of some communities, the "river rats" and "ne'er do wells" of other communities, the people who live on the "wrong side of the tracks," and in the ghettos and slums of our great cities. Middle classicists speak of these children as "the culturally deprived," the "culturally disadvantaged," for whom the middle-class-oriented school should provide "compensatory education." It is estimated that, by 1970, there may be one deprived child for every two enrolled in the schools of our large cities.[2]

AN INTERVIEW WITH SMITH BROWN OF JONESVILLE

"Since I made that crack about class to you the other day . . . I've done a lot of thinking about this class business. First thing, I want to say there's no use talking about people being in a certain class and in a certain portion of a class unless they are accepted by the people in that group as equals. If they are not accepted, they just don't belong. . . .

"The society class around here is the 400 class. In the main, it's rooted right over there in the Federated Church. It comes from the Federated Church. Now, Bill, a lot of these people are 398's, but they think they're 400's. With a few exceptions, no one who's not in the Federated Church is in this class. . . .

"The Volmers from top to bottom are in; the Friedricks from top to bottom are in; the Caldwells—all of them are in. Now, there's a case of two families getting together and keeping the money in the family. You know, Ted Caldwell married the Volmers girl. As far as I can figure out, that was pretty well arranged by the old folks. You know, here for years, the Caldwells and Volmers have been close business associates. They worked out a lot of deals together. . . .

"Now, here's an example of a big boost up, Mrs. A. B. Henderson. Now, Mrs. A. B. Henderson is in and her daughter's family is in. . . . I'm going to tell you some details on that just so you can get the picture. . . . Don't get the idea I am just gossiping for gossip's sake. I am giving you the facts so that you will be able to fit in the picture. Now, Mrs. A. B. Henderson was clerk in a store here in town before her marriage. She married A. B. Henderson. The Hendersons were in around here, and they have been in [the 400] for a long time. . . . Oh, yes, she was a Stillwell. She has

[2] Frank Riessman, *The Culturally Deprived Child* (New York: Harper, 1962), p. 1.

some sisters around here and some brothers who were down there, and they stayed there. They have never done anything.

"Some of the Stocktons do and some of them don't [belong to the upper class]. You've always got to make a division in the Stocktons. . . . Here are the Stocktons who don't. . . . Mrs. Helen Cross, she doesn't. Now, she is Carl Stockton's sister, but she's not in. Now, there's the case of a girl who married down and stayed there. . . .

"I think that's just about all the society class. There may be one or two that I have overlooked, but that's all I can think of.

"The next class down is what we call the fringe of society around here. . . . The fringe of this thing has a lot of families on it who have had money and lost it.

"The Robert Claytons were former members of the 400, but they failed in business and he was dropped. Oh, hell, he got to owing everybody around town, and he just wasn't worth a damn, and they just got left out of things. Mrs. Tom Cooper and her sister, Mrs. Henry Gardner, are on the fringe, too. Mrs. Gardner is a nice person, but she had a cousin, Everett Roberts. He never was in. He was just a no-good-so-and-so. . . . They both inherited a lot of money. Hell, they both just ran through it. Just phlooey. Just threw it away. . . . Everett was no good from the beginning. . . . He was just never accepted. Just as I told you, the whole thing is based on money, but it isn't money alone. You've got to have the right family connections, and you've got to behave yourself, or you get popped out.

"Now, the Halls are another family who were never in. They never did move in that set, but they had a hell of a lot of money at one time. Old man Hall was never liked around here. I don't know just what it was, but he was just excluded. Oh, if they had big parties or something, they might invite him; but they were never accepted by the society class."

"Then, there was the Adams family. . . . Arthur was the black sheep of the Adams family. He was just a wastrel; he never amounted to anything. . . . Now, Henry was a nice fellow, but he was tighter than hell. He was too niggardly and pinch-penny to be in. He could have been in the fringe, but he just didn't spend on anything.

"The next stratum starts with the fringe and takes in certain other elements. This is what you'd better call the upper-middle class. This level is made up mainly of the women who dominate the Country Club, along with some other groups, especially the top and the fringe. The top dominates the Country Club; at least they are in, but they're not active. They're the ones who, you might say, are behind the scenes and really control things. The fringe is pretty active, and this group of women are active, too. The women in this group just seem to split a gut to do things right. It's amusing as hell. We used to belong to the Country Club, but we don't any more. This Country Club is, of course, quite cosmopolitan. It's got a lot of people in it and diverse elements. Anybody who thinks he can afford to get in and play golf, and so on. But it's this bunch of women who really dominate the club and keep the activities going, although I'm pretty damned sure they don't have as much say-so in it as they think they do. . . .

"Now, here is another group that's all about at this same level, and my wife and I are in this group some of the time. It's not in a different class from the others. Now, we don't have any money, and our being included in these groups is due wholly to my professional position and the fact that my wife and I belong to several good organizations. Hell, if it weren't for them we wouldn't be in anything. . . .

"Now, we come to the working class. The working class is made up of good, solid people who live right but they never get any place. They never get in real trouble. They are the ones who work down at The Mill and the other factories. They are the ones who work around as clerks in the stores, own little trucks and maybe little businesses. . . . These neighborhood grocers, and so on. . . .

"Well, while they're fixing supper for us I just want to mention one more class. Now, this one is really a lulu. These are the families that are just not worth a goddam. Now, they're not immoral—they're not unmoral—they're just plain amoral. They just simply don't have any morals. I'll tell you they just have animal urges, and they just respond to them. They're just like a bunch of rats or rabbits.

"There's the Jones family. My God, that Jones outfit! . . . All their kids . . . are tougher than hell. They never went any place in school, and they're always getting into jams. Another family that's in the making is that Kraig family. Those poor little kids are half-frozen and ragged all the time, and they come along one after the other. I've seen them go to the store with a nickel or a penny to buy some candy and that type of thing. Every morning they come down to the store and buy five or ten cents' worth of sweet rolls for breakfast.

"Now, another family that's in the same class is the Rain family. They're Kentuckians and, I'll tell you, they're really something. Then, there's the Jackson family that live down south of The River. Well, they're lulus, too. Then, there's that John Harding bunch that live in back of the tannery. Old John Harding and his family have been in more trouble around here than you can really think about. Then, there's the Kilgore family. Old Tom's got four or five girls. They've got into trouble. Some of them are about half-witted, and Harry himself is not any too bright. They aren't worth a damn."*

* Note that Smith Brown was only able to identify five social classes in the middle western city of Jonesville.

W. Lloyd Warner, Marchia Meeker, Kenneth Eells, *Social Class in America,* Harper Torchbooks, Harper and Row, New York, 1960.

Who Teaches Whom? Public school teachers seldom will have upper-upper children as pupils, and seldom either do lower-upper children go to public school except possibly in elementary school. Usually by the seventh grade the two upper classes send their children to prep schools from which they go on to private colleges and universities to complete their education. In exclusive suburbia some youngsters from the upper classes attend public schools, but the chances are that most new teachers will begin their careers in schools with children from the upper-lower and lower-lower social classes because these classes are the two largest in the general population, and they have more children per family than do the middle classes. These are the youngsters that middle-class teachers generally do not understand and are not sympathetic with because they are so different from the kind of children the teachers themselves once were.

The teaching of lower-class youngsters is one of the great problems and challenges of teaching. During the next decade, the matter of coping effectively with lower-class children is one of the great educational tasks facing the nation—if not the greatest one. Every day, in the press, at the supermarket, on television, what one reads and hears is the uproar resulting from the inability of the school and its middle-class teachers to cope successfully with the problems of educating lower-class pupils. For example, much is heard and written about the high school drop-out. Who is the drop-out? He has been described in various ways, but one element all descriptions have in common is that the drop-out is from the lower social classes.

Social Class Determinants

What determines which social class a person falls in? One basic determinant is occupation and income. Specifically, what kind of work does the father do? The unskilled worker is at the bottom of the stratification ladder because he works primarily with his hands: the more theoretical and "clean" the work, the higher one's socioeconomic status. Occupation ratings, as developed by Warner, are shown in Figure 3. Besides occupation, particularly the father's, other sources of income count heavily.

Many of the determinants of social class are the "badges" that identify one's class:

Father's occupation

Source of income

Area of town in which residence is located

Type of dwelling

Affiliations, i.e., the social groups and organizations to which you belong (your clubs and church) and the people you associate with (your friends and social acquaintances).

Another basic determinant of social class is amount of education. Because amount of education is so important in today's scientific and technological world and because it is such a forceful determinant of social class, the concept of equality of educational opportunity becomes the cornerstone of American free public education. An A.B. degree once was considered sufficient for a person to go out and succeed in the workaday world. Today it is in the same category as a high school diploma was 30 or 40 years ago. Today a person gets an A.B. degree and then immediately wants to go on to a Master's or a higher degree or for some kind of professional degree before he feels he is ready for work. This is all because of the importance of education in determining one's job, "life-style," and status in society.

Rating Assigned to Occupation	Professionals 1	Proprietors and Managers 2	Businessmen 3	Clerks and Kindred Workers 4	Manual Workers 5	Protective & Service Workers 6	Farmers 7
1	Lawyers, doctors	Of very large businesses	Regional & divisional managers of large enterprises	Certified public accountants			Gentlemen farmers
2	High school teachers, graduate librarians, undertakers		Ass't managers, office and dept. managers of large businesses	Accountants, postmasters			Large farm owners, farm owners
3	Social workers, grade school teachers, librarians (not graduate)	Of moderate-sized businesses	All minor officials of businesses	Bank clerks, secretaries to executives	Contractors		
4			Stenographers, sales people in dry goods stores		Factory foremen, plumbers (own business)	Dry cleaners, railroad conductors	
5			Dime store clerks, telephone operators		Carpenters, medium-skilled workers	Barbers, cooks, bartenders	Tenant farmers
6		Of very small businesses			Ass'ts to carpenter, semi-skilled workers	Baggagemen, gas station attendants	Small tenant farmers
7					Heavy labor, odd-jobs men	Janitors	Migrant farm laborers

Figure 3. Warner's Scale for Rating Occupations. Abridged and simplified from the scale found in W. Lloyd Warner *et al.*, *Social Class in America* (Chicago: Science Research Associates, 1949), pp. 140–41.

As long ago as 1927, the sociologist Pitrim Sorokin described the crucial role of education this way:

In present Western societies, the schools represent one of the most important channels of vertical circulation. This is manifested in hundreds of forms. Without university or college graduation, an individual can not factually (in some European countries even juridically) be appointed or obtain any prominent place among the high ranks of government or of many other fields; and contrawise, a graduate with a brilliant university record is easily promoted and given a responsible position, regardless of his origin and family. Many fields of social activity (especially professions) are practically closed to a man who does not have a corresponding diploma; a graduate is often paid better than a non-graduate at the same position. . . . This "channel role" of the present schools has now become much greater than before because the present schools have taken many functions previously performed by the Church and family and some other organizations.

Sorokin refers to the school system as a "social elevator whose effectiveness depends somewhat on the extent to which education is available to all classes in society." The school also represents, in his view, a "testing, selecting, and distributing agency. . . . a very complicated 'sieve,' which sifts 'the good' from 'the bad' future citizens, 'the able' from 'the dull,' 'those fittest for high positions' and those 'unfitted.' " [3]

Vertical Mobility

In contrast to many other countries which have a "closed" social class system, the American system is "open." Thus, it is possible for a person to move from one social class to another in America by way of vertical mobility. The chief social elevators are schooling (i.e., brightness), talent, beauty, marriage, luck. These elevators can bring a person from the bottom to the top of the social ladder, except for the upper-upper class. As mentioned earlier, only time makes it possible to move from lower-upper to upper-upper—usually three generations.

Because American schools are supposedly free and open to all, a person from the lower-lower class can, through getting an education for himself, move from one social class to another. Thus, schooling is one important element in vertical mobility. Similarly, a boy endowed with special talent may rise rapidly. For example, Jackie Robinson and Willie Mays happened to have a great talent for professional baseball and this enabled them to move quickly up the social ladder.

Let's take the girl who happens to be beautiful. She may come from a lower-class family and live on the wrong side of the tracks, but once she is crowned Miss America at Atlantic City she is on her way up to the middle classes and perhaps beyond.

Marriage also is a way up and out for both boys and girls, as typified by parents who want to see that their children "marry well," by which they mean to an equal or better—that is, higher—social class. Several years ago the newspapers were headlining the marriage of one of the Rockefellers to the family's Swedish maid. By the fact of her marriage vows, she moved into a higher social class.

[3] Pitrim A. Sorokin, *Social Mobility* (New York: Harper, 1927), pp. 170–71.

There always is the possibility that sheer luck will supply the push up. Being in the right place at the right time, having a winning ticket on the sweepstakes, hitting the jackpot at Reno, making a "killing" on the stock market—all these can change one's life-style.

Implications for Education

"The American public school is a curious hybrid: it is managed by a school board drawn largely from upper-class circles; it is taught by teachers who come largely from middle class backgrounds; and it is attended mainly by children from working class homes." [4] Thus, the overriding educational issue is "reconciling the unreconcilables"—that is, the value systems of school boards, teachers, and students.

Specifically then, these four implications for teachers emerge from the existence of social class patterns in most American communities:

1. The upper classes set the policies for the management of public schools and employ the superintendent as the executive officer to carry out their policies. On the other hand, they do not use the schools. Thus, they are generally parsimonious about voting new taxes or bonds for school support, because they send their children to private schools.

2. The middle classes supply the values to be inculcated and sustained, and the curriculum to be studied; they write the textbooks to be mastered, and they establish and administer the system of rewards and punishments for student conformity and adherence.

3. The lower classes furnish the children, who are reared within their parents' value system; to these children the teachers' values are artificial, the curriculum unrealistic, the textbooks nonunderstandable, the system of rewards distasteful. Lower classes tend to defy teachers as authority figures and to balk at the schools, yet they are the group which has the most to gain from the schools.

Millions of disadvantaged Americans are congregated today in congested sections of the large cities and in the rural areas. It is valid to ask what America means to these millions of people. Certainly it has not been for them a land of equal opportunity. The schools present the best hope for overcoming their cultural handicap. This has been demonstrated repeatedly wherever the efforts of skillful educators and the support of an understanding community have combined to make schools the mighty instruments which only schools can be. If the public fully backs its schools—and only if it does—the time may come when no American is culturally disadvantaged.[5]

4. The school is a microcosm of the larger society; the groups, the cliques, the friendship patterns, the gangs, the homogeneous groupings of students for

[4] Goodwin Watson in Riessman, *op. cit.,* p. x.
[5] Educational Policies Commission, *Education and the Disadvantaged American* (Washington, D.C.: National Education Association, April, 1962), p. 25.

instruction—all these realities in every school are miniature social classes. A good example is "The Parking-lot Crowd," immediately below.

THE PARKING-LOT CROWD

About one-fourth of the four hundred juniors and seniors [at Hill High School] belong to the Parking-lot set. It is the only group readily recognized by everyone due to their dress, haircuts, and indifferent attitudes toward school. Also, it is the only school group that initiates its members. About the tenth or eleventh grade a "promising" student is watched. If one of the Parking-lot members gets to know and to like him, he is brought in. As long as he is okayed by one, he is accepted by all. The Parking-lot girls feel the social differences within the school more keenly than the boys, and this awareness of the girls is true in all groups.

The teenagers who make up the Parking-lot crowd are stereotyped by other students as nonconformists who are contemptuous of authority and consider themselves too adult to engage in high school activities. They are rightly regarded as unkempt: the boys looking sloppy in clothes they seem to have slept in, with long greasy mops of hair, and the "taps on their shoes that make them sound like horses" because of their shuffling walk; the girls looking cheap in tight sweaters and short skirts and the stacked Brigitte Bardot hairdoes. To the other groups the label of "Parking-lot member" is definitely uncomplimentary and undesirable because of this image. However, all agree that Parking-lot members when considered individually rather than en masse are cooperative and genial.

It is in the Parking-lot crowd that you find the students least interested in textbooks, unwilling to work for good grades. They are contemptuous of teachers who assign heavy homework. Many of the boys would like to drop out of school but are forced by their parents to stay and work enough in shop courses to earn a diploma. The girls, however, know the value of a high school diploma in holding jobs and earning promotions and so work just hard enough in their business courses to graduate.

The poorest students are found in this group. In the main, their lack of interest in studying is the result of family influence. Their parents would like to see their children further their schooling, but do not expect it or cannot afford it. Also, parents are anxious to have another member of the family earning his own way. The teenagers themselves want a paycheck in order to be on their own, buy cars, and marry.

Members say that they get together just to smoke. Smoking publicly is one way of attracting attention since they take no part in and therefore receive no recognition in school activities. Another bid for attention is in their constant use of bad grammar, swearing, and profanity. Gang fights express their rebellion against the role of students. These are started by the girls, resenting some catty or jealous remark, with their boy friends and pals joining in headlong. Occasionally switchblades appear and mob feeling takes over. At such times only the police can quiet them.

Nearly every member also drinks occasionally, and parents try only to limit consumption. Some boast that they can get drunk without parental punishment. However, this is the exception to the rule, as most of the parents disapprove of excess drinking. The reaction of one mother was typical: "I'll slap you down if you ever come home drunk!"

The members of the Parking-lot have lots of free time, for they do little homework and do not participate in school sports or clubs. They associate only with their immediate friends, and most of their dates and steadies come either from within the ninth and tenth grades or from outside the school and city. The girls prefer older boys with jobs; three have steadies in the military service whom they plan to marry. Dating usually means going to the movies or private parties or just driving around; very rarely does it mean attending a school dance and never, any athletic event.

The girls are characterized by heavy make-up that includes elaborate eyeshadow. They wear their hair long, and, while some copy Brigitte Bardot's beehive, many prefer well brushed and neatly kept ponytails or fashionable bouffants. Clothes verge on the daring with low necklines on blouses and dresses, sweaters a size too small, and short tight skirts. Although tennis shoes are now the fashion, girls in the Parking-lot insist on wearing "flats," hard-soled ballerina slippers. The boys like the fancy "duck-tail" and "Elvis Presley pompadour" haircuts. Leather jackets and heavy boots are also favorites.

Members of the Parking-lot crowd know that they are looked down upon by most of the students and faculty, but blame a small group within theirs for "making a spectacle" of themselves and for giving them all a bad name. They feel that they are as good as the rest of the school except for the troublemakers in their own group on whom they also look down. However, should anyone of their set get into a quarrel or fight, the rest do not hesitate to join in and help their friends. On the whole, they are willing to abide by school rules with the exception of the two that prohibit smoking on school property and taking cars out of the lot at noon. Some resent Traffic Control members because they don't like to take orders from other students and feel they are too free with their citations. On the other hand, they all resent Student Court, feeling that students should not be allowed to punish others and believing that the court is easier on the good students but ready to "throw the book" at any of their crowd.

Excerpt from "The Social Structure of Hill High School," unpublished paper, author unknown.

CLASS AND CASTE

Up to now, we have been discussing socioeconomic status and its implications for education. When you add to the problem of social class the problem of color-caste—i.e., race—the social and educational implications become explosive. In some eastern cities, it is the bronze-skinned Puerto Ricans; in some western communities, it is the amber-skinned Oriental or Mexican. But by far the most numerous, the most ubiquitous, and most explosive is the Negro. Because of indigenous and historical factors, this group more than any other continues to be found in the lower social classes and to remain there from one generation to another, whereas many other racial groups that once were on the bottom of the socioeconomic totem pole have moved up from there. This then leads us to the problem of what the school can do and ought to be doing about lower-class youngsters who have the additional stigma of dark skins.

Vice President Hubert H. Humphrey, a leader in the nation's efforts to obtain equality for those economically disenfranchised, has said:

The civil rights movement of the 1950's and 1960's is sometimes referred to as the Second American Revolution. Perhaps more accurately, it may be seen as a major phase in the continuing revolution upon which the American people embarked in 1776. In the abolition of slavery in the 1860's, in the women's suffrage movement of the late nineteenth and early twentieth centuries, and in the great struggle for the right of workers to organize for free collective bargaining that reached a climax in the 1930's, America continued its successive assaults on the citadels of inequality and injustice. The campaign for equal justice and opportunity for minority groups—particularly the Negro—marks the latest battle in the long struggle of this nation toward a genuine, working democracy.

To some Americans, the key to solving the many and vexing problems of the Negro and other caste groups is by means of equal employment opportunities and better housing. To others, like Humphrey, the key lies in equal educational opportunity.

Without educational equality there can be neither equal opportunity in employment nor real equality at the ballot box. To the man lacking the . . . training to qualify for most jobs, "fair" employment practices can be hollow benefits indeed. And the right to vote is scarcely a full achievement . . . for those not educated to understand the importance of the ballot. In establishing equal educational opportunity, the desegregation and integration of our schools are major and indispensable steps.[6]

The fate of our nation, industrially, politically, and in case of war depends primarily on the ability of the public schools to help large numbers of children from slum and farm-tenant groups to learn the basic skills of our society.

Allison Davis, *Social Class Influences upon Learning* (Cambridge, Mass.: Harvard University Press, 1948), p. 23.

While many educators continue to shout "No" to George Counts' challenge of a generation ago, *Dare the Schools Build a New Social Order?*, there is a growing group who believe that teachers are in the best position to see the effects of unequal educational opportunities for caste groups and, thus, because of their professional training and commitment, best equipped to take the lead in saying and *demonstrating* what must be done.

[6] Hubert H. Humphrey, ed., *School Desegregation: Documents and Commentaries* (New York: Thomas Y. Crowell, 1964), p. 1.

What Must Be Done

All authorities agree that the color-caste groups, suffering as they do from social and economic deprivation, are not "ready" for school. In particular, they have not had the experiences which bring them up to the point of their Caucasian contemporaries when it comes to learning to read, write, and calculate. Various kinds of compensatory and remedial teaching and enriching out-of-school experiences are needed. The earlier these start, the better. In some schools, this means special preschool reading readiness classes; in all it means smaller classes, teachers trained in remedial skills, and the assistance of a corps of specialized personnel such as psychologists, nurses, social workers, doctors. All these things cost money, far more than many schools now have or can afford.

In general, the schools in the depressed areas attended by Negroes, North and South, lack the physical facilities they should have. The buildings are old, dirty, and run-down. Experienced teachers who have caused problems in other assignments often are dumped into these schools as "courts of last resort." At best their teaching can be described as a holding action. Beginning teachers, the other main source of supply for slum schools, often are overwhelmed by the challenge and quit from discouragement or request transfer to an all-white school.

So much for *what* to do. Now let's consider how to do it.

How It Should Be Done

The only way out of the impasse in the caste schools of the South and the slum and ghetto schools of our great cities in the North and on the West Coast is to improve the schools radically and quickly by retooling the educational program—both *what* is to be taught and *how*—through providing additional and better trained staffs and improved physical facilities. *This is easier said than done.*

A significant aspect of the "how to do it" problem is involved in what psychologists call *self-image*. Many Negro children come to school with (or soon develop from their initial experiences in school) an evil self-image because of middle-class-instigated frustration—from deprivation and persecution—and rebellion. Without a good self-image, the Negro says, "I don't care" and "I do something about it." The color-caste child's "D-P" (deprived and persecuted) image can be measured by a Richter scale in terms of the (1) distance from the Dick and Jane image, (2) amount of economic deprivation, (3) recency of immigration, (4) degree of prejudice against his particular race, and (5) extent to which there is no male status figure in the family.

The hostile middle-class culture represented by the school provides few benefits and incentives for the Negro. Because it condemns him to an unending succession of failures, he leaves school at the first opportunity. A successful school program must attack this problem on three fronts simultaneously: it will show that the school situation is very similar to what the life situation is and will be, and that by living in the school situation, the child is preparing for the life situation; it will include the remedial services necessary for academic progress; and it will arouse aspirations which can alter constructively the courses of young lives.[7]

Some states and some school districts provide extra funds for "compensatory education." Some schools are using foundation monies from Ford and Carnegie to experiment with various ways to resolve the basic school problems; for example, in New York City there is the Higher Horizons Program, and in Oakland, California, the Community Inter-Agency Project.

Some school districts are attempting to resolve the problem by changing "the mix" in schools. Civil rights groups charge that depressed city schools are practicing de facto segregation. Achieving racial balance in such schools is accomplished by bussing students from another area or by changing school attendance boundaries so that whites and Negroes in equal numbers attend the same school, thus eliminating the traditional "neighborhood school." Others have "open" schools—to be attended by anyone regardless of where he lives. Some provide a mix of white-Negro teachers in the same proportion as the students.

The underlying assumption in such school integration efforts is that enough "good" will occur in relations and understandings which are developed between the two groups to overcome the "bad" effects. By "bad" effects are meant the holding back of white middle-class students while the Negroes catch up.

There is increasing evidence, however, that the integrated education drive and its concomitant—concern for the education of the urban disadvantaged child—is actually powering educational benefits for *all* children, not only Negro children. For example, the great hue and cry that arose regarding the "segregated" white-face, white-theme "Dick and Jane" readers led to the development of a variety of new "urban" readers that appear not only to improve the reading ability of the Negro children but lead also to the improvement of the white children's reading. . . .

It is extremely important that there be a carefully planned approach for the period in which the Negro youngster, moving from a segregated school to a desegregated one, catches up:

1. Most of the catching up should be done in intensive after-school programs—afternoons, week ends, summers, vacations can all be utilized. Homework helpers, tutors, teaching machines, educational TV, specially trained teachers . . . should be utilized. The assumption should be made that these students are ignorant and uninformed rather than unintelligent, nonverbal, lacking in motivation. . . .

2. Any catching up within school hours must guard zealously against the possibility that supposedly temporary homogeneous grouping does not develop into intraschool *de facto* segregation. . . . The Negro children must contantly be moving out of the "lowest" ranks into the mainstream. . . . The more ad-

[7] Educational Policies Commission, *op. cit.*, p. 39.

vanced pupils can be encouraged to assist the less advanced ones (actually, teaching others is a splendid learning device, so the advanced youngster should benefit considerably)....

3. Teaching techniques (such as role playing, the use of games, films, and programmed learning) strongly suited to low-income urban youngsters will also revolutionize the rather dull school curriculum. . . .[8]

Those closest to the situation are aware, however, that merely changing the mix will not solve the problem—a problem which in both the North and South has been generations in the making. It is a long, hard, often cruel road from *mere presence* to *full acceptance*. To achieve the latter requires a new social milieu—in both the school and the larger community.

Obviously, there is no sure or generally accepted answer on "how it should be done." The present unresolved situation is neatly summarized by Hubert Humphrey when he says:

The fact is that today, so long after the [Supreme] Court's ruling, only a lamentably small proportion of our minority-group children find any marked improvement in their opportunities for educational equality. Most of the victories, for most Negroes, have been moral victories. Though such gains may lift the spirit, they cannot be considered adequate progress toward providing the equal educational and economic opportunity, and the equality in political life of our communities, that must remain our goal.[9]

A WEEK WITH WILLIAM

William is a ninth-grade colored boy, aged fifteen and a half years, and with an intelligence quotient of 96. He is a big, mature, handsome boy. He has nine brothers and sisters, eight of them younger than himself. The exception is Tom, one year older, who works. His father has not lived with the family for about three years. He resides with another woman, so William says. The family all live in three rooms. They are supported by relief. William's clothes are always well-pressed and he is always neat and clean, facts which belie his home environment. He does odd jobs, for spending money and clothes. He plans to go to work to help support the family when he finishes the ninth grade. He is probably representative of the poorest [Cincinnati] community pattern in the school population.

A.M.	TYPICAL WEEKDAY
8:00- 8:30	Got up, washed, pressed pants, dressed.
8:30- 9:00	Stopped in at the bakery and bought some cup cakes and ate them on the way to school.
9:00-12:00	In school.
P.M.	
12:00-12:30	Did not eat lunch. Played volleyball on the playroof.

[8] Address by Frank Riessman of the Columbia University department of psychiatry at a Michigan State University symposium on school integration as quoted in *The National Observer*, July 13, 1964, p. 13.

[9] Humphrey, *op. cit.*, pp. 2–3.

12:30- 3:30	In school.
3:30- 4:30	Walked his girl home. Talked and "made love."
4:30- 5:00	Went home, split wood, brought up coal, ate.
5:00- 6:00	Listened to the radio program, "Jam for Supper."
6:00- 6:30	Read a funny book.
6:30- 7:00	Played cards.
7:00- 7:30	Ate supper and helped with the dishes.
7:30- 8:00	Went to the "hang-out" where his gang loafs.
8:00-10:30	Went with the gang over to the home of one of the girls. Played cards, listened to the victrola and the radio, danced, played kissing games, "necked."
10:30-11:00	Bummed around the street corner.
11:00-11:30	Hung around the "hang-out" and finally went home.
11:30- 8:00 A.M.	Asleep

A.M.	SATURDAY
9:00- 9:30	Got up, washed, dressed, ate breakfast, made his own bed.
9:30-11:30	Scrubbed floors, swept and dusted.
11:30-12:00	Ate lunch and got dressed to go out.
P.M.	
12:00- 4:00	Went to the show by himself.
4:00- 4:30	Went home and listened to the radio.
4:30- 5:00	Read a funny book and the funny paper.
5:00- 5:30	Ate supper.
5:30- 6:00	Took a nap.
6:00- 7:00	Went over to his boy friend's, shot crap and played cards.
7:00- 7:30	Read a funny book.
7:30- 8:00	Went over to his girl's house, listened to victrola records, and danced.
8:00-11:00	Went to the "hang-out" where his gang meets, talked, danced, ate, listened to the radio, played pin-ball machines, and the like.
11:00-12:00	Took his girl home, played cards, "necked."
A.M.	
12:00- 1:30	Left girl's house and just walked around for about an hour to see what was going on. Talked on the corner until the "cops" came along. Went home and went to bed.
1:30-11:00	Asleep.

A.M.	SUNDAY
11:00-11:30	Got up, washed, dressed, ate breakfast.
11:30-12:00	Read a funny book.
P.M.	
12:00- 4:30	Went to the show by himself and met his girl inside.
4:30- 5:00	Walked his girl home, "made love" to her.
5:00- 5:30	Went home and ate.
5:30- 6:00	Went over to the "hang-out." Hung around playing cards.
6:00- 7:30	Went back to his girl's house with his crowd. Danced, played records and kissing games.
7:30-11:30	Worked as a pin-boy at the bowling alley.

11:30-12:30   Loafed around on the street with the fellows and went home
     and to bed.
A.M.
12:30- 8:30   Asleep

Commentary on William's Activities. The great bulk of William's leisure time is consumed in activities involving girls, such as dancing, "necking," "dating," kissing games, and various sex activities, and activities of the loafing kind, which are predominant, such as walking around, "bumming" and sitting around at the "hang-out." He listens to the radio, especially "jazz" music, and often uses the victrola for supplying dancing music. Like the other boys interviewed, he reads comic books and little else. He goes to the movies three times a week, on an average. Physical activities are conspicuous by their absence. . . .

. . . His daily leisure activities are almost routine in their regularity.
William keeps late hours, and seems to be "on his own" so far as home supervision is concerned. . . .

. . . . .

In general, the picture presented [by studies of William and his peers] is of young adolescent boys living in an environment extraordinarily bare of opportunities . . . and the inability of home, school, and community to do anything about it. . . .

James C. Stone, "The Leisure-time Activities of Junior High School Boys in a Basin Area of Cincinnati," unpublished Master's thesis, University of Cincinnati, 1943, pp. 123–26.

CONCLUSION

Social class is a fact of American life; the classes differ in many ways about many things, including schools and schooling, yet all are required to pay taxes to support essentially middle-class schools and most send their children to them. For the schools, the greatest unmet and unfaced challenge is presented by the lower-class student. While much is made of the problem of the Negro in the lowest socioeconomic class, *it is important to remember that the lower classes show no partiality—all races, nationalities, religions are found there—because economic deprivation, the basic cause of low-class status, is color-blind.*

There are many reasons why the school has left unsolved year after year the problem of adequately educating the slum child and his farm-tenant "country cousin." Some of the most relevant ones discussed in this chapter include the following:

Number. Lower-class children are the *most* numerous, their parents the *least* vocal; the upper classes with the fewest children are the most vociferous.

Cost. The old inadequate buildings in the depressed parts of town are already there; it would be a double expense to tear them down and build new ones in their place; remedial instruction means smaller classes, expensive instruction; books and teaching materials are written and directed toward the middle and upper classes.

Teachers. Their middle-class attitude on such basic questions as morality, sex, eating, fighting, swearing, motivation, reading, schooling, etc., is as different from that of lower-class pupils as day from night. To the teacher, lower-class culture is immoral, "dirty"; hence its pupils are rejected. By contrast, the values of the lower classes should be considered amoral and the teaching of such youth a great opportunity with only one direction in which to go—*Up.*

The school's job is of the utmost importance and teachers with the commitment to teach the "4D" children—the deprived, depressed, depraved, disadvantaged—are difficult to recruit and train and are doomed to rendering a most significant social service without the glamour of the Peace Corps. Yet their job may be infinitely more important.

What dedicated and understanding teachers *can* accomplish is beautifully and fittingly told by Billie Davis immediately below.

The Hobo Kid—Billie Davis

. . . When I was a small ragged hobo, sitting on the ground beside a campfire, hungrily licking the fishy oil from the lid of a sardine can as I studied my history lesson, I was beginning to understand the relationship between public education and personal liberty. I want to tell the American people something about our schools . . . something they must have forgotten. Or it may be that some have never recognized that which I consider to be the greatest value of our system. I want to make certain that they recognize it now, and I can show them plainly by telling them my story.

. . . Every school held for me a mystical secret beauty. Every school was my personal friend. It wanted me. There were laws that said so. It wanted to make me smart and pretty and smooth, like the people who lived in houses. And in each town I strolled serenely up the walk to the school building, almost forgetting that I was a camper. I found a teacher and said again, as I had on that first day, "I would like to go to school here, please."

Without exception, I was greeted with kindness. Of course there were some startled exclamations, some smiles and some slightly irritated mutters. . . . All this talk of poorly trained, underpaid teachers, striving for the privilege of becoming mechanical robots enslaved by some insensitive assembly line for a good union wage per hour, cannot drive from my mind the memory of the teachers who have shaped my life. There was Miss Williams, kind and motherly, who let me stay in at recess and water her plants. She had found me hiding in the fire escape. It was a big round pipe on the outside of the building, through which pupils could slide to the ground in case of fire. I could crawl up inside at recess to hide, so the children on the playground could not tease me. Miss Williams saw me through her window and let me climb in over the window sill as though we were playing a game. She did not scold, but rather laughed with me about it. She did not ask a question, but always after that, she had some work for me to do at recess. I understood her motive, and yet it did not crush my spirit to accept her favor. I felt that she knew. I understood and we shared a plot together. The whole situation was simply a temporary inconvenience which a camper kid had to put up with until she could get enough schooling to catch up with the people who lived in houses. . . .

. . . [On the evening of graduation from high school] I looked at the row of solemn teachers and wondered if they realized the potential power of their influence to shape a life, to change a destiny, to free a world. I wish that I could help them to recognize their power and encourage them to use it with wisdom and purpose. I longed to express my appreciation and pay them some appropriate tribute. I looked down at the notes of my speech: "What East High Has Meant to Me." Childish. Inadequate. Someday I would write a real tribute to the teachers and to the public schools of the United States of America.

Many times since that night I have remembered the vow. I have picked up a pen or sat at the typewriter and tried to think of a fitting tribute. But proper words have never come. There is so little that I can say concretely. Except I am not a Hobo Kid now. I am a citizen, clean and smooth, equal to other citizens. And I live in a house.

> Billie Davis, "I Was a Hobo Kid," *The Saturday Evening Post,* December 13, 1952, pp. 25, 107–8. The daughter of an itinerant farm worker who made furniture from willows as he followed the crop-pickers up and down the San Joaquin Valley in the 19—'s, today Miss Davis is a well-known writer and lecturer.

Questions for Discussion

1. If we could recruit teachers from the lower rather than the middle classes, would this solve the problem of providing understanding teachers for slum children? How might the recruitment be done?

2. If our schools are free but actually unequal in the opportunities they provide children from the lower socioeconomic levels, what ought to be done about it? How realistic a hope is true equality within your lifetime?

3. Study the 1949 "Warner's Scale for Rating Occupations," page 170. If he were to revise it in terms of today, what changes might he make? Why?

4. Does your state or district provide extra funds for "compensatory education"? Find one which does and review the provisions. What is your opinion of this form of special education?

5. How far should a community go to provide racially integrated schools, K–12? Are there some other factors to be taken into account besides the desirability of the mix? What are they?

6. Since "mere presence" *ipso facto* will not guarantee acceptance among students from varying socioeconomic backgrounds, what can teachers do to promote greater acceptance?

7. Discuss various plans for redoing school boundaries such as the Princeton Plan, the Berkeley Plan, and others. Which one do you favor? Why?

8. Suppose your child had to spend 45 minutes in the morning and 45 minutes in the afternoon on a school bus in order to attend a racially integrated school. How would you feel about it? How might this affect his attitude?

9. Should teachers of lower-class children accept them as they are or attempt to change their values, or both, or neither? Why?

10. What are the great independent foundations like Ford and Carnegie doing to aid Negro education? What is the reason for their expenditure of such vast sums for this purpose?

Activities and Projects

1. Make a case study of some famous person whose sudden luck or outstanding talent dramatically altered his life-style.

2. Read John P. Marquand's *Point of No Return,* Sloan Wilson's *Man in the Gray Flannel Suit,* or Budd Schulberg's *What Makes Sammy Run?* and prepare an oral report, emphasizing particularly aspects of the story that pertain to social class.

3. Visit a school in the slums of your city. How closely do the neighborhood, school, curriculum, teachers, and pupils fit the patterns discussed in this chapter?

4. Analyze the friendship patterns or social cliques of a school class of your choice. Should the teacher provide more mix within the class? If so, how?

5. Study the social class structure of a comprehensive-type school of your choice, and do an analysis similar to "The Parking-lot Crowd" (page 173).

6. Interview several Negroes or several students from another lower class-caste group. Concentrate particularly on how they feel about school, their teachers, their classmates.

7. Read Counts' *Dare the Schools Build a New Social Order?* If Counts were commenting on the current state of racial segregation, what would he say about the school's responsibility?

8. Interview a teacher from a "hilltop school." Find out how she feels about the way the youngsters she has behave. Find out why she is teaching at the "hilltop" and whether she would accept an assignment in a slum school.

9. Inspect the textbooks used at a particular grade level or for a particular course. How accurately do they reflect a "white, Protestant, middle-class" culture bias?

10. Take two lower-class youngsters from the same block or neighborhood, one white, the other Negro. Talk to each one individually and compare their reactions on a set list of questions which you have prepared ahead of

time. To what extent are the similarities and differences in their responses the result of skin color and social class differences?

References

"SOCIAL CLASS"

BERNSTEIN, BASIL, "Social Structure, Language and Learning," *Educational Research*, 3:163, June, 1961.

BROOM, LEONARD, and PHILIP SELZNICK, *Sociology*, 3d ed. (New York: Harper & Row, 1963), Chapter 6.

COLEMAN, JAMES S., *Social Climates in High Schools* (Washington, D.C.: U.S. Department of Health, Education and Welfare, 1961).

DAVIS, ALLISON, *Social-Class Influences upon Learning* (Cambridge, Mass.: Harvard University Press, 1948).

———, *et al., Deep South* (Chicago: University of Chicago Press, 1941).

———, and JOHN DOLLARD, *Children of Bondage* (Washington, D.C.: American Council on Education, 1940).

———, and ROBERT HAVIGHURST, *Father of the Man* (Boston: Houghton Mifflin, 1947).

DOBRINER, WILLIAM M., *Class in Suburbia* (Englewood Cliffs, N.J.: Prentice-Hall, 1963).

DOLGER, LAURA, and JANET GINANDES, "Children's Attitude toward Discipline as Related to Socioeconomic Status," *Journal of Experimental Education*, 15: 161–65, December, 1946.

HANDLIN, OSCAR, *The Uprooted* (New York: Grosset & Dunlap, 1951).

HAWES, GENE R., "The Colleges of America's Upper Class," *Saturday Review*, Vol. 46, No. 46, November 16, 1963.

HOLLINGSHEAD, AUGUST B., *Elmtown's Youth* (New York: Wiley, 1949).

OSTRACH, HERBERT F., "English and the Lower-Class Student," *English Journal*, 52:196, March, 1963.

SCHMUCK, RICHARD A., and ROBERT W. SCHMUCK, "Upward Mobility and I.Q. Performance," *Journal of Educational Research*, 55:123–28, November, 1961.

SOROKIN, PITRIM A., *Social Mobility* (New York: Harper, 1927).

STENDLER, CELIA, *Children of Brasstown* (Urbana: Bureau of Research and Service, College of Education, University of Illinois, 1949).

STONE, JAMES C., "The Leisure-time Activities of Junior High School Boys in a Basin Area of Cincinnati," unpublished Master's thesis, University of Cincinnati, 1943.

TUNLEY, ROUL, "The Delinquent: Do We Hate Our Children?" *The Nation*, 199:5–6, July 13, 1964.

VOTAW, ALBERT V., "The Hillbillies Invade Chicago," *Harper's Magazine*, 216:64–67, February, 1958.

WARNER, W. LLOYD, ROBERT J. HAVIGHURST, and MARTIN B. LOEB, *Who Shall Be Educated?* (New York: Harper, 1944).

———, MARCHIA MEEKER, and KENNETH EELLS, *Social Class in America* (Chicago: Science Research Associates, 1949).

WHYTE, WILLIAM FOOTE, *Street Corner Society* (Chicago: University of Chicago Press, 1960).

WILSON, ALAN B., "Residential Segregation of Social Classes and Aspirations of High School Boys," *American Sociological Review*, 24:836–45, December, 1959.

WYDEN, PETER, *Suburbia's Coddled Kids* (New York: Avon Books, 1962).

"COLOR CASTE"

BALDWIN, JAMES, "A Talk to Teachers," *Saturday Review*, 46:42, December 21, 1963.

BARTKY, JOHN A., *Social Issues in Public Education* (Boston: Houghton Mifflin, 1963), Chapters 16, 19.

CONANT, JAMES B., *Slums and Suburbs* (New York: McGraw-Hill, 1961).

COOPER, SOPHIA, "Employment of June 1960 High School Graduates," *Monthly Labor Review*, 84:463–70.

DRAKE, ST. CLAIR, and HORACE R. CAYTON, *Black Metropolis.*

Education and the Disadvantaged American (Washington, D.C.: Educational Policies Commission, NEA, 1962).

GREENE, JAMES E., "Disciplinary Status of White and Negro High School Students in a Large Southeastern School System," *Journal of Negro Education*, 31:25–29, 1962.

HUMPHREY, HUBERT H., *School Desegregation: Documents and Commentaries* (New York: Thomas Y. Crowell, 1964).

KRAMER, JUDITH R., and SEYMOUR LEVENTMAN, *Children of the Gifted Ghetto* (New Haven: Yale University Press, 1961).

RIESSMAN, FRANK, *The Culturally Deprived Child* (New York: Harper, 1962).

———, "Teaching the Culturally Deprived," *NEA Journal*, 52:20, April, 1963.

TAYLOR, DALMAS A., "The Relationship between Authoritarianism and Ethnocentrism in Negro College Students," *Journal of Negro Education*, 31:455–59, 1962.

THOMPSON, DANIEL C., *The Negro Leadership Class* (Englewood Cliffs, N.J.: Prentice-Hall, 1963).

WOLFE, DEBORAH P., "Curriculum Adaptations for the Culturally Deprived," *Journal of Negro Education*, 31:139–51, 1962.

> Promote then, as an object of primary importance, institutions for the general diffusion of knowledge. In proportion as the structure of a government gives force to public opinion, it is essential that public opinion be enlightened.
>
> GEORGE WASHINGTON

the past

The growth of American education—which, in reality, dates back before the days of ancient Greece and Rome and continues through such important eras as the Renaissance and the Reformation in Europe and the Colonial and Revolutionary periods in this country to the present—is without question one of the great epics of modern civilization. Teachers, as well as physicians, lawyers, and ministers, can have but little real understanding and appreciation of their chosen profession without some knowledge of the historical development and significance of their profession. If education is to move from its traditional conservative position toward one of improvement consistent with America's social, political, and governmental progress, teachers need constantly to evaluate and alter their philosophies and procedures in the light of the events of the past.

In the few short years since this nation was born, there have been many improvements in the status of teachers and their profession. A thumbnail comparison of teachers in the early days of America's history with those who are employed in twentieth-century schools may make some of these improvements explicit:

	Colonial Teachers	*20th-century Teachers*
Sex	Predominantly men, except in "dame schools" and in certain Quaker schools and in some schools in the South.	Mixed, with women predominant in the elementary schools, though in recent years men have become much more in evidence. Men predominate in high schools, colleges, and universities.

Experience	Teachers considered their work as temporary rather than a life's vocation, though some were permanent members of the profession with as many as 50 years of service.	The average teacher in the 1960's has taught for 13 years. The greatest loss of professional personnel occurs within the first 3 years of teaching.
Salaries	Varied greatly, ranging between 10 and 100 pounds annually ($50 to $500), depending greatly upon the size of the community. Frequently salaries were paid in kind (wheat, corn, furs, etc.) on a semiannual or quarterly basis. Sometimes board and room was part of a teacher's compensation.	The typical salary for the American teacher of the early 1960's is a little more than $5,700 annually, paid usually in 10 or 12 monthly pay checks. There is, however, a wide range in salaries, extending from under $4,000 to more than $10,000 annually.
Education	Varied greatly—from college graduates to those barely able to read and write, with the lesser educated assigned to lower grades. College graduates were trained in the standard areas of Latin, Greek, and religion. No professional education until Franklin established his Academy—later to become the University of Pennsylvania—in 1750.	Teachers in America currently average 4.7 years of college education, and are rapidly approaching an average of 5 years of preparation for both elementary and secondary teaching. Their college work typically provides a fairly balanced array of general education, arts and sciences, and professional education courses.
Licensure	Licenses were not required of teachers in the colonies. There were, however, a few unsuccessful attempts at requiring licenses of school masters.	All teachers have licenses to teach issued by authorities in the states where they teach. There are a number of kinds of "certificates," and the requirements for obtaining them are far from standardized.
Work Load	Many teachers held classes from 7 A.M. to 5 P.M. in the summer and from 8 A.M. to 4 P.M. in the winter, and then did the usual "homework" during the remaining waking hours. Teachers often were required or expected to serve in many capacities in the community and church, as	Mid-twentieth-century teachers work up to 50 hours a week in managing the classroom, grading papers, and planning lessons. They often participate in community and church activities of their own choice.

grave-diggers,   bell-ringers,
choir directors, church custodians, town-criers, etc.

HISTORICAL PERSPECTIVE OF EDUCATION

The history of American education, as indicated previously, really dates back to ancient Greece and Rome. Of course, education has been in existence since the beginning of man: in prehistoric times, parents taught their children; so do they also today. Education in prehistoric times and in ancient countries such as China and Japan, while important, contributed little, if anything, to education in America. This discussion, then, will be limited to the countries and leaders of Europe which have made direct contributions to our educational system; it will then proceed to an overview of the course education has taken in the United States since the early days of our history.

The modern world's educational systems are indebted to the Greek city-states of Sparta and Athens for a number of their policies and practices. In Sparta, physical education was an important part of the training of men, and even of women, whose function was to bear children. Since the educational aim was the development of soldiers, boys, after beginning their education at home, received military training when they were between the ages of seven and twenty, and they were taught military science or served in the army until they became full-fledged citizens of the city at age thirty.

The great Greek philosophers, poets, and artists came from democratic Athens, where the educational aim was the preparation of citizens, not that of the preparation of soldiers, as in Sparta. Children were educated in the home until age seven, at which time their formal training began. Then the girls remained at home under the guidance of their mothers and slave-nurses, while the boys attended various private schools until they attained age sixteen. They were acompanied to and from school by slaves called *paidagogos*, hence the origin of the term "pedagogues," sometimes applied to teachers. Individualized instruction was a feature of Athenian schools; the subjects were music, literature, and physical education. At age sixteen, boys attended the gymnasium, a state-supported school, where the principal subject studied was physical education. Eight- to sixteen-year-old students in Athens studied a wide range of subjects, including grammar, literature, poetry, rhetoric, drama, mathematics, and oratory. Athens produced such outstanding philosophers and teachers as Socrates, Plato, and Aristotle. The writings of the latter two, particularly, give insight as to the prevailing philosophies of education in Athens.

In Rome, the patterns of education largely were borrowed from the Greeks. Rome developed an intensive concentration in the field of oratory. With the spread of Christianity in the Roman Empire, the early church set up its own schools; finally, about A.D. 491, all except church schools were abolished by the Emperor Justinian after Christianity became the state religion. During the Dark Ages, when the Roman Empire was overthrown by invading barbaric tribes, the only learning activities took place in Christian centers, usually the monasteries. Here churchmen attempted to preserve the culture and learning that had been developed, but education generally was virtually at a standstill for several hundred years.

The Renaissance

What might be considered the beginning of "modern" education occurred in the last half of the fifteenth century with the period called the Renaissance. At that time a new interest in education accompanied new emphasis on such academic studies as literature, architecture, arts, and sciences. Beginning in Italy, the revival of learning spread north into central Europe, and eventually to the British Isles. The most famous educational philosopher of the Renaissance period was Desiderius Erasmus (about 1469–1536), a Roman Catholic priest born in Rotterdam and educated in the Netherlands, at the University of Paris, and in schools in Italy. But it was his work in England at St. Paul's School and at Cambridge, where he instituted a humanistic curriculum with an emphasis upon classical languages and literature, that had the most direct effect on American schools. His efforts in the English schools resulted in the establishment of English academies, and this type of institution, which stressed sciences and arts as well as the classics, eventually became the pattern of schools transplanted to some of the colonies. Erasmus' writings revealed that he believed in such modern educational practices as universal education, condemnation of corporal punishment, and the study of foreign languages (in his case, Greek and Latin), with the emphasis upon conversation rather than upon memorization of rules of grammar. It was during the Renaissance period that the humanities came into existence; these were the forerunners of such modern studies as social studies, political science, government, sociology, psychology, education, and languages.

The Reformation

The Protestant Reformation, a movement in Europe during the fifteenth and sixteenth centuries, had many aspects and resulted from religious, political, economic, and social causes. Although not totally a progressive movement, it nevertheless produced the real pattern for education in a number of the American colonies. The actual break with the Roman Catholic Church came in 1517 when Martin Luther (1483–1546), a Catholic monk, nailed his famous theses questioning certain religious practices to the church door in Wittenburg, Germany.

Luther's translation of the Bible into the German language provided a very strong incentive for the people to learn to read. Indeed, the Bible became the most-used textbook in the German nation, what Luther considered the core of the university curriculum. Luther encouraged the teaching of religion in the schools and translated the catechism into the vernacular language so that it could be taught to children. He also believed that sacred music should be included in the school's curriculum because it would inspire moral sentiments in pupils. And very significantly for American schools, he proposed that control of the schools be in the hands of civil authorities rather than of church leaders.

Three important aspects of modern American education are the direct result of the Protestant Reformation: (1) the growth of civil control of education as opposed to religious and private control (the so-called doctrine of separation of church and state); (2) the idea that each state should control education within its boundaries, and (3) the dominance of the subject of reading in the elementary schools.

Among the important educational leaders in Europe during the Reformation period, in addition to Luther, were Melancthon, Bugenhagen, Sturm, Calvin, Knox, and Comenius. As the student progresses in his professional education program, perhaps he will take a course in the history of education and pursue in detail the study of these men and their educational contributions. In this volume, space allows for a cursory discussion of only one, the last.

Comenius

John Amos Comenius (1592–1670), a member of a small religious sect that grew out of the Reformation in Moravia, a part of Czechoslovakia, was one of the greatest educational leaders of the post-Reformation era. He was a bishop in his church, but because his religious group was despised in his native Moravia, he had to go to Poland and Sweden before his educational ideas bore fruit. He was the first European to make use of pictures in his teaching—the result of his attending school at age sixteen and observing young boys at ages nine and ten years struggling with their study of Latin. His book *Orbis Pictus* (pictured world), with illustrations, was a primer for teaching Latin. Comenius' educational principles, contained in his book *The Great Didactic*, resemble the objectives of schools in twentieth-century America. He advocated that *all* children—boys and girls alike—should be educated and that each should have his own textbook. Believing that universal education is impossible unless there is simultaneous instruction of numbers of pupils, Comenius was the first to advance the idea of teaching large groups of children together at the same time. He also recommended that the school year begin on a specific date, and that lessons be divided into daily, weekly, and monthly plans. Humor has a place in education, advocated Comenius, and he made great use of fairy tales, play, music, and manual instruction in his teaching. His method was teaching from the known to the unknown, and he made extensive use of sensory learning in his classrooms.

NATURE IS OUR GUIDE

Let us then commence to seek out, in God's name, the principles on which, as on an immovable rock, the method of teaching and learning can be grounded. If we wish to find a remedy for the defects of nature, it is in nature herself that we must look for it, since it is certain that art can do nothing unless it imitate nature.

We find on investigation that the principle which really holds together the fabric of this world of ours, down to the smallest detail, is none other than order; that is to say, the proper division of what comes before and what comes after, of the superior and the subordinate, of the large and the small, of the similar and dissimilar, according to place, time, number, size, and weight, so that each may fulfill its function well.

. . . Very aptly does Cicero say: "If we take nature as our guide, she will never lead us astray."

The art of teaching, therefore, demands nothing more than the skillful arrangement of time, of the subjects taught, and of the method.

M. W. Keatinge, *The Great Didactic of John Amos Comenius* (London: A. & C. Black, 1896), pp. 250, 245, 252, 248.

Other Early European Educators

Following the era of Comenius were four European leaders in the field of education who are worthy of some note. Jean Jacques Rousseau (1712–1778) was an extreme critic of the conditions that were to be found in France in areas of religion and government as well as in the field of education. He protested against the humanist, formal-discipline educational theories that were in vogue in his time and against the treatment of children as "little adults." Rousseau's theory, explained in his famous book *Emile,* was that children should develop naturally, instead of in accordance with stiff, unnatural, meaningless situations. Among Rousseau's ideas held in high repute in education today are that the school's curriculum should be planned according to the needs and interests of boys and girls, and that reason and experimentation should replace authority. Rousseau's philosophy of education spread throughout France, into Germany and other European countries, and eventually to the United States.

One of Rousseau's disciples was Johann Heinrich Pestalozzi (1746–1827), a Swiss educator who was greatly inspired by reading *Emile* and by the teachings of the French reformer. Pestalozzi experimented with Rousseau's methods on his own children and on children in five different schools in Switzerland, the most famous of which was that at Yverdon, which he directed for twenty years. Like Rousseau, he believed in the natural development of children and in the doctrine of interest as a means of motivation for learning. Pestalozzi made great use of "object lessons," in which real articles—such as oranges, tools, etc. were used as teaching aids. His most famous book, *Leonard and Gertrude*, is a novel dealing with peasant life in his native country and with functional home education; his book on educational philosophy and method is *How Gertrude Teaches Her Children*. Many of Pestalozzi's ideas were transplanted directly to American schools.

A pupil of Pestalozzi was the German educator Friedrich Froebel (1782–1852), who conceived the idea of the kindergarten and who opened the first school of this type in 1837 in Blankenburg. Froebel's educational philosophy quite naturally fell in line with that held by his teacher in Switzerland as well as those held by his predecessors, Comenius and Rousseau; he believed in the natural development of children. Teachers from all over the world attended Froebel's school for kindergarten teachers, and the rapid growth in the establishment of kindergartens throughout the world is attributed to the zeal of the graduates of Froebel's school. His philosophy of education is expressed in his book *The Education of Man*.

THE EVILS OF EDUCATION

Nature requires children to be children before they are men. By endeavoring to pervert this order, we produce forward fruits, that have neither maturity nor taste, and will not fail soon to wither or corrupt. Hence it is we have so many young professors and old children. Childhood hath its manner of seeing, perceiving, and thinking, peculiar to itself; nor is there anything more absurd than our being anxious to substitute our own in its stead. I would as soon require an infant to be five feet high, as a boy to have judgment at ten years of age. In fact, of what use would reason be to him at that age? Reason is given us as a check upon our power; a child has no need of such restraint.

Jean Jacques Rousseau, *Selections from Emilius* (1773).

In 1831, Johann Friedrich Herbart (1776–1841), a German professor of philosophy and education, published a book entitled *Letters Dealing with the Application of Psychology to the Art of Teaching*, and thus was planted the seed which eventually became the foundation for modern empirical psychology. Herbart's work was principally in the areas of psychology and method; his thesis with respect to the purpose of education was that it should help children develop moral character. Educational and psychological innovations by this German scholar included the establishment of the first demonstration school connected with a university, and replacement of the old "faculties of the mind" theory—which held that the mind is divided up into compartments, such as memory, reasoning, and will, and each operates as a separate entity—with the currently accepted idea that the mind functions as a unit. Herbart and his disciples viewed educational method as a science and devised the five formal steps in teaching: (1) preparation, (2) presentation, (3) comparison, (4) conclusion, and (5) application. The National Society for the Study of Education, currently an important professional organization in the United States, had its beginning as the National Herbartian Society, organized in America in 1895 by educators who had studied under Herbart's followers in Germany.

DEVELOPMENT OF AMERICAN EDUCATION

The settlers of the early American colonies brought with them the languages, religions, customs, and educational systems they had known in their homelands. As a result, many different types of schools, most of them largely unsatisfactory, were established on the new continent. Most authorities, however, have defined three important patterns of education: that found in the New England colonies, in the Middle Atlantic colonies, and in the Southern colonies.

New England Colonies

Since religious freedom was one of the strong motives of the English colonists for settling in the New World, it was natural for them to establish schools so that their children might be able to read, because the early settlers, following the concepts of the European reformers, believed that the only way to salvation was through individual interpretation of the Scriptures. In 1635, fifteen years after the Pilgrims landed at Plymouth Rock, they established the Boston Latin School, the first organized school in New England to be successful. While the educational policy of the New England colonists was different from the European system, the schools themselves were simply transplants of similar schools in the mother country.

Latin grammar schools, the predominant type of educational institution prior to the Revolutionary War, had as their objective the preparation of boys for college, where the emphasis was upon preparation for the ministry. The curriculum of these forerunners of secondary schools in America thus consisted primarily of Latin, Greek, and theology. The Latin grammar school was a seven-year institution, which boys usually entered at age seven. Although some money for the support of the Latin grammar schools was raised through taxation, they were chiefly private schools charging tuition, and thus were attended principally by children of the élite in the New England colonies. Remnants of the grammar schools which remain in today's public schools include the emphasis upon a classical education, the rigid graduation requirements channeled toward admission to college, and the emphasis upon a logical rather than a psychological approach to learning.

Some children of both sexes attended "dame schools" in New England. Here they received their elementary education from housewives or mothers who taught the rudiments of reading and arithmetic and the catechism, and who usually charged a small tuition fee. Other children studied under private tutors when their parents could afford them.

The first legislation affecting education in the New England colonies, the Massachusetts School Law of 1642, passed by the Massachusetts Bay Colony, encouraged the education of children. It provided that town magistrates periodically check up on the education of children, and, if found wanting, the town officials could attempt to force parents to see that their children learned to read. This law was not strictly enforced, however, so the Massachusetts Law of 1647, better known as the "Old Deluder Satan Law," was passed. With its requirement that each town of 50 householders provide a teacher for its children, and that each town of 100 families provide a Latin grammar school came the first "compulsory" school legislation.

Middle Atlantic Colonies

In the Middle Atlantic colonies, the schools were organized by churches instead of by civil authorities, but, of course, the motive remained the same: that children learn to read so that they might read the Bible. Whereas the Puritan-Calvinist influence was felt in church and civil organizations in New England, such a single influence was not possible in the Middle Atlantic colonies, where there was a mixture of Protestant denominations. The result was the establishment of private schools by each particular religion to teach each denomination's specific beliefs. Civil authorities had little, if any, responsibility for the support of education.

Teachers were usually clergymen until regular instructors were obtainable. Children, both boys and girls, were taught in their native tongues—Dutch in New York, English in Pennsylvania, and Swedish in Delaware—and the emphasis was upon reading, writing, arithmetic, and catechism.

Southern Colonies

Virginia and the other Southern colonies were principally settled by Englishmen of some means who became the aristocracy and who operated large plantations. These colonists hired private tutors for their own children, but they provided no education for the children of slaves whom they had imported to work on the plantations. When their children reached a certain age, they were usually sent back to England to finish their education. Since the colonists in the South came to America primarily to improve their economic conditions, their government took little interest in education.

A few free schools, however, were established in the Southern colonies, principally through contributions of individuals interested in schools. These became known as "pauper schools," because parents whose children attended were required to declare publicly that they were paupers.

Early American Schools

Elementary education in the early days of our country's history was, to say the least, hard and crude. The school buildings themselves contained one room with the barest of furniture and educational equipment. Reading, writing, arithmetic, and religion were the principal subjects taught, and these in a way which today seems crude and wasteful. Textbooks were practically non-existent, the earliest ones being hornbooks consisting of a sheet of paper attached to a wooden paddle and protected by a thin, transparent sheet of horn. These books usually bore the alphabet, a set of syllables, and the Lord's Prayer. *The New England Primer,* which made its debut in the colonies in 1691, was the predominant textbook for 150 years.

Teachers in colonial schools, except in dame schools, were usually men not particularly prepared for their work. None was licensed for teaching. There were no grades per se in the early schools; all children were placed in one large room, and each progressed at his own rate.

While the Colonial period in America produced no really great leaders in the field of education, the early national era immediately following the Revolutionary War and leading up to the Civil War saw a few luminaries come forward as statesmen, philosophers, and educators.

Benjamin Franklin (1706–1790), born and educated in Boston, believed that education was an individual instead of a state function, that schools should be established by individual contributions, and that public monies should be used only for the education of the poor. Convinced that children should be taught practical instead of classical subjects and that they should be taught in English, Franklin established the first public academy in 1751 in Philadelphia, a secondary school which eventually became the University of Pennsylvania.

Thomas Jefferson (1743–1826), one of the nation's earliest and greatest statesmen, had considerable effect on the development of education in America, particularly in his native state of Virginia. He believed in universal education so that enlightened human beings could govern themselves, and his suggestions led the way for the establishment of the first state school system. The education bill which Jefferson introduced in 1779 in the Virginia legislature proposed a democratic school system in which the state would be divided into sections corresponding to school districts; the bill also would provide for the education of both boys and girls, would provide free education for the first three years of primary school, would set up the provisions whereby a superintendent of schools would be elected, and would include provisions for secondary education. Worthy graduates of Virginia's high schools would be sent at public expense to the College of William and Mary. Because of the plantation owners' opposition, Jefferson's bill did not pass the Virginia legislature, but a great deal of credit is due him for implanting the idea of a complete state system of education into the minds of leaders of other states, and eventually of the entire country.

The "Father of American Public Education," Horace Mann (1796–1859) was a lawyer who served his state of Massachusetts in the House of Representatives and in the Senate prior to his appointment in 1837 as first secretary of the newly created Massachusetts state board of education, a position he held for twelve years. At the end of each year in this position, Mann published a report on the accomplishments and needs of the state schools; his most famous report is the seventh, made following five months' study of various schools in Europe. A forerunner of modern teachers' colleges and schools of education was the normal school established by Mann in 1839 in Lexington, Massachusetts. Among the innovations and reforms which Mann instigated in his own and other states were the following: improvement of buildings and physical equipment, higher standards for the training of teachers and greater care in the selection of trainees for the profession, higher standards in supervision of instruction, the encouragement of the establishment of libraries in schools and towns, improvement of classroom instruction, the consolidation of small school districts into larger ones, the introduction of vocal music, history, geography, physiology, and hygiene into the public school curriculum, the insistence upon regular attendance, higher teachers' salaries, inauguration of uniform textbooks, and the abandonment of corporal punishment.

THE COMMON SCHOOL

Without undervaluing any other human agency, it may be safely affirmed that the common school, improved and energized as it can easily be, may become the most effective and benignant of all the forces of civilization. Two reasons sustain this position. In the first place, there is a universality in its operation, which can be affirmed of no other institution whatever. If administered in the spirit of justice and conciliation, all the rising generation may be brought within the circle of its reformatory and elevating influences. And, in the second place, the materials upon which it operates are so pliant and ductile as to be susceptible of assuming a greater variety of forms than any other earthly work of the Creator. The inflexibility and ruggedness of the oak, when compared with the lithe sapling or the tender germ, are but feeble emblems to typify the docility of childhood when contrasted with the obduracy and intractableness of man. It is these inherent advantages of the common school, which, in our own state, have produced results so striking, from a system so imperfect, and an administration so feeble. In teaching the blind and the deaf and dumb, in kindling the latent spark of intelligence that lurks in an idiot's mind, and in the more holy work of reforming abandoned and outcast children, education has proved what it can do by glorious experiments. These wonders it has done in its infancy, and with the lights of a limited experience; but when its faculties shall be fully developed, when it shall be trained to wield its mighty energies for the protection of society against the giant vices which now invade and torment it—against intemperance, avarice, war, slavery, bigotry, the woes of want, and the wickedness of waste,—then there will not be a height to which these enemies of the race can escape which it will not scale.

Horace Mann, *Twelfth Annual Report*

Henry Barnard (1811–1900) did for education in Connecticut and Rhode Island what Horace Mann had done in Massachusetts. A scholar who graduated from Yale at the young age of nineteen, Barnard's writings are valuable as a comprehensive story of the field of education. He started the *American Journal of Education* in 1855, and in 1867 he was appointed the first United States Commissioner of Education, a position he held for three years.

The Academy

The school that replaced the Latin grammar school in the early days of our Republic was the academy. After Franklin sparked the establishment in 1751 of the first academy in Philadelphia, many schools of this type were initiated throughout the country. They were patterned after the academies in England, with a curricular emphasis upon "everything that is useful and everything that is ornamental." The curriculum of the academy represented a radical departure from that of the Latin grammar school, which was strictly classical in nature. Classes in the academy were conducted in English, and the courses included grammar, arithmetic, accounting, geometry, astronomy, public speaking, writing, history, penmanship, composition, English literature, drawing, science, modern foreign languages, bookkeeping, and navigation. Boys and girls alike attended. While the academies served a need in the eighteenth century and provided schooling for more children than ever before, still, since they were private schools and charged tuition, they did not provide education for all children of secondary school age. It was not until the first quarter of the nineteeth century that the dream of making secondary education available to all children in our country was realized.

First Public High School

Pressures from citizens for free public secondary schools for their children after they had completed the common schools resulted in the establishment of the Boston English Classical School in 1821; three years later the name was changed to English High School. College-entrance subjects were omitted from the high school curriculum, but otherwise the new school's program resembled that of the academy. English, mathematics, science, logic, and history were stressed in the school which, at first, admitted only boys. In 1826, a girls' high school was opened in Boston, but not until thirty years later did the first coeducational public high school open in Chicago. The new secondary school movement spread slowly at first: by 1840, only fourteen towns and cities in Massachusetts had public high schools, and by 1860 more than 300 such schools existed, chiefly in Massachusetts, New York, and Ohio; but by the turn of the century the number had increased to about 6,000, enrolling 80 per cent of the nation's youth. In 1827, the Massachusetts legislature passed a law which required every town of 500 or more families to maintain a high school which would teach American history, bookkeeping, algebra, geometry, and surveying, and in towns of 4,000 or more, Greek, Latin, history, logic, and rhetoric were to be included.

A number of people in the nineteenth century protested against the free public high schools, principally because of the taxation necessary for their maintenance. The famous Kalamazoo case, a test case of public-supported schools, tried in 1874 before the Michigan Supreme Court, resulted in the court's ruling that the city of Kalamazoo could levy taxes to support free public secondary schools. The case, and others that followed, settled the question in America of a community's right to tax its citizens for the support of free public high schools.

Early Colleges

Several colleges and universities were established in the Colonial and early national eras of our country's history. Harvard College, founded in 1636 "to advance learning, and perpetuate it to Posterity, dreading to leave an illiterate Ministery to the Churches, when our present Ministers shall lie in the Dust," was the first institution of higher learning in America. Others—like Harvard open only to young men aspiring to the ministry—included William and Mary in Virginia, 1693; Yale in Connecticut, 1701; Princeton in New Jersey, 1746; Columbia in New York City, 1754; University of Pennsylvania in Philadelphia, 1755; Brown in Providence, Rhode Island, 1764; Rutgers in New Jersey, 1766; and Dartmouth in New Hampshire, 1769.

Education of Women

Higher education for women was unthought-of for a half-century after the Revolution. But through the untiring efforts of women like Emma Willard (1787–1870), Catherine Beecher (1800–1878), and Mary Lyon (1797–1849), the education of women in secondary school and college became an established reality in the United States. In 1821 Mrs. Willard established the Troy (New York) Female Seminary, in which many teachers of the time were educated. Seven years later, Miss Beecher opened the Hartford, Connecticut, Female Seminary for the training of teachers, nurses, and homemakers, and after she moved in 1838 to Cincinnati, Ohio, she founded the Western Female Institute. At the college level of education, Mary Lyon established Mount Holyoke Seminary in 1836.

The Early National Period

It may be seen from the foregoing paragraphs that from the time of the Revolution to the War between the States (1776 to 1860), education saw some forward-looking advancements. The curriculum of the secondary schools was broadened in the academies and the public high schools, the schools became tax-supported and free, and the education of women at secondary and college levels began to receive attention.

The Post-Civil War Period

The years between 1860 and 1918 were marked by some great strides in the development of education in this country. Three emerging philosophies influenced education: idealism, with its emphasis upon the spiritual rather than the material; classical humanism, which advocated hard, unpleasant tasks for pupils; and pragmatism, with its practical application of learning and its insistence upon experimentation and research. The ideas and methods of such European educators as Pestalozzi, Herbart, and Froebel began to be adopted in the schools during this period, and several Americans who appeared on the scene profoundly affected education in the United States. Elementary education was expanded greatly during the period, partly because of the rapid growth of urban areas, and the kindergarten became a part of the public school system in several communities, beginning in St. Louis, Missouri.

America's first real titans in the promotion of educational philosophy, psychology, and methodology made their influence felt in schools throughout the nation during this period. Francis W. Parker (1837–1902), after serving as superintendent of schools in Quincy, Massachusetts, went to the Department of Education at the University of Chicago in its early days and there established some innovations in teaching methods which led to less artificiality in the classroom. William T. Harris (1835–1909) was superintendent of St. Louis schools when Froebel's kindergarten plans were first introduced into American public schools. G. Stanley Hall (1844–1924) contributed the theory of genetic psychology, concerned with developmental aspects of psychology—tracing processes whereby individual and racial behavior modes are developed—and stressed the idea that methodology needs to be related to the subject being studied, the age of the learner, and the predominant psychology of the era. In 1829, Samuel R. Hall wrote and published the first professional book in education, *Lectures on School Keeping*.

William James (1842–1910), America's first great psychologist, published in 1890 a two-volume work entitled *Principles of Psychology*, which forcefully pointed up the relationship between psychology and education. In collaboration with John Dewey and C. S. Peirce, he successfully developed the philosophy of pragmatism, the only American educational ideology. James' writings, including his *Talks to Teachers*, provided the basis for many of the theories and practices of progressive education in this country.

John Dewey (1859–1952) was the first great American educator who was educated entirely in the United States. Formerly an idealist, Dewey came to pragmatism from idealism. The most important part of his life was the years 1895 to 1905 when he was a professor of philosophy at the University of Chicago. There, in 1896, he opened his famous experimental school where, in an ideal school environment, the children studied the great social needs of mankind through an interest approach.

Definition of Education

We reach a technical definition of education: it is that reconstruction or reorganization of experience which adds to the meaning of experience, and which increases ability to direct the course of subsequent experience. (i.) The increment of meaning corresponds to the increased perception of the connections and continuities of the activities in which we are engaged. The activity begins in an impulsive form; that is, it is blind. It does not know what it is about; that is to say, what are its interactions with other activities. An activity which brings education or instruction with it makes one aware of some of the connections which had been imperceptible. To recur to our simple example, a child who reaches for a bright light gets burned. Henceforth he *knows* that a certain act of touching in connection with a certain act of vision (and *vice-versa*) means heat or pain; or, a certain light means a source of heat. The acts by which a scientific man in his laboratory learns more about flame differ no whit in principle. By doing certain things, he makes perceptible certain connections of heat with other things, which had been previously ignored. Thus his acts in relation to these things get more meaning; he knows better what he is doing or "is about" when he has to do with them; he can *intend* consequences instead of just letting them happen—all synonymous ways of saying the same thing. At the same stroke, the flame has gained in meaning; all that is known about combustion, oxidation, about light and temperature, may become an intrinsic part of his intellectual content.

The other side of an educative experience is an added power of subsequent direction or control. To say that one knows what he is about, or can intend certain consequences, is to say, of course, that he can better anticipate what is going to happen.

John Dewey, *Democracy and Education* (New York: Macmillan, 1916), pp. 89–90.

To Dewey, every problem was different, requiring a fresh approach and a fresh solution. The basis of his educational philosophy was change, and the learner, rather than the subject matter, was the important concern in the learning process. Dewey promoted the method of scientific problem-solving in the teaching-learning situation, and he had real concern for the use of critical inquiry in all problematic arrangements.

Dewey was a voluminous writer in the fields of both philosophy and education. His outstanding contributions in the latter area are *School and Society, Democracy and Education,* and *Experience and Education.* Among the organizations inspired by this foremost American educational thinker are the Progressive Education Association and the John Dewey Society, which has been in continuous existence since it was founded in 1927.

Among the disciples of Dewey who made an impact upon education in this country are William Heard Kilpatrick, the leading exponent of the concept that the curriculum should be the total range of experiences involved in the school's activities, and Boyd Henry Bode, a progressive education exponent who emphasized a methodology based on the students' interests as well as the democratic approach to learning.

During the post-Civil War period, the government became more active in educational affairs. In 1862, Lincoln signed the Morrill Act establishing a federal fund for vocational education and providing for the education of larger numbers of students. The Supreme Court of Michigan in 1874 handed down the famous decision in the Kalamazoo case which made it legal for communities to tax themselves for the support of secondary schools. The Committee of Ten on Secondary School Studies of 1893 and the Committee of Thirteen on College Entrance Requirements of 1895 were charged by the National Education Association to study and define the college preparatory curriculum.

Modern Education in the United States

Since the end of World War I, education in this country has been marked by further important changes. Beginning with the Seven Cardinal Principles proposed in 1918 by the Commission on Reorganization of Secondary Education, several efforts have been made by various groups to define specifically the purposes of public education in the United States. Interest in education has been at a peak; this, in addition to a population explosion, has resulted in increased enrollments at all levels of schools as well as in experimentation and research in the techniques of teaching.

Since 1918 there has been an increased emphasis upon the scientific education of pupils; the concern of teachers has been upon the education of the whole child and providing for the individual differences of children. The federal government has taken an increased interest in education and has provided federal funds for programs in vocational education, through the Smith-Lever Act of 1914, the Smith-Hughes Act of 1917, and the Civilian Conservation Corps Act of 1933; for aid for students in higher education through the National Youth Authority of 1935; for assistance to veterans through the Servicemen's Readjustment Act of 1944 (the G.I. Bill of Rights); and for programs in foreign languages, science, and guidance through the National Defense Education Act of 1958. Philanthropic foundations, such as the W. K. Kellogg Foundation and the Ford Foundation, have provided funds to public schools and institutions of higher education for the purpose of promoting research and experimentation to improve education.

The emphasis in education in recent years has been upon quality rather than quantity; this implies that each child needs to be challenged to his fullest potential, that the creative abilities of youngsters need to be developed, and that children need to be taught how to think rather than what to think. Our democracy can afford no less than the best education for all children; quality education is essential to the very survival of our free way of life.

ARE THE QUESTIONS ASKED
ABOUT EDUCATION TODAY NEW?

Although the preceding broad overview of the history of education, with special emphasis upon the development of schools in America, has not precisely pointed up that specific questions existed in the minds of citizens of the various eras with respect to the schools and their effect on children, such questions are quite readily implied. There is little doubt that since the dawn of civilization people have questioned schools and what they are trying to accomplish and how they are going about it.

Over the past few years the authors have collected several references to people's questions relative to schools and the schooling of their children. Among them is the following, attributed to Socrates, some 2,500 years ago:

The children now love luxury, they have bad manners, contempt for authority, they show disrespect for elders, and love chatter in place of exercise. Children are now tyrants, not servants of their households. They no longer rise when elders enter the room. They contradict their parents, chatter before company, gobble up dainties at the table, cross their legs, and tyrannize over their teachers.

THE FEDERAL GOVERNMENT AND EDUCATION

While the United States Constitution does not mention education, since the early days of our history the federal government has been friendly toward public education and has, in fact, encouraged its promulgation by a number of actions. Following is a chronology indicating its most important activities and their dates:

1787   Northwest Ordinance. This act provided for one section of each township in the Ohio territory to be given for maintaining public schools in that township.

1791   Tenth Amendment included in Constitution. Control of education left to the states.

1802   Establishment of the U.S. Military Academy at West Point, N.Y.

1803   When Ohio was admitted to the Union, Congress extended the policy stated in Northwest Ordinance to other states.

1818   First federal financial aid to states for education.

1819   Dartmouth College case. New Hampshire legislature attempted to change Dartmouth College from a private to a public college. U.S. Supreme Court ruled that a college charter is a charter which legislatures may not impair; higher education in this country cannot be entirely a state activity.

1845   Establishment of the U.S. Naval Academy at Annapolis, Maryland.

1862   Morrill Act, which provided that each state should receive 30,000 acres for each senator and representative in Congress. Money received from the sale of this land was to be invested, and the interest was to be used for agricultural and mechanical arts colleges. Such colleges continue to receive federal money for their maintenance.

1865   Establishment of Freedmen's Bureau to assist schools for Negro children.

1867   Creation of the U.S. Office of Education in the Department of the Interior. In 1939, the office was moved to the Federal Security Agency, and in 1953, it came under the Department of Health, Education, and Welfare. The U.S. Commissioner of Education, the chief executive officer in the office, is appointed for an indefinite tenure by the President of the United States. The office is maintained to promote the cause of education in the country and to diffuse information about the condition of education.

1874   Kalamazoo case. The Michigan Supreme Court ruled that it was legal for the public to be taxed to support public secondary schools.

1887   Hatch Act. The federal government appropriated $15,000 annually to each state maintaining an agricultural college, and established agricultural experimental stations.

1909   First White House Conference. Called by President Theodore Roosevelt, the meeting was held in Washington, D.C. Other meetings were held in 1919, 1931, 1940, 1950, 1955, and 1960.

1914   Smith-Lever Act. Provided for matching federal funds with state monies for the promotion of extension work in agriculture and home economics at the college level.

1917   Smith-Hughes Act. Provided for matching federal and state funds to promote agricultural education, manual arts, and home economics at the high school level.

1918   Compulsory education effective in all states.

1920   Vocational Rehabilitation Act. Federal money provided to states for educating handicapped persons.

1920   Reserve Officers' Training Corps program initiated. Personnel and equipment for training programs in secondary schools and colleges provided by federal government.

1925   Oregon case. U.S. Supreme Court ruled unconstitutional a law, passed by the Oregon legislature in 1922, which required every child in the state to attend public schools. Private and parochial schools can exist in the states, in addition to public schools. The state, however, supervises and inspects all schools.

1933   Federal Emergency Relief Act provided for nursery school program.

1933   Civilian Conservation Corps. Among other things, this program provided for education and employment of young people.

1937   George-Deen Act. Provided further federal funds for vocational education.

1944   Servicemen's Readjustment Act. The G.I. Bill of Rights supplied federal monies for veterans' education. A second act was passed in 1952.

1946   Congress approved this country's membership in the United Nations Educational, Scientific and Cultural Organization (UNESCO).

1947   National School Lunch Act. Public and parochial schools were provided federal funds on a permanent basis for school hot-lunch programs.

1952   Zorach case (New York City). U.S. Supreme Court ruled released time for religious instruction off school property was constitutional. This reversed a decision in 1948—the McCollum case—in Champaign, Illinois.

1954   Supreme Court ruled segregation in public schools was unconstitutional.

1955   White House Conference on Education called by President Eisenhower in Washington, D.C. About 2,000 educators and laymen representing all states and territories discussed aims of education, school organization, school building needs, teacher supply, school finances.

1958   National Defense Education Act. Provided federal funds for the promotion of science, foreign languages, guidance, and audio-visual aids in the schools; also funds for student loans and fellowships.

1960   Golden Anniversary White House Conference on Children and Youth. Provided further attention to education.

1961   Congress turned down President Kennedy's program of federal assistance for public school construction and teachers' salaries.

1964   NDEA extended and antipoverty bill passed.

Another reference is the following attributed to Confucius (551–478 B.C.):

The teachers of today just go on repeating things in a rigmarole fashion, annoy the students with constant questions, and repeat the same things over and over again. They do not try to find out what the students' natural inclinations are, so that the students are forced to pretend to like their studies, nor do they try to bring out the best in their talents. What they give the students is wrong in the first place and what they expect of the students is just as wrong. As a result, the students hide their favorite readings and hate their teachers, are exasperated at the difficulty of their studies and do not know what good it does them. Although they go through the regular courses of instruction, they are quick to leave them when they are through. This is the reason for the failure of education today.

Some persons in Aristotle's day (384 B.C.) complained that children preferred sitting and chatting to participation in physical education activities and that they had unsavory manners. Complaints were so numerous that the famous Greek philosopher wrote, "There are doubts concerning the business of education, since all people do not agree in those things they would have a child taught."

Every generation has had its critics of the schools; the literature abounds with indications of profuse criticism of schools in the United States from Colonial times through the present era, with such current gadflies as Vice Admiral H. G. Rickover, Arthur Bestor, and James B. Conant. The nature of the criticisms has been, generally, that schools are not as good as they once were, that they do not teach the fundamentals, that progressive education has taken over the schools.

ARE THE QUESTIONS THE RESULT OF MISUNDERSTANDINGS?

There can be little question that a great deal of the objective, unemotional criticism that has originated with many thinking critics of education has merit. Some teachers are not properly prepared—just as some practitioners in any profession or vocation are not properly prepared. Progressive education (whatever that means!) is something that almost everyone opposes—for different and often contradictory reasons. This educational ideology has been held responsible for almost every social evil of the twentieth century. When John Dewey, who formulated the basic principles of progressive education, stated that education should concern itself with the whole child, he meant that development of the child's physical, intellectual, emotional, social, and spiritual being must take place simultaneously; one aspect of a child's being, such as the intellectual, is not isolated from another. Teachers must, thought Dewey, take advantage of the natural interests of children and place as few artificial restraints upon these interests as possible. Some followers of Dewey, however, interpreted this idea to mean that children's interests should reign supreme—a theory which Dewey himself violently opposed, accusing these followers of carrying freedom to a point of near anarchy.

When Dewey and the original progressives proposed that education is life itself, not a preparation for life, some disciples assumed that the curriculum should be based on real needs of children at present. Others, however, carried this idea to the point of expounding that such subjects as social dancing and driver training were more important that the more "solid" academic subjects. To this Dewey strongly objected, indicating that the absence of intellectual control through significant subject matter was deplorable.

Currently, the term "progressive education" has no specific meaning. Critics have made it mean almost anything that they wish it to mean.

So it is with many of the other questions that today are being raised with respect to public education. There can be little question but that today's schools are far superior to those of earlier days; children are receiving a better education now than they did formerly, as many studies bear out. There has never been a time but that teachers accepted as a major part of their responsibility the teaching of the fundamental subjects. But the emphasis upon teaching these fundamentals in a meaningful manner sometimes leads people to suspect what they are doing, because of the sharp contrast between this methodology and that of the first quarter of this century.

ARE THE QUESTIONS UNHEALTHY?

A school system is only as good as the teachers and administrative and supervisory officials who make up its personnel. It is natural for professional people to tend to invoke a counterattack when numerous emotional charges, especially those having little or no foundation, are hurled in their direction. Such actions and reactions usually generate more heat than light, however; confusion and discontent rather than enlightenment and improvement are too often the result. Actually, it is during a time of dynamic social change, when questions are raised about everything, that educators have their greatest opportunity to improve the schools.

Criticisms of and questions about the education of children indicate a real concern for and interest in the schools and what they are trying to accomplish. Throughout the length and breadth of this land there is ample evidence to the effect that concern and interest are at a peak now: newspapers and magazines publish countless reports concerning education in America; statewide conferences and two national White House Conferences on education are further indications of the heights to which concern and interest have ascended.

Such times present excellent opportunities for professional educators to evaluate what they are actually accomplishing in the schools and to invoke improvements where the need is indicated. Generally speaking, the American people are interested in having education for their children that is second to none in the world, and are willing to pay for it. And as long as there are schools, there will always be room for improvement in their programs.

WILL THESE AND OTHER QUESTIONS CONTINUE?

As indicated in the preceding paragraph, there will always be room for improvement in the school programs in the United States; thus, there is no reason to assume that the time will come when people no longer will question and criticize their schools. In the foreseeable future, with dynamic social changes in our culture almost inevitable, there is little to indicate that pressures on schools to provide stronger programs will abate.

It is reasonable to expect the questions and criticisms of education to continue as long as the concern and interest remain at their peak, as long as certain inadequacies actually do exist, as long as a certain portion of the country's population questions the advisability of operating *public* schools at public expense, and as long as a nostalgic reactionary belief exists in the minds of some individuals. A needed innovation in most public school systems in America is the establishment of a faculty evaluation organization to keep constant vigilance for forthcoming questions and to relate them to possible program improvements in their systems.

THE ADEQUACY OF AMERICAN EDUCATION

By now, it should be evident to the future teachers of the United States that the professional educator's great dream of the attainment of excellence has not been realized. Nor is there evidence at hand that the pursuit of excellence is near its end. In education, as in most of the physical and life sciences, each advancement serves only to open up wide new vistas of what might be tried in the future to provide better school programs for America's most precious natural resources—its boys and girls. However, when American education is evaluated in the light of unemotionally arrived-at criteria, criteria that are measured objectively, the picture of the school's accomplishments appears bright and clear.

What Is Meant by "Progress"

At one time in the history of American education, progress in the education of students referred to their increasing ability to memorize and verbalize; this was measured by tests which placed a premium on pupils' ability in these two types of activities. Today, "progress" is considered multidimensional. With greater emphasis on quality than on quantity in our education, the thinking with respect to progress is focused on trying to challenge each child to his fullest potential, to develop the creative abilities of youngsters, and to help prepare children and youth to meet the changing and challenging needs of our society. We are now more concerned with teaching children how to think rather than what to think.

For convenience sake, most studies and textbooks on child growth and development utilize case studies and other techniques to indicate children's progress in physical, mental, social, personality, and language development, among others, and present frequency distributions and other statistical data resulting in the establishment of norms at certain chronological ages. Few studies have dealt with individual children and their unique total growth patterns. Most teachers can attest to the fact that no one child in the classroom conforms to the average performances reported as norms in these studies.

According to Frank,

. . . It is what is taking place in the intact functioning child that is significant; this cannot be found in frequency distributions, in each of which a child may occupy a wide range of rank orders because he has been fractionated into a series of discrete variables. The clue to his makeup and functioning is how he attempts to encompass these divergencies and incongruities within his growing organism and emerging personality.

Along this developmental path there are innumerable obstacles, hazards, blocks, and impediments, and also a series of acute transitions with which the child must cope in order to grow up. We may think of this as a maturational process, of relinquishing, giving up, abandoning and rejecting what the child has often laboriously achieved in order that he may replace what he has learned with a new pattern, a new ability, a new way of perceiving the world and coping with the transitions. . . .[1]

Progress, then, takes place in each of several behavior dimensions simultaneously, and it is the responsibility of the teacher to try to encourage this process. To determine the amount of progress made by pupils in the several behavior dimensions, it is necessary for the teacher to evaluate gains made in each dimension for which he has responsibility. In some areas—primarily those in which information is learned—it is relatively simple to assess pupil progress through the use of standardized or teacher-made tests. In other areas, however, measuring pupil progress is not so easy; these involve the measurement of real understanding and the ability to use the information which the pupil assumedly has learned. It is clear that teachers must learn to use a wide variety of evaluative techniques and also must attain an understanding of instruments used by specialists in testing, guidance, and diagnosis. Most important, teachers need to consider values held by the culture and by children and to translate these into aspects of desirable behavior.

Are Our Students More Poorly Educated than Their Forebears?

There has always been, in the United States, a sentimentality toward the schools which is perfectly normal and understandable. Almost everyone in our communities at one time or another was a pupil in the public schools; in earlier days, and even in the present era in many parts of our country, the school was the center of social life in the community. Pleasant memories are usually the only ones recalled when present-day pupils' parents and grandparents reminisce about the "good old days" and the activities that took place in the school they attended. It is quite natural for an adult to feel that his education was superior and that a similar education should be "good enough" for his offspring.

A number of documented studies in existence reveal that modern schools *are* doing a better job of educating the boys and girls of the land than did the schools of the past. Shane and McSwain present some samplings of modern education's results in the one aspect of academic accomplishments:

[1] Lawrence K. Frank, "Four Ways to Look at Potentialities," in *New Insights and the Curriculum,* 1963 Yearbook (Washington, D.C.: Association for Supervision and Curriculum Development, NEA, 1963), p. 25.

1. At least 17 research studies have demonstrated that, from 1844 to the present, children consistently have improved academically. Despite the fact that a less-selected group of children attend the elementary school than attended a century ago, today's youngsters make better scores than did their parents or grandparents when given the same tests.

2. The test scores of 230,000 children, chosen as a representative national sample, were found to have improved 12 percent in a given grade when the same test was used. This remarkable increase was made in a single 10-year period and despite crowded schools and a shortage of teachers.

3. The strong academic gains registered over the years were made by increasingly younger children. The average fourth grader, for example, is one full year younger today than the average fourth grader of 35 years ago! [2]

An article in a recent issue of *Changing Times* magazine reveals,

. . . . There's evidence that the average twelfth grader is weak in both reading and math. Nevertheless, many test scores show that youngsters do better now than they used to. For example, the same tests in reading, arithmetic and language usage given to elementary school children in different years yield higher scores for today's pupils.

Similar results turned up when U.S. Armed Forces Institute tests in English, social studies, science and math were given to a cross section of high school seniors in 1955. They scored better on all subjects, especially math, than seniors who took the same tests in 1943. And James Conant compared the teaching of math and physics in 13 comprehensive high schools with instruction at four well-known, excellent high schools from which the vast majority of students go to college. When he matched the test scores of students with equivalent basic abilities he found no important differences between the two types of schools. In fact, students in one of the comprehensive schools achieved better in both trigonometry and physics than students in any of the "excellent" schools.

. . . . In a recent article, the president of the California Institute of Technology, known to be one of the most rigorously demanding colleges in the country, declared that teachers are preparing students so well that many of the most difficult colleges have had to upgrade their freshman courses. Cal Tech has dropped its remedial reading course, and the chemistry and physics departments have revised their freshman offerings. Each year thousands of high school seniors take placement tests and wind up in advanced courses in college.[3]

Despite the fact that there is always room for improvement in American schools, the facts—objective and unemotional truths—indicate that today's teachers are doing a better job of teaching boys and girls than did their predecessors of some years ago. The demands of the present and future, however, make increasingly better teaching and school programs an absolute necessity.

[2] Harold G. Shane and E. T. McSwain, *Evaluation and the Elementary Curriculum*, rev. ed. (New York: Holt, 1958), pp. 103–4.

[3] "How Good *Are* Our Teachers?" *Changing Times*, 17:30–31, June, 1963. Reprinted by permission. Copyright 1963 by The Kiplinger Washington Editors, Inc., 1729 H St., N.W., Washington, D.C. 20006.

Are We Losing the Educational Race in the World?

One of the favorite pastimes of critics of American education is to compare our schools unfavorably with those of European nations. Admiral Hyman G. Rickover, USN, one of the most vociferous of the critics, for example, recently made such statements as "it is time we look around and see what is being done in other countries," and "rightly, Sputnik has been seen as a triumph of Russian education." But on the worldwide educational scene, a great paradox seems to exist: while many educators and lay persons in the United States are rushing madly to make changes in our educational pattern so that it will resemble that of certain of the European countries, leaders in those nations are fashioning their education systems to correspond to that of the United States. This paradox was expressed eloquently recently by Stanley Elam, editor of *Phi Delta Kappan* magazine, in an editorial in that journal:

It is one of the ironies of our time that in the decade of the Fifties, while domestic critics were castigating American schools for "anti-intellectualism" and comparing them unfavorably with those of Europe, the liberal democracies of that continent were abandoning their rigid caste system, with its emphasis on advanced education for the élite only, and beginning to adopt the kind of free, universal, public, unitary, comprehensive school we take so much for granted.[4]

Countless articles and speeches made by firsthand observers of school systems in other countries bear out the truth that this paradox does, in fact, exist.

To objectively compare the educational systems of foreign countries and the United States is a task of no small proportion. If such a comparison were to be made accurately, it would require, in the words of Medlin, Lindquist, and Schmitt,

. . . *first*, an extensive and intensive investigation into every subject area at every level of the education structure, in order to establish an inventory of quantity and quality, and, *second*, research into the historical, philosophical, social, and economic foundation of the . . . societies from which the schools are created and which they must serve.[5]

After spending several years as director of the Technical Assistance Department of UNESCO in Paris, Hollinshead wrote, upon his return to the United States:

If observations comparing European and American education are to be useful, then it is of first importance to know something of the scope of what is being compared. . . .

. . . in the United States, some seven times as many of the age group attend

[4] Stanley Elam, "Editorial," *Phi Delta Kappan*, 43:49, November, 1961.

[5] William K. Medlin, Clarence B. Lindquist, and Marshall L. Schmitt, *Soviet Education Programs* (Washington, D.C.: U.S. Department of Health, Education and Welfare), pp. 201–10.

high school and at least five times as many attend college as in Europe. Or, to think of it in another way, we have almost as many students in the national honor societies in high schools, and in Phi Beta Kappa, Sigma Xi, and Phi Kappa Phi in our colleges as Europe has in its entire student bodies.[6]

Hollinshead continues to the effect that the only real comparison that can be made between the educational systems of any two nations is in the area of philosophy. He points out that the educational purposes of the United States have always been, in addition to teaching the fundamentals, that of uniting a highly diverse population, mostly of European background, and that of providing everyone a chance for obtaining an education.

European education, on the other hand, as one is told frankly in Europe, is to train an élite, usually recruited from the higher social ranks, which will govern social, political, and economic life. To some degree its purpose is to maintain the existing class structure rather than to break it up. . . . One can be full of admiration for the hard work and high standards involved in this program, without believing that rote learning and a heavy emphasis on past civilizations constitute the best preparation for solving modern problems.[7]

With particular respect to Russian education Mayer, a professor of humanities at the University of Redlands, California, has this to say:

. . . . Through extreme rigor they [the Russians] have almost wiped out illiteracy. As we know, the Russian teacher occupies a high place. Russian achievements in technology and science are not to be underestimated. Their language training is excellent. . . .
But ultimately, our system of education is far superior. It is superior because it is based upon individuality. It is superior because it centers less upon standards. It is superior because it expresses the spirit of democracy.[8]

We are not losing the educational race in the world today. *For us,* the educational system we have is best, and it has played a large part in making this nation the leading one in the world in any aspect one could mention.

Are We Sacrificing Quantity for Quality?

Earlier in this chapter mention was made of the pursuit of excellence in education and of the fact that educators, above all people, realize that the goal of excellence is far from attainment. The publication in 1958 of *The Pursuit of Excellence* by the Rockefeller Brothers Foundation (see Chapter 2, page 39) has challenged the thinking of educators with respect to the responsibilities of the schools and their personnel to students and to the general public.

Having been much used in the literature and in speeches since the publi-

[6] Byron S. Hollinshead, *Is European Education Better?* (Washington, D.C.: American Council on Education, 1958), pp. 1–8.

[7] *Ibid.*

[8] Frederick Mayer, *A History of Educational Thought* (Columbus, Ohio: Charles E. Merrill, 1960), pp. 459–60.

cation of the Rockefeller report, the term "excellence" has taken on several different meanings. To certain individuals, the term means that the quantity of work required of students should be increased; to these persons, excellence would be achieved if students spent a greater amount of time and effort on their school work. To others, "excellence" means a greater emphasis in school upon the teaching of foreign languages, sciences, and mathematics, and consequently a radical alteration of existing curricular patterns. Still other proponents of "excellence" in education advocate leaving the responsibility for character development and for citizenship training to the home and church, with the school concentrating exclusively upon the intellectual development of children and youth.

Excellence in education is a complex concept involving much more than simply the instigation of a "get tough" policy on the part of teachers. Quantity of work must not be confused with quality of work; the increase in academic efforts must not result simply in increased busy work, and no stone should be left unturned in an attempt to help students develop their abilities in such areas as creative and critical thinking. According to Misner, Schneider, and Keith:

What students are expected to learn is important. At a time when areas of knowledge have become so vast and so complicated it is the responsibility of the schools to determine and attach priority to those fields of knowledge that are of greatest significance both to students and to society. Recognizing that some fields of knowledge are of greater importance than others does not imply that all students should be expected to acquire the same knowledge without any consideration to individual interests, aptitudes and abilities. To expect a student whose interests and aptitudes clearly suggest a successful career in the creative arts to acquire mastery of the same scientific subjects required of a potential research chemist is totally indefensible. Excellence in education can be achieved only to the extent that it is sought with reference to the individual student. What may be excellent achievement for one individual may be mediocre or dissipated achievement for another.[9]

Excellence in education, while undeniably a meritorious goal, poses many problems in the course of its pursuit. It cannot be denied that learning *really is* an individual matter, and since education is involved in the business of learning, excellence in education can be attained only to the degree that schools provide for experiences which will result in the optimum development of each student. In a democratic society, excellence in education cannot be attained by the education of the élite only; schools must provide worthwhile learning experiences for "all the children of all the people." The future of our nation and our way of life depends upon the ability of our people to think independently, critically, and creatively.

[9] Paul J. Misner, Frederick W. Schneider, and Lowell G. Keith, *Elementary School Administration* (Columbus, Ohio: Charles E. Merrill, 1963), p. 8.

CONCLUSION

To trace the history of education from ancient times to modern twentieth-century schools is to relate an inspiring story of progress and achievement. Through study of the contributions of the great leaders in education and philosophy, present-day American educators can profit from the accomplishments, as well as the errors, of their predecessors so that education in the world's greatest nation may continue to progress unabated toward an ever-elusive goal of excellence.

The years since World War II have seen the rise of many critics of public education in America. These critics have raised many questions with respect to the programs being offered to children and youth in this country, and in so doing, they have perhaps rendered public education a very real service.

Questions for Discussion

1. In what ways are teachers' situations in modern schools like those of teachers in colonial schools? In what ways are they different? In which aspects of the profession have we apparently made the most progress as far as the teaching situation is concerned?
2. What has the modern American school system inherited from ancient Greece and Rome? the Renaissance period? the Reformation?
3. Which of the early European educators do you think contributed most to the development of America's educational system? What was his contribution?
4. American colonists were "on fire" in favor of freedom of religion, speech, and assembly. Do you think they also were "on fire" to establish democratic schools? What evidence do you have to substantiate your answer?
5. What remnants of the early schools in this country are still in evidence in modern schools? Do you think that schools of the future are likely to retain these remnants? Why?
6. In what ways do you think recent criticisms of the public schools have resulted in changes in their curricula, methods, organization, and administration?
7. What implications for today's teachers are contained in John Dewey's definition of education?
8. To what extent have the goals that Horace Mann envisioned for the common school been accomplished? Why do you think they have not all been accomplished in the more than 100 years since Mann presented them?
9. What is the importance of the Kalamazoo case?
10. What is your attitude toward federal activity in the field of education?

Activities and Projects

1. Consulting history books, state departments of education, and "old timers" in your community, write a paper on the historical development of education in your state.

2. After consulting current periodicals and textbooks containing information on comparative education, prepare a chart on education in the United States and in two countries of your choice. Arrange your paper in three columns, each headed by the countries, and cover items such as Elementary or Common School Program, Secondary School Program, Number of Years Included, Predominant Philosophy, Method of Financing, Primary Control (National, State, Local, etc.), Education of Teachers, Salaries of Teachers, Types of Local Administration, and others you may wish to pursue. The arrangement of your page might be as follows:

Topics	Soviet Union	France	United States
Elementary Program			
Secondary Program			

3. Prepare a time chart of the part the federal government has played in the development of education in the United States.

4. Choose one of the European educational leaders mentioned in this chapter and write a biographical paper emphasizing his contributions to American education. Use the term paper format acceptable in your college's education department.

5. Do the same thing as in number 4 with one of the current leaders in American education.

6. If possible, secure copies of textbooks used in early American schools (or those in use when your grandparents or parents were in school). Compare with books currently in use, noting differences and what the changes are intended to accomplish.

References

"EUROPEAN INFLUENCES AND THE HISTORY OF AMERICAN EDUCATION"

BUTTS, R. FREEMAN, A Cultural History of Western Education, 2d ed. (New York: McGraw-Hill, 1955).

——, "Search for Freedom—The Story of American Education," NEA Journal, 49:33–48, March, 1960.

CALLAHAN, RAYMOND E., An Introduction to Education in American Society, 2d ed. (New York: Knopf, 1960).

GOOD, H. G., *A History of American Education*, 2d ed. (New York: Macmillan, 1962).

GRAMBS, JEAN D., and L. MORRIS MCCLURE, *Foundations of Teaching* (New York: Holt, Rinehart & Winston, 1964), Chapters 11, 12.

KNELLER, GEORGE F., ed., *Foundations of Education* (New York: Wiley, 1963), Chapter 1.

MASSEY, HAROLD W., and EDWIN C. VINEYARD, *The Profession of Teaching* (New York: Odyssey, 1961), Chapters 2, 3.

MAYER, FREDERICK, "Education and the Crisis of Our Times," *Phi Delta Kappan*, 43:300–302, April, 1962.

———, *A History of Educational Thought* (Columbus, Ohio: Charles E. Merrill, 1960).

MESSENGER, JAMES F., *An Interpretative History of Education* (New York: Thomas Y. Crowell, 1931).

MULHERN, JAMES, *A History of Education*, 2d ed. (New York: Ronald, 1959).

POUNDS, RALPH L., and JAMES R. BRYNER, *The School in American Society* (New York: Macmillan, 1959), Chapter 3.

RICHEY, ROBERT W., *Planning for Teaching*, 3d ed. (New York: McGraw-Hill, 1963), Chapters 11, 12.

THAYER, V. T., *The Role of the School in American Society* (New York: Dodd, Mead, 1960), Parts 2 and 4.

THUT, I. N., *The Story of Education* (New York: McGraw-Hill, 1957).

WILDS, ELMER H., and KENNETH V. LOTTICH, *The Foundations of Modern Education* (New York: Holt, Rinehart & Winston, 1961).

"CRITICISMS, QUESTIONS, ISSUES AND TRENDS"

CHANDLER, B. J., *Education and the Teacher* (New York: Dodd, Mead, 1961), Chapter 3.

———, *The Contemporary Challenge to American Education* (Washington, D.C.: Educational Policies Commission, NEA, 1958).

———, *Contemporary Issues in Elementary Education* (Washington, D.C.: Educational Policies Commission, NEA, 1960).

CRESSMAN, GEORGE R., and HAROLD W. BENDA, *Public Education in America* (New York: Appleton-Century-Crofts, 1961), Chapter 17.

DOWNEY, LAWRENCE W., "Direction Amid Change," *Phi Delta Kappan*, 42:186–91, February, 1961.

GRAMBS, Chapters 13, 14, 16.

HASKEW, LAURENCE D., and JONATHON C. MCCLENDON, *This Is Teaching*, rev. ed. (Chicago: Scott, Foresman, 1962), Chapter 13.

HOLLINSHEAD, BYRON S., "American and European Education—Why the Differences?," *NEA Journal*, 48:56–59, February, 1959.

KALLENBACH, WARREN W., and HAROLD M. HODGES, eds., *Education and Society* (Columbus, Ohio: Charles E. Merrill, 1963), Chapter 9.

LEE, J. MURRAY, "Elementary Education, 1985," *Educational Leadership*, 17: 475–79, May, 1960.

MILLER, RICHARD I., "An Approach to Teaching about Communism in Public Secondary Schools," *Phi Delta Kappan*, 43:189–92, February, 1962.

MISNER, PAUL J., FREDERICK W. SCHNEIDER, and LOWELL G. KEITH, *Elementary School Administration* (Columbus, Ohio: Charles E. Merrill, 1963), Chapter 17.

NIEMEYER, GERHART, "Problems of Teaching about Communism," *Phi Delta Kappan*, 43:193–96, February, 1962.

PARKER, J. CECIL, T. BENTLEY EDWARDS, and WILLIAM H. STEGEMAN, *Curriculum in America* (New York: Thomas Y. Crowell, 1962), Chapters 15, 16.

PERKINSON, HENRY J., "The Future of American Education," *Phi Delta Kappan*, 41:398–402, June, 1960.

Phi Delta Kappan, volume 40, October and November, 1958, and volume 43, November, 1961, entire issues.

RICCIO, ANTHONY C., and FREDERICK R. CYPHERT, eds., *Teaching in America* (Columbus, Ohio: Charles E. Merrill, 1962), Part VI.

RICHEY, Chapter 15.

ROCK, WILLIAM C., "Automation Challenges Education," *American School Board Journal*, April, 1961.

SHANE, HAROLD G., "We Can Be Proud of the Facts," *The Nation's Schools*, 60:44–47, September, 1957.

——, and E. T. MCSWAIN, *Evaluation and the Elementary Curriculum* (New York: Holt, 1958), Chapters 1, 2, 4, 15.

STINNETT, T. M., and ALBERT J. HUGGETT, *Professional Problems of Teachers*, 2d ed. (New York: Macmillan, 1963), Chapter 1.

VANTIL, WILLIAM, "Is Progressive Education Obsolete?" *Saturday Review*, February 17, 1962.

WIGGIN, GLADYS A., *Education and Nationalism* (New York: McGraw-Hill, 1962).

X

Philosophers sit in their sylvan hall
And talk of the duties of man,
Of Chaos and Cosmos, Hegel and Kant,
With the Oversoul well in the van;
All on their hobbies they amble away
And a terrible dust they make;
Disciples devout both gaze and adore,
As daily they listen and bake.

PHILOSOPHERS

the philosophies

In speaking of the scope of educational philosophy, Adler says, "It addresses itself only to professional educators; it is even written in a peculiar technical language, which is called 'pedaguese' and is almost totally unintelligible to anyone who has not 'done time' in a school of education." [1] But even many of these who have "done time" in a school of education find difficulty in working out *a* specific philosophy that is workable within a classroom and that can be described in down-to-earth terms in answer to that favorite question of school district panels interviewing applicants: "What is your philosophy of education?" It would be interesting if the applicant were to turn the tables on his interrogators!

A philosophy may be drawn from several schools, not just one. It may be of the teacher's own making and hence couched in a language all its own. Furthermore, it may vary from situation to situation, tending on *la race, le milieu,* and *le moment.*[2]

"Passion for Life," a French educational film of 1920 vintage, presents a

[1] Mortimer J. Adler, "In Defense of Philosophy of Education," *Philosophies of Education,* Forty-first Yearbook, National Society for the Study of Education (Bloomington, Illinois: Public School Publishing Company, 1942), p. 218.

[2] The French philosopher Hippolyte Taine used these terms in his literary works to explain mechanical action. Their use here is in a different context to point out three factors: the sociological, *la race;* the philosophical, *le milieu;* the psychological, *le moment.*

good example of the quest for an applicable philosophy of education. As a fledgling, the new teacher standing before his motley crew of boys inwardly soliloquized: "How does one reach the educational soul of each youth; how does one put the element of inquiry into the mind of this one or that one; how does one kindle the spark that unlocks enthusiasm for learning? Look at ——, his pastime is chasing flies on the ceiling; and ——, he is still fishing by the stream where I first met him; and ——, his bewildered look bespeaks of what is in his mind; and ——, already a man and still here; and ——, so shy that the slightest motion on the part of the teacher unnerves him."

This new teacher had the very essence of a philosophy of education, "to take a student where he is and bring him where he ought to be and could be, and to make it possible for him, in every way, to open the door to knowledge." But what would this teacher have answered to the question "What is your philosophy of education?"

To provide for a more meaningful overview of the philosophies of education two questions must be resolved. The first, "What is a philosophy of education?" The second, "Who has a philosophy of education?" A philosophy of education is any reasonably coherent set of values and fundamental assumptions used as a basis for evaluating and guiding educational practice. And every person who has a reflectively held point of view about basic values and assumptions in education has a philosophy of education.[3]

Before any attempt can be made to determine the applicability of a philosophy of education to the classroom, account must be taken of the fact that the writers of philosophies of education did not expound their concepts with a clear-cut picture of the public school teacher or his school student. They were in a sense issuing learned statements from the podium of wisdom directed for the intellectual consumption of other philosophers.

To develop this thought further and to justify the philosopher's point of view, let us consider the following observation.

But when the philosopher, for example, tries to answer the question of what education is, he does not set out to observe something called education. This question . . . cannot be answered by observation. Rather, the philosopher seeks to answer his questions by construing definitions and making conceptual and linguistic analyses, by arguments that involve cases and counter-examples, by the use of particular facts and cases, as well as by other logical and linguistic techniques. Educational questions answered in these ways come within the scope of educational philosophy.[4]

Applicability of a philosophy of education is relative to the situation within which application can be found. That is to say that the philosophy—or offshoots thereof—must be shaped to the situation, not the situation to the philosophy. It would seem, then, that when the advocate of a particular philosophy of

[3] Philip H. Phenix, ed., *Philosophies of Education* (New York: Wiley, 1961), p. 4.

[4] Chester W. Harris, ed., *Encyclopedia of Educational Research*, 3d ed. (New York: Macmillan, 1960), p. 957.

education states that he unflinchingly adheres, without deviation, to the tenets of *his* philosophy of education, his contention may lack probability.

The question of how to classify the various philosophies of education is difficult to answer, because there are no clear-cut schools of educational philosophy. One of the more widely used classifications is based upon the principles which distinguish the various schools of general philosophy. Thus, as schools of educational thought, there are to be found idealism, scholasticism, realism, experimentalism, and forms of naturalism.

But even schools of general philosophy are not themselves mutually exclusive. Only when each school is considered in bold outline and its principles are taken in their totality as a system of thought can one school be set apart from another. Even so, in their details, there are still similarities among these schools.

Different philosophical positions bring about differing answers as to what a philosophy of education ought to be and ought to do. The following philosophies of education will be considered in the light of this statement: (1) idealism, (2) scholasticism, (3) realism, and (4) experimentalism.

THE PHILOSOPHY OF IDEALISM

Its Tenets

Idealism has come to be used for all philosophic theories which give priority to the mind. There is no single meaning for idealism, but a family of meanings; and, therefore, no single inclusive definition but a family of definitions.[5] Although there are different kinds of idealism, they all stress the reality of personality, though in unequal degrees.

Plato's expression, "To see with the eye of the mind," adapts itself well to the main concept of idealism when added to it is the meaning of the word *idea*, of Greek origin, "things clearly seen." Seeing clearly with the mind's eye means to *see* in a very personal manner. Thus, the idealist can conceive of nothing higher or more valuable than personality. Personality is defined as "that which has value in itself, that for which other values exist, and that which is deserving of respect above all things." [6] In point of origin personality is conceived as descending from the super-personal or an original Person. The personality of man is a part of the infinite mind that comprehends the entire universe in personal terms. As Horne has defined the term, "To think of the universe in terms of an original Person expressing himself in finite persons is idealism as a philosophy." [7]

[5] Hobert W. Burns and Charles J. Brauner, *Philosophy of Education* (New York: Ronald, 1962), p. 237.

[6] Herman H. Horne, "An Idealistic Philosophy of Education," *Philosophies of Education*, Forty-first Yearbook, National Society for the Study of Education (Bloomington, Illinois: Public School Publishing Company, 1942), p. 152.

[7] *Ibid.*, p. 147.

The idealist's world is thus a world in which personality is not only supreme but enjoys freedom, a world of the nature of the mind. In this world mind explains matter, and personality counts for most as it shapes the world to suit its own cosmic purposes. In such a world the destruction of selfhood is unthinkable, and lack of consideration for the personalities of other racial, religious, and ethnic groups is inconsistent with the ideal of the immortality of human personality. To the idealist, the individual must always be considered an end and can never be treated as a means.[8]

Idealists claim that ultimate reality is spiritual or ideal. But idealists, like realists, exhibit wide variations in beliefs about philosophical and educational questions. Even so, idealists subscribe in one way or another to the view that consistency and correspondence to reality, as they see reality, are the primary criteria of true ideas.

Mind is the principle of explanation. We live, and move, and have our intellectual being in a world of mind. There is no adequate denial of this fact. Mind, subjectively used and objectively applied, is the sole principle of explanation.

Implications for Education

To idealists the chief purpose of education is to develop the individual as a finite personality, and to do so in such a way as to bring him into harmony with a superior life. Only if the person is so developed can he enjoy the basic well-being of which he is capable. This aim is to be achieved partly through positive expression of the self, partly by use of the dialectic methods to develop judgment and reasoning, and partly by teaching those skills, knowledges, and ways of thinking essential to responsible citizenship.

Applied to the educational process, this philosophy of personality means that *the learner is an individual who counts for something in the creation of values in the world.* But more than this, the idealist sees the learner not only as an individual but also as a person. The distinction here is one of socialization.

For the idealist, the method (or means) of education is relatively unimportant in the light of the end, i.e., the cultivation of the personality of the pupil. *The idealist teaches pupils, not subjects.*

To summarize the idealist's position, the individual is a finite person capable of growth, under guidance, into the image of a finite person, and nothing is higher or more valued than personality. Respect for personality in feeling and behavior is the highest virtue and, if practiced, would solve all human problems.

Implications for Teaching

"I want to see you think," said the seventh-grade teacher to her pupils. The teacher uses this expression as an attention-getting device to impress

[8] James C. Stone, "A Curriculum for American Ideals," unpublished doctoral dissertation, Stanford University, 1948, p. 14.

upon her charges at the beginning of the school year and many times through-out just what she expects of them. She wants to see all eyes, ears, and minds open. She does not want to sense that some of her students are out of the learning situation.

In speaking with the above teacher (who is not letting the approach of retirement take away two of the marks of good teaching, namely, youthful zest and unlimited enthusiasm), one is not aware that she espouses a particular philosophy of education or that she works toward the implementation of facets of more than one philosophy. As a matter of fact, she leaves one with the impression that her answer to "What is your philosophy of education?" would probably be, "Let the 'pedaguesists' express their concern for philoso-phies of education; my job is teaching pupils." Yet this teacher has adopted and put into use two of the basic principles of idealism, to wit, priority of the mind and priority of the individual. She is in effect bringing about "positive expression of self." [9]

Many conversations with her over a period of years indicate that she adapts herself to the situation (culturally disadvantaged students), that she uses well the method she has adopted, that she gets both her subject and herself liked. And as Horne continues to say along this line of thought, "It is not enough to know method. We must know our pupils and our subjects, and we must be likable people. The objective of all method in teaching is the cultivation of the personality of the pupil." The main thing to remember is that we are teaching students, not subjects.

There is perhaps no other philosophy of education which has a greater impact on the beginning teacher, yet the neophyte is frequently not aware of it. A number of first-year teachers were asked which of the four philosophies of education was likely to exert the greatest influence on their teaching. Al-though eclecticism was apparent in their answers, the mode of expression, such as "concern for my students," "raise their level of thinking," "reach the individual," etc., indicated tendencies to favor idealism.

Some teachers confused ideals with idealism. "My most serious setback," remarked one, "was to find that the high ideals which I brought to the class-room could find no applicability with some of my classes." In her case, it turned out that she was assigned to two kinds of students, the academically oriented or college preparatory, and the nonacademically oriented or noncollege. An-other teacher who had excelled throughout her own scholastic years could not find continuous application for the high standards under which she herself had worked.

While there is some affinity, in a broader sense, between ideals and ideal-ism, the ideal defined as something in its most perfect or excellent form is not compatible with idealism, which can make allowance for the less than perfect and the less than excellent.

[9] Harris, *loc. cit.*

THE PHILOSOPHY OF SCHOLASTICISM

Its Tenets

Scholastic philosophy is theocentric; it has God as its basis. This corner-stone of scholasticism is apt to prove irritating to the modern secularist who either ignores God or relegates Him to lower case. Secularism and naturalism, so characteristic of other schools of educational philosophy, make it exceedingly difficult for the modern mind trained in these philosophies to understand the Catholic position on this important matter. Without God, the Catholic maintains, there is no ultimate purpose in life, no ultimate purpose in education.[10]

Like the idealist to whom he is closely allied, the scholastic also believes in a hierarchy of values. But the supreme value in this instance is union with the Church rather than respect for personality per se. "Supernatural values are obviously more important than the natural; spiritual values of greater import than the bodily and eternal of more significance than temporal."[11] Although personal identity is fused in a unity of thought, this still leaves freedom of will and freedom of choice unimpaired.

Scholastic philosophy teaches that there is a yardstick with which to measure the good and the bad. This yardstick deals with the formation of the whole man, body and soul, intellect and will. This yardstick is fixed and un-changing, suitable for all ages and all countries. Scholastic philosophy teaches that there is such a yardstick, such a norm of morality, one eminently usable, namely, man's rational nature taken in its entirely.

The scholastic holds firm that it is by no happenstance that man was placed on the face of this earth. His goal is clear-cut: to be saved. Thus his educational goal must be fused with his spiritual and must be one, inseparable.

On this very point a first-year teacher had this to say: "We are called, in fact admonished, to be perfect as our heavenly Father is perfect (Matt. 5:48). Moreover, experience has shown that the pursuit of perfection, if properly controlled both exteriorly by those concerned with the life of an individual, and interiorly by the individual himself, can be made a source of enduring happiness and fulfillment. Of course, there are various levels of perfection, i.e., religious, social, moral, political, physical, mechanical, intellectual, etc." Since education encompasses all these levels, it would seem to follow that its goals should be the perfecting of the individual on as many levels as possible with proper respect for the person's ability, obligations, and—by no means least— freedom to choose whether he will be perfect or not.

In reaffirmation of what has been previously stated, the philosophy of education most akin to scholasticism is idealism. The most striking thing to

[10] William J. McGucken, "The Philosophy of Catholic Education," *Philosophies of Education,* Forty-first Yearbook, National Society for the Study of Education (Bloomington, Illinois: Public School Publishing Company, 1942), p. 252.

[11] *Ibid.,* p. 265.

the idealist is his own ideas, his mind. Mind, however, is not just composed of ideas; it is the thinking, feeling, purposing self which everyone introspectively knows himself to be. As such it is the strongest conviction of reality that he has. Both the Catholic and the idealist are concerned to explain the origin of mind.

To summarize, the whole educational aim of scholasticism is to give new life to all persons, restoring them to their high position as children of God, citizens of the kingdom of God. For the scholastic, education is the organized development and equipment of all the powers of a human being, moral, intellectual, and physical, by and for their individual and social uses, directed toward the union of these activities with their Creator as their final end.

Implications for Education

It is the function of education to aid and guide the individual in attainment of "the true, the beautiful, and the good," which possess an inherent value. Knowledge is not considered the final end of education. Rather, the aim of education is a gestalt—the formation of the whole man into the likeness of God, "better still, transformation of Christians into other Christs." [12]

Quite independently of any dogmas of faith, or any calling on truths known through revelation, the scholastic can formulate a definition of education: "Education is the organized development and equipment of all the powers of a human being, moral, intellectual, and physical, by and for their individual and social uses, directed towards the union of these activities with their Creator as their final end." [13]

Such an end justifies any method of learning that is based on the theory that all education is ultimately self-education and should eventuate in a self-disciplined individual. Thus are included the full range of teaching methods from the most traditional to the most progressive.

There has been acrimonious debate within the Catholic Church at various periods of history as to what the child should be taught, but the attitude of the Church in the matter of the child's nature has never changed. Every child born into this world is regarded as a child of Adam. And the Church's whole educational aim is to restore the sons of Adam to their high position as children of God.

Hutchins, in *Higher Learning in America*, points out that modern man is obliged to go to metaphysics to draw education out of its disorder and chaos. He says that in the modern world theology, the principle of order in the medieval university, cannot be an integrating force in education. This is in contradiction to the Catholic viewpoint which holds that metaphysics necessarily deals with the existence and nature of God. The dispute over the definition of *metaphysics* is typical of the secularism of this period, which threatens

[12] Stone, *op. cit.*, p. 17.
[13] T. Corcoran, S.J., *Private Notes* (Dublin, n.d.), as quoted by McGucken, *op. cit.*

to become so dominant that scholasticism will no longer find any expression in the public schools.

Implications for Teaching

Two questions about values and ethical ideals have claimed the interest of educational philosophers. These are (1) what values and rules of conduct are to be taught in the public schools? and (2) how are these values and rules to be taught? Answers to each of these questions have tended to follow differences among philosophers as to the source of values. Those who hold that spiritual values are rooted in the supernatural maintain that moral and spiritual education divorced from religion and religious instruction is inadequate if not impossible. The position of the scholastic is clear: secular education cannot meet the values and rules of scholasticism. These views are exemplified in the American Catholic elementary and secondary schools.

On the other hand, some—those who believe in a naturalistic theory of value, for example—insist upon the view that the secular school can and does develop the highest type of moral as well as spiritual character. "All education is moral, for the end of all teaching is to complete the moral growth of the child, and to impart to him the moral ideals of the race. No knowledge is merely for its own sake, but all must in some way affect conduct. Children act as they have been taught, or as society has let them teach themselves. Honesty, truthfulness, industry, and the other essential virtues of the moral life can be taught. Moreover, the ethical end is not a far-off culmination of

---

SCHOLASTICISM: AN EXAMPLE FOR ILLUSTRATION AND COMMENT

(A Sister, in garb, is teaching a class in a Roman Catholic school. The room is adorned with a crucifix and pictures of Christ, as well as the usual maps, blackboard, etc.)

Sister: Children, we have been discussing what will happen to us when we receive Confirmation. We said that Confirmation does these things for us: It makes us stronger Christians, more perfect Christians, and soldiers of Christ. Today we have been discussing this third point—being soldiers of Christ. The first two we said have to do only with ourselves. You children know that Christ did not just say, "Be strong Christians, be perfect Christians," but He gave us, first of all, His example, secondly, His Commandments and directions, and thirdly, some special helps. What did we say those special helps were, Jean?

Jean: The seven gifts of the Holy Ghost.

Sister: Good, Jean. The first of these two points have to do only with ourselves, to be strong Christians, perfect Christians. Today we talked about that third point: a soldier of Christ. The first quality of a soldier must always be what?

Sam: Courage.

Sister: Yes, now let's look at that last point. A soldier of Christ is responsible for others. Let's take that idea and apply it to our social studies. Look at the map for a moment. We have been studying the Eastern States, and we have noticed how these people depend on each other and need each other. All year in our various units we have discovered how interdependent the sections of the United States are. Now children, can you see what the attitude of a Catholic should be toward these interdependent people? Interdependence is not just being a good American. Realizing our interdependence, the need for justice and charity, is part of our Confirmation, part of being a good soldier of Christ. Can you think of some special ways in which these people of the Eastern States depend on each other and depend on other parts of our country?

First, it should be pointed out that this example is taken from a catechism class. It illustrates the teaching of doctrine, which is done formally in classes of this sort. This is not a class in arithmetic or social studies as such, which would probably be taught in a more formal fashion. The presence of various religious symbols in the classroom helps to remind everyone of the religious beliefs which permeate the school. The example also illustrates the effort of the Catholic educator to put Catholic faith and principles into all of the child's obligations, his civic as well as his religious ones.

Finally, I would mention that while the classroom technique suggested in this example is typical of many Catholic schools, as well as of others, further examples would show that a great variety of techniques are used in the Catholic schools.

Robert J. Henle, "A Roman Catholic View of Education," in *Philosophies of Education*, ed. Philip H. Phenix (New York: Wiley, 1961), pp. 81–82.

---

one's education, but an idea that is to be realized in every step of the educational process. The child is to grow continuously in the moral as in the intellectual life, and these two aspects of life are inseparable.[14] The contentions of both sides are clear. But the Catholics have a better chance of achieving their aims because they have their own school system that is dedicated to their one purpose in education.

That the "yardstick" of the scholastic has breadth and depth is reaffirmed by Pope Paul VI. Holding that young people tend to be conformists, he said that teachers ought to try to develop their individual personalities and self-affirmation. He remarked to a delegation of teachers active in the youth movement of Italian Catholic Action that an educator should not be "a passive observer of the phenomena of the life of young people." "There is nothing like young people—impatient and rebellious toward principles of the past, and particularly the recent past—for acquiescing to fashion, for fearing being

[14] George E. Partridge, *Genetic Philosophy of Education* (New York: Macmillan, 1912), p. 167.

different from others, and for being prone to imitation." The Pope warned the educators against mistaking action for thought and "of making experience the fount of truth." The teacher's goal, he said, must be to train a man to act as he thinks.[15]

A first-year teacher, although espousing idealistic naturalism, seemed, by her own admission, to be groping for something more: "My broader goal as a functioning teacher is an attempt to develop in each student an awareness of self as an individual, *but* an individual who can attempt responsibility for himself and his actions within the society of which he is a member—thus necessitating a keen awareness of self-control for successful interaction within the society. The future of the world lies with those we educate today who will become the ministers, the lodge leaders, the corporation presidents, the parents, the professors—the educators of tomorrow!"

THE PHILOSOPHY OF REALISM

Its Tenets

Modern realists hold ultimate reality to be the objective world, a world independent of any and all human experience. Although realists disagree among themselves on many important points, they seem all to agree that not only the true but also the desirable educational ideas and doctrines are those which correspond to the structure of the objective world. In the realistic view of education, theory and reason play a central role. Since right conduct as well as knowledge is grounded in reality, the chief purpose of education is to enable the student to understand the world as it really is. Hence the basic ideas which make up our knowledge of all forms of reality, including the common purposes and points of view which characterize society, should constitute the content of the educational program. Logic, grammar, and mathematics are to be taught, not only as tools of communication but also as instruments for the apprehension of reality.

Thus, in the pursuit of education, the modern realist makes no allowance for the supernatural. His objectivism is purely external. This externalism has for its credo the central role of theory and reason.

In realism, a familiar as well as useful starting point is the nature of experience. The realist holds that experience is a secondary notion, that a subject and an object must exist in reality before an experience can take place between them. Experiencing, in the realist's view, is the process by which these two independent, antecedent entities come together into a knowing relationship. Thus, the purpose of experiencing is to gain knowledge of what is. In contrast, the experimentalist regards experience as much broader than conscious awareness.

[15] *The Catholic Voice*, April 3, 1964, p. 18.

Realism is a gospel not devoid of discipline in the sense of external pressure—even accepting the idea of compulsion from without, a factor in method derided by experimentalists. The teacher operates not only *in loco parentis*; more fundamentally still, he operates *in loco naturae*. The laws of nature provide the basis for discipline in life. A teacher guilty of arbitrary compulsion would be looked down upon by many of his colleagues, but not a parent using rational compulsion in keeping junior from jumping out of the moving family car.

Realism is more realistic than idealistic, that is, more occupied with things as they *are* than with things as they *should be*, and the realist is frank to admit that if anything is unknown, it cannot at the same time be known, and hence, on the basis of direct knowledge, the truth of the principle of independence—the principle above all others that unifies the realists—cannot be asserted. But the realist does not claim to prove his truth in this impossible way. The principle is not an established generalization from fact. Indeed, realism in its totality is an hypothesis.[16] This theory can be exemplified by examining generic traits of reality as in the following example.

In searching for the reasons to support his practices, the teacher seems ultimately to come to reasons that are basic, beyond which he cannot go or does not care to go. He finally comes to "The world just is that way" or "That is just the nature of things." In other words, there are generic traits of reality which constitute the data, the "givens," of the educative process. If the course of education be set in accordance with them, it can have reasonable assurance of succeeding.

To accept something the way it really is, at face value, that is, to accept it with the finality of reasoning, spells the prerogative of the realist. The realist is a fellow close to common sense and to the common man in his attitude toward knowledge. He observes things coming into his ken, then going out, or so it seems, without suffering any significant modification as a result of such experiencing.

To the writer pounding away at the typewriter in his study, the typewriter does not become less real—does not seem to vanish from the world—when he leaves his study to answer the front doorbell. The configuration of the typewriter—its keys, space bar, ribbon, etc.—can form an instant picture in the mind of the realist, the observer.

To summarize, realism confines itself to the realm of the natural, to the act of knowing—a form of reaction of the organism to a problem situation. To the realist, the problem method in teaching is the one demanded by the nature of the situation.

Respect for the individual is central in the realist's point of view—an individual whose growth is bidirectional in origin—resulting from both the

[16] Frederick S. Breed, "Education and the Realistic Outlook," *Philosophies of Education*, Forty-first Yearbook, National Society for the Study of Education (Bloomington, Illinois: Public School Publishing Company, 1942), p. 102.

demands of society from without and the needs and pressures from within the individual.

Implications for Education

The realist finds educational value in everything that contributes to his intellectual development. The philosopher's terminology for theory of knowledge is epistemology; whatever else education deals with, knowledge certainly has been its central interest through the centuries. For the curriculum of the schools, sound knowledge provides a most important objective.

The realist believes in an educational program which is conceived as a middle-of-the-road pattern between the point of view of the experimentalist on the one hand and the idealist on the other. The one emphasizes the method of education; the other the materials of knowledge.

The realist accepts as an equal aim of education—along with individual development—the acquisition of and adjustment to the group culture. The individual develops through adapting to social pressures so that in the final outcome the demands of the individual and the demands of society have been blended into one.

The aim of education, as the realist sees it, is fourfold: to discern the truth about things as they really are and to extend and integrate such truth as is known; to gain such practical knowledge of life in general and of professional functions in particular as can be theoretically grounded and justified; and finally, to transmit this in a coherent and convincing way both to young and old throughout the human community.

Education is the art of communicating truth. It has not been fully achieved until this truth not only lies within but actually possesses the mind and heart of the student. This process of communication is both theoretical and practical, but the theoretical is prior. The child, of course, should be interested in what he is learning. But it does not follow that whatever the child is interested in is, therefore, valuable. This is absurd. The skill of the teacher lies in eliciting the interests of the child in the right things, especially in grasping the truth for its own sake.[17]

The accidental interests of children should not determine the direction of education. These interests furnish only the point of departure. The teacher who said, in reply to a visitor's question about the program for the morning, "I don't know what it will be; the children haven't come in yet," does not meet the requirements of the realist's theory of education. For the realist, the function of the teacher is not that of an impartial or inert observer, but that of an intelligent guide who directs the process of learning in the light of both the present status of the learner and the important ends to be achieved.

[17] John Wild, "Modern Philosophies and Education," Fifty-fourth Yearbook, National Society for the Study of Education (Chicago: University of Chicago Press, 1955), p. 31.

Implications for Teaching

The "Spare the rod and spoil the child" adage does not hold true for the realist since he substitutes reason for the rattan. The student is given a glimpse of higher wisdom.

The general assumption is that if a thing is worth doing, a good teacher can prove it; and if so, an intelligent class, like an intelligent community, will approve it. It is the doctrine of consent.

The student who enrolls in a foreign language class just to study, to provide mental challenge, or—in the common vernacular—to fulfill a requirement, will not do nearly as well as the one who is keenly motivated by the fascinatingly exciting appeal of communicating with someone from another culture, or of serving his country as a career diplomat, or of becoming a teacher of the foreign language.

"*L'art pour l'art,*" Théophile Gautier's poetic doctrine of art for the sake of art, although realistic in art, finds little applicability in the central role of realism. How much interest holds "math for the sake of math," "chemistry for the sake of chemistry," "biology for the sake of biology"? However, to the magnitudes of the operation of mathematics, the formulas of chemistry, and

---

REALISM: AN EXAMPLE FOR ILLUSTRATION AND COMMENT

(This is a portion of the discussion in a high school physics class.)

Teacher: Today in physics lab we are going to devote our time to a preliminary study of Sir Isaac Newton's three laws of motion. If you have read your homework carefully you will be able to tell me which law I shall be illustrating as I roll this ball across the table. Mary Ann?

Mary Ann: The law of inertia. This means that when something is moving it does nothing itself to change its motion.

Teacher: That is half of it. Can you tell me the other half?

Mary Ann: Yes. When something is at rest it remains that way until something moves it.

Teacher: Good. This ball will continue to roll until it is stopped by me or by some other force. This brings us to Newton's second law of motion. Arnold, will you state it for us?

Arnold: When anything is made to move, its motion is in strict proportion to the force acting on it.

Teacher: Exactly. You boys on the baseball team will know what I mean when I explain the theory of the fast ball and the slow ball. That brings us to the third law of motion. Mary Ann?

Mary Ann: I don't really understand this one. But it says that the action and reaction are equal and opposite.

Teacher: Let me illustrate it for you. It has to do with the truth that rest is a balance of forces. For instance, this book as it stands on the table is attracted by the force of gravitation, but the strength of the table resists this force, so the book remains at rest. Arnold?

Arnold: May I ask a question?

Teacher: Yes.

Arnold: Well, Sir Isaac Newton lived a long time ago. Why are we studying about him today?

Teacher: That is a good question, Arnold. In any field of learning, whether it is mathematics, science, or even music, there are certain basic fundamentals and truths. Sir Isaac Newton, though more of a mathematician than an astronomer, discovered the laws that explain why the moon goes around the earth and the planets revolve around the sun. Now, our whole modern machine world also exemplifies the same Newtonian principles. For instance, modern rocketry is an application of Newtonian physics. So Newton is really very modern after all.

In this example we have a teacher trying to induct the class into a field of knowledge, an organized, systematic body of knowledge, physics in this case. They are discussing the laws of Sir Isaac Newton, who illustrates one of the peaks of excellence in the development of physics. This is certainly compatible with the emphasis of classical realism. Notice also the concern for the theoretical, for understanding general laws, which is also characteristic of the classical realist approach.

What the example does not and really could not show, because of its brevity, are the arts of learning: the forming of habits of acquiring, using, and enjoying knowledge through engaging in these acts day after day until the student becomes adept at them. Among these are the arts of reading, of studying, of research, of deliberation, and of discussion. Nor does the example show the arts of imagination being developed. For that we might use a different kind of lesson, such as one in the fine arts, in literature, or even in history.

Harry S. Broudy, "A Classical Realist View of Education," in *Philosophies of Education,* ed. Philip H. Phenix (New York: Wiley, 1961), pp. 22–23.

---

the language of biology, add the proper ingredients of interest on the part of the student (for career or professional attainment), and knowledge of subject matter, suitable methodology, and creativity on the part of the teacher, and there evolves a recipe conducive to separating the known from the unknown.

THE PHILOSOPHY OF EXPERIMENTALISM

Its Tenets

Experimentalism as an explicit and systematic theory of education stems primarily from the work of John Dewey. It belongs to the twentieth century, and, like Dewey, it is characteristically American in its temper and outlook. The full realization of experimentalism as a comprehensive philosophy came with the advent of industrialism, modern science, and technology.

According to some educational philosophies, the doctrines and practices of education find their ultimate vindication in the analysis, criticism, and organization of human experience. Other philosophies hold that some of these doctrines are rooted in a conception of an ultimate reality which transcends ordinary experience. A general view which finds acceptance by experimentalists is that philosophers who stress experience as the final court of appeal in the justification of educational ideas look to practical consequences. For experimentalists the test of educational doctrines is to be found in how they work out at the level of observation and practice.

In further substantiation of this approach is a statement of the viewpoint of the experimentalist Hullfish:

The experimentalist turns *to* experience rather than *away* from it in order to find values that are to direct this experience. Experimentalists . . . turn to experience, believing that values emerge in the stresses and strains and in the hopes and aspirations of daily life and that these, when further reflected upon and refined, are then set up as ideals to serve until such time as it seems necessary for them to undergo reconstruction in order that they may guide human activities more effectively.[18]

Knowledge for the experimentalist does not exist objectively as its does for the idealist. Knowledge exists only within experience—as a process of interaction between the individual and his environment. "We always live at the time we live and not at some other time, and only by extracting at each present time the full meaning of each present experience are we prepared for doing the same thing in the future. This is the only preparation which in the long run amounts to anything." [19] It is by and through this process of interaction between a person and social group of which he is a part that personality of selfhood is formed—"a being able to think itself of what it knows of itself." [20]

It is certain then that, for the experimentalist, experience assumes both an organism and an environment and is the outcome of their continual interaction. Furthermore, experience is not just something which is privy to the person who has it. Experience is what it is largely because of the social context in which it takes place. Indeed, if experience did not occur in a common culture it would have far less meaning than it does. One's knowledge of himself is enhanced by his knowledge of others and his knowledge of others by knowledge of himself. Since the breadth and depth of experience depend on the culture context in which it occurs, preparing the individual to participate in that culture is the main objective of education. Only as it is experienced and lived does this culture enter into experience, and it can be lived only as the school enters into community activities, takes field excursions, has shops, and the like.

[18] Phenix, *op. cit.*, p. 11.

[19] John Dewey, *Intelligence in the Modern World* (New York: Random House, 1939), p. 673.

[20] William H. Kilpatrick, "Philosophy of Education from the Experimentalist Outlook," *Philosophies of Education*, Forty-first Yearbook, National Society for the Study of Education (Bloomington, Illinois: Public School Publishing Company, 1942), p. 41.

To the experimentalist the sum total of experience, its aggregate, can find realization within the individual always as an end and never merely as a means. In this regard the experimentalist outlook is interwoven with the following three conceptions from Kilpatrick:

1. Ideas mean only their consequence in experience.
2. Experience is essentially social in origin and predominantly social in purpose.
3. We find out what to expect in life by studying experimentally the uniformities within experience.[21]

To summarize, the experimentalist stresses both the experience of the individual and the experience of the group, but sees the growth of the individual as the end, and the social order as the instrument for achieving the development of personality.

Implications for Education

On the strictly pedagogical side, experimentalism holds the view that the method of problem-solving, by which science has progressed in its conquest of nature, is the best method of learning. It claims that the standards of intellectual discipline to be developed through education are determined by the demands of the problematic situation and the process of its resolution. Pragmatism holds that the end of education is growth, and that the optimum conditions of growth consist of freedom to investigate, together with an absolutely free sharing and exchange of ideas. The most widespread objection to the pragmatic theory of inquiry is that voiced by philosophers who insist upon absolute standards of conduct and upon some conception of knowledge as *transcending* ordinary experience. Other critics, holding man's fundamental knowledge to be metaphysical, insist that scientific knowledge is secondary.

We may see both how the child learns the culture and how to state the correlative aim of education. The child shares in the life of the family and neighborhood; he must do so; his existence depends upon it. This surrounding life goes on, as we saw, in terms of the culture. The child in living this life lives it as shaped and permeated by the cultural distribution. What is thus lived is not lost, as Clifford says, but retained, built at once into the child's organism, into the very structure of his being, to serve as the foundation for future action.[22]

In brief, any adequate educational program will thus be concerned to help each individual child grow up from his state of initial dependence into full participation in the richest available group life, which, in a democratic country, includes a full share in the active management of group affairs. Such an educational program will go on further in an active effort to improve the group culture.

The social concept of experimentalism was nurtured by new interpretations

[21] *Ibid.*, p. 44.
[22] W. K. Clifford, *Lectures and Essays* (London) as quoted by Kilpatrick, *op. cit.*

of the school institution, which in turn gave birth to the term "progressive education." Most of the educational reforms of the first half of the twentieth century were loosely grouped under this term, as the movement had its greatest influence between 1918 and 1935. Progressivism in education rested in part upon new psychological evidence about the nature of the learner and the learning process and in part upon new interpretations of the school as a social institution.

Implications for Teaching

It is not the business of the school to transport youth from an environment of activity into one of cramped study of the records of other men's learning; but to transport them from an environment of relatively chance activities, into one of activities selected with reference to guidance of learning. The most direct blow at the traditional separation of doing and knowing and at the traditional prestige of purely "intellectual" studies has been given by the progress of experimental science. If this progress has demonstrated anything, it is that there is no such thing as genuine knowledge and fruitful understanding except as the offspring of doing. Men have to do something to things when they wish to find out something; they have to alter conditions. This is the rule of the laboratory method, and the lesson which all education has to learn.[23]

In short, *"You live what you learn, and you learn what you live,"* as Dewey pragmatically put it!

In an experimentalist classroom, two things would be expected to predominate. The first of these may be called the "continuity of a reflective atmosphere," where students are not merely engaged in fruitless memorization but are thinking through problems of concern and are being helped to do so by the knowledge they bring to bear on them. The second expected thing, if we take seriously the development of the quality of human relationships, may be called the "continuity of a democratic atmosphere." [24]

There are problems which may easily become too personal for free study, for example, local political problems. But the deeper problems of civilization have to be studied and our citizens must become intelligent about them. Thinking through problems, or the continuity of a reflective atmosphere, and developing human relationships, or the continuity of a democratic atmosphere, are basic to the "Seek and you shall find" theory of experimentalism.

EXPERIMENTALISM: AN EXAMPLE

The course of study for fifth-grade social studies in the Bluegrass public schools requires a unit on the community. To introduce it, the teacher took the class on a field trip. The class spent part of a day busing about the city,

[23] John Dewey, *Democracy and Education* (New York: Macmillan, 1915), pp. 320–22 *passim*.

[24] Phenix, *op. cit.*, p. 12.

observing its geographic features and its industrial complex, and hearing about such things as its unique form of city government.

Now the class has divided into interest groups at work on various projects. One group is concerned with the historical development of the city, another with its economy, another with its cultural features. Each group is responsible to make a detailed study of its topic and to devise a means of writing it up and presenting it to the entire class. Some of the students are working with reference books, others have gone to the library or to interview resource persons, still others are making charts, exhibits, posters, or are writing up materials.

The teacher moves from group to group, assisting, suggesting, encouraging. The students move about freely. Some work at committee tables in groups; some work individually, then consult and talk with each other.

In the illustration, several features are apparent:

1. The pupils are learning from direct experiences as a prelude to or in conjunction with indirect or vicarious experiences.
2. They are working on problems they have chosen—problems which are therefore real to them ("lifelike") and for which they have considerable inherent motivation.
3. Their intellectual skills are developing, as are their skills of cooperation and deportment.
4. The role of the teacher is that of stimulator, activator, group leader; always in control, but usually from behind the scenes.

To the above implications for classroom teaching, a teacher's reaction may well be, "How can I put all this theory into practice? How can I—a kindergarten teacher, an elementary grade teacher, a junior high or senior high school teacher—practice what the experimentalist preaches?" And the experimentalist will answer, "Go to the butcher, the baker, the kilowatt maker. Visit the courtroom, the city hall, the auto factory, the marina, the propulsion plant, the jet runway, etc., etc., etc., and take back to the classroom for exploration and experimentation the substance of your sorties." In addition, the experimentalist is bound to say, "Remember the experience of children is the curriculum of the classroom."

CONCLUSION

The irreducibles in the teaching process are the teacher, the learner, the thing taught and learned, the method used, the locale (where), and the time (when). Of these, the teacher and the learner are the most important. And of these two, the teacher is engaged only for the sake of the learner.[25]

Whether or not he is aware of it, Horne's "ultimate irreducible"—the teacher—must have a philosophy of education—a series of beliefs on the basis

[25] Horne, *op. cit.*, p. 158.

of which he makes educational decisions and which guide his actions. Similarly, every school faculty has a philosophy of education and every school district has one.

The four philosophical schools reviewed in this chapter agree on the (1) importance of the individual or respect for personality as a basic value; (2) need for an understanding of the social and cultural development of our civilization, as well as of the development of the intellectual powers of the child; and (3) necessity for preparing the student for his future role in life.

The traditionist schools (idealism, scholasticism, realism) are at opposite poles from the experimentalists on such points as the (1) place of fixed standards in guiding behavior, (2) importance of knowledge as an end rather than as means, and (3) contribution of the present to the process of learning. Applied to teaching, the traditionist philosophies place top priority on the student's knowledge of the cultural heritage and on a curriculum aimed at preparing students for the future by gaining an understanding of the accumulated wisdom of the past. The progressive's philosophy, applied to teaching, places top priority on the student's studying directly the problems of his own environment and mastering the understandings and skills necessary to work cooperatively with his peers in the solution of these problems.

By both direct and implicit statements, this chapter has emphasized that few teachers have a philosophy of education that can be tied directly to one school; most are eclectic in their point of view. But all have one, usually unexpressed or implied, to guide them.

Questions for Discussion

1. Look over the various statements of goals in Chapter 2. To what school of philosophy would you assign each one?
2. How would you classify the educational philosophy of the instructor of this course? Why?
3. What are the chief sources of one's philosophy? Home? School? Religious affiliation? College? Or what?
4. Can an adherent of the Aristotelian philosophy be a satisfactory public school teacher? Do you know of any? What adjustments or concessions might such a person have to make?
5. To what extent do your local newspapers reflect a school of philosophy in their editorials on educational matters?
6. What about the curriculum of the college or university you now are attending? What philosophy of education does it reflect?
7. What parts of the local school curriculum reflect what school of philosophy?
8. Examine the list of activities and projects in an elementary or secondary school textbook. To what extent do they reflect the influence of progressive education?

9. Should the schools teach democratic values? How is your answer a reflection of a particular school of philosophy?
10. To what extent should a teacher try to get his students to adapt to his own philosophy?

Activities and Projects

1. Write to a school district of your choice and obtain a statement of their philosophy of education. To what extent would you say it is eclectic?
2. Prepare a report on the life and times of John Dewey, showing in particular how his philosophy was a reaction to the social milieu of his times.
3. Visit a kindergarten and spend a day observing the program. How does it reflect the concepts of progressive education?
4. Observe a class in vocational education in a nearby secondary school. To what extent is the program a reflection of the influence of John Dewey and company?
5. Observe some college preparatory junior high school classes of English. To what extent is the teaching a reflection of the traditionist philosophies?
6. Visit a Catholic school in a nearby community. To what extent are what is taught and how it is taught a reflection of scholasticism?
7. Interview the superintendent or principal of a public school. Inquire about his philosophy of education and then try to classify it.
8. Interivew the Mother Superior of a Catholic school, and ask her for a brief statement of her philosophy of education. How does it differ from that of a realist?
9. Interview the headmaster of an independent elementary or secondary school. Ask about his philosophy of education. How does it fit into this chapter's classification of schools?
10. Prepare a report on a philosopher of distinction such as John Dewey, William H. Kilpatrick, Boyd Bode, Comenius, Aristotle, Plato, Rousseau.
11. Write an essay on "Current Philosophies of Education" in which you compare the principles of idealism, realism, and pragmatism. Include the names of philosophers associated with each school, together with some of their theories.

References

"IDEALISM"

ADLER, MORTIMER J., "In Defense of Philosophy of Education," *Philosophies of Education*, Forty-first Yearbook, National Society for the Study of Education (Bloomington, Illinois: Public School Publishing Company, 1942), Chapter 5.

BARRET, CLIFFORD, ed., *Contemporary Idealism in America* (New York: Macmillan, 1932).

BESTOR, ARTHUR, "Education for Intellectual Discipline," in *Philosophies of Education*, ed. Philip H. Phenix (New York: Wiley, 1961), Chapter 4.

BRAMELD, THEODORE, *Philosophies of Education in Cultural Perspective* (New York: Dryden, 1955), Part III, "Education as Cultural Conservatism."

BUTLER, J. DONALD, *Four Philosophies and Their Practice in Education and Religion* (New York: Harper, 1957).

———, "Idealism in Education Today," *School and Society*, 87:8–10 (January 17, 1959).

HORNE, HERMAN H., "An Idealistic Philosophy of Education," *Philosophies of Education*, Forty-first Yearbook, National Society for the Study of Education (Bloomington, Illinois: Public School Publishing Company, 1942), Chapter 4.

KIRK, RUSSELL, "A Conservative View of Education," in *Philosophies of Education*, ed. Philip H. Phenix (New York: Wiley, 1961), Chapter 10.

LIGON, ERNEST M., "Education for Moral Character," in *Philosophies of Education*, ed. Philip H. Phenix (New York: Wiley, 1961), Chapter 6.

ROYCE, JOSIAH, *Lectures on Modern Idealism* (New Haven: Yale University Press, 1919).

"SCHOLASTICISM"

BUTLER, J. DONALD, *Four Philosophies and Their Practice in Education and Religion* (New York: Harper, 1957). Chapter 6, "Scholasticism."

HENLE, ROBERT J., "A Roman Catholic View of Education," in *Philosophies of Education*, ed. Philip H. Phenix (New York: Wiley, 1961), Chapter 8.

MC GUCKEN, WILLIAM J., "The Philosophy of Catholic Education," *Philosophies of Education*, Forty-first Yearbook, National Society for the Study of Education (Bloomington, Illinois: Public School Publishing Company, 1942), Chapter 6.

MARITAIN, JACQUES, *Education at the Crossroads* (New Haven: Yale University Press, 1943).

OUTLER, ALBERT C., "Quid Est Veritas," *Christian Century*, 76:258–60, March 9, 1959.

PARTRIDGE, GEORGE E., *Genetic Philosophy of Education* (New York: Macmillan, 1912).

WILDS, ELMER H., and KENNETH V. LOTTICH, *The Foundations of Modern Education*, 3d ed. (New York: Holt, Rinehart & Winston, 1961), Chapter 7, "Spiritual Discipline for the Soul's Salvation."

"REALISM"

BRAMELD, THEODORE, Part IV, "Philosophic Foundations of Perennialism."

BREED, FREDERICK S., *Education and the New Realism* (New York: Macmillan, 1939), Chapters 1, 10.

——, "Education and the Realistic Outlook," *Philosophies of Education,* Forty-first Yearbook, National Society for the Study of Education (Bloomington, Illinois: Public School Publishing Company, 1942), Chapter 3.

BROUDY, HARRY S., *Building a Philosophy of Education* (Englewood Cliffs, N.J.: Prentice-Hall, 1954), Chapters 1, 2.

——, "A Classical Realist View of Education," in *Philosophies of Education,* ed. Philip H. Phenix (New York: Wiley, 1961), Chapter 2.

——, "Realism in American Education," *School and Society,* 87:11–14, January 17, 1959.

BUTLER, J. DONALD, *Four Philosophies and Their Practice in Education and Religion* (New York: Harper, 1957), Chapter 3, "Realism."

"EXPERIMENTALISM"

BODE, BOYD, *Modern Educational Theories* (New York: Macmillan, 1927), Chapters 4–6.

CHILDS, JOHN L., *American Pragmatism and Education* (New York: Holt, 1956), Chapter 11.

——, *Education and Morals: An Experimentalist Philosophy of Education* (New York: Appleton-Century-Crofts, 1950).

——, *Education and the Philosophy of Experimentalism* (New York: Century, 1931).

DEWEY, JOHN, *The Child and the Curriculum* (New York: Macmillan, 1920).

——, *Democracy and Education* (New York: Macmillan, 1916).

——, *Intelligence in the Modern World* (New York: Random House, 1939).

——, *The School and Society* (New York: Macmillan, 1915).

HANDLIN, OSCAR, *John Dewey's Challenge to Education* (New York: Harper, 1959).

KILPATRICK, WILLIAM H., "Philosophy of Education from the Experimentalist Outlook," *Philosophies of Education,* Forty-first Yearbook, National Society for the Study of Education (Bloomington, Illinois: Public School Publishing Company, 1942), Chapter 2.

SMITH, B. OTHANEL, "Philosophy of Education," *Encyclopedia of Educational Research,* 3d ed., ed. Chester W. Harris (New York: Macmillan, 1960), 957–63.

STRATEMEYER, FLORENCE B., "Education for Life Adjustment," in *Philosophies of Education,* ed. Philip H. Phenix (New York: Wiley, 1961), Chapter 3.

"ECLECTICISM AND GETTING INTO THE CLASSROOM"

BRACKENBURY, ROBERT L., *Getting Down to Cases* (New York: Putnam, 1959).

BRUBACHER, JOHN S., ed., *Eclectic Philosophy of Education* (Englewood Cliffs, N.J.: Prentice-Hall, 1951).

BUSH, ROBERT, *The Teacher-Pupil Relationship* (Englewood Cliffs, N.J.: Prentice-Hall, 1954).

GRAMBS, JEAN D., and MORRIS L. MCCLURE, *Foundations of Teaching* (New York: Holt, Rinehart & Winston, 1964), Chapter 16, "The Need for Philosophy and Values in Education."

HARRIS, RAYMOND P., *American Education: Facts, Fancies, and Folklore* (New York: Random House, 1961).

KING, EDMUND J., *World Perspectives in Education* (Indianapolis: Bobbs-Merrill, 1962), Chapter 11, "Philosophy, Psychology, and Programmes."

MOORE, HARRY R., *Modern Education in America* (Boston: Allyn & Bacon, 1962), Chapter 7, "Philosophical Foundations."

PARKER, J. CECIL, T. B. EDWARDS, and WILLIAM STEGEMAN, *Curriculum in America* (New York: Thomas Y. Crowell, 1962), Chapter 2, "Philosophies and Aims of Education."

PHENIX, PHILIP H., ed., *Philosophies of Education* (New York: Wiley, 1961).

THELEN, HERBERT A., *Education and the Human Question* (New York: Harper & Row, 1960).

WOODRING, PAUL, and JOHN SCANLON, eds., *American Education Today* (New York: McGraw-Hill, 1963), Part Two, "The Changing Philosophies."

If society clearly defines the new duties it wishes our schools to fulfill and if it steadfastly supports them not only with money but also with faith, they will surely justify that faith in the future as they have in the past.

HENRY STEELE COMMAGER

the system

ORGANIZATION OF THE SCHOOLS

As indicated previously, there are fifty separate systems of education in the United States—one for each state—instead of one system for the entire country. Since the nation's Constitution makes no mention of education and its control, this aspect of the culture has been considered an implied power of the states and falls under the provisions of the Tenth Amendment. Thus, education legally is a function of each state, and each has made provisions in its constitution for the establishment of public schools. The states, in turn, have delegated a large part of their responsibility in education to local school districts, which elect directors who are state officials. The federal government, too, has, since the earliest days of this nation's history, played an important role in the development and operation of public schools. Thus, public education in the United States is, in reality, a function shared by the federal and state governments and the local districts; legally, however, it is a function of the states, and the state legislatures have complete control over public education within their boundaries, subject, of course, to limitations of the federal and state constitutions.

The number of local districts within each of the states varies considerably; for example, whereas in 1962 the state of Nevada had only 17 districts, the state of Nebraska had more than 3500. In 1962, the total number of districts throughout the United States stood at 35,330, having been reduced from 125,000 in 1933 through consolidation and reorganization. By 1970, the number of districts should be 10,000 if the recommendations of the President's Commission on National Goals (1960) are realized.

Most school districts provide for a program of instruction from kindergarten or grade one through at least grade twelve, with many districts extending to grades thirteen and fourteen. Though many other organizational schemes are in operation, typically the elementary school includes grades kindergarten or one through six; the junior high, grades seven through nine; and the senior high school, grades ten through twelve. Some districts employ an 8–4 structure, others use a 6–6 or a 6–2–5 plan; newer experimental plans use arrangements different from these, or none at all, as in the nongraded schools.

Elementary and secondary schools provide programs which meet the minimum standards prescribed by state codes, and embellish their curriculums in accord with their financial abilities. Thus, the offerings of these two school levels ordinarily provide for rather complete educational programs and services, including special classes at various age levels for physically and mentally handicapped and mentally superior students, guidance and counseling services, health services, and remedial programs commensurate with the district's initiative and capabilities. Though some secondary schools specialize in vocational training, most operate as comprehensive high schools, offering a complete program of studies suitable for all students—those going to college, those undecided about college, and those going to work after high school. Of the comprehensive high schools' programs, Conant suggests that they:

> . . . have three main objectives: first, to provide a general education for all the future citizens; second, to provide good elective programs for those who wish to use their acquired skills immediately upon graduation; and third, to provide satisfactory programs for those whose vocations will depend on their subsequent education in a college or university. . . . This high school should have no less than 100 students in its graduation class.[1]

It is recommended that each elementary and secondary attendance unit employ a full-time principal and sufficient supervisory personnel to care for its needs in this area. If the staff of a building exceeds 25 persons, the principal should have additional administrative personnel to assist with his work. To be self-sufficient—that is, to be economically able to offer a wide range of special services, including health personnel, a psychological consultant, etc.—it has been suggested that school districts should have at least 10,000 students, or 2000 pupils if the district can obtain certain special services from other sources, such as a county or an intermediate unit.

FINANCING

School finance is one of the most important and, generally, one of the most complex aspects of public education. While financial matters are usually considered principally the concern of the superintendent or one of his assistants or the business manager, in reality they directly affect each teacher and each lay person in the community. Teachers are, of course, vitally interested in such

[1] James B. Conant, *The American High School Today* (New York: McGraw-Hill, 1959), pp. 14, 17.

financial aspects as salaries; amounts allocated for teaching-learning materials and equipment, including textbooks; and adequate physical facilities in which to work. Lay citizens, while normally interested in providing a good education for children in the community, are, at the same time, concerned with the costs of the school system's programs. In most communities in the United States, the public school is the largest of all business enterprises.

Although a great sum of money goes into the schools each year—currently about 18 billion dollars per year, representing about 6 per cent of the national income—it is still doubtful that enough is being spent for the education of America's most important natural resources. It is anticipated that by 1982 the cost of maintaining and operating all schools and colleges in the nation will exceed 50 billion dollars.[2] But compared to what our citizens spend on such items as tobacco, liquor, and cosmetics, the amounts expended for education are indeed meager.

Currently across the country, the local community pays about 56 per cent of the total cost of public school education,[3] and about 90 per cent of that amount is derived from taxes on local real estate. The states' share, nationally, approximates 40 per cent of the total school costs, though the proportion of support provided at that level varies widely, from 5 per cent in Nebraska and New Hampshire, to 89 per cent in Delaware. There is a need for action which will widen the local tax base to relieve real property of a disproportionate share of financing schools, and since most school districts are not empowered to devise new tax revenues, there is a need for increased state and federal support of education. In one way or another, however, there is no way to support public schools other than by taxation.

Many problems of the schools relate to the matter of their finances, or, rather, the lack of finances. The problems have become more numerous and critical in recent years with the trend toward extending school systems upward to include the junior college and downward to include the kindergarten and nursery school, the trend toward equalizing educational opportunity for all boys and girls in the country, colossal increases in enrollment, the attempt to provide more quality in the educational program, tremendous increases in school building construction, and inflation.

The school budget is the instrument whereby the school systems cope with financial problems. Generally, the budget is prepared by the superintendent or his assistant in charge of finance and is presented to the board of education for approval. There is a current trend in budget preparation toward the cooperative involvement of representatives of all groups of school personnel and, in many instances, of lay people in the school community. A good budget includes not only an annual financial plan of educational program, receipts, and expenditures, but also a projection of these budgetary areas on a long-term basis, sometimes extending up to twenty years into the future. The educational program portion of the plan includes such factors as the curriculum, pupil

[2] *Changing Times*, 11:32, June, 1957.
[3] *Progress of Public Education in the United States of America, 1960–61* (Washington, D.C.: U.S. Department of Health, Education and Welfare, 1961), p. 26.

population, teacher-pupil ratios, and scope of offerings. The plan for receipts involves listing the sources of funds other than those to be raised by local taxes and the amounts estimated to be received from each source. Included in the expenditures section of the budget are classifications of instruction (which generally accounts for an average of 66.7 per cent of the total expenditures), administration (4.5 per cent), fixed charges such as rent and insurance (6.4 per cent), operation and maintenance of the physical plant (13 per cent), and special services such as health and school lunch, summer school, capital outlay, and debt services (9.4 per cent).

CONTROL

The American people are zealous in their desire to maintain the operation of their schools at a local level. As a result, people living in school districts establish their schools and provide buildings, materials, personnel, and programs for their operation and maintenance. The districts originally were formed by a vote of the people with approval of the state legislature. The boundaries of the districts vary to a great extent; sometimes they follow city, township, or county lines, sometimes not. Generally, counties are broken up into school districts, though in a number of southern states the local school district's boundaries are the same as those of the county. As indicated previously, there is a national trend toward consolidation of two or more local districts into one so that small, inefficient units might be replaced by larger ones which can provide improved educational programs. Some states have established intermediate units. In previous years these consisted of administrative units operating within county lines with a primary concern for schools in rural areas and small towns. Currently, the intermediate units assist the state office in supervising local schools, provide for special supplementary services to local districts which for some reason cannot provide these services for themselves, assume the responsibility of providing a special educational program for such areas as vocational training and handicapped youngsters, and provide an educational program for post-high school students who do not intend to go to college.

Boards of Education

The governing board for each school district is a five- to nine-member lay group known as the board of education. The board is usually elected by the citizens of the district and derives its powers from the state. Approving the system's annual budget and employing a district superintendent are the two primary responsibilities of the board of education, though it is charged also with hiring all school district personnel, levying taxes, contracting for school building construction, approving salary schedules, and generally setting school system policy. A board of education is a policy-making group, and its functions do not include administering the schools, though it does have the power to make and enforce reasonable rules and regulations. To carry out its policies, it names a chief executive officer, the superintendent of schools.

Superintendent of Schools

The superintendent of schools serves not only as the executive officer of the board of education, but also as the school system's chief administrator. Since the first professional superintendent was appointed in 1837 in Buffalo, New York, the person in this office generally has been charged with carrying out policies of the board and serving as educational leader of the community and of the professional staff.

The Building Principal

As the superintendent is the professional leader for the system, so the principal is the educational leader of an individual elementary or secondary school building. The principalship no longer is a teaching position from which a little time is released for care of administrative details; ideally, it is a full-time professional position, the holder of which is considered an educational states-man in his school community.

Today's principal is an instructional leader; national administrators' organizations are advocating that elementary and secondary principals spend at least 50 per cent of their time in supervisory activities. In addition to helping teachers through various supervisory activities, principals maintain records on pupils and staff, prepare schedules, employ substitute teachers, prepare various kinds of reports, provide teachers with teaching materials, spark curriculum improvement, and assist with hiring teachers.

State Departments of Education

The agency in state government which licenses public school teachers and issues their teaching credentials is the state department of education. Of course, this agency also carries out a number of other important functions besides that of licensing; these include providing adequate, balanced, comprehensive plans for the state's public school programs; proposing educational measures for legislative consideration and executing school laws that have been passed by the legislature; distributing monies from the state for support of local schools; establishing certain minimum regulations governing curriculums, building construction, and health and safety measures. In most states, the state department provides certain supervisory assistance, such as consultants and materials in various fields of knowledge, for the use of teachers in the state; professional information of all kinds is accessible in state department offices, also.

Chief State School Officer

The executive officer of the state department of education is called, variously, the state superintendent of schools, the state superintendent of public instruction, the commissioner of education, or state director of education. He is generally elected by the people or appointed by the governor, although there is a trend toward appointment by the state board of education. Generally, his tenure is for four years, though some states provide an indefinite term of office.

Among the duties of the chief state school officer are to have general supervision of the public schools; to act as the executive officer of the state department of education and the state board of education; to nominate (and remove from office) personnel for his professional and clerical staff; to organize the state department of education, subject to the state board of education's approval; to prepare outlines for state courses of study; to prepare and submit to proper state officials a budget for current expenses of the state department and for amounts of money to be appropriated to public schools and to institutions under control of the state department; to interpret school laws; to prepare forms for reports from school districts and state educational institutions; to evaluate credentials and issue licenses to certificated school personnel; to approve school sites and plans; to review proposals for school consolidations; to report state school status and needs to the legislature and the governor; and to approve teacher-education curriculums.

State Boards of Education

All states except Illinois, Michigan, North Dakota, and Wisconsin have state boards of education whose chief responsibility consists of interpreting the educational needs, practices, and trends of the schools to the people in the state, and of developing the educational policies desired by the people. In the four states mentioned, these responsibilities are carried out by the chief state school officials. Most members of the state boards are appointed by the governor or other state officials, but there seems to be a trend toward having the members elected by the people. The number on the boards and the tenure of the members vary widely among the states.

STATE CERTIFICATION

Enormous differences exist among the fifty states in the certification of teachers and other school personnel such as principals, guidance workers, and superintendents. So great is the variation in requirements that about all one can say the various states have in common is the requirement that the teacher be issued some type of license before he can commence to practice his profession.[4]

In such "low-standard states" as Mississippi, Alabama, and the Dakotas, a person may be issued a regular certificate even if he does not possess a bachelor's degree. At the other extreme are the "high-standard states," such as Arizona, California, New York, and Washington, in which a regular certificate is issued

---

[4] See Elizabeth H. Woellner and M. Aurilla Wood, *Requirements for Certification,* 27th ed. (Chicago: University of Chicago Press, 1962).

only after the completion of five years of preparation. There also are wide variations in the specific requirements for a teaching certificate. For example, no two states have the same requirements for an elementary school certificate. To add to the lack of agreement on what constitutes essential minimum preparation for a teacher, even the high-standard states have loopholes and "escape hatches," which permit teaching on less than the regular fifth-year standard. Sometimes these forms of substandard certification are called "provisional" or "emergency," and in other cases a so-called "standard" certificate is issued with the fifth-year requirement "postponed," that is, to be completed during the ensuing five years of teaching service.

While the wide variation in practices and requirements leads to the conclusion that licensing by the states can best be described as a "state of confusion," there is an important concept that should not be overlooked, the one requirement that all states have. It is that all states require teachers to be licensed. States do this to assure the public that only properly qualified and properly educated persons will teach their children. Some states, like New York, even require teachers in private schools to be licensed.

Fortunately, there are statewide and national movements looking to reform in certification. Let us look briefly at four developments which seem to be having the greatest influence. These are (1) reciprocity, (2) political action, (3) recommendations of scholars, (4) experimental programs of teacher preparation.

Reciprocity

It seems ludicrous that a person who is certifiable in one state and thus considered a competent practitioner of his art and craft turns out to be a substandard and noncertifiable teacher in a neighboring state. But each state sets up its own qualifications for teachers' certificates just as it does for drivers' licenses. Since teachers, like all other Americans, are an increasingly mobile group, the variety in state certification requirements has become a serious obstacle in their movement from state to state. Reciprocity—the acceptance by a state of a teacher licensed by another state—is an effort to resolve the problem. Some states have achieved reciprocity by developing "compacts" in which the certifying authorities of a group of neighboring states with somewhat comparable standards have agreed to accept any teacher certified by a member of the group. If there are minor differences in requirements, these are worked out during the initial teaching service.

A bolder step to achieve the goal of reciprocity is by national accreditation of the colleges and universities that prepare teachers. The rationale of this approach is that a graduate of an approved institution, with its approved program, should *ipso facto* be certifiable in any state of the union. This means that state boards of education must accept the stamp of the teaching profession's accreditation as meeting their own legal definitions of minimum teaching qualifications.

For the past fifteen years, a national agency known as the National Council for Accreditation of Teacher Education has been established. It has approved the institutions in the United States in which approximately 75 per cent of the nation's teachers are educated. For an illustration of the colleges and programs approved by NCATE, see Figure 4, which shows acceptable institutions in the representative states of Florida, New York, Ohio, Oregon, and Texas.

Although fewer than one-fourth of state certifying boards or commissions accept this form of accreditation, it is nevertheless both an important and a controversial development in the professional standards movement and represents a significant breakthrough in the certification confusion.

Institutions	Elementary	Secondary	School Service Personnel	Highest Degree
Florida				
Florida State University, Tallahassee	X	X	X	D
Stetson University, DeLand	X	X	X	M
University of Miami, Coral Gables	X	X	X	D
New York				
Cornell University, Ithaca	X	X	X	D
Hofstra University, Hempstead	X	X	X[2]	M
State University of New York:				
State University at Buffalo	X	X	X	D
State University College at Albany		X	X[24]	D
at Brockport	X	X		M
at Buffalo	X	X		M
at Cortland	X	X[25]		M
at Fredonia	X	X		M
at Geneseo	X	X		M
at New Paltz	X	X		M
at Oneonta	X	X		M
at Oswego	X	X		M
at Plattsburgh	X	X		M
at Potsdam	X[26]			M
Syracuse University, Syracuse	X	X	X	D
University of Rochester, Rochester	X	X	X	D[8]
Ohio				
Central State College, Wilberforce	X	X		B
Hiram College, Hiram	X	X		B
John Carroll University, Cleveland		X		M
Miami University, Oxford	X	X	X	6
Ohio University, Athens	X	X	X	6
St. John College of Cleveland, Cleveland	X		X[19]	M
University of Akron, Akron	X	X	X[2]	M
University of Dayton, Dayton	X	X		B
University of Toledo, Toledo	X	X	X	M
Wittenberg University, Springfield	X	X		B

Those institutions not yet evaluated or action pending are not included in the list.

Institutions	Elementary	Secondary	School Service Personnel	Highest Degree
Oregon				
Eastern Oregon College, La Grande	X	X		M
Lewis and Clark College, Portland	X	X		B
Marylhurst College, Marylhurst	X	X		B
Oregon College of Education, Monmouth	X	X		M
Oregon State University, Corvallis	X	X	X^7	D
Portland State College, Portland	X	X		B
Southern Oregon College, Ashland	X	X		M
University of Oregon, Eugene	X	X	X^{18}	D
Texas				
Abilene Christian College, Abilene	X	X		B
East Texas State College, Commerce	X	X	X^2	M
Incarnate Word College, San Antonio	X	X		B
North Texas State University, Denton	X	X	X	D
Our Lady of the Lake College, San Antonio	X	X	X^1	M
Prairie View Agricultural and Mechanical College, Prairie View	X	X		B
Sam Houston State Teachers College, Huntsville	X	X		M
Southwest Texas State College, San Marcos	X	X	X^7	M
Texas Christian University, Fort Worth	X	X	X	M
Texas Southern University, Houston	X	X	X	M
Texas Wesleyan College, Fort Worth	X	X		B
Texas Woman's University, Denton	X	X		M
Trinity University, San Antonio	X	X	X	M
University of Texas, Austin	X	X	X	D
West Texas State College, Canyon	X	X	X^2	M

1) Elementary and secondary principals
2) Elementary and secondary principals; guidance counselors
6) Sixth collegiate year is highest level approved
7) Guidance counselors
8) Including music teachers
18) Elementary and secondary principals; school psychological personnel; superintendents
19) Elementary principals
24) Superintendents
25) English, mathematics, science, social studies, and physical education
26) Including music for grades 1–12

Figure 4. Colleges and Universities Accredited by NCATE, Effective 1963–64

Political Action

The increasing importance of education in America's technological development, and the sudden surge in the sheer number of bodies to be educated, coupled with the increased cost of education, have brought public education, kindergarten to the university, into the center of the political arena in a number of states.

As a consequence of the people's interest and legitimate concern, reflected in the behavior of their elected representatives, a number of states have sought to bring greater flexibility in certification standards by taking direct legislative action to minimize the minutiae of state credential requirements. By so doing, laymen have sought to make teaching more available to an increasing number of applicants, with varying but acceptable qualifications. Reducing the specificity of state requirements through such means helps bring state licensing closer to the purpose for which it is basically intended—to assure the public that the holder of the license has the minimum qualifications to be a teacher.

Recommendations of Scholars

Recently outstanding scholars have devoted major attention to the need for certification reform. James B. Conant, former president of Harvard University, proposes some radical alterations in his book *The Education of American Teachers*. He raises certain basic questions and then proceeds to answer them. Who is responsible for the education of teachers? The state. Who ought to be responsible? The institutions *and* the school district.

Conant proposes:

For certification purposes the state should require only (a) that a candidate hold a baccalaureate degree from a legitimate college or university, (b) that he submit evidence of having successfully performed as a student teacher under the direction of college and public school personnel in whom the State Department has confidence, and in a practice-teaching situation of which the State Department approves, and (c) that he hold a specially endorsed teaching certificate from a college or university which, in issuing the official document, attests that the institution as a whole considers the person adequately prepared to teach in a designated field and grade level.[5]

Another question Conant raises is how well state regulations protect the public against ignorant or incompetent teachers. His answer: not very well. Why this is not done very well is lucidly discussed and historically documented by Lucien Kinney in his treatise *Certification in Education*. Taking several states as examples, he shows how state legislatures, supported by vested interest groups, have used certification to achieve their own ends and how present practices cannot guarantee competence. Kinney's answer: have the profession disregard and look beyond state systems and establish its own licensure system. "Only when the profession has control of the quality of its membership can it take over its proper responsibilities."[6]

Kinney's proposal, like Conant's, will be widely discussed (and cussed); each is bound to shake up the status quo in teacher certification.

[5] James B. Conant, *The Education of American Teachers* (New York: McGraw-Hill, 1963), p. 210.

[6] Lucien B. Kinney, *Certification in Education* (Englewood Cliffs, N.J.: Prentice-Hall, 1964), p. 132.

Experimental Programs of Teacher Preparation

Beginning in a small way in the early 1950's and continuing in an accelerated way in the 1960's, a number of the nation's best-known colleges and universities have carried on experimental programs of teacher preparation. The Ford Foundation alone has given over 70 million dollars to institutions to encourage them to develop and try out "breakthrough" programs of teacher education. Because experimental curriculums differ from standard or regular curriculums—often involving teaching internships, for example, in lieu of student teaching [7]—many of these programs initially ran head on into the inflexible requirements of state certification. As a result of the persistence of the colleges and the recognition by state authorities of the place of experimentation in teacher education, a number of states revised their requirements so that teachers prepared in other than conventional or traditional programs could be certified.

While these four developments—experimentation, political action, reciprocity, and the interest of scholars—are having the effect of liberalizing the certification requirements in a number of states, there still remains the confusion caused by lack of interstate agreement on what it takes to become a teacher.

There exists *general* agreement that a teacher should be (1) well versed in the subjects he is to teach; (2) broadly educated through undergraduate study in the humanities, the arts, and the sciences; (3) professionally knowledgeable about the social and psychological foundations of education, the school curriculum, and the methods and materials of instruction; and (4) professionally "tried out" through an assignment as a student or practice teacher or teaching intern.

But when it comes to the *specific amount* of each of these essential ingredients, states differ considerably and generally are gun-shy about stating their requirements in such broad terms. The variation among and between states on certification standards is not likely to be reduced in the near future.

EMPLOYMENT PRACTICES

A school district's ability to compete for the less than adequate supply of new teachers each year depends on its (1) salary schedule, (2) geographic location, (3) availability of cultural advantages, (4) physical facilities, and (5) general reputation. It is not surprising to find that the practices of recruiting and employing teachers vary widely. Within this range of diversity, it is pos-

[7] A teaching internship is a new type of teacher preparation program in which (1) actual teaching (with pay and full responsibility) is substituted for practice teaching, (2) the school district and the college share supervision responsibility for the trainee, and (3) seminars drawing on the problems of teaching and designed to illuminate these problems replace formal education courses.

sible, however, to discuss employment practices which are applicable in a majority of the nation's larger, or at least "better," school districts.

Teacher Personality

"It's up to you!" This is the bold truth of the matter of getting a teaching post. Whether the individual strikes out on his own and presents himself to the superintendent unannounced (a bad practice, by the way), or whether he goes through the college placement office or the county superintendent's office (both good practices), it is the kind of person he *is* which counts most. *Proper grooming, good manners, cultural background, and pleasing personality* are the *sine qua non* of employability.

What Administrators Want

In employing new teachers, school administrators usually interest themselves in the following items:

1. Certificate held: Does the applicant have a valid state certificate? What kind? Is it a regular or standard teaching license?

2. College or university attended: At what institution did the applicant prepare for teaching? (The institution's status and reputation and the administrator's experience with other teachers from the same institution weigh heavily.)

3. Student teaching record: At what levels and in what fields did he do his student teaching? How successful was the applicant in student teaching? (Administrators have learned that the test of the pudding is in the eating!)

4. Teaching experience: Has the applicant had any? In what kinds of schools and where? With what success? (Letters of verification are necessary to prove the case.)

5. Academic interests: What subjects is the applicant best qualified to teach? What others could he teach, if necessary? (Grades earned in college in the applicant's teaching field are important, although many administrators assume that a college degree is sufficient evidence of academic or scholarly capability.)

6. Extracurricular specialties: In what extracurricular activities did the applicant participate? What other hobbies does he have? Could he supervise such activities for school-age pupils? (When other things are equal, this ability counts heavily with administrators.)

Related to the preceding six rather basic items are the findings of a survey of 108 principals in five large metropolitan school districts.[8] The answers to the

---

[8] James C. Stone, "Factors Related to Success of Beginning Teachers," *Research Résumé* of the California Teachers Association, May, 1961, pp. 56 ff.

question "What characteristics do you consider most important in selecting beginning teachers?" could be grouped under these categories:

1. Professional preparation
2. Personality
3. Academic preparation
4. Interest in children
5. Related experiences—for example, scout work, camp counseling, Sunday-school teaching, and the like
6. Mental and physical health
7. Attitude toward colleagues
8. Appearance
9. Cultural and social background
10. Moral and ethical values
11. Age

The percentages of principals responding with statements that could be included in the above eleven categories are shown in Figure 5. Professional preparation, personality, academic preparation, and interest in children were mentioned by half or more of the principals at each grade level (elementary, junior high, senior high).

Professional preparation was mentioned by the largest percentage of princi-

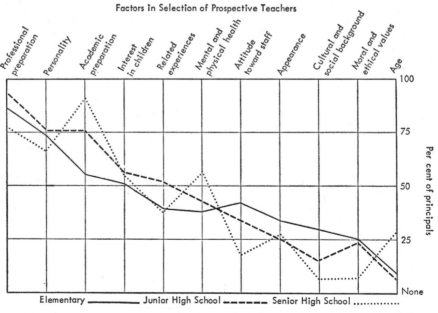

Figure 5. Per Cent of Principals, According to Grade Level, That Referred to Various Factors as Important in Selecting Beginning Teachers. From James C. Stone, *California's Commitment to Public Education,* Thomas Y. Crowell Company, p. 56.

pals at the elementary and junior high school levels (87 and 95 per cent, respectively). Academic preparation was mentioned by the largest percentage of senior high school principals (95 per cent). Evidently, academic background was of more concern to senior high school principals than to elementary and junior high school principals. Conversely, less importance was attached to related experiences by senior high school principals than by elementary and junior high school principals. At the other end of the scale, a smaller percentage of senior high school principals than of elementary and junior high school principals mentioned cultural and social background or moral and ethical values as important considerations in the employment of beginning teachers.

Candidates for teaching positions might well keep these divergent emphases in mind when seeking teaching positions.

Applying

All districts have some kind of job application form which must be filled out. This should be done prior to an interview. The application usually requires official record transcripts (every applicant should have a half-dozen sets handy) and letters of recommendation attesting to the applicant's teaching experience or teaching potential. General letters "To whom it may concern" are of little value, and character letters from ministers, friends, business acquaintances, or former employers are worthless *unless* they contain *specific* comments on the candidate's promise as a teacher.

The Interview

School officials usually interview applicants if there are openings for which they are qualified. The interview serves the purpose of allowing the employer and the teacher to make a face-to-face assessment of one another. It also permits verification of the statements made on the teacher's application and gives an opportunity for securing additional information on various points. If the interview ends with any of the following phrases, the teacher can cross the school district off his list of possibilities: "We'll get in touch with you if (when) . . .;" "Have you thought of applying at . . .;" "Perhaps you'd be interested in being on our substitute list." If, on the other hand, the interview concludes with, "We'll call you as soon as we receive your confidential file from your college placement office" or "We'd like to offer you a contract," then you're in!

PLACEMENT AGENCIES

Colleges and universities preparing teachers maintain a teacher placement service. In small colleges, the service is rendered as a part of the Department of Education. In large colleges and universities, there is either a separate teacher placement office, or the service is rendered by a general placement bureau serving all graduates of the institution.

An additional placement service is rendered in some states by the employment agency of the U.S. Department of Labor. Another placement agency in most states is the state education or teachers' association, which usually charges a fee of 1½ to 5 per cent of the first year's salary.

How It Works

The purpose of the college placement office is to serve as middleman between employer and applicant. Prospective employers make known their openings, known as "calls," to the placement office, which nominates for each call those persons in its files whom it deems best qualified and forwards a set of their confidential papers to the prospective employer. The employer reviews the papers and notifies the placement office of those in whom he is interested. Interviews are then arranged, generally at the placement office. Usually an employing school official will have interviews with applicants from several colleges before arriving at a decision. He then notifies both the candidate and the placement office of his decision.

The Confidential File

In every college placement office, there is a qualified professional person in charge who knows the education field and the importance of establishing a confidential file or dossier. The forms to be filled out by the teacher candidate are extensive and time consuming, and the pages of information which the candidate must give (and he should do so with great care) will require several hours of work. Once done, however, the task usually is finished for one's professional life (except for keeping it up to date as advanced degrees are secured and the teacher becomes qualified for advanced nonteaching positions in guidance, supervision, administration, and the like).

Letters of Recommendation

The final step in the establishment of the confidential file is securing letters of recommendation. The placement officer will furnish each candidate with envelopes and forms on which the letters of recommendation are to be written. The completed forms are mailed directly to the office by the writer of the letter.

No candidate should merely drop such forms off to selected people, or have the placement office send them for him, unless he has first asked individuals if they will be willing to write a letter of recommendation for him. This is not only common courtesy; it also avoids the embarrassment of having letters filled with generalities, which might be interpreted negatively by the employing official. The candidate should remember that these letters are confidential and that, once received, they are the property of the placement office, to be used as the placement director, in his professional role, may see fit.

All these admonitions emphasize the importance of securing the right kind of letters. The beginning teacher should seek letters from (1) the public school teachers under whose supervision he did his student teaching, and (2) college or university supervisors of student teaching. Letters from other college faculty members who can attest to the candidate's promise as a teacher are an appropriate supplement, but are never a substitute for those written from firsthand experience about the candidate's abilities in actual teaching situations.

The experienced teacher should secure letters from (1) officials of the school district in which his last teaching was done, and (2) if the past teaching experience was in a state other than the one in which the candidate is now applying, general letters from local residents attesting to teaching promise are a good supplement to the above.

The intern program candidate should use (1) academic faculty who know him well enough to tell how acceptable he might prove as a teacher, and (2) former employers or lay leaders who also know him well enough to tell how promising he might be as a teacher.

Selective Placement

Mention has been made of the professional qualifications of the placement officer and of his role in the handling of confidential letters. One additional aspect of his professional role should be made clear—his responsibility for "selective placement." This responsibility enables him to reserve the right to exercise his professional judgment in recommending candidates to employers for available positions. If, for example, he has ten kindergarten teacher candidates and only one call for kindergarten teachers, it is his privilege to recommend to the employing official the two or three candidates he thinks are best qualified for the job. A candidate not nominated may request that his papers be forwarded to the school employer for consideration. Papers so sent, however, are marked "Sent at candidate's request."

Out-of-state Reciprocity

Most college and university teacher placement agencies belong to the National Institutional Teacher Placement Association. Through the national agency, affiliated institutions have agreed to assist the graduates of an out-of-state institution who wish to seek positions in their state. To secure the assistance of the in-state institution, the candidate's out-of-state college or university placement office must initiate the request to the in-state institution of choice. There usually is no charge for this reciprocal service.

Follow-up Services

Placement offices usually carry on follow-up studies of their graduates. One reason for this activity is sheer interest in their alumni, but another is to secure information to feed back to the college in order to improve its program of preparation. Studies of the number of students each year who qualify for certificates but do not enter teaching are examples of placement offices' follow-up work. Another is the study of reasons why candidates are not placed.

SCHOOL DISTRICT SELECTION PROCEDURES

Small Districts

In small school districts the governing board itself selects the teaching staff, without professional assistance, since districts of this size usually do not employ a superintendent. If the district is large enough to employ a superintendent, it may delegate to him the responsibility of selecting teachers. In most cases, the board acts in matters of personnel selection only on the recommendations of the superintendent.

Medium- and Large-sized Districts

In medium- and large-sized districts, central office personnel do the initial screening of teacher applicants. The titles of such persons are numerous—assistant superintendent, personnel director, or curriculum coordinator. The most likely candidates chosen by the central office staff usually are then interviewed by the principal in whose school the vacancy exists. Since the principal is the person who will be responsible for the teacher's success or failure, his decision is the critical one.

A growing trend in both medium- and large-sized districts is the use of personnel selection committees made up of both teachers and administrators. These committees do the "second stage" interviewing and prepare priority lists for consideration by the central office in making recommendations for board action.

In some of the nation's largest urban districts, such as New York and Los Angeles, written examinations are required as a part of the screening process. On the basis of the written examination and a selection committee's interview, each applicant is assigned a position on an eligibility list. Recommendations to the board are then made by the central office staff on the basis of placement on the list.

Contracts

When a teacher has been selected for employment, he usually is offered a contract, a legal document specifying the terms of employment, conditions of work, and compensation. The terms of the contract are legally binding on both parties and may be enforced by court action, if necessary. In any event, the contract can be terminated only by mutual agreement of both parties. Before signing a contract, a teacher should carefully consider its provisions, because failure to live up to them may be cause for revocation or suspension of his credentials.

It is not unusual for a teacher to sign a contract one day, only to learn the next day of a position he would prefer. Nor is it unusual for a teacher to sign a contract and, upon later visiting the school and the community, wish he had not acted so hastily. Such "20-20 hindsight" may be avoided if, ahead of signing on the dotted line, the teacher weighs carefully such items as (1) the terms of the contract, (2) the kind of community, (3) the climate of the school, (4) the type of assignment, and (5) available housing and cultural opportunities.

PROMOTION, TRANSFER, MOBILITY, PROFESSIONAL MORTALITY

Assumed Promotions

Despite the single salary schedule (equal pay for equal qualifications regardless of grade level taught), unfortunately the idea still persists in the minds of some people that a person is a "better" teacher if he teaches at the higher grade levels. In all too many districts, moving from elementary to junior high is assumed to be a promotion, as is moving from junior high to senior high or from senior high to junior college.

Recognition Promotions

Recognition type promotions are the kind associated with being named department chairman (junior high school, senior high school, or junior college); a supervising teacher of student teachers; a demonstration teacher; an institute, extension, or college summer-session teacher; or a consultant teacher (for elementary school music, art, physical education, exceptional children). Usually a modest additional stipend is paid for such services.

Real Promotions

Actual promotions which involve substantial salary increases are those in which the successful and experienced classroom teacher is appointed to an administrative position, such as counselor, assistant principal, dean, curriculum coordinator, principal, superintendent, and the like.

Transfers

Transfers from one school to another *within* a district are common. Request for transfer may be initiated by the teacher to the superintendent. It is wise for the teacher to discuss his desire to transfer with his current principal since few districts will honor such a request unless the teacher's present principal approves. Acceptable reasons for transfer include moving to a school which (1) is near the teacher's home or a college or university, (2) provides a welcome change of student or faculty climate, (3) avoids his having a personality conflict with principal or colleagues.

A transfer also may be initiated by the principal and the central office. Typical reasons are personality conflicts, inability to work well with certain cultural or socioeconomic groups, parental discontent, and the need to balance school staffs between young and old teachers, strong and weak, expert and inexperienced, men and women. Some districts make it a practice to transfer a certain proportion of their experienced teachers as a means of in-service education.

A transfer *between* school districts can be made only by resignation in the teacher's current district and employment in the new district.

Mobility

Like Americans generally, teachers are a mobile group.

In the category of *professional mobility,* an undetermined proportion of the nation's teachers (1) move from lower grade levels to higher levels and from teaching to advanced nonteaching responsibilities, and (2) move in and out of the profession. Since a majority of America's public school teachers are women, this possibility is one of teaching's recruitment incentives. Young married women resign to raise a family, but many return to teaching at a later date.

In the category of *geographic mobility,* an undetermined proportion of the nation's teachers (1) move from school to school or from one district to another within the state, or (2) move from their "home" state to another state.

Professional Mortality

The professional mortality rate among teachers is believed to be high, especially at the beginning stages of service. The drop-out rate of teachers who complete preparation but do not take a teaching position is approximately 27 per cent. The current rate is considerably better than it was five to seven years ago, when studies showed that 50 per cent of secondary and 25 per cent of elementary certificate candidates did not take teaching positions. The improved holding power of the teaching profession today may be due to higher salaries and increased status.

TENURE

One of the significant protections of public school teachers in many states is the tenure law. This statute probably has contributed more to the stability and general health of the teaching profession than any single factor. "In 1920 only five states recognized by law the principle of permanent tenure for public school teachers. By 1955 there were 32 states with tenure laws." [9] And by 1964, 37 states had tenure laws.[10]

Although, like certification, tenure regulations vary in details from state to state, a teacher usually has tenure after three years of teaching in a state. Typical reasons for dismissal of tenured teachers include (1) dishonesty, (2) incompetence or other evident unfitness for service, (3) persistent violation of or refusal to obey regulations, (4) immoral or unprofessional conduct, (5) conviction of a felony or of a crime involving moral turpitude, (6) membership in the Communist party, the refusal to answer questions regarding same, or the indoctrination of pupils with communism.

Two actions to dismiss a permanent teacher were filed recently by a board of education and consolidated for trial. The first action charged the teacher with immoral conduct, unprofessional conduct, and dishonesty. All three charges were based specifically upon the fact that the teacher, in order to sustain adequate enrollment figures in her class for adults and prevent its discontinuance for lack of pupils, intentionally falsified the attendance records by signing the names of absent students. The second action charged evident unfitness for service and unprofessional conduct, based upon letters written by the teacher which contained statements of a defamatory and degrading nature concerning her associates and administrative superiors. These letters also revealed such violent prejudices that she could not have been expected to deal fairly with mixed classes.

Each of the charges, supported by evidence, was held to be grounds for dismissal. In this case the falsification of records constituted immoral conduct, unprofessional conduct, and dishonesty; the defamatory statements constituted unprofessional conduct and evident unfitness for service.[11]

Over the years, tenure decisions have been made by the courts to the extent that (1) it has become forbiddingly costly for a district to dismiss a tenured teacher, and (2) it has become almost equally costly to dismiss a probationary teacher from a regular position prior to the expiration of his annual contract, because such dismissal must be for the same causes and follow the same legal procedures as for tenured teachers.

Recognizing these facts about the dismissal of teachers, many groups acting on behalf of governing boards have advocated greater flexibility in tenure laws.

[9] Edgar B. Wesley, *NEA: The First Hundred Years* (New York: Harper, 1957), p. 337.

[10] The states without tenure provisions are Arkansas, Nevada, North Dakota, Oklahoma, South Dakota, Virginia, Mississippi, North Carolina, South Carolina, Texas, Utah, Vermont, Wyoming. Those states in which tenure is available only in certain places within them are Georgia, Kansas, Missouri, Nebraska, Oregon, and Wisconsin.

[11] Lawrence Kearney, "Interpretations of Law," *California Schools*, 31:489, December, 1960.

RETIREMENT

Before 1917 no state had a retirement plan for teachers, by 1957 such plans were operating in 45 states,[12] and today all states have retirement plans. A number of trends and changes are evident:

Adoption of social security coverage for all or some teachers in 37 states. An estimated 50 to 60 percent of all instructional employees in the nation's public elementary and secondary schools are now covered.

Adoption of survivor benefit programs in 14 states whose teachers have no protection under the survivors' insurance provisions of the social security system. These programs are designed to provide monthly payments to dependent survivors of members who die while in active teaching service. Seven states added this feature to their retirement laws since 1958. Only Alaska and Puerto Rico have yet to provide such survivor benefits although Puerto Rico continues monthly payments of part of the life annuity of a deceased retired teacher to the surviving widow and minor children.

At present 23 state retirement systems pay a lump-sum death benefit in addition to refunding the member's accumulated contributions to the estate or beneficiary of a member who dies before retirement. In 1950 only seven states did so.[13]

The California State Teachers' Retirement System—which we shall discuss as a typical, although somewhat generous, plan—requires a minimum of five years of teaching service within the state. Service outside the state is noncreditable. A teacher must have reached the age of fifty-five to be eligible for retirement benefits. There is no mandatory retirement age, although a teacher loses his tenure status at the age of sixty-five.

A teacher's retirement pay is based on the average of the highest salary earned over his "best" three years. Upon retirement:

1. At age sixty, with twenty years of service, a teacher receives twenty-sixtieths (one-third) of the average of the "best" three years.

2. At age sixty, with thirty years of service, a teacher receives thirty-sixtieths (one-half) of the average of his "best" three years.

3. At age sixty-five, with twenty-two years of service, a teacher receives one-half of the average of his "best" three years.

4. At age sixty-five, with thirty years of service, a teacher receives two-thirds of the average of his "best" three years.

5. At age sixty-five, with forty-four years of service, a teacher receives 100 per cent of the average of his "best" three years.

A teacher may retire for disability at any age. In general his benefit is about equal to one-fourth of his annual compensation.

If the teacher dies before retirement, his beneficiary may receive a lump-sum

[12] Wesley, *loc. cit.*
[13] *NEA Research Bulletin,* 42:99, December, 1964.

payment which is equal to (1) all his contributions with interest *and* (2) one-twelfth of his annual salary at the rate at which he was last employed but for no longer than six years. In addition, if the surviving spouse has one child under eighteen, the spouse will receive $180 per month; two or more children under eighteen, $250 per month. When the retired teacher dies, his estate receives $400 in addition to the other benefits to which he is entitled.

Should the teacher decide to drop out of teaching after five or fewer years of service (and many do), he must withdraw all his retirement contributions with interest. Should he drop out after five years of service, he may either remain in the system or withdraw all his retirement contributions with interest. Upon reentry into teaching service, a teacher may redeposit his withdrawn contributions plus interest if he so chooses, thus gaining for retirement the benefits of his previous years of service.

IN-SERVICE GROWTH

In-service education is the *planned* education, after service begins, which continues to promote professional growth. Professional growth, in turn, encompasses activities that extend one's liberal education, increase his competence in a subject area, enlarge his professional knowledge, and refine his professional skills.

This definition admittedly is a broad one and runs counter to the conception of in-service education in some school districts which either define it so narrowly as to limit it to upper-division or graduate courses, or so broadly as to include almost anything a teacher does outside the walls of his classroom.

Individual Responsibility

As professionals using a specialized body of knowledge and technical skills, it is incumbent on teachers to maintain, improve, extend, and update their store of knowledge and technical skill. And it is the individual teacher's *own* responsibility to make himself a more competent professional practitioner. Expertness is acquired through consistent, organized, and purposeful professional study, which is central to the teacher's claim of membership in a profession.

School District and College Responsibility

Since most school districts measure teacher merit for salary increases by units of credits held and by successful teaching service, it follows that school districts share some responsibility for providing organized opportunities for teachers to meet these salary hurdles.

A practical guideline for evaluating a school district's in-service offerings follows:

1. Individual teachers should have opportunities to work on their own problems. (This includes opportunity to plan for themselves, to participate voluntarily rather than be required to do so.)

2. The regular administrative and supervisory organization of the school system should be fully utilized. (This includes curriculum development, instructional improvement programs, workshops, institutes, conferences, the special assistance of principals, supervisors, and department heads.)

3. The school system insures time, facilities, and resources to stimulate and strengthen the program. (This refers to time for curriculum study groups within the teacher's normal work day, conferences within the normal work week, use of specialized resource personnel, and the like.)

4. The program must provide for communication and interaction among all persons in the school system. (This includes all grades, all subject fields, all teachers and principals, and representatives of laymen, such as board and PTA members.)

5. The role of the chief administrative officer in the school system is that of facilitator and coordinator as contrasted to "guiding and directing genius." (This refers to encouraging development of good organization and procedures for in-service education, facilitating the work of groups, and creating a climate for professional growth.) [14]

Usually school districts provide opportunities for in-service education in cooperation with higher education institutions. In part, this is done to eliminate the squabble in the district over the "credit" problem, that is, what an acceptable unit of in-service credit is. Many colleges and universities have extension services specifically designed to provide off-campus courses within the proximity of school districts. In some states the county superintendent, too, plays a significant role in arranging in-service training opportunities.

Typical School District Programs

A recent survey of the in-service education programs of 383 school districts showed that the most frequently used activities were (1) faculty meetings, (2) conferences, (3) workshops, (4) consultant services, (5) teacher orientation programs, (6) institutes, (7) preparation and evaluation of instructional materials. These seven forms of in-service education were reported the preference of 60 per cent or more of the districts included in the survey.[15]

Teacher Preference

A survey of all teachers in one city school district showed that teachers themselves expressed somewhat different preferences for in-service education

[14] National Society for the Study of Education, *In-service Education* (Chicago: University of Chicago Press, 1957), Part 1, Chapter 12.

[15] "District In-service Training Programs—A Survey of Policies and Practices," *Research Bulletin* of the California Teachers Association, April, 1959.

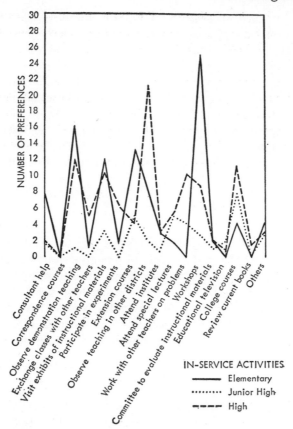

Figure 6. Teachers' Preferences for In-Service Education Activities. From James C. Stone, *California's Commitment to Public Education*, Thomas Y. Crowell Company, page 179.

activities. It also showed some interesting differences between elementary and secondary teachers. These preferences are shown in Figure 6.[16]

By combining similar activities (i.e., "extension course" with "college course" and "observe demonstration teaching" and "observe teaching in other districts"), the teachers' in-service education preferences appear in this order of priority: (1) observe teaching, (2) take college extension or campus courses, (3) participate in workshops, (4) visit exhibits of instructional materials and devices, (5) work with other teachers studying special problems.

Academic Organizations

A number of nationally organized academic groups are active in the in-service field. These include the National Council of Mathematics Teachers,

[16] Unpublished study. Office of the Superintendent of Schools, Martinez City Schools, Martinez, California.

the National Council of Teachers of English, the American Association for Health, Physical Education, and Recreation, to name a few. These organizations conduct workshops, conferences, institutes, and summer session programs for teachers.

In addition, college and university professors who are authorities in various academic fields are working with classroom teachers in school districts, through county offices, and at state and national levels.

The question of who is responsible for in-service education begets the qualified answer, the teacher, but everybody is in the act to help him, including the federal government through the National Defense Education Act.

Relation of In-service Education to the Salary Schedule

Most districts have related their in-service program to the salary schedule as a form of incentive for participation. In doing so, districts have had to face the question, "Is everything a teacher does by way of professional growth creditable in-service education?" A few districts have decided yes. More districts, however, have attempted to distinguish between "regularly expected" activities and "credit for salary" activities. An example from the Board of Education Policies Handbook for the Bluegrass school district follows:

1. *Regularly Expected Activities*: Regularly expected in-service education activities are those which all teachers engage in as a normal part of their assigned responsibilities. These include a variety of activities, such as daily preparation for teaching, participation in professional organizations, observing teaching demonstration lessons, faculty committee work, attending conferences, extracurricular assignments, and similar matters. Such activities are rewarding to the teachers in and of themselves. It shall be the policy of this board to encourage such activities on the part of all teachers and to expect the administrative staff of the district to provide leadership and support for such activities on the part of all teachers. Such activities, however, shall not normally be considered for salary credit.

2. *Credit for Salary Activities*: As professional practitioners, teachers are expected to participate in extensive and formal study and comparable forms of professional growth. These types of in-service growth activities are clearly those which are *not* normally done by teachers in the regular performance of their assigned responsibilities. The purpose of such activities is to increase teaching abilities and broaden teachers' educational backgrounds, thereby increasing their worth to the district. These activities shall be of a type meriting *either* or *both* classification and/or hurdle credit [17] on the salary schedule. Since these in-service growth experiences will vary with the individual needs of teachers, they may encompass a wide range of activities such as college and university courses, travel, community services, organized workshops, curriculum committees, and the like. Such activities shall extend over a recognized period

[17] Hurdle credit is credit that must be earned to obtain the normal increment.

of time and be of a comprehensive nature. It shall be the policy of this board to delegate the approval of credit for these activities to an evaluation committee.

Districts using policies of either the limited type or the comprehensive type establish evaluation committees of teachers and administrators to determine the amount of credit to be given for noncollege work and the criteria to be used in making such judgments. Bluegrass school district, which has adopted the following criteria, grants credit if:

1. The overriding purpose of the activity is clearly one of increasing the teacher's professional competence.
2. The activity extends over a definitely recognized and designated period of time, is of a comprehensive nature, and, if repetitious of a previously engaged-in activity, is clearly justifiable by new conditions.
3. The activity is planned and undertaken in an organized manner, in contrast to one in which participation is unorganized, informal, or incidental.
4. The activity is clearly related to the needs and interests of the teacher so that he may become a more competent practitioner and is designed to provide an opportunity for the fulfillment of these needs and interests in a systematic way.
5. The activity is not only of value to the individual teacher, but is also of value to other teachers in the district with whom it is shared.

CONCLUSION

In this chapter, we have discussed "the system," that is, the manner in which public education is organized in the United States, including local, state, and national agencies, and professional processes like placement, tenure, inservice education, certification, and accreditation.

Taken together, the dedicated people who make up the organizational structures of these various agencies and who are responsible for these processes have been referred to as "the apparatus" by Conant in his critical review, *The Education of the American Teacher*. Like any organized activity of importance on the American scene, the profession's zeal for better schools has brought with it loyalties and interrelationships which appear to the outsider to constitute an interlocking directorship. However, even a critic like Conant recognizes that it is the dedication and loyal service of these professionals which have given teaching in America its stability and its powerful voice at local, state, and national levels.

Questions for Discussion

1. How do you explain a statement of the Rockefeller Brothers Foundation to the effect that all problems in education lead us back sooner or later to the basic problem of financing?

2. What procedure does a prospective teacher take to become licensed in the state in which you plan to teach? Does your state grant life certificates? How are they obtained? What is your opinion of teaching licenses granted for life?

3. What is your reaction to the idea of merit ratings for teachers? Of relating salary increases to merit ratings?

4. What resources are available to you in your college community that would be helpful to you in your growth toward becoming a teacher? Explain how you have taken, or could take, advantage of these resources.

5. Do you favor state teacher tenure laws? Why or why not? Why do you think some states have them while others do not?

6. What kind of teacher retirement plan would not penalize teachers who wish to move from one state to another?

7. Why are in-service education programs important to experienced teachers? Which of several techniques and media used in in-service programs seem to you of most value to teachers? Why? Should in-service education be related to salary schedules? Why?

8. What are the advantages and disadvantages of having a state chief school officer appointed by the state board of education as opposed to having one elected by the people?

9. How do you account for the significant decrease in number of school districts in the United States in recent years?

10. Find out what institutions in your state are accredited by NCATE. Talk to a professor of education about this and then to one in a subject matter field. Do they agree on the place of NCATE in approving institutions for teacher education?

Activities and Projects

1. Obtain current charts showing the amount of money spent by the various states for education within their boundaries, and the amount of money raised to support education. How does your state compare with others? How does your state compare with the national average? How does your state compare with other states in the country and with the national average in the efforts made to support public education?

2. Obtain a copy of the latest edition of Woellner and Wood's *Requirements for Certification*. What are the requirements for obtaining a license in several states in which you have an interest in teaching? How do they compare in such aspects as number of years to complete the license, the degree needed, the number of semester hours required in professional education courses and in the liberal arts, the requirements for teaching in elementary school and in secondary school?

3. Write a news article for your community's local newspaper supporting the single salary schedule which, hypothetically, your school district is desirous of adopting.

4. Secure from your college's teacher placement office data concerning the probable supply and demand figures at the level at which and/or in the subject fields which you plan to teach when you finish your college work. What can be done if the supply appears to exceed the demand in your field of interest?

5. Write to the state departments of education in three states where you have considered employment to secure information about their retirement plans. How do they compare?

6. Compare the fringe benefits available in a large district that you know of with those in a small district with which you are acquainted or which you can find out about.

7. Obtain the names of the board of education members in your home community. What are their occupations? How do you think they are representative of the entire community? What are the qualifications for effective board members?

8. How is the public school system in the community in which you live organized? Draw a chart indicating the system's organizational structure from the board of education to the pupils, and share this with others in your class.

9. Contact the superintendent of schools in a district with which you are acquainted. If possible, arrange for him to visit your class and explain the problems he has with respect to financing education in his district and with respect to organization of the schools in the district.

References

"ORGANIZATION OF THE SCHOOLS"

ABRAHAM, WILLARD, A Time for Teaching (New York: Harper & Row, 1964), Chapters 2, 3.

BROWN, B. FRANK, The Nongraded High School (Englewood Cliffs, N.J.: Prentice-Hall, 1963).

CONANT, JAMES B., The American High School Today (New York: Mc-Graw-Hill, 1959, pp. 14, 17.

GOODLAD, JOHN I., and ROBERT J. ANDERSON, The Nongraded Elementary School (New York: Harcourt, Brace & World, 1963).

GRAMBS, JEAN D., and L. MORRIS MC CLURE, Foundations of Teaching (New York: Holt, Rinehart & Winston, 1964), Chapter 9.

MAYER, MARTIN, The Schools (New York: Harper, 1961).

MISNER, PAUL J., FREDERICK W. SCHNEIDER, and LOWELL G. KEITH, Elementary School Administration (Columbus, Ohio: Charles E. Merrill, 1963), Chapter 4.

MORSE, ARTHUR D., Schools of Tomorrow—Today (New York: Doubleday, 1960).

RICHEY, ROBERT W., Planning for Teaching, 3d ed. (New York: McGraw-Hill, 1963), Chapter 16.

TRUMP, J. LLOYD, and DORSEY BAYNHAM, *Focus on Change: Guide to Better Schools* (Chicago: Rand McNally, 1961).

U.S. Office of Education, *Programs '63* (Washington, D.C.: U.S. Government Printing Office, 1963).

"FINANCING SCHOOLS"

BARR, W. MONFORT, *American Public School Finance* (New York: American Book, 1960).

BENSON, C. S., *The Economics of Public Education* (Boston: Houghton Mifflin, 1961).

Does Better Education Cost More? (Washington, D.C.: Committee on Tax Education and School Finance, NEA, 1959).

Financing Education for Our Changing Population (Washington, D.C.: Committee on Educational Finance, NEA, 1961).

Financing the Public Schools, 1960–70, Special Project on School Finance (Washington, D.C.: National Education Association, 1962).

GRIEDER, CALVIN, T. M. PIERCE, and W. E. ROSENSTENGEL, *Public School Administration*, 2d ed. (New York: Ronald, 1961).

HUNT, HEROLD C., *Becoming an Educator* (Boston: Houghton Mifflin, 1963), Chapter 9.

HUTCHINS, CLAYTON D., and DOLORES A. STEINHILBER, *Trends in Financing Public Education*, U.S. Office Circular 666 (Washington, D.C.: U.S. Government Printing Office, 1961).

RICHEY, Chapter 17.

"CERTIFICATION OF TEACHERS"

ABRAHAM, Chapter 4.

CONANT, JAMES B., *The Education of American Teachers* (New York: McGraw-Hill, 1963).

GRAMBS, Chapter 4.

HODENFIELD, G. K., and T. M. STINNETT, *The Education of Teachers* (Englewood Cliffs, N.J.: Prentice-Hall, 1961).

KINNEY, LUCIEN B., *Certification in Education* (Englewood Cliffs, N.J.: Prentice-Hall, 1964).

MC GRATH, EARL J., and CHARLES H. RUSSELL, *Are School Teachers Illiberally Educated?* (New York: Bureau of Publications, Teachers College, Columbia University, 1961).

MISNER, Chapter 3.

New Horizons for the Teaching Profession (Washington, D.C.: National Commission on Teacher Education and Professional Standards, NEA, 1961).

RICHEY, Chapter 4.

STONE, JAMES C., "Teacher Certification, Supply and Demand," *Review of Educational Research,* pp. 343–54, October, 1963.

TRUMP, J. LLOYD, *New Directions to Quality Education* (Washington, D.C.: National Association of Secondary School Principals, NEA, 1960).

WOELLNER, ROBERT C., and M. AURILLA WOOD, *Requirements for Certification,* 27th ed. (Chicago: University of Chicago Press, 1962).

"EMPLOYMENT PRACTICES"

ABRAHAM, Chapter 5.

Classroom Teachers Speak on Teaching as a Profession (Washington, D.C.: Department of Classroom Teachers, NEA, 1961).

Economic Status of Teachers in 1962–63 (Washington, D.C.: Research Division, NEA, 1963).

GORDON, GARFORD C., "Conditions of Employment and Service in Elementary and Secondary Schools," *Review of Educational Research,* p. 385, October, 1963.

KERSHAW, JOSEPH A., and ROLAND N. MCKEAN, *Teacher Shortages and Salary Schedules* (New York: McGraw-Hill, 1962).

LINDSEY, MARGARET, ed., *New Horizons for the Teaching Profession* (Washington, D.C.: National Commission on Teacher Education and Professional Standards of NEA, 1961).

MASON, WARD S., *The Beginning Teacher—Status and Career Orientations* (Washington, D.C.: U.S. Department of Health, Education and Welfare, 1961).

MISNER, Chapters 14–16.

MORRIS, VAN CLEVE, *Becoming an Educator* (Boston: Houghton Mifflin, 1963), Chapter 11, "Teaching as a Career."

PETERSEN, DOROTHY G., *The Elementary School Teacher* (New York: Appleton-Century-Crofts, 1964), Parts I and IV.

A Position Paper on Teacher Education and Professional Standards (Washington, D.C.: National Commission on Teacher Education and Professional Standards, NEA, 1963).

RICHEY, Part III.

STILES, LINDLEY, ed., *The Teacher's Role in American Society* (New York: Harper, 1962).

STINNETT, TIMOTHY M., *The Profession of Teaching* (Washington, D.C.: Center for Applied Research in Education, 1962).

———, and ALBERT J. HUGGETT, *Professional Problems of Teachers,* 2d ed. (New York: Macmillan, 1963).

STONE, JAMES C., *California's Commitment to Public Education* (New York: Thomas Y. Crowell, 1961).

Teaching Career Fact Book (Washington, D.C.: National Education Association, 1962).

White House Conference on Children and Youth, *Conference Proceedings* (Washington, D.C.: The Conference, 1960).

xii

The services of teachers are vital for the welfare of the country and of every individual. Beyond this, the nation's teachers directly influence the quantity and quality of the services provided by all the other professions.

NATIONAL MANPOWER COUNCIL

the profession

What is teaching? A profession comparable to other professions like medicine, law, the ministry? Or is teaching merely a trade, albeit a highly important one, which offers, as the National Manpower Council puts it, services "vital for the welfare of the country and of every individual," but nevertheless a vocation which more closely resembles and has more in common with the trades than with the professions?

This is the question to be discussed in this chapter. In so doing, we present first the writings of an author whose basic leaning is in the direction of answering "Yes." In developing his case, this author draws on one state, California, as his example.

In the second part of the chapter we present a point of view which holds that teaching is *not* now a profession nor is it likely to become one in the foreseeable future. The status of teachers in New York City is an example of this point of view.

The chapter will conclude with the authors' own observations on the issues involved.

THE CASE FOR TEACHING AS A PROFESSION

There are five important hallmarks of professional status. Each will be discussed in terms of the extent to which elementary and secondary school teaching appears to meet the criteria.[1]

[1] The material in the following discussion is adapted from James C. Stone, *California's Commitment to Public Education* (New York: Thomas Y. Crowell, 1961), pp. 162–64.

CRITERION 1. The members of a profession perform an essential social service—one which is fundamental to the welfare of society.

Pro: Since teaching is the "mother" profession on which all others depend, it certainly qualifies here. Few will doubt that most teachers are more dedicated to their vocation than to economic gain. Because society recognizes the importance of public school teaching to its well being, the state distinguishes between those who are qualified teachers and those who are untrained laymen or even charlatans. This distinction is made through the licensing of qualified practitioners and the legal requirement that only those so licensed may perform the service. The distinction is also made through the process of state accreditation of teacher-education institutions.

Con: The practice of permitting unqualified laymen to teach in periods of shortage, rather than discontinuing the service, denies, in part, the necessity for strictly qualified practitioners.

CRITERION 2. The essential social service rendered by members of a profession is based on intellectual techniques and abilities.

Pro: Few will deny that teaching requires intellectual qualities based on the ability to impart subject matter in ways appropriate to children of a particular age level.

THE AMERICAN TEACHER

There is no office higher than that of a teacher of youth; for there is nothing on earth so precious as the mind, soul, character of the child. No office should be regarded with greater respect. The first minds in the community should be encouraged to assume it. Parents should do all but impoverish themselves, to induce such to become the guardians and guides of their children.

WILLIAM ELLERY CHANNING

Con: Some kinds of public school teaching border on vocationalism. These may include the teaching of manual skills in shop courses, and trade and industrial education.

CRITERION 3. The members of a profession have undergone an extended period of specialized preparation.

Pro: This formal preparation includes the mastery of specialized knowledge and the acquisition of specialized skills. The specialized knowledge is represented in the teacher's academic subject background (majors and minors) and the professional education subject matter included in the psychological and sociological foundations of education. The acquisition of specialized skills is gained in the laboratory experiences of teacher assistantship, student teaching, and internship, with accompanying work in methods and materials of instruction. The whole idea of in-service education is proof of the relevance of this criterion for teaching.

Con: Since some individuals have gone into teaching without these knowledges and skills and apparently have "gotten by," it may be argued that they are not as essential as some would have us believe.

CRITERION 4. The members of a profession associate together as a self-governing organization of practitioners for such purposes as (1) defining the scope of individual and group autonomy, (2) disciplining their members, (3) maintaining and improving standards, and (4) participating in decisions affecting professional practice.

Pro: 1. Teachers have long held to the concept of academic freedom—what the teacher does within the four walls of a classroom is pretty much up to him. This feeling grows stronger as one moves up from elementary to university teaching.

WHAT'S A GOOD TEACHER?

See what students themselves say as quoted in the recent book *High School Students Speak Out,* by David Mallery, a report on interviews in high schools around the country.

"The most important thing," goes a typical comment, "is a teacher's personality—its interplay with ours—his ideas—the way he gets us to think —the way he shows his interest in us . . ."

"Mr. Sullivan in music—there's a marvelous man. He teaches us about life. I've got a whole new set of standards for myself . . ."

"Miss Carlson could get you excited about the dullest subject!"

"I know a teacher who could take the best book written and kill it dead as a doornail in one class period."

"A teacher should give you confidence that you can do it."

"Being recognized as a person by a teacher," says Mallery summarizing the interviews, "was deeply valued. In fact, it seemed fundamental to many a student's whole motivation in school." And he says, "The experience with the subject consistently took second place to the encounter with the teacher."

"How Good *Are* Our Teachers?" *Changing Times,* 17:27, June, 1963. Reprinted by permission. Copyright 1963 by The Kiplinger Washington Editors, Inc., 1729 H St., N.W., Washington, D.C. 20006.

---

2. Recent legislation in a few states permits panels of teachers to investigate instances of professional "malpractice," and this evidence is considered "expert testimony" if a teacher appeals to a court of law.

3. Since World War II, teachers themselves at long last are taking an active part in the movement toward higher professional standards. Being informed about the status of one's profession is a first step in this direction.

4. Active participation by members of professional groups at local and state levels is necessary for decision-making. For example, over four-fifths of California's public school teachers are associated in a single professional body for this purpose.

Con: Teachers are far from being comparable to other groups in meeting Criterion 4, largely because teachers are public employees. As such, many of the decisions made autonomously by other professions are made for teachers by public bodies such as the state legislature and county and district lay boards.

CRITERION 5: The members of a profession develop and are guided in their professional and personal behavior by a code of ethics.

Pro: Codes of ethics for teachers are established by the National Education Association and the American Federation of Teachers.

Con: Until a single code is established and receives actual rather than verbal support, teaching has a long way to go before qualifying on this criterion.

THE CASE FOR TEACHING AS A TRADE

In the analysis which follows, we shall regard a profession as an occupation which exhibits all the following eight characteristics. Each criterion will be discussed in terms of the extent to which teaching possesses these essential qualities.[2]

CRITERION 1. *A unique, definite, and essential social service.*

Pro: Education services are so important in the welfare of children and of society that they must be made available to all children rather than limited only to those children whose parents can afford to pay for them.

Con: What is clear and definite about the "social service" rendered by teachers? Is the public sure of the functions which teachers perform or is it substantially divided on this matter—from those who consider the function as custodial ("baby-sitting") and those who consider it character building ("education for democratic ideals"), to those who consider the function as pupil achievement of academic subject matter? As an occupational group, teachers themselves are not agreed on this matter. By contrast, the functions of the medical profession are obvious: to prevent illness, prolong life, eliminate pain.

Teaching *is* a means to "something." But "that 'something' is often referred to as 'the end of education,' 'the objectives of education,' 'the purposes of education,' or 'the aims of education.' "[3] We don't agree within the profession, nor does the public agree, on what the "something" is. "Where the occupational group itself or the public is not sure of the function of the group, or is substantially divided on this matter, it is impossible to agree on issues of professional training, ethics, compensation, and so on. Professionalization is inevitably delayed where there is substantial disagreement and uncertainty over the function of an occupational group."[4]

The word *essential* is crucial in this criterion. It must be so considered by

[2] The eight criteria are taken from Myron Lieberman, *Education as a Profession* (Englewood Cliffs, N.J.: Prentice-Hall, 1956), pp. 2–6.

[3] *Ibid.*, p. 19.

[4] *Ibid.*, p. 2.

the public *and* the practitioners. When teachers engage in strikes, boycotts, lockouts, etc., they are in effect denying the essentiality of their service.[5]

CRITERION 2. *An emphasis upon intellectual techniques in performing its service.*

Pro: The criterion is so obviously met in teaching as to need no elaboration.

Con: What, for example, is very intellectual about the elementary school teacher who spends so much of her working day putting galoshes on, then taking them off, dispensing milk and cookies, supervising naps, *et al.*, or the high school shop teacher, be his medium metal, wood, or plastics? Only when we get to those who teach the high school academic subjects of foreign languages, math, science, English, and history can the teacher qualify as performing a role which involves "an emphasis upon intellectual techniques."

CRITERION 3. *A long period of specialized training.*

Pro: Entry into a profession requires a long period of preparation. All states set such requirements for teachers for a standard or permanent certificate.

Con: No one would care to employ a physician who did not have an extensive education, including a number of years beyond the bachelor's degree. But what about teachers? There are some with no collegiate preparation, some with only two years, some with bachelor's degrees but no professional preparation. And in private elementary and secondary school teaching, only in a few states like New York are there state standards for teacher employment based on an extensive education.

A number of nonprofessional occupations require long periods of specialized training. However, most of the training is not intellectual. Doesn't this apply to some of the professional training of teachers? Certainly some aspects of professional education such as observation, participation, student teaching, and intern teaching are more physical than intellectual activities. The same has been said by some students of some of their education courses: "just busy work," "survey of basket weaving," "elaboration of the obvious." Professional training to qualify under this criterion must be required of all practitioners *prior* to entry into service (not, as with interns, *during* teaching service) and must be *primarily*, though not wholly, intellectual.

CRITERION 4. *A broad range of autonomy for both the individual practitioners and the occupational group as a whole.*

Pro: Within the four walls of his classroom, the teacher is "king." If no principal is looking over his shoulder, he alone decides what to teach, when, how, and to which pupils.

Con: The main job of the principal is the supervision of instruction. In

---

[5] Ironically, those who believe in the right of any working group to strike use the same argument on the essentiality of their service to justify their position; for example, it is because the service is essential that the strike is the appropriate technique for securing action. Thus peach pickers go out on strike only when the trees are ripe, dock workers only when the ships arrive in port, teachers at the opening of the school year, doctors when socialized medicine legislation is about to be voted on.

the professions "lack of autonomy in the form of supervision usually does great harm and is strongly resented." [6] Real professional work is not amenable to the close supervision principals and instructional supervisors are expected to give. Moreover, what is to be taught is not determined by the teacher but by the public acting through legislative mandate and the local governing board acting through adopted curricula, courses of study, textbooks, and the like. Failure to follow these dictums is grounds for suspension or dismissal in most states and communities. Since there is wide disagreement on what teachers are supposed to accomplish, it follows that there isn't much room left for "professional autonomy." "The more disagreement as to function, the more interference with WHATEVER teachers do." [7]

As stated above, at the present time the public decides most things about teachers and teaching. Efforts by the profession to move into decision-making have met a wall of opposition. Recent efforts of teachers' organizations to be active in policy formation in certification is an example of the public's *unwillingness* to trust the autonomy of the organized teaching profession. There is no trend in the wind to change this. On the other hand, the concept that the "schools belong to the people" is deeply embedded in American tradition. It isn't likely to change and those who write and preach about movements toward autonomy for the teaching profession are merely whistling in the dark, or kidding themselves, or both.

CRITERION 5. *An acceptance by the practitioners of broad personal responsibility for judgments made and acts performed within the scope of professional autonomy.*

Pro: In the eyes of most students, the teacher is an authority figure. In the realm of academic affairs, grading for example, the teacher usually is the sole authority. Largely he alone decides on the how of his teaching.

Con: Professional responsibility for judgments and acts performed involves two kinds of authority—intellectual (example, "What do I teach?") and moral (example, "What is good to do in this situation for this child?"). By and large teachers have been gun-shy to accept responsibility for either important intellectual or moral judgments. On moral issues, the typical teacher relies on "the front office" for taking authoritative responsibility. On curriculum matters, he relies on the authority of the central office and the textbook authors. Seldom does a teacher assume responsibility beyond these minimum and narrow confines. Seldom does he speak out. And when he does, many formal and informal pressures are brought to bear to keep him in line, to prevent him from rocking the boat. It is the unusual teacher today who takes responsibility for judgments and acts which involve matters of professional judgment beyond the "9 to 3" teaching day.

CRITERION 6. *An emphasis on the service to be rendered, rather than the*

---

[6] *Ibid.*, p. 4.
[7] *Ibid.*, p. 87.

economic gain to the practitioners, as the bases for organization and per-formance of the social service delegated to the occupational group.

Pro: The phrase "Lo, the poor teacher" is eloquent testimony on the extent to which teaching meets this criterion.

Con: The protagonist here pleads *nolo contendere* (no plea).

CRITERION 7. *A comprehensive self-governing organization of practitioners.*

Pro: Teachers are organized into a powerful group known as the National Education Association. In turn, the NEA has strong organizations in each of the states, and in many local communities the NEA chapter is a rallying point for teachers.

Con: All professions have more than a single national organization to which the practitioners may belong. For example, the M.D. may belong to both the AMA and a national specialist group, such as the Academy for Internal Medicine. Similarly, teachers who belong to the NEA also may be members of the National Council of Teachers of English, for example. The several memberships become a problem to the concept of "self-governing organization of practitioners" only when the two organizations are philosophically in conflict. Then the concept of an autonomous voice for the profession goes out the window. The recent rise to power of the AFT, particularly in large urban centers of the United States, has obliterated the hope that teachers in America could ever have *a* "self-governing organization of practitioners." The NEA and AFT are in a death struggle which may last decades. If, as some predict, the AFT grows at the expense of the NEA and one day all teachers are unionized, the teachers will have met this criterion of "a comprehensive self-governing body of practitioners." But by then teaching also will no longer be a profession!

CRITERION 8. *A code of ethics which has been clarified and interpreted at ambiguous and doubtful points by concrete cases.*

Pro: The NEA has adopted a code of ethics, generally regarded as "the" code for teachers. It provides the guide for the prospective teacher and the beginning teacher to his professional rights and privileges. It is designed to serve as a behavioral reference point for the experienced teacher. It provides the profession with a basis for excluding the unscrupulous, the incompetent. It protects the competent teacher from unfair attacks. State teachers associations also have adopted the same or similar codes.

Con: Teachers not only have NEA-derived code(s), but AFT-derived code(s). And they differ markedly on such fundamental matters as the right to strike, collective bargaining, sanctions, *et al.* In addition to differences on these matters, there also is a basic difference over the question "Who is a teacher?" For the NEA, a teacher is both one who teaches within the four walls of a classroom and the other school personnel who carry on so-called "non-teaching" functions, such as principals, superintendents, and the like. For the AFT, "nonteaching" school personnel are not eligible for membership since they are deemed a part of management and hence inherently hostile to workers. Thus, the AFT would drive a wedge between teachers and administrators. Donovan puts the issue well when he says:

The school administrator is likely to find himself the target of teacher animosity as though he were the bearer of all the ill will that some teachers imagine exists against them. It has always been amazing to me how that creative, noble, judicious and angelic creature as each creature describes himself automatically, upon assuming an administrative position, becomes stubborn, stupid, dictatorial and biased. And this apparently happens with no extra effort on the part of the administrator.[8]

Bad as these philosophical differences between the two major organizations are, this is not the most serious argument against the criterion. As Lieberman points out, "unless codes are enforced, they are practically worthless." This is the nub of the problem. With a few exceptions, as we have seen, codes of ethics for teachers have *not* been enforced by courts, nor have they been enforced by teacher groups. The code's existence is known by teachers, but very few could tell you what's in the code and fewer still could give an example of how the code ever influenced their behavior. Like the teacher's certificate, it is form without substance.

SOME OBSERVATIONS ON THE TWO "CASES"

From a careful reading of these two "cases," certain observations are in order:

1. There is more agreement than disagreement in the pro and con arguments and also in the criteria which each protagonist establishes as his baseline.

2. The concept of a profession is a loose one, many people using the word *profession* as a synonym for occupation. Thus we hear such expressions as the "acting profession," the "professional football player," the "profession of social work," the "business profession," and the like.

3. While teaching may not qualify completely on all professional criteria, it should be kept in mind that few of the well-known professions qualify 100 per cent either. Many are still evolving toward complete professionalization.

4. What is important is the activity engaged in and not the word used to describe it.

Teaching, whether termed trade or profession, remains an important, challenging, intellectual calling requiring considerable investment in preparation time and considerable individual responsibility. Undoubtedly, like the other so-called professions, it is in a state of flux—hopefully, though perhaps not actually, in a state of becoming more professional in the sense of the classic criteria.

[8] Address of Bernard E. Donovan, Executive Deputy Superintendent of Schools, New York City—"The School Administrator and Teachers' Organizations"—before the California Association of Secondary School Administrators, March 24, 1964.

No Other Sure Foundation

We can, I think, now state the conditions which if achieved would guarantee teaching the prestige, status and public recognition enjoyed by the traditional learned professions. The nature and importance of the teacher's task is such that its practitioners must be intellectually able, must possess a defined body of subject matter and skill, must pursue their work as a career, must undergo a long and arduous period of preparation, must be dedicated to the welfare of those they teach, must be accorded a high degree of autonomy in day-to-day practice, must participate in the development of necessary group solidarity and subject themselves to the discipline inherent in such solidarity, and must be well paid and professionally secure. This definition of what we mean when we use the term "teaching profession" becomes a statement of aims and objectives of any professional teachers organization.

Arthur F. Corey, *Your AASA in 1957–58,* official report of the American Association of School Administrators, p. 147.

We say "hopefully, though perhaps not actually" because we are disturbed over the recent actions of certain teacher groups and the effect of their activities on their professional image. The strike of New York City teachers in 1963 was a serious blow to their status as professionals. Similarly, in 1964 the two-day "holiday" taken by the teachers of Utah in protest against the governor's actions was a serious blow to their professional image. In turn these isolated examples of unprofessional behavior dampen the professional image of all teachers.

Victory—At What Price?

The threatened teachers' strike, with all the bitterness and bickering it implied, has been averted. The education of a million children went along without interruption. Teachers got a pay raise—not all their union had demanded, but a substantial gain.

But there's another side to this picture of first-day jubilation.

What was the price of this victory? Does it mean that the City must reconcile itself to a periodic show of raw force every time a contract comes up for negotiation?

Editorial, *The New York World-Telegram and Sun,* September 9, 1963.

In Place of Reason

The teachers' strike which began in New York [City] yesterday is a tragedy for the whole city—for its citizens whose irresponsible lethargy is one of the causes of the strike, for the teachers themselves whose action, born of desperation, mars the high pretensions of their calling, and for the children, of course, who are the helpless victims of this undisciplined adult strife. . . .

The Washington Post

TEACHERS' STRIKE

The teachers' strike in New York [City] is a bitter blow against the city's million school children. It is also a bitter blow against the image of the dedicated teacher.

Dallas Times Herald

As quoted in *Saturday Review*, 45:52, May 19, 1962.

The recent strike of M.D.'s in British Columbia and Belgium and the threat of one in England were a serious blow to the professional image of medicine. As a matter of fact, this action by members of the top-status profession has done irreparable damage to the entire concept of what constitutes a profession and what is acceptable practitioner behavior, if one accepts the classic definition and values the general public's acceptance of his group. How long the public will continue to give professional privileges to practitioner groups which behave like tradesmen is a moot question.

The concept that teaching is a profession, however short it may fall in measurement against the established criteria, is important to society and its future well-being. *Professions organize and, through their organization, help to regulate the service rendered to society. Professions also work to increase the quality of the services they render. A profession can perform these functions for society better than society can do them by itself.*

The concept that teaching is a profession is also important for teachers. *It denotes a behavioral level of expectation.* If teachers feel professional, they will more likely act like professionals. Thus they are more likely to be esteemed by others as professionals.

RE STATUS

The status of the teacher in American society does merit our concern and attention. Plato observed that "what is honored in a country will be cultivated there." If one measures honor by emoluments, then teaching, and by extension education, is not honored here.

The current tendency to suspect education as a center of subversion is a demonstration, not of honor, but of a disrepute which has dangerous implications for our country. For either education is to be cultivated here or we are lost. In Whitehead's phrase: "In the conditions of modern life the rule is absolute, the race which does not value trained intelligence is doomed."

The problem of the teacher is a complex one, and defies the laws of supply and demand. He is in short supply; he is underpaid; he lacks status. It is common to explain the first and third by the second. But to give him greater income he must first win the respect of the public, for the public pays the bill. Status then seems to control. But it is argued status is a reflection of income; so we box the compass but make no progress toward solving the problem.

Status and money will follow when in his profession the teacher can command respect. He professes knowledge. We would try to break the circle by making the teacher more wise. When his neighbors turn to him for advice as naturally as they now turn to the physician and banker the battle will be half won.

> O. Meredith Wilson, "Program of the Fund for the Advancement of Education," Minutes and Proceedings of the California Council on Teacher Education, April, 1953, *Report of the General Session*, pp. 33–35.

PROFESSIONAL PROBLEMS AND WAYS OF ATTACKING THEM

As the reader will have gleaned from the discussion of professional status, there is no dearth of problems needing solution by teachers. Solutions to professional problems will come as teachers (1) belong to professional groups, (2) actively participate in the groups' deliberations and decisions, (3) take individual responsibility for implementing the groups' decisions, and (4) always act as the professional people their leaders purport them to be.

A noteworthy example of teachers in action is the following. A local board of education summarily decided to release a nontenured teacher simply because he had been asked to testify at a hearing of the House of Representatives' Un-American Activities Committee.

The local teachers' association investigated the case thoroughly, through its professional relations committee, and recommended:

1. That the board not take on a task which rightfully should be performed by law enforcement agencies.
2. That teachers, when brought before the board of education, have the same judicial protection as the citizens in a court of law, as guaranteed under the Bill of Rights, pertaining to:
   (a) The right to counsel.
   (b) The right to call witnesses.
   (c) The right to cross-examine witnesses.
   (d) The right to have evidence weighed.
3. That when questioning a teacher, the board should consider him innocent until proven guilty, or it will infringe upon his dignity and self-respect.
4. That when being called before the board, a teacher is given a reasonable time for preparation.
5. That having signed the oath, a teacher in this district need not reaffirm his loyalty and good faith.

6. That the board reopen and completely review this case.

Action by the local association resulted in the rehiring of the teacher. Here is a Professional Relations Committee in action with a capital "A"!

Professional Organizations

As seen in the previous discussion, there are several all-encompassing teacher organizations and many specialized ones. In many communities, teachers who join such groups may have their dues paid through payroll deduction.

Teacher organizations. The largest professional all-encompassing teacher organization that cuts across professional lines is the 1,006,970-member National Education Association. The NEA operates through a representative assembly of 5,707 delegates, a board of directors of eighty-five members, twenty-seven commissions and committees, thirty-two departments, and thirteen headquarters divisions. Examples are its Commission of Education Policy, Teacher Education and Professional Standards; Department of Classroom Teachers, Social Studies Teachers, Mathematics Teachers; Division for Legislation, Research, and Adult Education Services. Approximately one-half of the nation's public school teachers hold membership in the NEA.

On the state level is the State Professional Teachers Association, which also operates through commissions and committees; examples include the Commission on Personnel Standards, the Commission on Higher Education, and committees on retirement, tenure, and legislation.

Nationally there also is the American Federation of Teachers, affiliated with the American Federation of Labor and Congress of Industrial Organizations. It has a membership of approximately 100,000 teachers, mostly confined to large industrial urban centers in the North.

Both the NEA and AFT have local and regional as well as state subgroups to which teachers may belong. A group promoting a world unification of existing professional organizations is the World Confederation of Organizations of the Teaching Profession.

Specialized organizations. There are both national and state organizations of specialized professional groups. Some examples include the American Association of School Administrators, National Association of Secondary School Administrators, National Association of Elementary School Administrators, American Junior College Association, The Association for Supervision and Curriculum Development, Association for Early Childhood Education.

In subject fields, there are such groups as the National Council of Teachers of English; National Council for Teachers of Mathematics; American Association for Health, Physical Education and Recreation; National Association for Industrial Arts Teachers; Homemaking Education Teachers; Business Education Teachers; and the like.

All these organizations present teachers with ample opportunities to participate as members of a profession working on large-scale problems which are of the utmost importance. This point could not have been asserted with equal conviction twenty-five years ago.

The Professional Standards Movement

World War II was responsible for many lasting effects on the nature and character of the teaching profession. First, it created a critical shortage of teachers as men and women left the classrooms to join the war effort. Secondly, there was an unprecedented increase in the birth rate. After the war, when the elementary schools were beginning to feel the impact of the new population increase, many of the young men and women did not return to teaching. A crisis faced the schools as a result of the continued and worsening shortage of qualified personnel, a crisis which has continued up to the present, but which, surprisingly enough, has also had a few positive effects on the teaching profession as well.

States attempted to meet the critical shortage of teachers by adopting plans for the issuance of emergency credentials based on no other standard than a statement by the employing school superintendent that no regularly certified applicant of the type needed was available. While this policy did provide a means of manning the classrooms, it also brought professionally minded teachers to the realization that, having some responsibility in this matter, they needed to exercise influence on the licensing policies of the states and on employment practices at local levels.

The National Education Association organized a National Commission on Teacher Education and Professional Standards. This, in turn, was followed by similar organizations in each state. Teachers with similar concern spoke, too, through the voice of the American Federation of Teachers.

The minutes of these organizations over the past twenty years show that much of their concern and effort has been in the direction of upgrading the standards of the teaching profession. This kind of organized effort by teacher groups, which did not exist before World War II, has become known as the professional standards movement and traces its origin to the effects of conditions initiated on Pearl Harbor Day, 1941.

The individual and his group responsibility. The individual teacher has a stake in the standards governing his profession, which can be stated simply: it is by professional standards that the quality of the membership is determined. In a word, the caliber of the colleagues who will be working side by side in each school is the result of the quality controls in selection, admission, and retention practices in the profession. Thus it is clear that each teacher needs to exercise some responsibility in preserving his interest.

Expression of this responsibility is evinced most readily through participation at the local level in some kind of organized effort related to the improvement of standards of the profession. Teacher participation may be manifested on several levels. On the first level, one must study the system of standards, find out what it is, and determine in which direction it ought to be going. Secondly, one must do something about it by accepting individual responsibility that extends beyond the four classroom walls or the school environs. One must give time for work and leadership in professional groups, organizing the thinking of teachers on issues, and voicing these thoughts in the councils where major decisions affecting the standards of the profession are made. Decision-making bodies include the office of the district superintendent of schools, local school boards, county boards of education, the state department and state board of education, and the state legislature.

The old bromide, "The chain is only as strong as its weakest link," is certainly pertinent here. It is only when teachers become enterprising in professional groups that they can expect to influence effectively the decisions relating to the standards of *their* profession. The extent to which teachers are charged with the obligation to assume individual responsibility for strengthening the image of the profession is illustrated in the following conception of the truly professional teacher:

A Member of the Profession
1. Demonstrates an appreciation of the social importance of the profession.
    (a) Renders appropriate service to society beyond that for which he has contracted.
    (b) Contributes to the honor and prestige of the profession by his personal conduct.
    (c) Actively seeks to upgrade professional standards through selective recruitment and retention programs.
    (d) Interprets to others the goals and practices of the profession.
2. Contributes to the development of professional standards.
    (a) Takes part in the development of a functional code of ethics.
    (b) Adheres to the accepted code of ethics.
    (c) Helps to enforce the code of ethics in upgrading standards of professional behavior.
    (d) Supports an adequate system of certification and accreditation.
    (e) Helps improve pre-service and in-service programs of preparation.
3. Contributes to the profession through his organizations.
    (a) Becomes a member of the organization.
    (b) Takes active part in the formulation of the organizational policies.
    (c) Supports the policy once formed until it is changed by the democratic process.
    (d) Seeks and supports legislative programs to improve the program of education as well as the economic and social status of the profession.
4. Takes a personal responsibility for his own professional growth.
    (a) Develops and tests more effective classroom procedures.
    (b) Keeps informed on current trends, tendencies, and practices in his field by use of professional literature.
    (c) Participates in conferences, workshops, etc., dealing with professional problems.
    (d) Enlarges his horizons through academic and nonacademic experiences.

5. Acts on a systematic philosophy, critically adopted and consistently applied.
   (a) Expresses a systematic philosophy of education held with deep personal conviction.
   (b) Identifies and clarifies the philosophical assumptions underlying various and conflicting policies for his work. . . .
   (c) Utilizes explicitly his philosophical view in making consistent choices of educational policies and practices.[9]

I am not willing that this discussion should close without mention of the value of a true teacher. Give me a log hut, with only a simple bench, Mark Hopkins on one end and I on the other, and you may have all the buildings, apparatus and libraries without him.

PRESIDENT JAMES A. GARFIELD

Questions for Discussion

1. Reread the cases for teaching as a profession and as a trade. Where do you stand on this issue? Why?
2. What is good teaching? Is it the same for all grade levels and subject matter fields?
3. Does "essentiality of the service" of a profession give it the right to strike or deny it this right?
4. Do you agree with Wilson, page 279, that "It is common to explain the first and third by the second"? How would you "unbox" the compass?
5. Are the importance of education and the status of teaching increasing? Marshal the evidence to support your conclusion.
6. Teaching has ben described as "like nursing—a woman's profession." What implications does this have for the reality of Kinney's definition of the role of a teacher as member of the profession (page 283)?
7. Is education an academic discipline? What are the implications of your answer for teaching as a profession?
8. What are the major roadblocks education faces in its striving for more complete professional status?
9. Is professionalism the opposite of amateurism? What, then, is the consequence as regards the role of the teacher in our society?
10. Is intellectualism the cornerstone of professionalism? If not, what is?
11. Teachers no longer should be "recruited"; they should be selected. What differences are implied here?

[9] Lucien B. Kinney, in *Six Areas of Teacher Competence* (Burlingame: Commission on Teacher Education, California Teachers Association, 1964), pp. 25–26.

Activities and Projects

1. In the company of two other students, observe several experienced teachers of the same grade level or subject field. To what extent do you agree that each is a "good teacher"?
2. Interview the superintendent of a school system of your choice. Find out how he selects new teachers and how he evaluates their success.
3. Visit a local teachers' professional association meeting. What were their chief concerns? How does your conclusion fit the professional image?
4. Conduct a survey among PTA members on their image of teachers. How does it square with your own image?
5. Interview a doctor or lawyer about his "role" as member of the profession. How does it square with the competencies listed on page 283?
6. Talk to a union member and find out what his union does for him, how he feels about it, and what part he takes in decision-making in the organization.
7. Ask the principal of a school of your choice to read and react to Donovan's statement on page 277.
8. Write to Ford Foundation, 477 Madison Avenue, New York City, for materials describing their "breakthrough" programs of teacher education. Prepare a report on the significance of these experiments.
9. Investigate what such organizations as the following do for education as a profession "in the process of becoming": Phi Delta Kappa, Kappa Delta Pi, and Student NEA.

References

"STATUS, ET AL."

ANDERSON, ARCHIBALD W., "The Teaching Profession: An Example of Diversity in Training and Function," *Educational Theory*, 12:1–33, January, 1962.

BARZUN, JACQUES, *The Teacher in America* (New York: Doubleday, 1959).

BROUDY, HARRY S., *Paradox and Promise* (Englewood Cliffs, N.J.: Prentice-Hall, 1961), "Teachers, Strikes, and the Art of Payment," pp. 125–37.

BRYSON, LYMAN, "The Arts, the Professions, and the State," *Yale Review*, 36:633, Summer, 1947.

CARR-SAUNDERS, A. M., and P. A. WILSON, *The Professions* (Oxford, England: Clarendon, 1933).

CHRISTENSEN, EDWARD L., "Is Teaching a Genuine Profession?" *Business Education World*, 35:18–19, November, 1954.

KING, EDMUND J., *World Perspectives in Education* (Indianapolis: Bobbs-Merrill, 1962), Chapter 9, "Teachers and Their Recruitment."

KINNEY, LUCIEN B., and L. G. THOMAS, *Toward Professional Maturity in Education* (Burlingame: California Teachers Association, 1955).

LIEBERMAN, MYRON, *Education as a Profession* (Englewood Cliffs, N.J.: Prentice-Hall, 1956).

——, *The Future of American Education* (Chicago: University of Chicago Pres, 1960), Chapter 5, "The Myth of the Teaching Profession."

RICHEY, ROBERT W., *Planning for Teaching*, 2d ed. (New York: McGraw-Hill, 1958), Part III, "Economic Aspects of Teaching."

"Yardstick of a Profession," *Institutes on Professional and Public Relations* (Washington, D.C.: National Education Association, 1948).

STINNETT, T. M., and A. J. HUGGETT, *Professional Problems of Teachers*, 2d ed. New York: Macmillan, 1963), Chapter 3, "The Profession of Teaching."

THOMAS, L. G., L. B. KINNEY, *et al.*, *Perspective on Teaching* (Englewood Cliffs, N.J.: Prentice-Hall, 1961), Chapter 13, "What Is the Significance of Status?"

"PROFESSIONAL PROCESSES"

ARMSTRONG, W. EARL, and T. M. STINNETT, *A Manual of Certification Requirements for School Personnel* (Washington, D.C.: National Commission on Teacher Education and Professional Standards, NEA, 1960).

KINNEY, LUCIEN B., *Certification in Education* (Englewood Cliffs, N.J.: Prentice-Hall, 1964).

SELDEN, WILLIAM K., *Accreditation* (New York: Harper, 1960).

STINNETT, Chapter 19, "Professional Certification of Teachers"; Chapter 20, "Professional Accreditation of Teachers."

STONE, JAMES C., "A School for Visitors," *Journal of Teacher Education*, 9:334, September, 1958.

——, "Seven Cardinal Principles of Certification," *Journal of Teacher Education*, 7:155–58, June, 1956.

THOMAS, Chapter 15, "How Do Teachers Enter the Profession?"

WIGGINS, SAM P., *Battlefields in Teacher Education* (Nashville, Tenn.: George Peabody College for Teachers, 1964).

"PROFESSIONAL EDUCATION"

BLAUCH, LLOYD, *Education for the Professions* (Washington, D.C.: U.S. Department of Health, Education, and Welfare, 1955).

BORROWMAN, MERLE L., *The Liberal and Technical in Teacher Education* (New York: Bureau of Publications, Teachers College, Columbia University, 1956).

CONANT, JAMES B., *The Education of American Teachers* (New York: McGraw-Hill, 1963).

COTTRELL, DONALD P., ed., *Teacher Education for a Free People* (Oneonta, N.Y.: American Association of Colleges for Teacher Education, 1956).

The Education of Teachers: Curriculum Programs (Washington, D.C.: National Commission on Teacher Education and Professional Standards, NEA, 1959).

HODENFIELD, G. K., and T. M. STINNETT, *The Education of Teachers* (Englewood Cliffs, N.J.: Prentice-Hall, 1961).

KOERNER, JAMES, *The Miseducation of Teachers* (Boston: Houghton Mifflin, 1963).

STONE, JAMES C., ed., "Symposium: The Internship in Teacher Education," *California Journal of Secondary Education*, 32:486–512, December, 1957.

WOODRING, PAUL, *New Directions in Teacher Education* (New York: Fund for the Advancement of Education, 1957).

"TEACHER ORGANIZATIONS"

American Federation of Teachers, Commission on Educational Reconstruction, *Organizing the Teaching Profession* (Glencoe, Ill.: Free Press, 1955).

LIEBERMAN, *Education as a Profession,* Chapters 9, 10.

———, *The Future of American Education,* Chapter 9, "Teachers Organizations —A Look at the Record."

NEA Handbook (Washington, D.C.: National Education Association, published annually).

STINNETT, Part III and Chapter 15, "Protecting and Disciplining Members of the Profession."

THOMAS, Chapter 16, "How and Why Is the Profession Organized?"

WESLEY, EDGAR, *National Education Association: The First Hundred Years* (New York: Harper, 1957).

"PROFESSIONAL RESPONSIBILITIES, PRIVILEGES, AND OBLIGATIONS"

Learning and the Teacher, 1959 Yearbook (Washington, D.C.: Association for Supervision and Curriculum Development, NEA, 1959).

LIEBERMAN, *The Future of American Education,* Chapter 8, "Employer-Employee Relations in a Public Profession"; Chapter 13, "Beyond the Cliché Barrier."

LINDSEY, MARGARET, ed., *New Horizons for the Teaching Profession* (Washington, D.C.: National Education Association, 1961).

MORSE, ARTHUR D., *Schools of Tomorrow—Today* (New York: Doubleday, 1960), Chapter 4, "Freeing the Teacher for Teaching"; Chapter 5, "Television Pioneer"; Chapter 9, "Teachers of Tomorrow."

Six Areas of Teacher Competence (Burlingame: Commission on Teacher Education, California Teachers Association, 1964).

STINNETT, Part IV.

THOMAS, appendix, "Outline of Teacher Roles," pp. 419–25.

index

index

ability:
  grouping by, 62, 152-153, 158
  individual differences in, 123, 142, 144
Abraham, Willard, cited, 119, 267
Abrahamson, David, 154n
academic freedom, 272, 274-275
academic subjects, priority for, 36-37,
    41, 42-43
  see also curriculum
academies:
  American, 195, 197
  English, 189
acceleration programs, 148, 149
accreditation, 247-248, 266, 271
achievement:
  grouping by levels of, 62, 153
  individual differences in, 61, 143-144,
    145-146, 158
Adler, Mortimer J., 217
  cited, 47, 236
administrators:
  in school organization, 241, 243-245
  teacher relationships with, 91-93
  in teachers' organizations, 276-277
adolescence:
  and the junior high school, 63
  and teen-age culture, 2-3
advanced placement plan, 149
Advise and Consent (Drury), 18-19
age differences:
  chronological, 142
  mental, 144
Ahman, J. Stanley, cited, 98
Aikin, Wilford M., cited, 47
Aims of Education, The (Whitehead),
    28-31
Alexander, William M., cited, 75, 119
American Association for Health, Physi-
    cal Education, and Recreation, 264

American Federation of Teachers (AFT),
    273, 276-277, 281, 282
American Journal of Education, 197
Anderson, Archibald W., cited, 285
Anderson, Robert H., cited, 75
Anderson, Robert J., cited, 267
application forms, 253
Aristotle, 24, 188, 205
Arlington, Va., salary scales in, 70-71
Armstrong, W. Earl, cited, 286
Arnold, Matthew, 36
artifacts, cultural, 4, 6-7
Association for Supervision and Curricu-
    lum Development, 146
average students, 145-146

Baldwin, James, 185
Barbe, Walter B., 149
Barnard, Henry, 197
Barr, W. Monfort, cited, 268
Barret, Clifford, cited, 236
Bartky, John A., cited, 185
Barzun, Jacques, cited, 285
Baynham, Dorsey, cited, 23, 268
Beauchamp, Mary, cited, 160
Beecher, Catherine, 198
behavior:
  change in, as learning, 59, 124, 128, 137
  classroom problems in, 54, 84, 85, 94,
    114
  and the creative student, 150
  influence by teacher on, 54, 59
behavioral sciences, and learning theory,
    127-128
Benda, Harold W., cited, 75, 97, 139,
    159, 215
Benedict, Ruth, cited, 21
Benjamin, Harold, 5-7
  cited, 22

291